クラウンメロン
クラウンメロン
クラウンメロン

I snapped this the other day when I was in a taxi passing by a greengrocer's [text on boxes: CROWN MELON] and realized how much I like Allen. But I like Tim even more! (Dadum! ★) We've been apart for a while, so I became all the more aware of his presence. This is volume 23, during which I discovered how healing it is for me to draw Tim.

—Katsura Hoshino

Shiga Prefecture native Katsura Hoshino's hit manga series *D.Gray-man* has been serialized in *Weekly Shonen Jump* since 2004. Katsura's debut manga, "Continue," appeared for the first time in *Weekly Shonen Jump* in 2003.

Katsura adores cats.

D.GRAY-MAN
VOL. 23
SHONEN JUMP ADVANCED
Manga Edition

STORY AND ART BY
KATSURA HOSHINO

English Adaptation/Lance Caselman
Translation/John Werry
Touch-up Art & Lettering/HudsonYards
Design/Matt Hinrichs
Editor/Gary Leach

D.GRAY-MAN © 2004 by Katsura Hoshino. All rights reserved.
First published in Japan in 2004 by SHUEISHA Inc., Tokyo. English translation rights arranged by SHUEISHA Inc.

The stories, characters and incidents mentioned in this publication are entirely fictional.

Printed in the U.S.A.

Published by VIZ Media, LLC
P.O. Box 77010
San Francisco, CA 94107

10 9 8 7 6 5 4 3 2
First printing, December 2012
Second printing, May 2016

www.viz.com

www.shonenjump.com

D.Gray-man

vol. 23

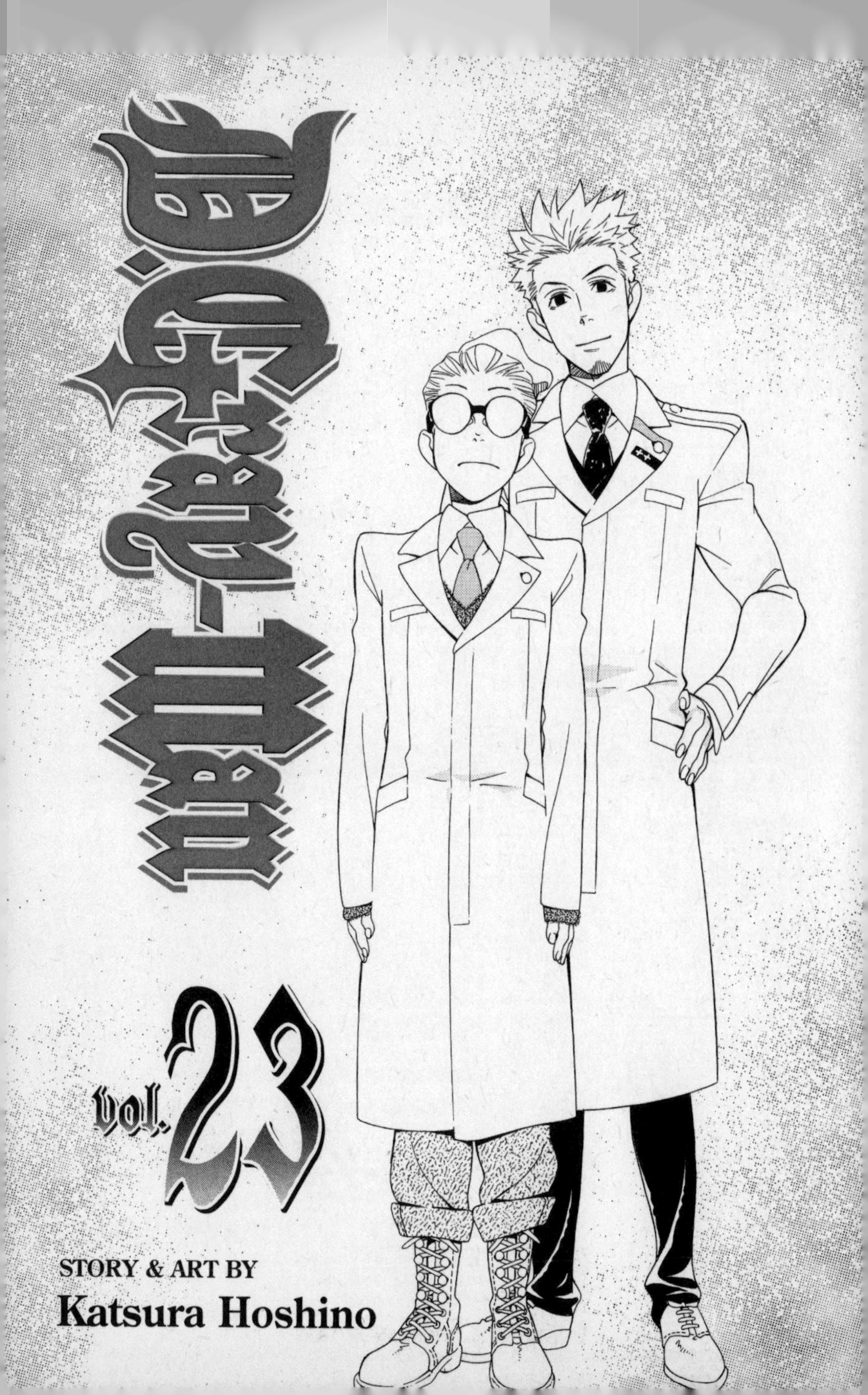

STORY & ART BY

Katsura Hoshino

D.Gray-man
CHARACTERS

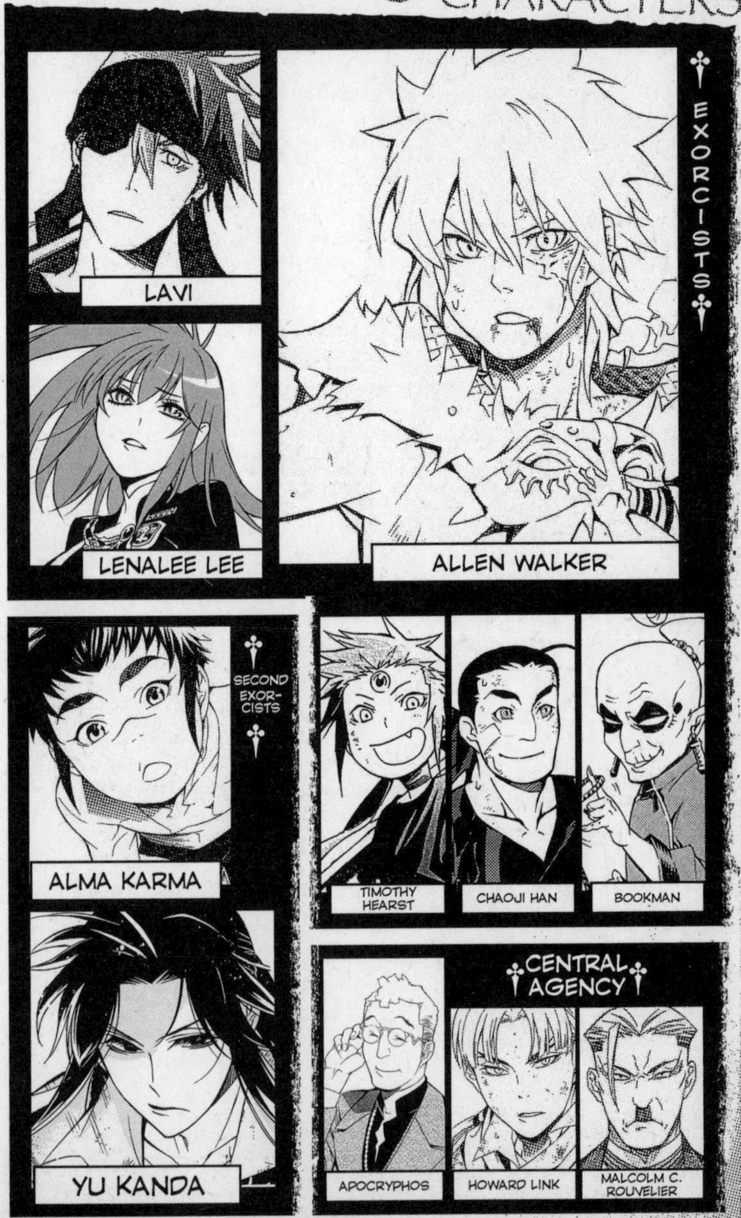
EXORCISTS
ALLEN WALKER
LAVI
LENALEE LEE
BOOKMAN
CHAOJI HAN
TIMOTHY HEARST
CENTRAL AGENCY
MALCOLM C. ROUVELIER
HOWARD LINK
APOCRYPHOS
SECOND EXORCISTS
ALMA KARMA
YU KANDA

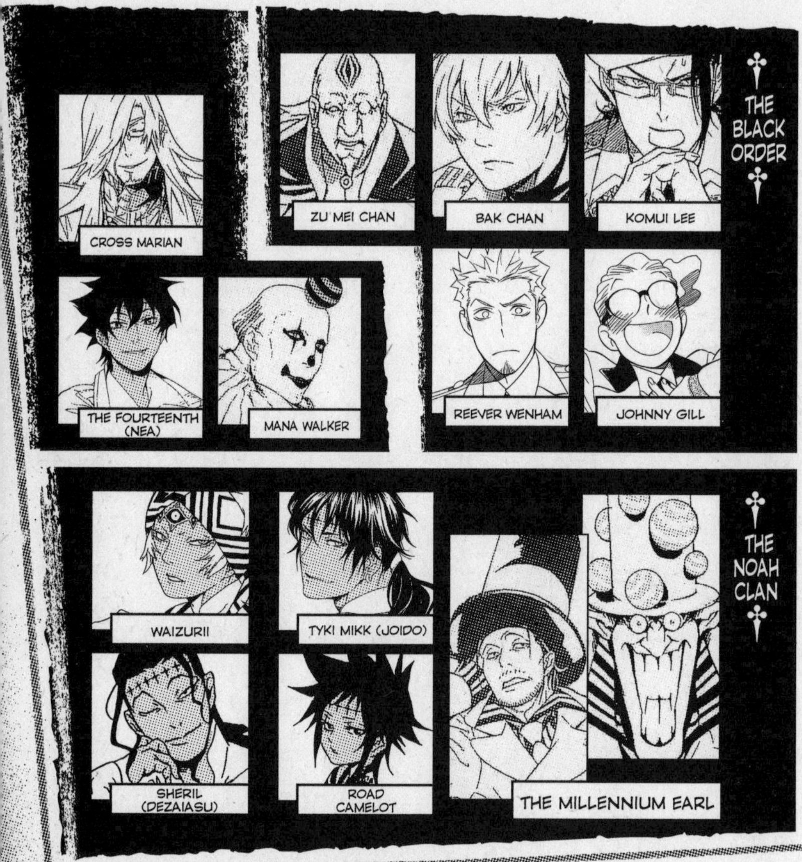
THE BLACK ORDER
KOMUI LEE
BAK CHAN
ZU MEI CHAN
CROSS MARIAN
JOHNNY GILL
REEVER WENHAM
MANA WALKER
THE FOURTEENTH (NEA)
THE NOAH CLAN
THE MILLENNIUM EARL
TYKI MIKK (JOIDO)
WAIZURII
ROAD CAMELOT
SHERIL (DEZAIASU)

STORY

IT ALL BEGAN CENTURIES AGO WITH THE DISCOVERY OF A CUBE CONTAINING AN APOCALYPTIC PROPHECY FROM AN ANCIENT CIVILIZATION AND INSTRUCTIONS IN THE USE OF INNOCENCE, A CRYSTALLINE SUBSTANCE OF WONDROUS SUPERNATURAL POWER. THE CREATORS OF THE CUBE CLAIMED TO HAVE DEFEATED AN EVIL KNOWN AS THE MILLENNIUM EARL BY USING THE INNOCENCE. NEVERTHELESS, THE WORLD WAS DESTROYED BY THE GREAT FLOOD OF THE OLD TESTAMENT. NOW, TO AVERT A SECOND END OF THE WORLD, A GROUP OF EXORCISTS WIELDING WEAPONS MADE OF INNOCENCE MUST BATTLE THE MILLENNIUM EARL AND HIS TERRIBLE MINIONS, THE APOSTOLIC NOAH AND THE DEMONIC AKUMA.

THE MILLENNIUM EARL AND THE NOAH ATTACK THE BLACK ORDER AND WREAK HAVOC WHILE ALMA KARMA, ASLEEP UNDER THE NORTH AMERICA BRANCH, CHANGES INTO AN AKUMA AND CLASHES WITH HIS FORMER FRIEND KANDA. ALLEN RECONCILES THEM AND SENDS THEM TO A PLACE FAR AWAY FROM IT ALL. LATER, THE INDEPENDENT-TYPE INNOCENCE KNOWN AS APOCRYPHOS TRIES TO FUSE WITH ALLEN AND AN ALL-OUT BATTLE ENSUES. AS A RESULT, THE ORDER DEEMS ALLEN TO BE ONE OF THE NOAH. FOR THIS AND OTHER REASONS, ALLEN LEAVES HIS FRIENDS BEHIND AND SETS OUT ALONE ON A NEW JOURNEY!

D.GRAY-MAN
Vol. 23

CONTENTS

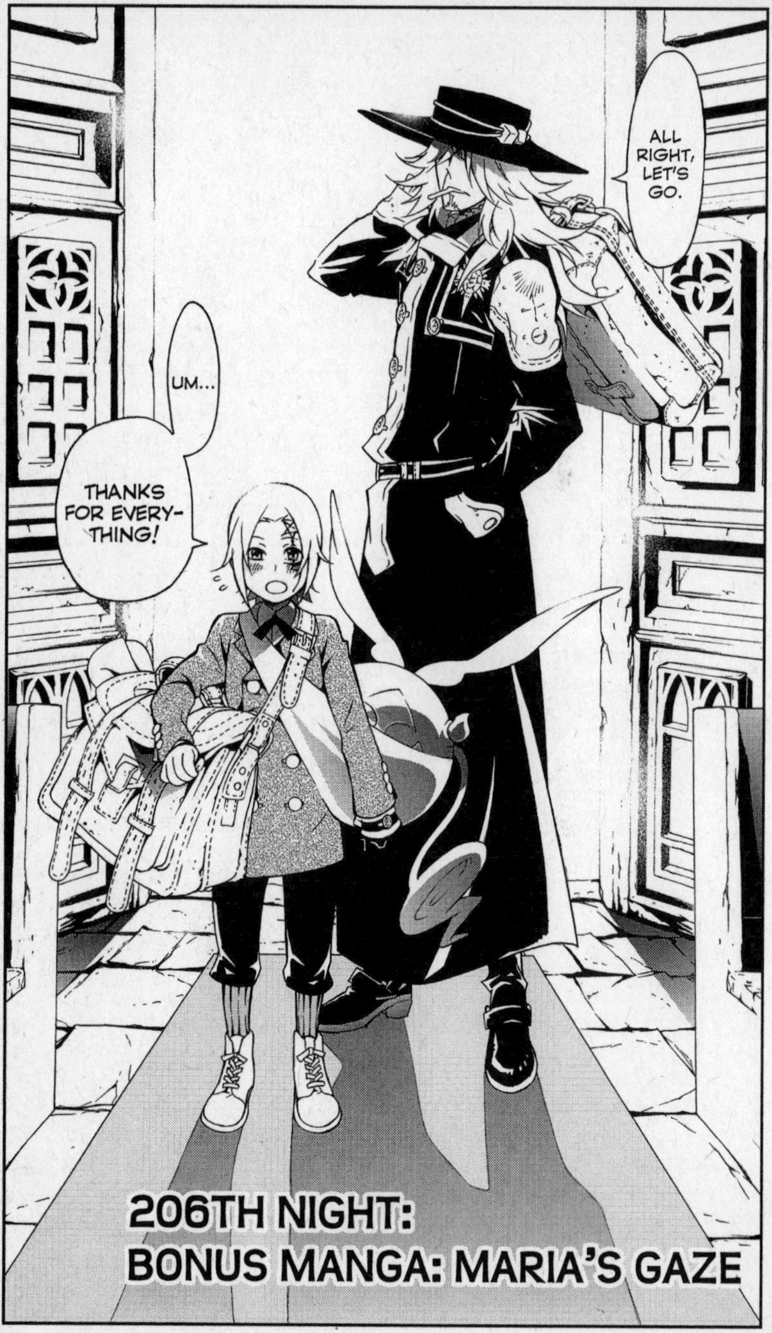
ALL RIGHT, LET'S GO.
UM...
THANKS FOR EVERY-THING!
206TH NIGHT:
BONUS MANGA: MARIA'S GAZE

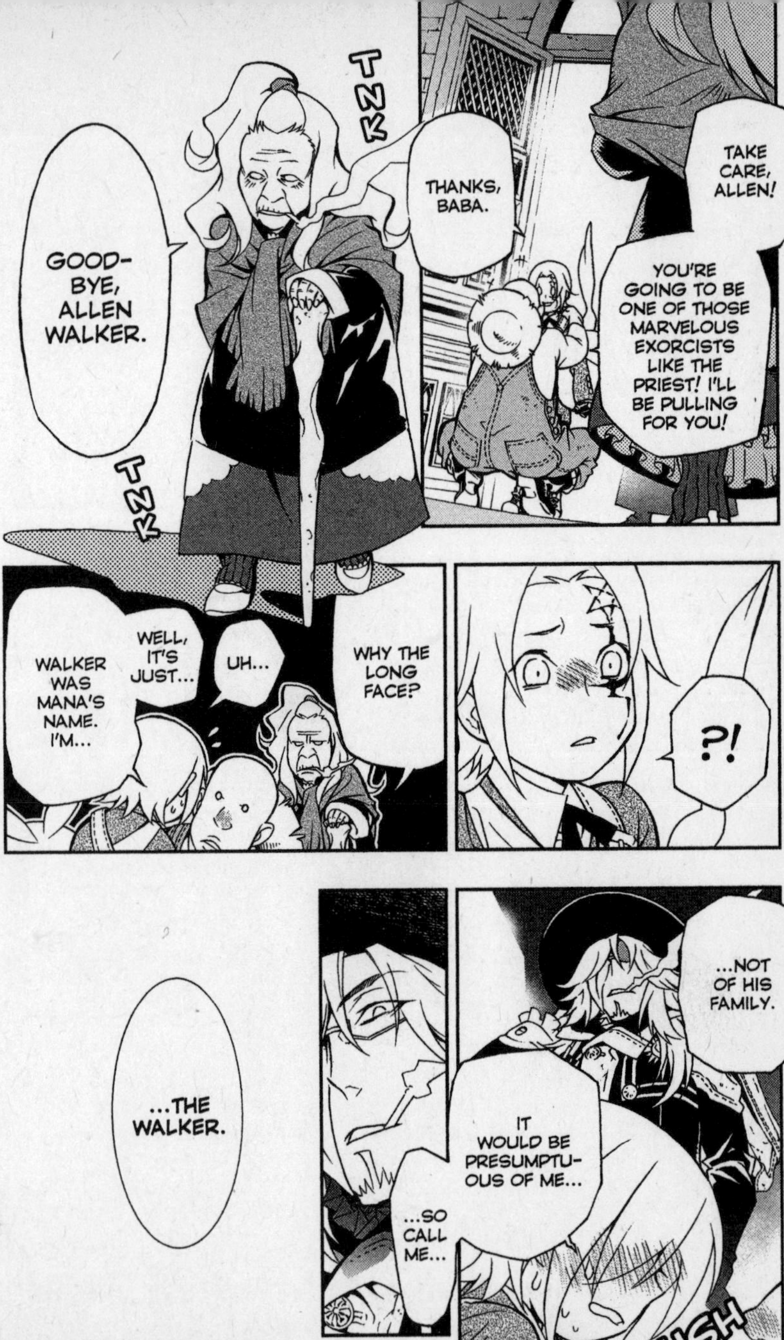
TAKE CARE, ALLEN!
YOU'RE GOING TO BE ONE OF THOSE MARVELOUS EXORCISTS LIKE THE PRIEST! I'LL BE PULLING FOR YOU!
THANKS, BABA.
TNK
GOOD-BYE, ALLEN WALKER.
TNK
?!
WHY THE LONG FACE?
UH...
WELL, IT'S JUST...
WALKER WAS MANA'S NAME. I'M...
...NOT OF HIS FAMILY.
IT WOULD BE PRESUMPTUOUS OF ME...
...SO CALL ME...
BLUSH
...THE WALKER.

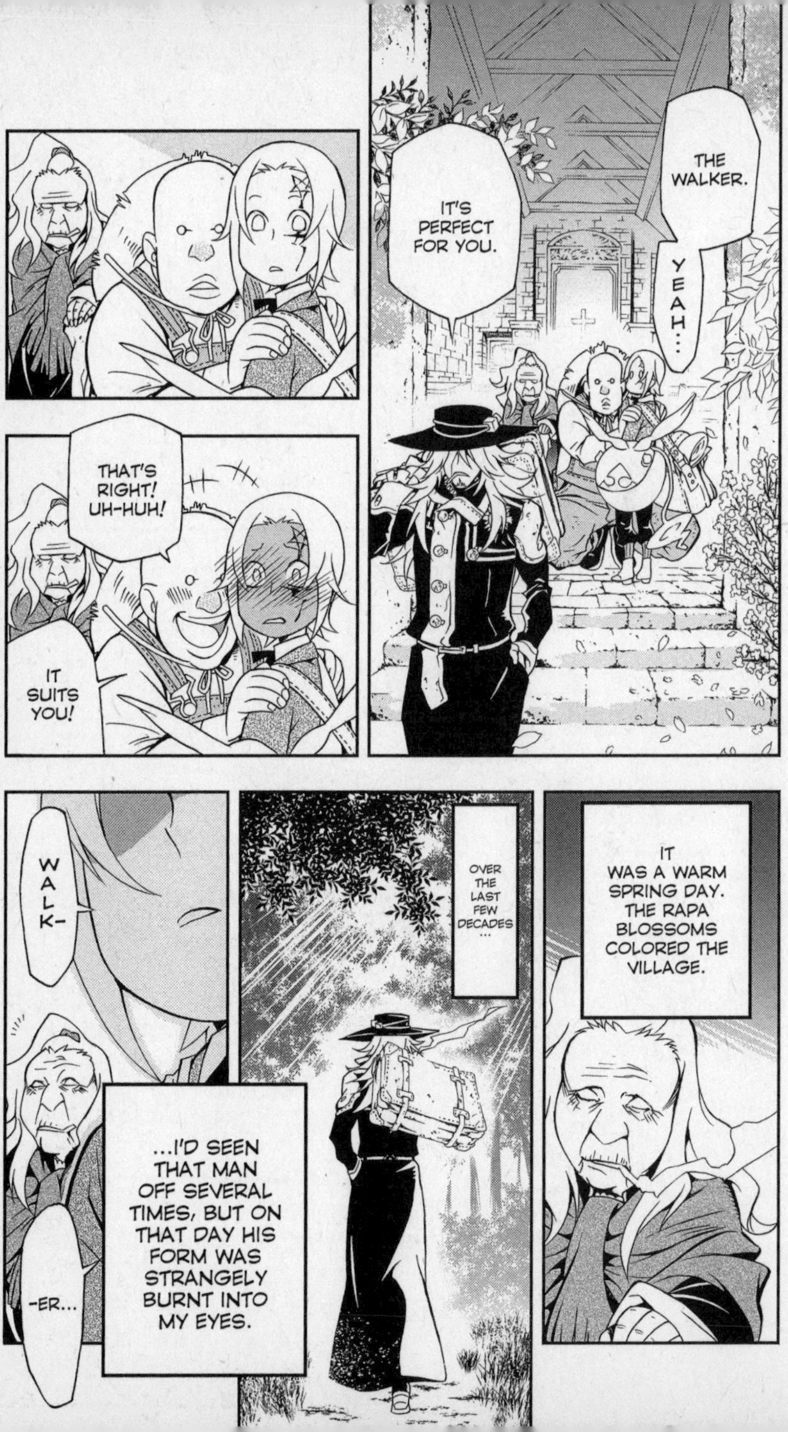
THE WALKER.
YEAH...
IT'S PERFECT FOR YOU.
THAT'S RIGHT! UH-HUH!
IT SUITS YOU!
IT WAS A WARM SPRING DAY. THE RAPA BLOSSOMS COLORED THE VILLAGE.
OVER THE LAST FEW DECADES...
WALK-
...I'D SEEN THAT MAN OFF SEVERAL TIMES, BUT ON THAT DAY HIS FORM WAS STRANGELY BURNT INTO MY EYES.
-ER...

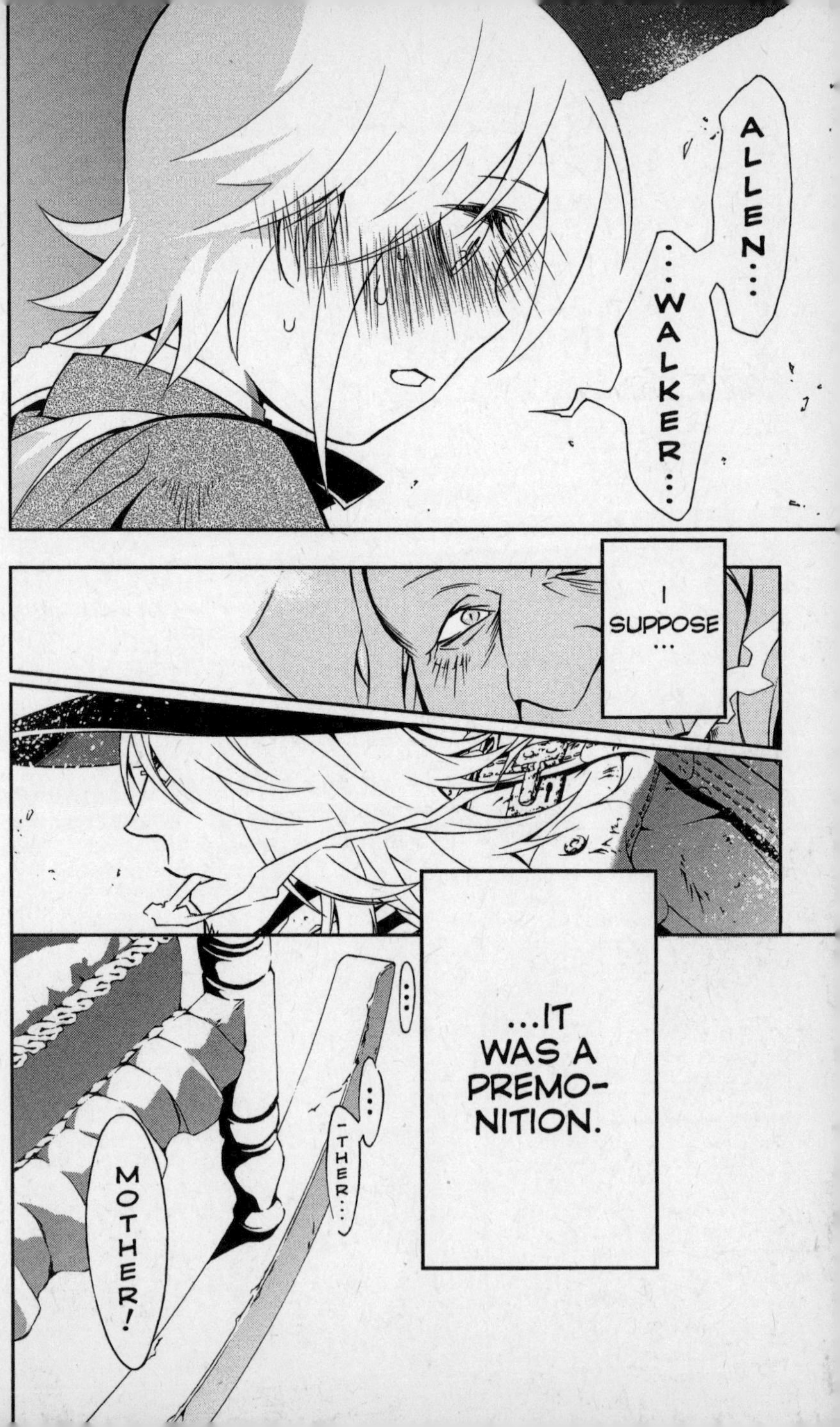
ALLEN... ...WALKER...
I SUPPOSE...
...IT WAS A PREMONITION.
...
...
-THER...
MOTHER!

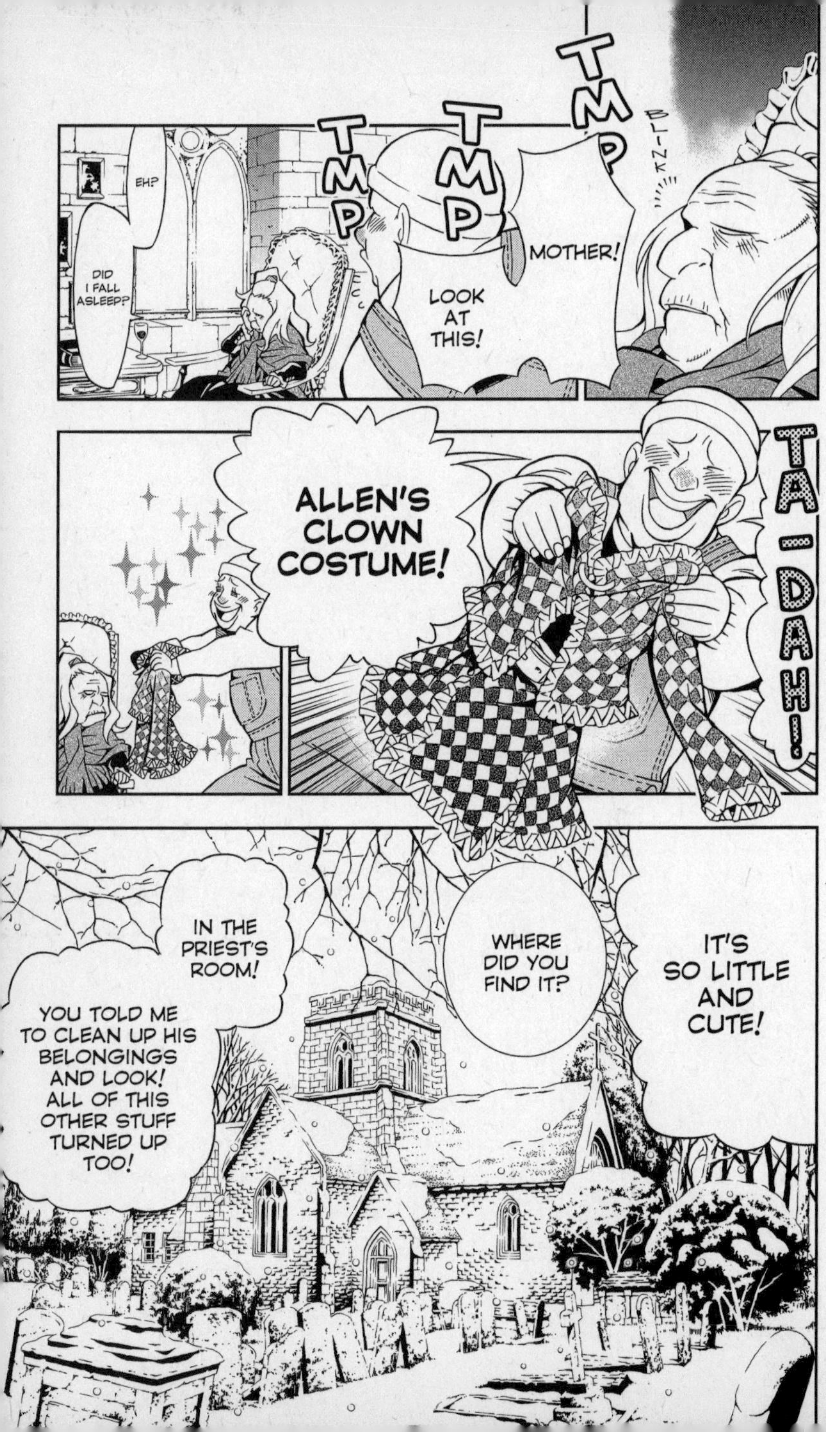
TMP
BLINK
TMP
TMP
MOTHER!
LOOK AT THIS!
EH?
DID I FALL ASLEEP?
TA-DAH!
ALLEN'S CLOWN COSTUME!
IT'S SO LITTLE AND CUTE!
WHERE DID YOU FIND IT?
IN THE PRIEST'S ROOM!
YOU TOLD ME TO CLEAN UP HIS BELONGINGS AND LOOK! ALL OF THIS OTHER STUFF TURNED UP TOO!

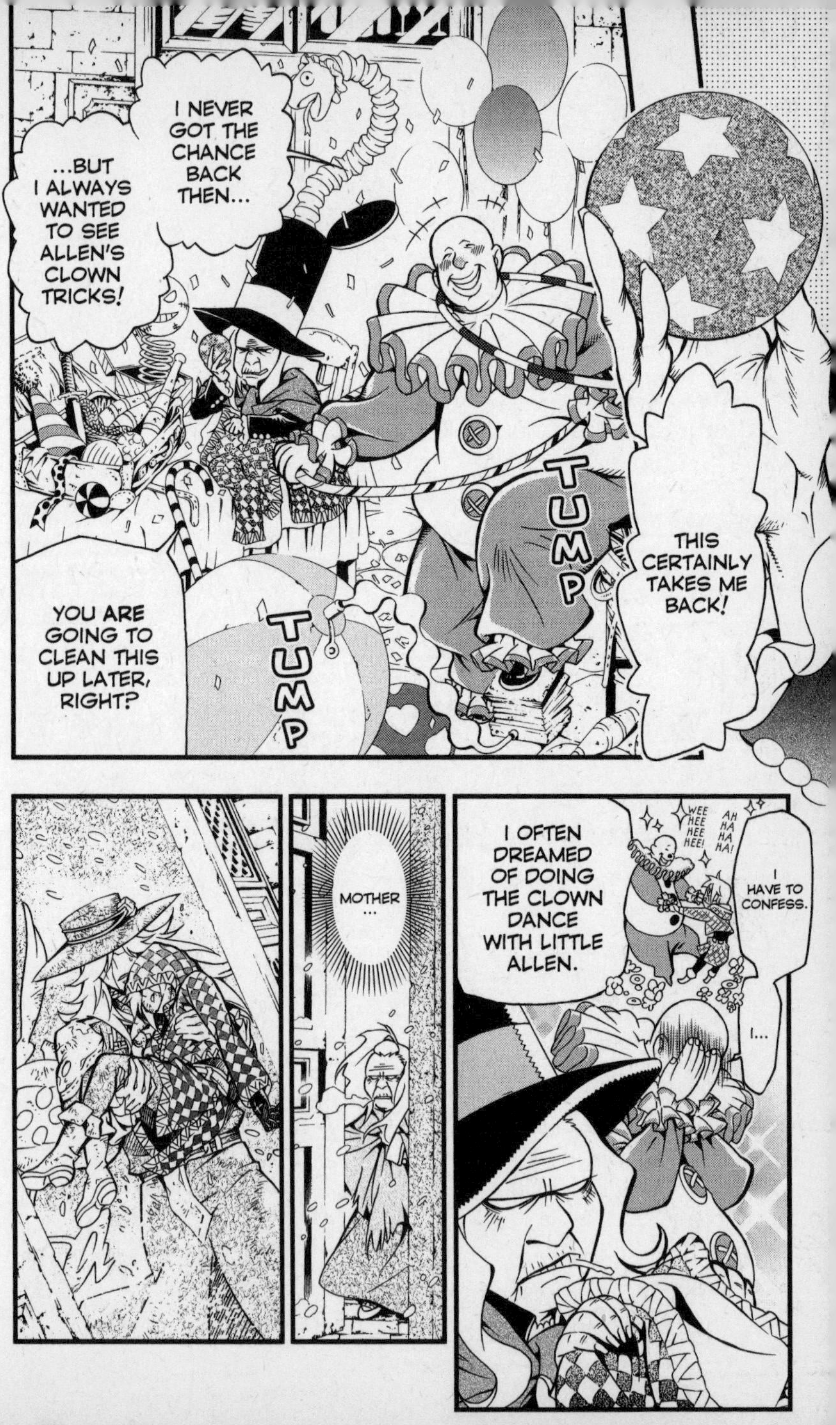
I NEVER GOT THE CHANCE BACK THEN...
...BUT I ALWAYS WANTED TO SEE ALLEN'S CLOWN TRICKS!
THIS CERTAINLY TAKES ME BACK!
TUMP
TUMP
YOU ARE GOING TO CLEAN THIS UP LATER, RIGHT?
I HAVE TO CONFESS.
I...
AH HA HA HA!
WEE HEE HEE HEE!
I OFTEN DREAMED OF DOING THE CLOWN DANCE WITH LITTLE ALLEN.
MOTHER ...

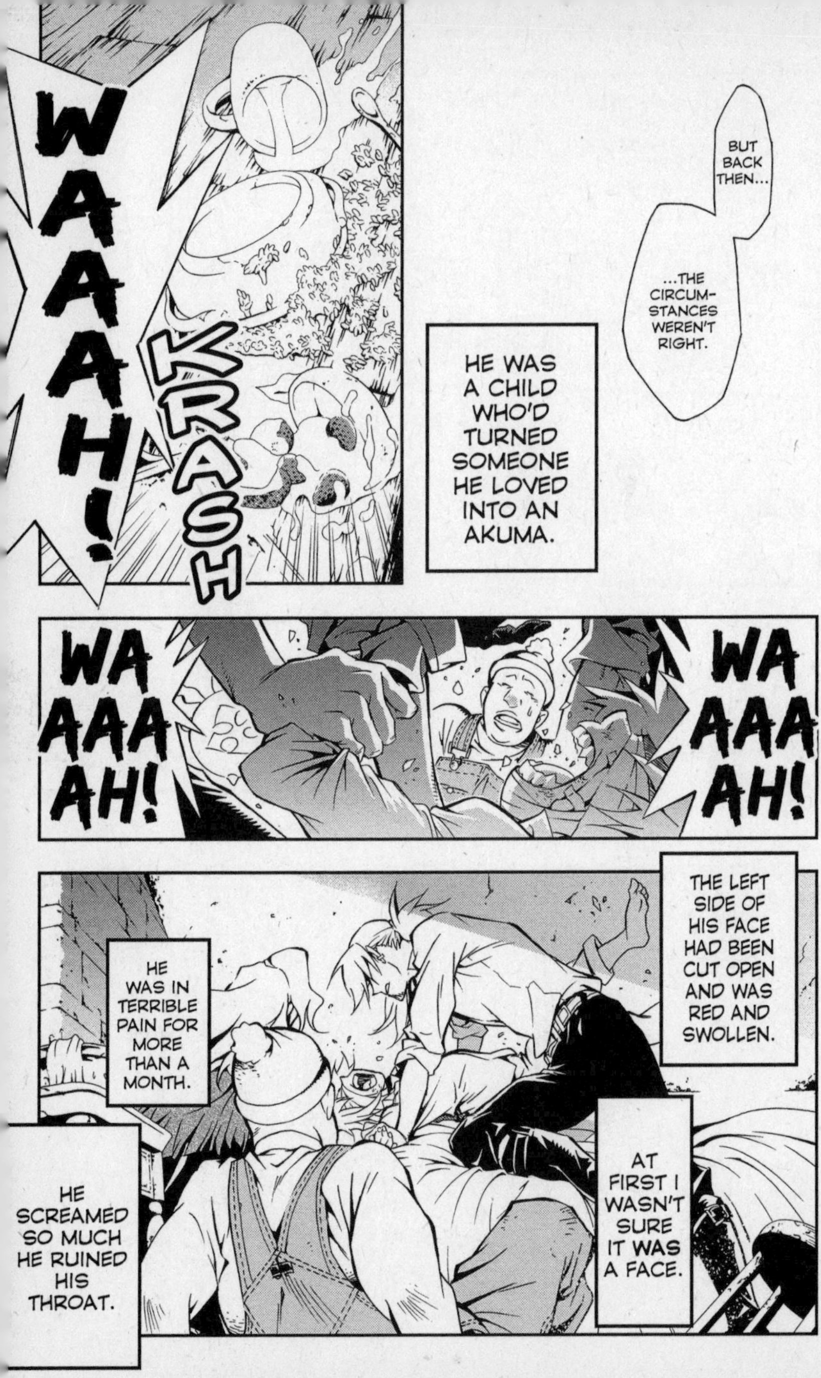
BUT BACK THEN...
...THE CIRCUMSTANCES WEREN'T RIGHT.
HE WAS A CHILD WHO'D TURNED SOMEONE HE LOVED INTO AN AKUMA.
KRASH
WAAAH!
WA AAA AH!
WA AAA AH!
THE LEFT SIDE OF HIS FACE HAD BEEN CUT OPEN AND WAS RED AND SWOLLEN.
AT FIRST I WASN'T SURE IT WAS A FACE.
HE WAS IN TERRIBLE PAIN FOR MORE THAN A MONTH.
HE SCREAMED SO MUCH HE RUINED HIS THROAT.

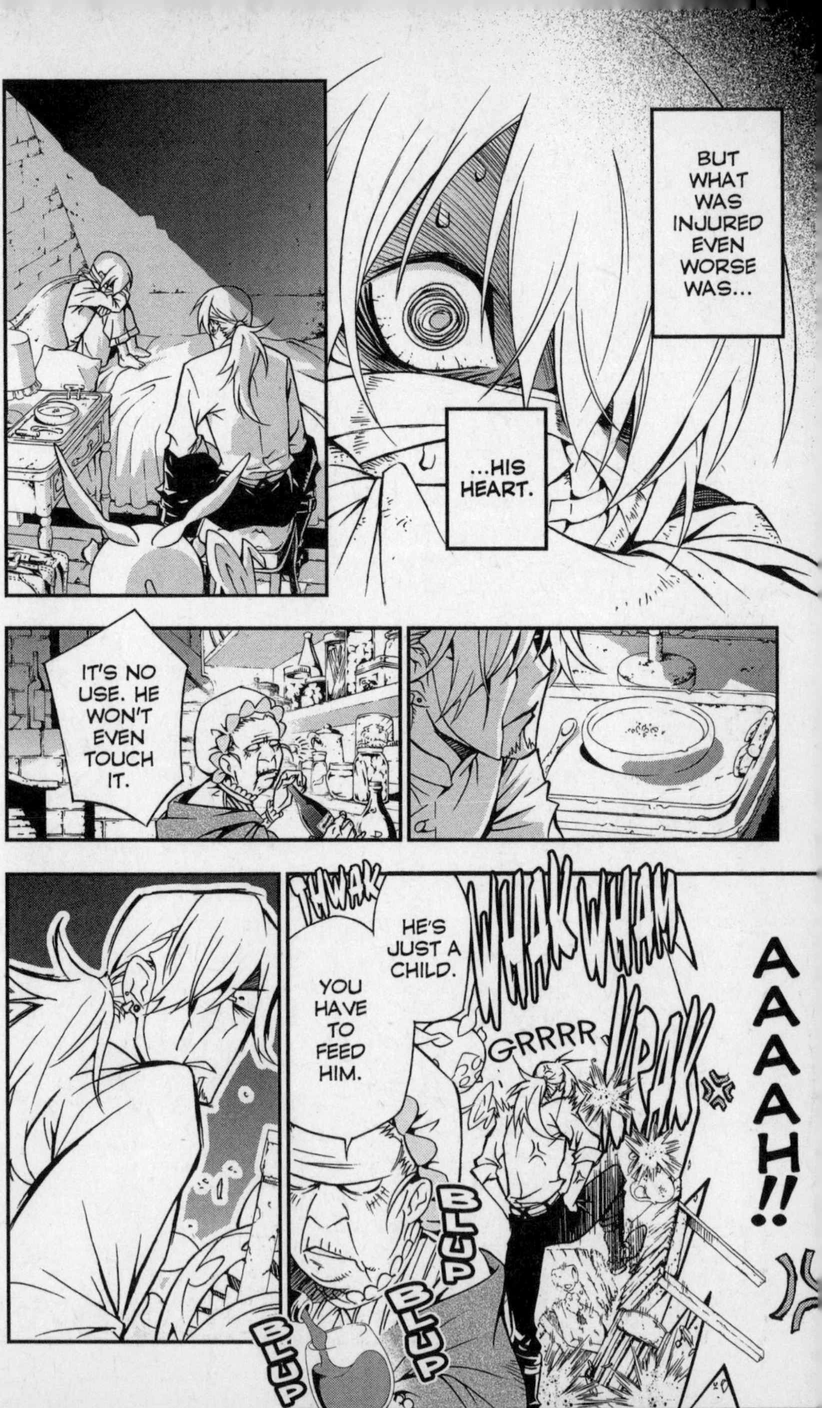
BUT WHAT WAS INJURED EVEN WORSE WAS...
...HIS HEART.
IT'S NO USE. HE WON'T EVEN TOUCH IT.
AAAAH!!
WHAK WHAM
THWAK
HE'S JUST A CHILD.
YOU HAVE TO FEED HIM.
GRRRR
BLUP
BLUP
BLUP
DESTROYING FURNITURE

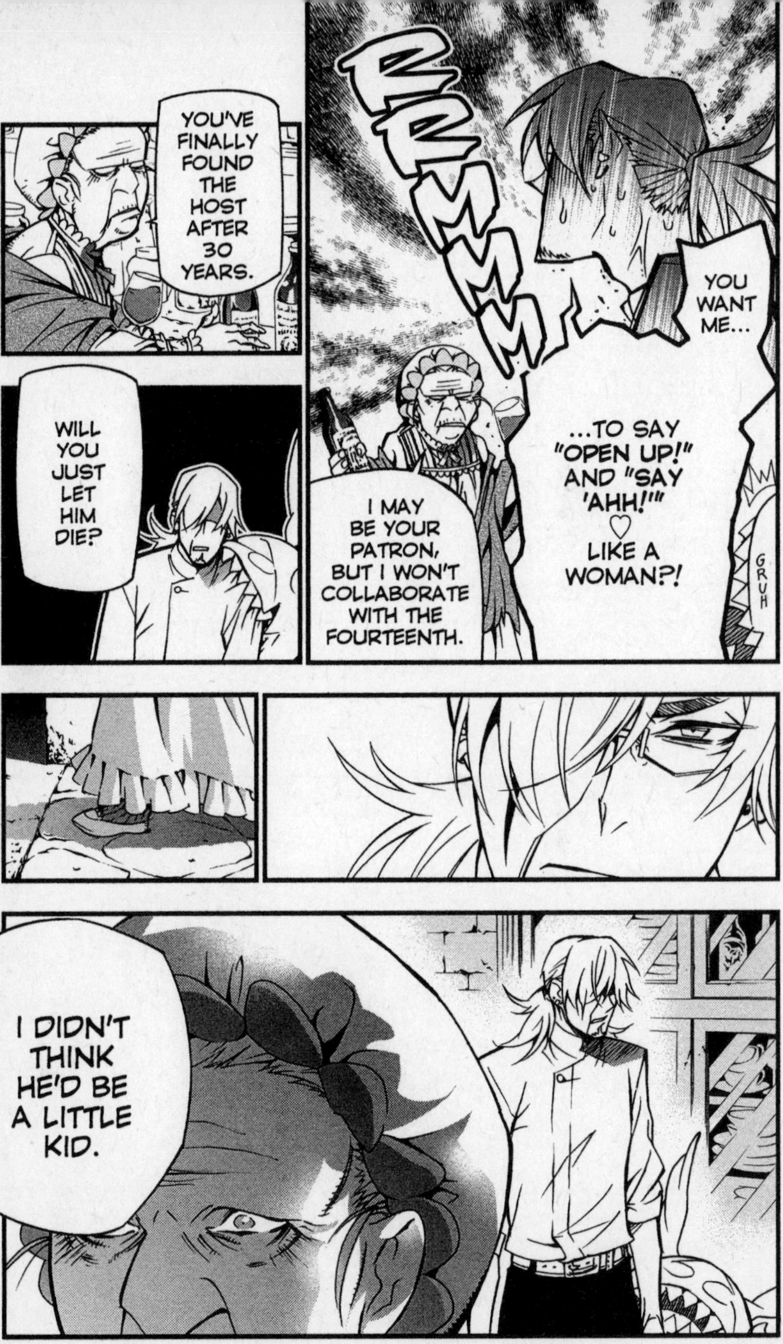
YOU WANT ME...
...TO SAY "OPEN UP!" AND "SAY 'AHH!'" ♡ LIKE A WOMAN?!
GRUH
I MAY BE YOUR PATRON, BUT I WON'T COLLABORATE WITH THE FOURTEENTH.
YOU'VE FINALLY FOUND THE HOST AFTER 30 YEARS.
WILL YOU JUST LET HIM DIE?
I DIDN'T THINK HE'D BE A LITTLE KID.

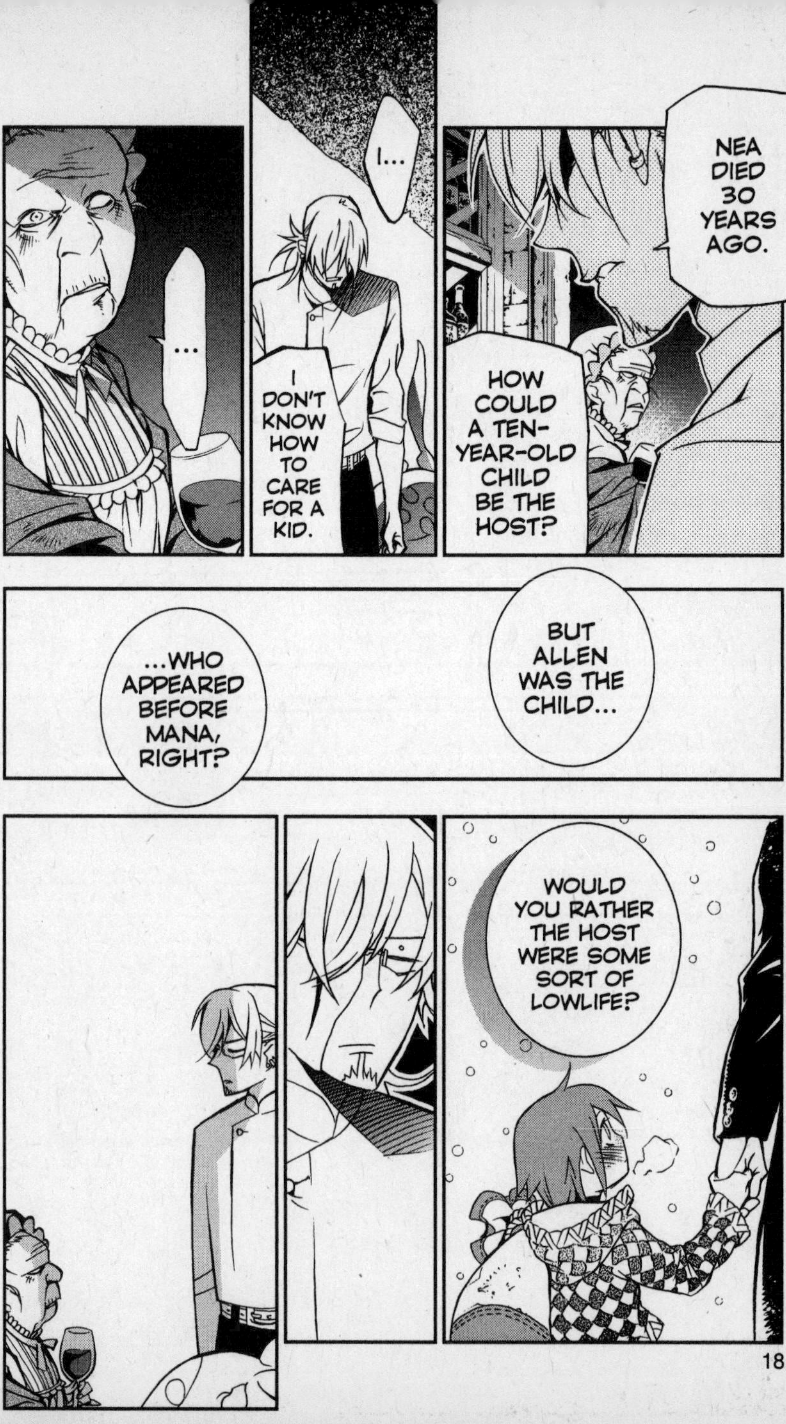
NEA DIED 30 YEARS AGO.
HOW COULD A TEN-YEAR-OLD CHILD BE THE HOST?
I...
I DON'T KNOW HOW TO CARE FOR A KID.
...
BUT ALLEN WAS THE CHILD...
...WHO APPEARED BEFORE MANA, RIGHT?
WOULD YOU RATHER THE HOST WERE SOME SORT OF LOWLIFE?

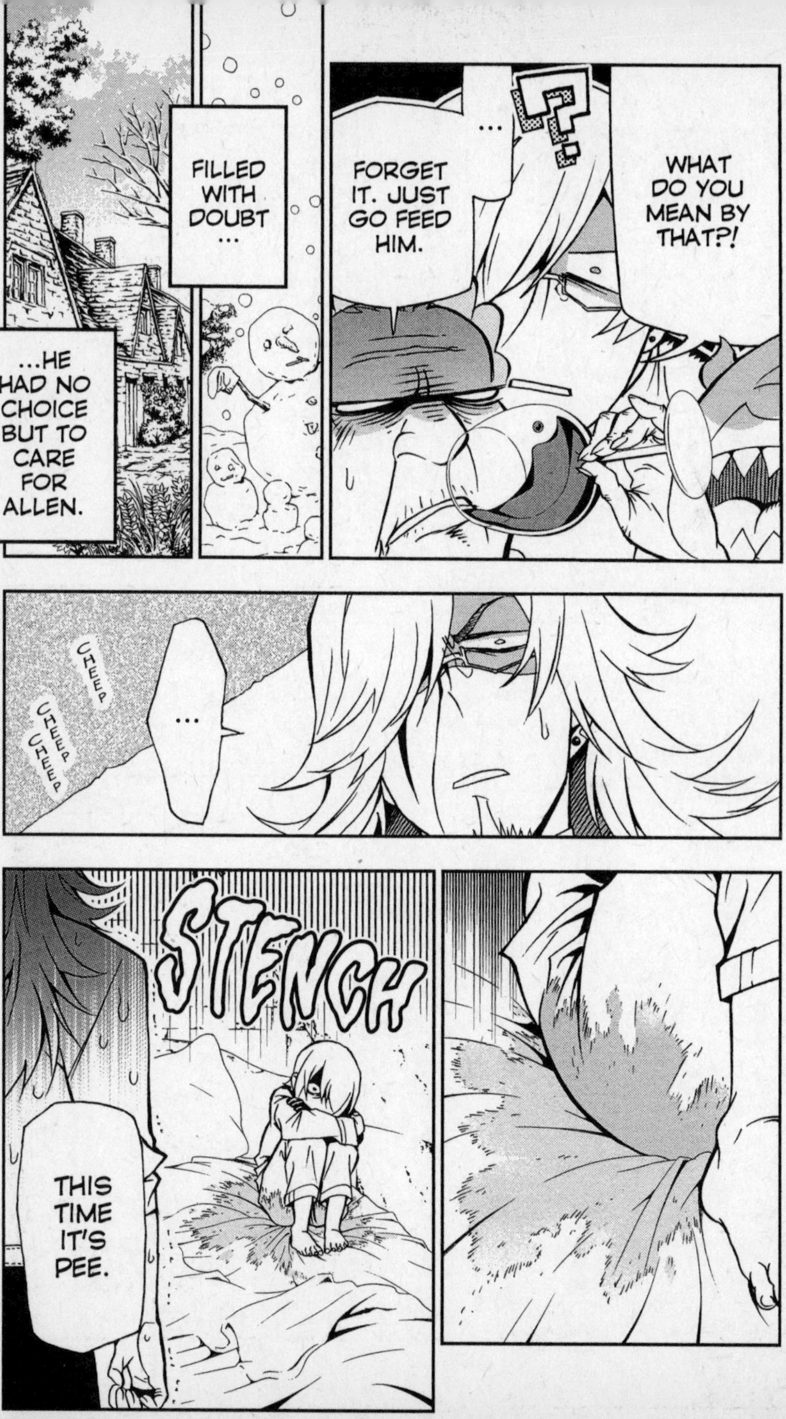
WHAT DO YOU MEAN BY THAT?!
...
FORGET IT. JUST GO FEED HIM.
FILLED WITH DOUBT...
...HE HAD NO CHOICE BUT TO CARE FOR ALLEN.
...
CHEEP
CHEEP CHEEP
STENCH
THIS TIME IT'S PEE.

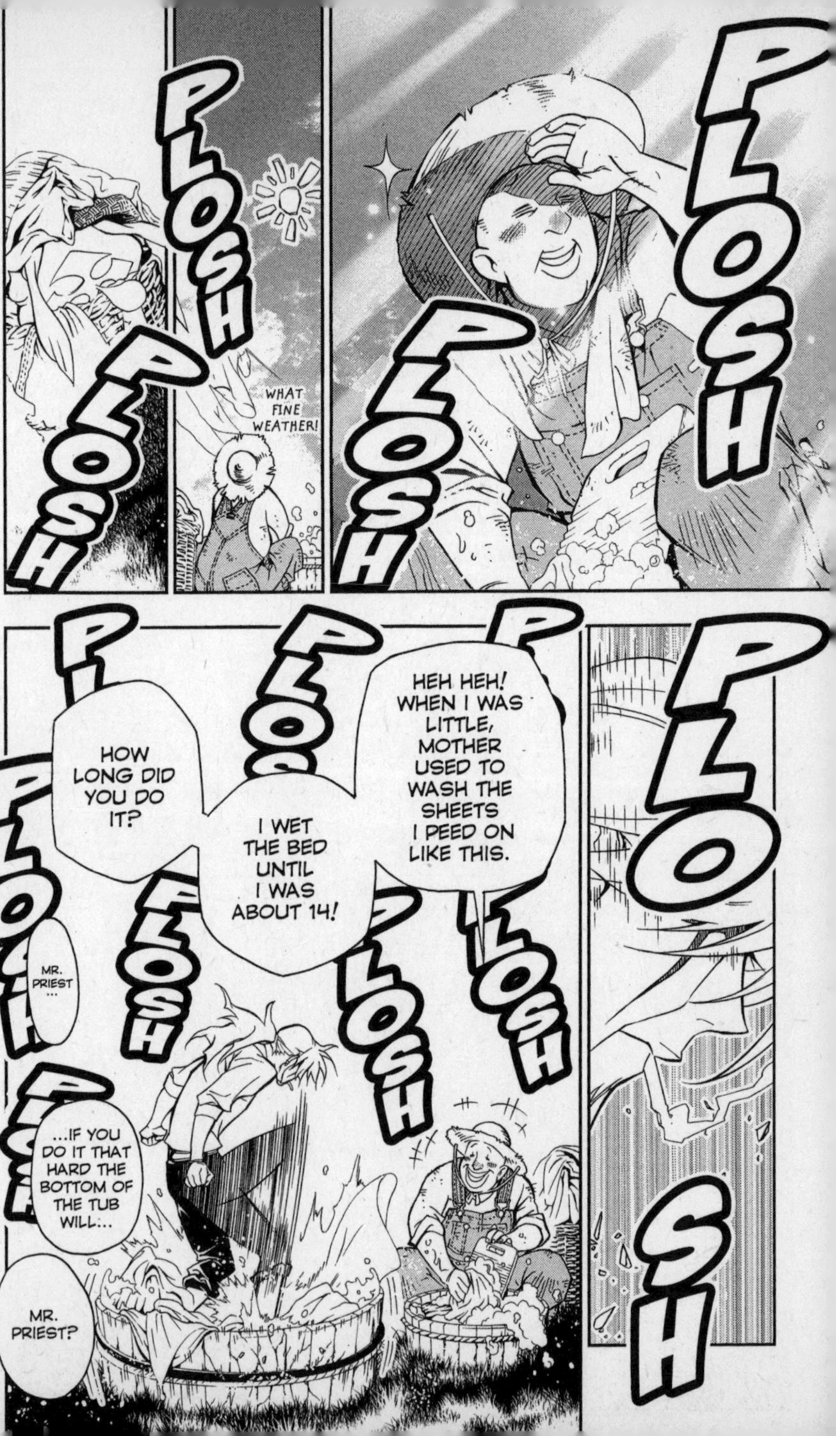
PLOSH
PLOSH
WHAT FINE WEATHER!
PLOSH
PLOSH
PLOSH
PLOSH
HEH HEH! WHEN I WAS LITTLE, MOTHER USED TO WASH THE SHEETS I PEED ON LIKE THIS.
PLOSH
I WET THE BED UNTIL I WAS ABOUT 14!
HOW LONG DID YOU DO IT?
PLOSH
MR. PRIEST...
...IF YOU DO IT THAT HARD THE BOTTOM OF THE TUB WILL...
MR. PRIEST?

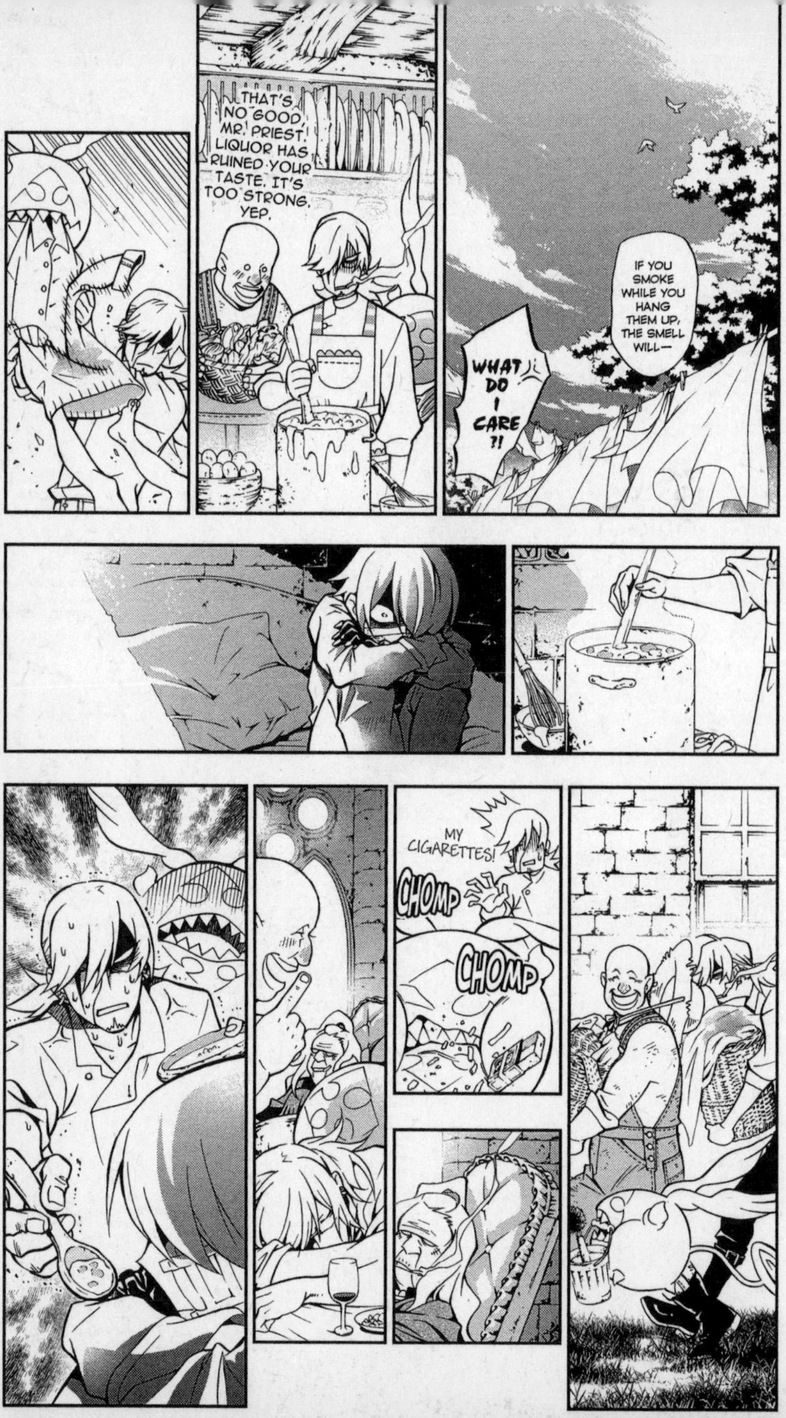
IF YOU SMOKE WHILE YOU HANG THEM UP, THE SMELL WILL—
WHAT DO I CARE?!
THAT'S NO GOOD, MR. PRIEST. LIQUOR HAS RUINED YOUR TASTE. IT'S TOO STRONG, YEP.
MY CIGARETTES!
CHOMP
CHOMP

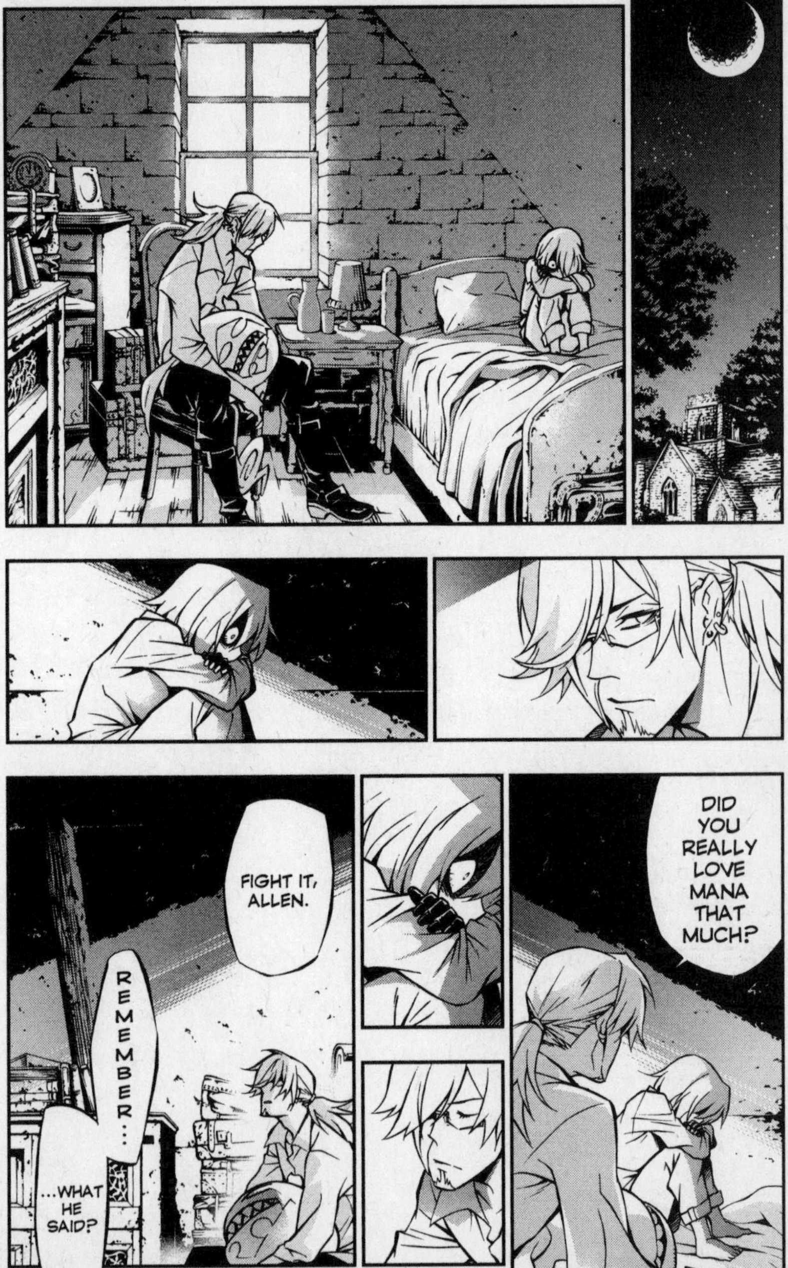
DID YOU REALLY LOVE MANA THAT MUCH?
FIGHT IT, ALLEN.
REMEMBER...
...WHAT HE SAID?

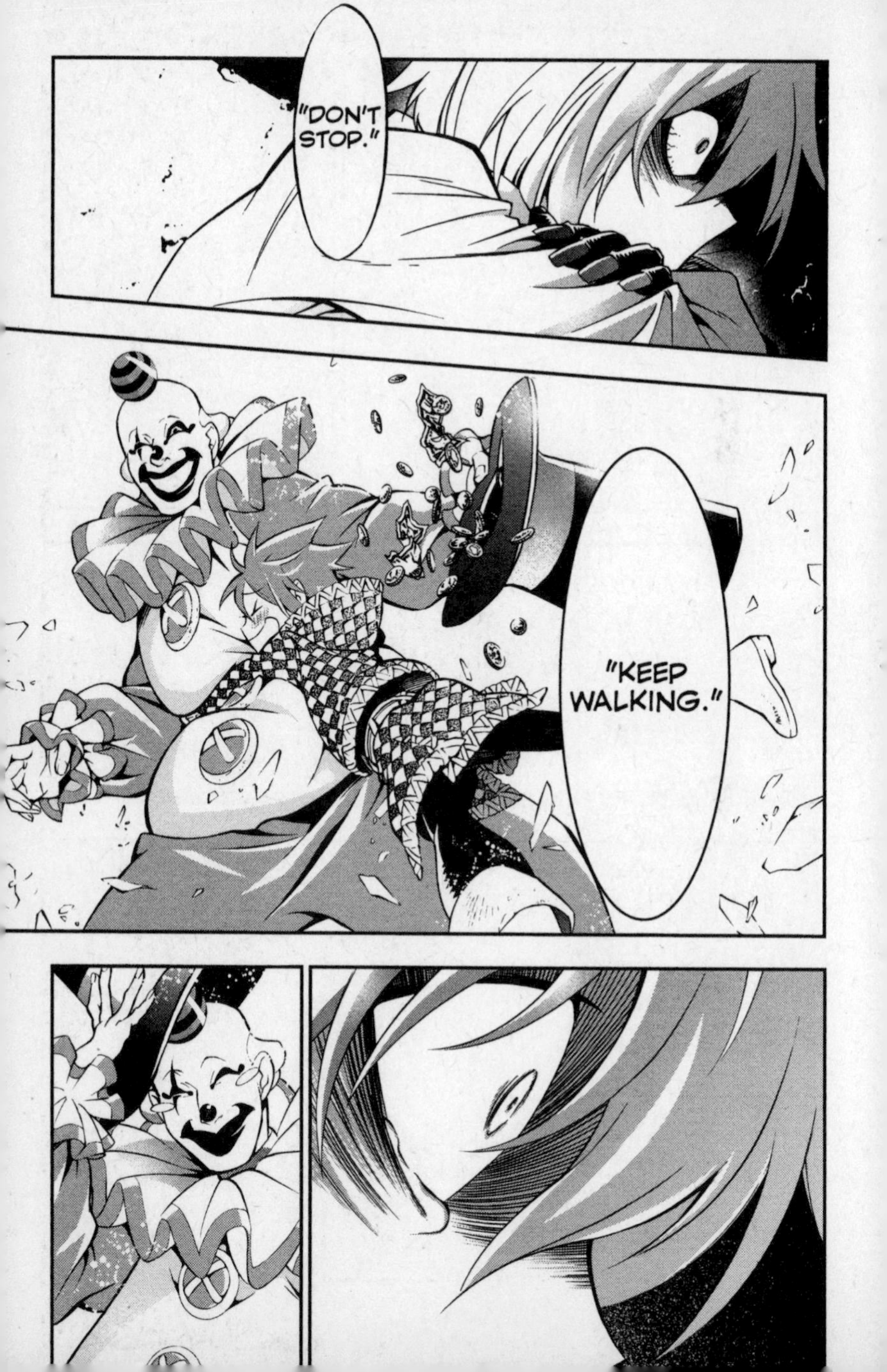
"DON'T STOP."
"KEEP WALKING."

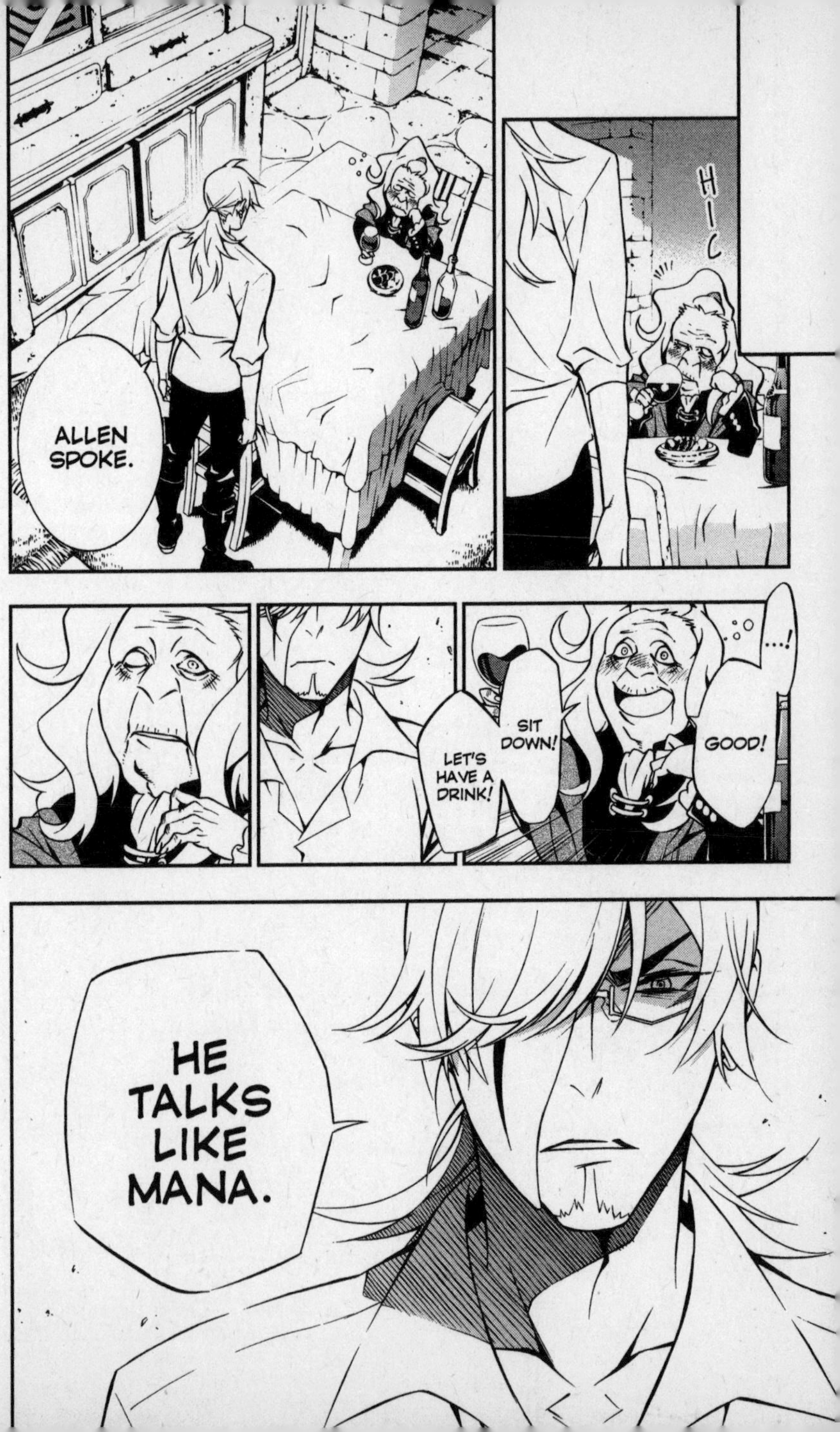
HIC
ALLEN SPOKE.
...!
GOOD!
SIT DOWN!
LET'S HAVE A DRINK!
HE TALKS LIKE MANA.

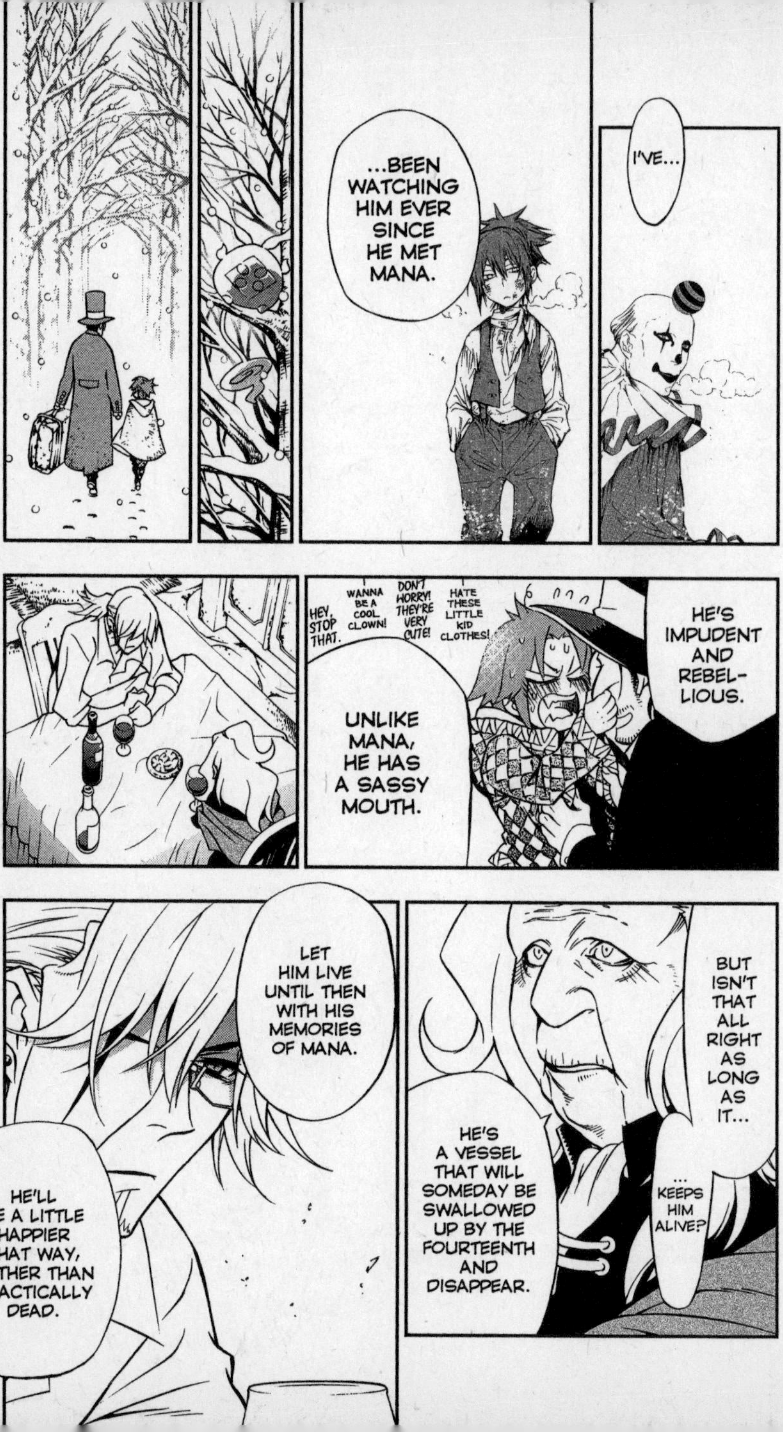
I'VE...
...BEEN WATCHING HIM EVER SINCE HE MET MANA.
HE'S IMPUDENT AND REBEL-LIOUS.
HATE THESE LITTLE KID CLOTHES!
DON'T WORRY! THEY'RE VERY CUTE!
WANNA BE A COOL CLOWN!
HEY, STOP THAT.
UNLIKE MANA, HE HAS A SASSY MOUTH.
BUT ISN'T THAT ALL RIGHT AS LONG AS IT...
...KEEPS HIM ALIVE?
HE'S A VESSEL THAT WILL SOMEDAY BE SWALLOWED UP BY THE FOURTEENTH AND DISAPPEAR.
LET HIM LIVE UNTIL THEN WITH HIS MEMORIES OF MANA.
HE'LL BE A LITTLE HAPPIER THAT WAY, RATHER THAN PRACTICALLY DEAD.

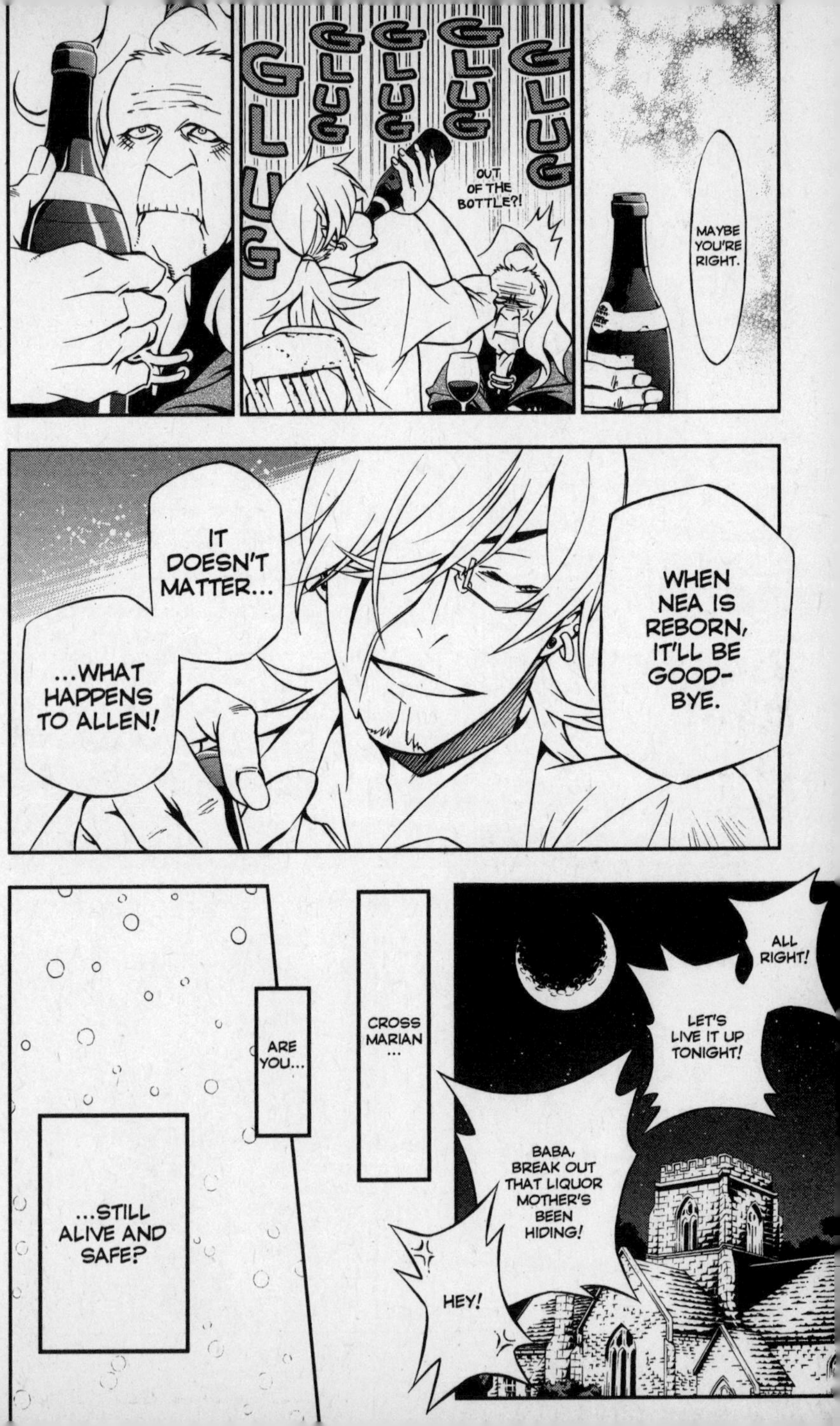
MAYBE YOU'RE RIGHT.
GLUG GLUG GLUG GLUG GLUG GLUG
OUT OF THE BOTTLE?!
WHEN NEA IS REBORN, IT'LL BE GOOD-BYE.
IT DOESN'T MATTER...
...WHAT HAPPENS TO ALLEN!
ALL RIGHT!
LET'S LIVE IT UP TONIGHT!
BABA, BREAK OUT THAT LIQUOR MOTHER'S BEEN HIDING!
HEY!
CROSS MARIAN...
ARE YOU...
...STILL ALIVE AND SAFE?

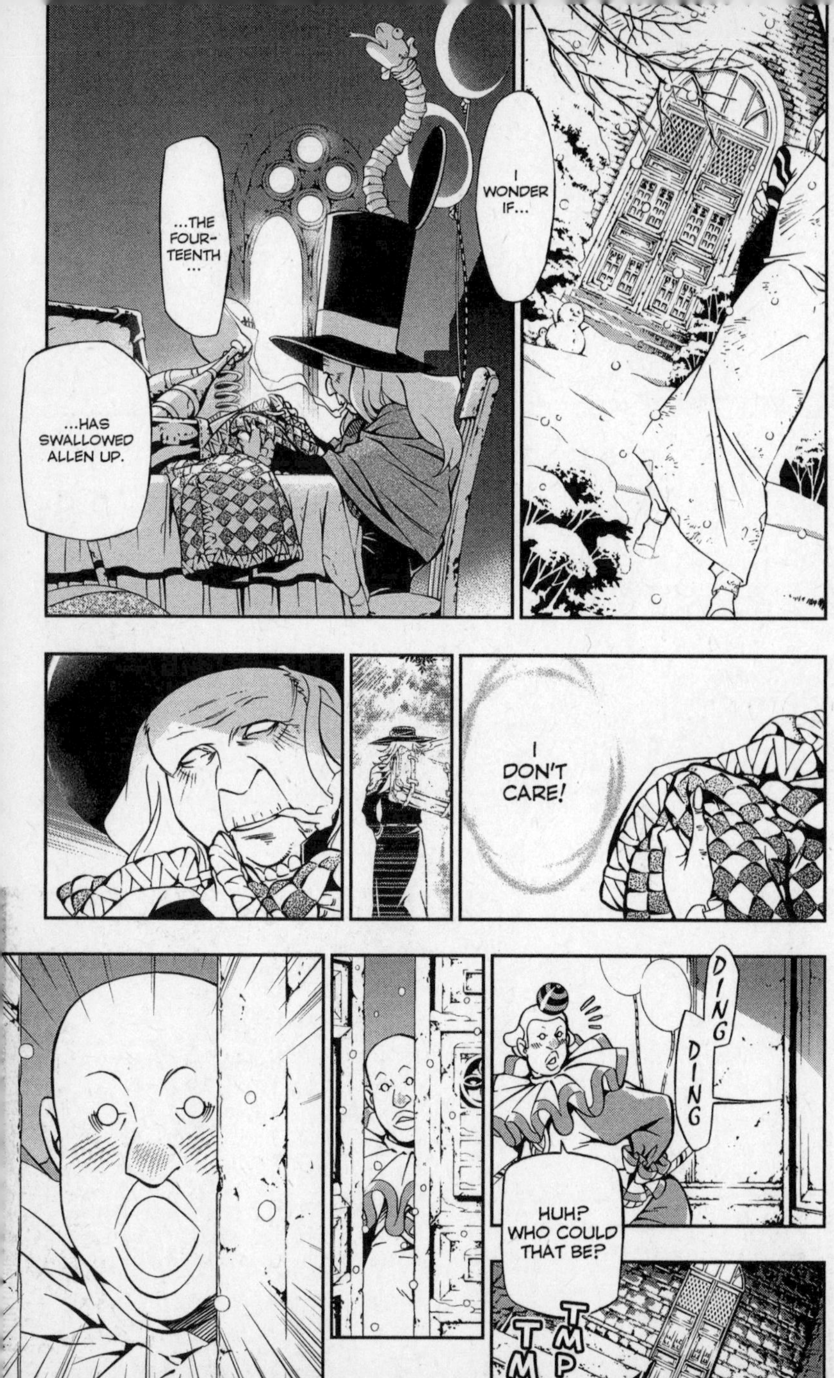
I WONDER IF...
...THE FOURTEENTH...
...HAS SWALLOWED ALLEN UP.
I DON'T CARE!
DING DING
HUH? WHO COULD THAT BE?
TMP
TMP

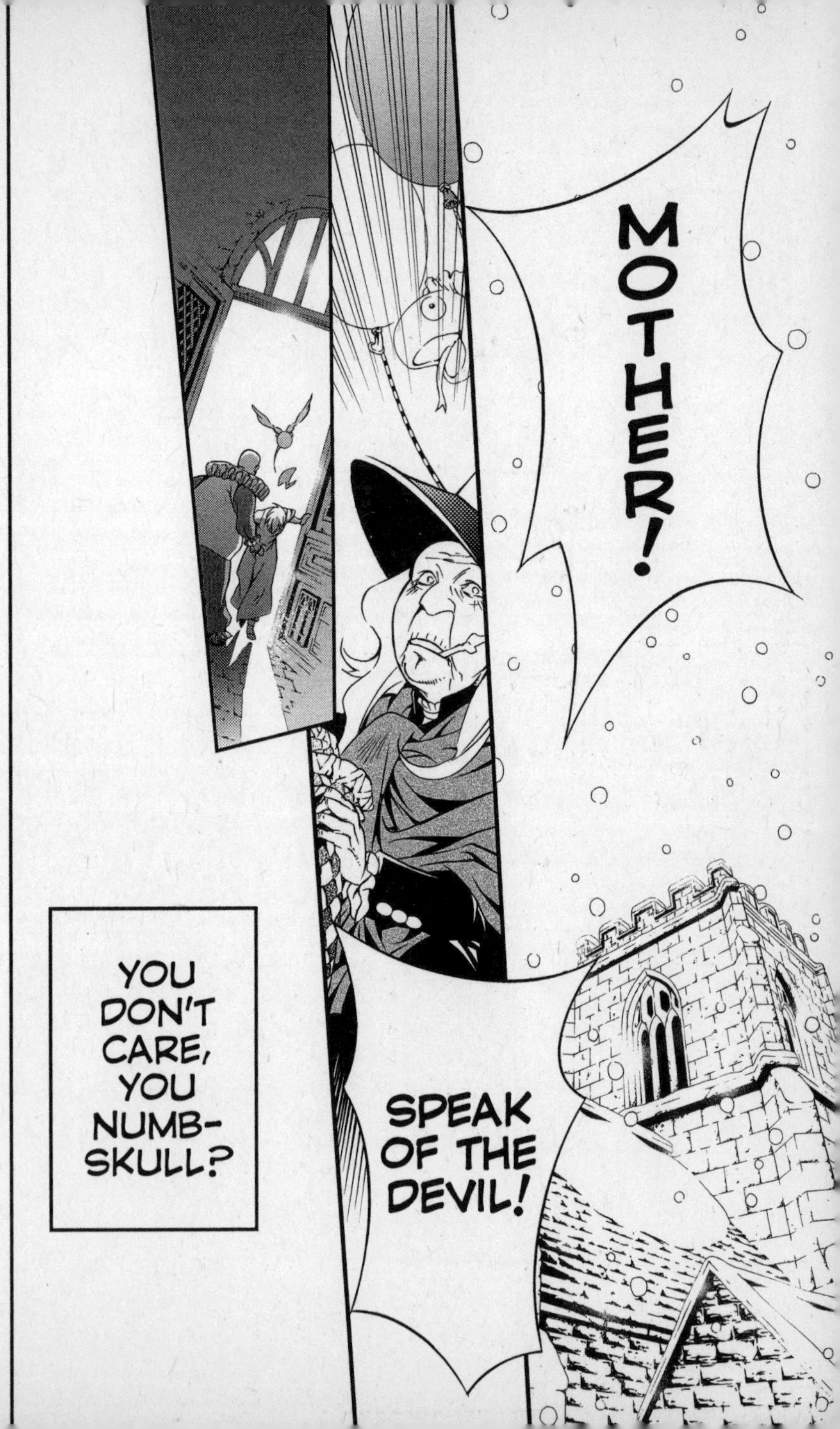
MOTHER!
SPEAK OF THE DEVIL!
YOU DON'T CARE, YOU NUMB-SKULL?

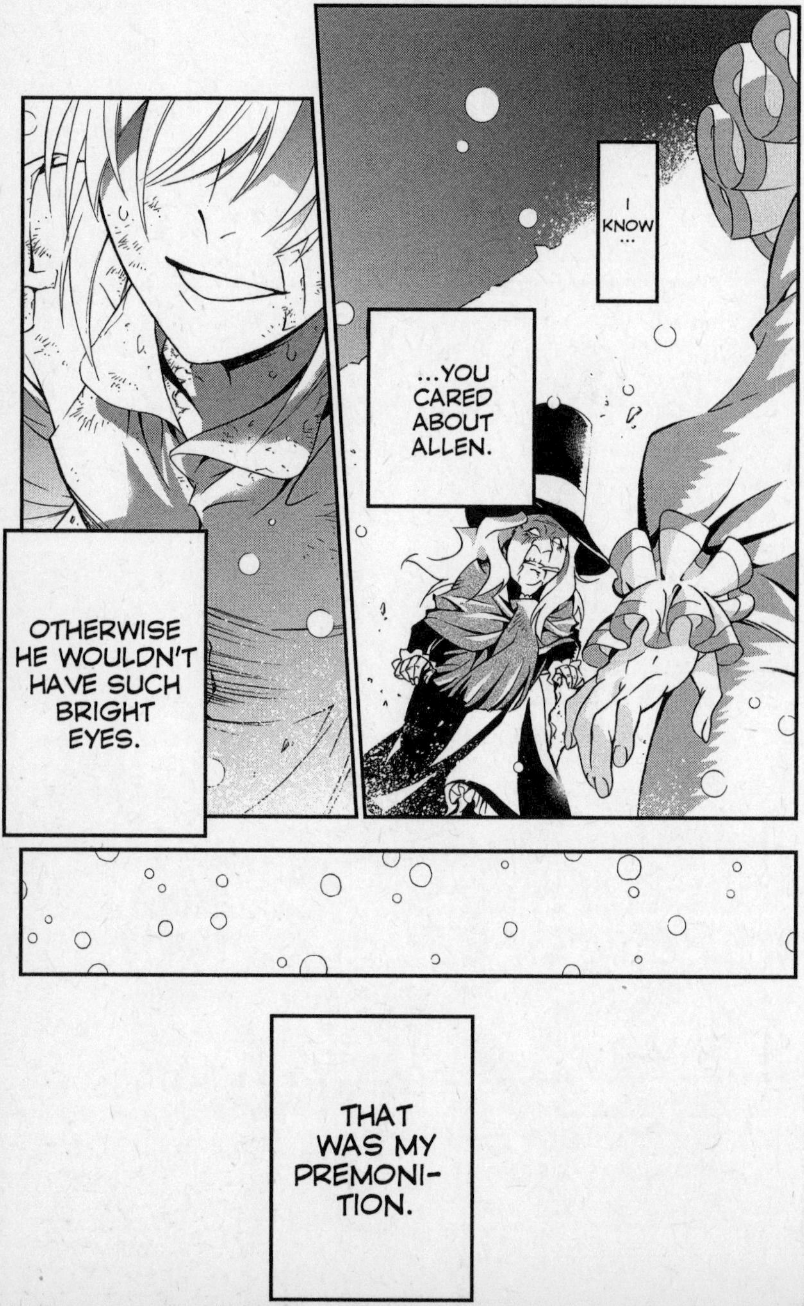
I KNOW...
...YOU CARED ABOUT ALLEN.
OTHERWISE HE WOULDN'T HAVE SUCH BRIGHT EYES.
THAT WAS MY PREMONI-TION.

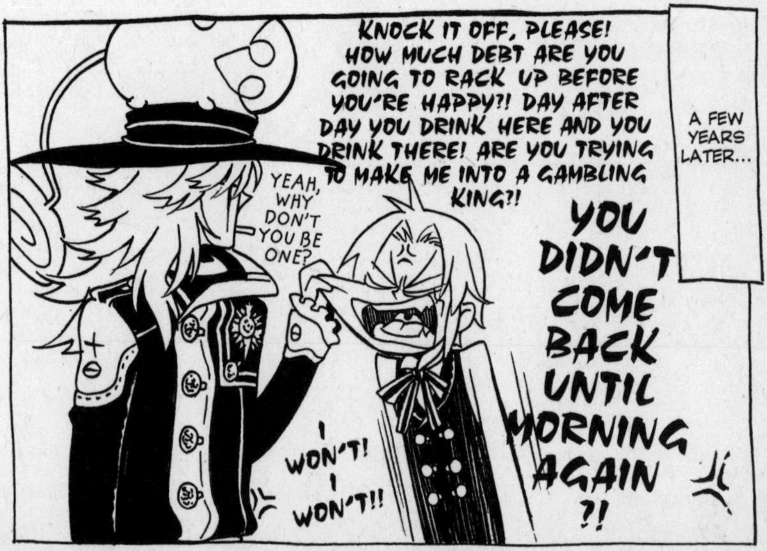

A FEW YEARS LATER...
YOU DIDN'T COME BACK UNTIL MORNING AGAIN?!
KNOCK IT OFF, PLEASE! HOW MUCH DEBT ARE YOU GOING TO RACK UP BEFORE YOU'RE HAPPY?! DAY AFTER DAY YOU DRINK HERE AND YOU DRINK THERE! ARE YOU TRYING TO MAKE ME INTO A GAMBLING KING?!
YEAH, WHY DON'T YOU BE ONE?
I WON'T! I WON'T!!

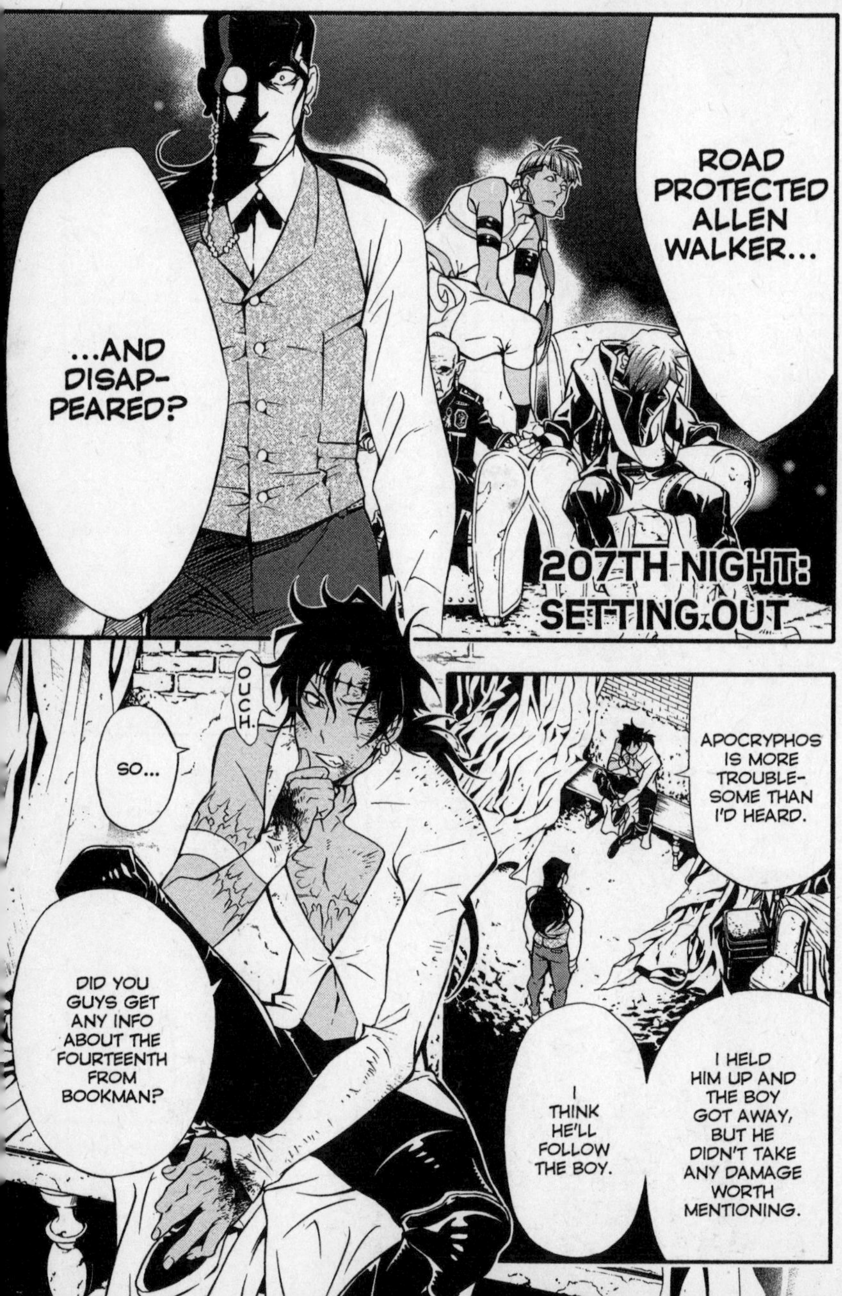
ROAD PROTECTED ALLEN WALKER...
...AND DISAP-PEARED?
207TH NIGHT: SETTING OUT
APOCRYPHOS IS MORE TROUBLE-SOME THAN I'D HEARD.
I HELD HIM UP AND THE BOY GOT AWAY, BUT HE DIDN'T TAKE ANY DAMAGE WORTH MENTIONING.
I THINK HE'LL FOLLOW THE BOY.
OUCH.
SO...
DID YOU GUYS GET ANY INFO ABOUT THE FOURTEENTH FROM BOOKMAN?

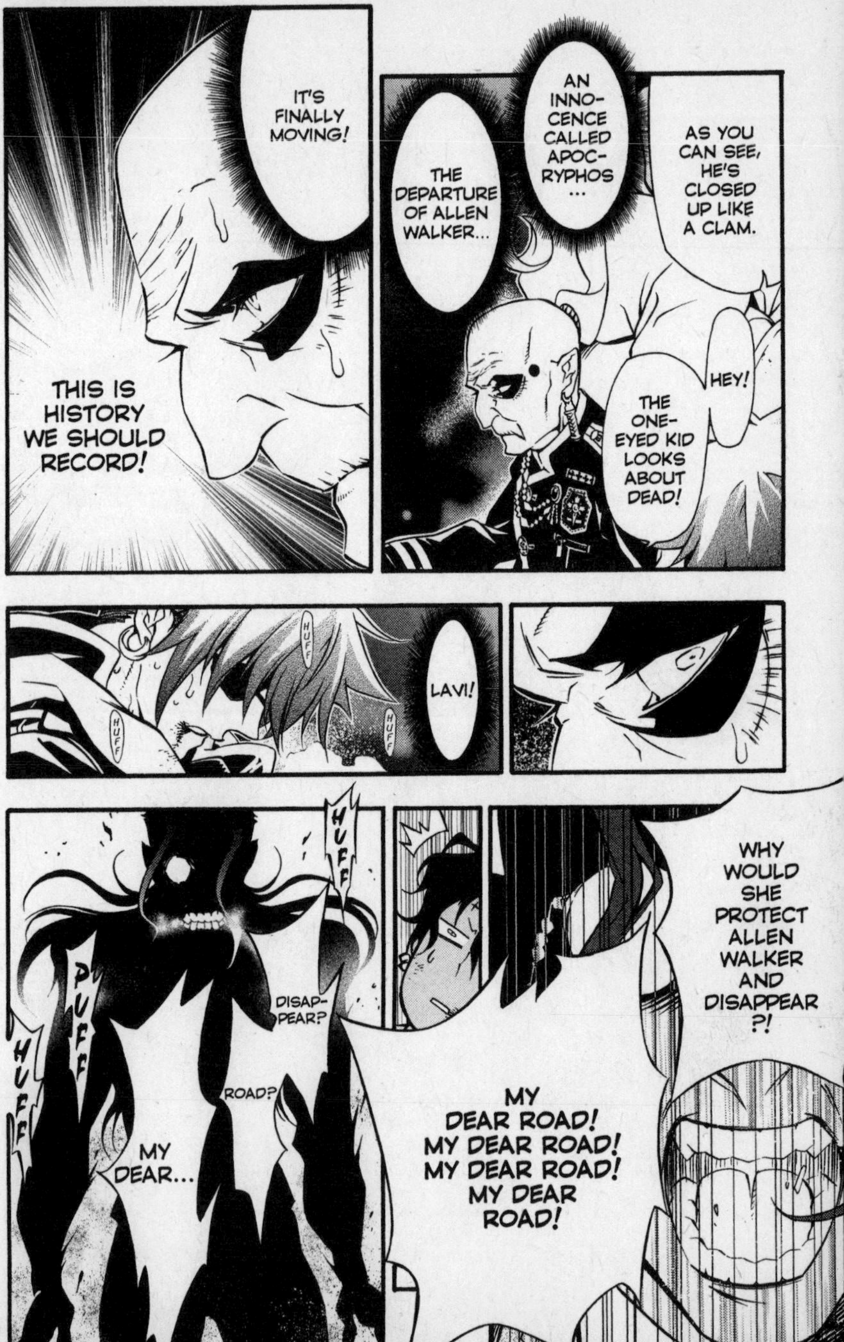
AS YOU CAN SEE, HE'S CLOSED UP LIKE A CLAM.
AN INNOCENCE CALLED APOCRYPHOS...
THE DEPARTURE OF ALLEN WALKER...
HEY!
THE ONE-EYED KID LOOKS ABOUT DEAD!
IT'S FINALLY MOVING!
THIS IS HISTORY WE SHOULD RECORD!
LAVI!
HUFF
HUFF
HUFF
WHY WOULD SHE PROTECT ALLEN WALKER AND DISAPPEAR?!
MY DEAR ROAD! MY DEAR ROAD! MY DEAR ROAD! MY DEAR ROAD!
HUFF HUFF
DISAPPEAR?
PUFF PUFF
ROAD?
HUFF HUFF
MY DEAR...

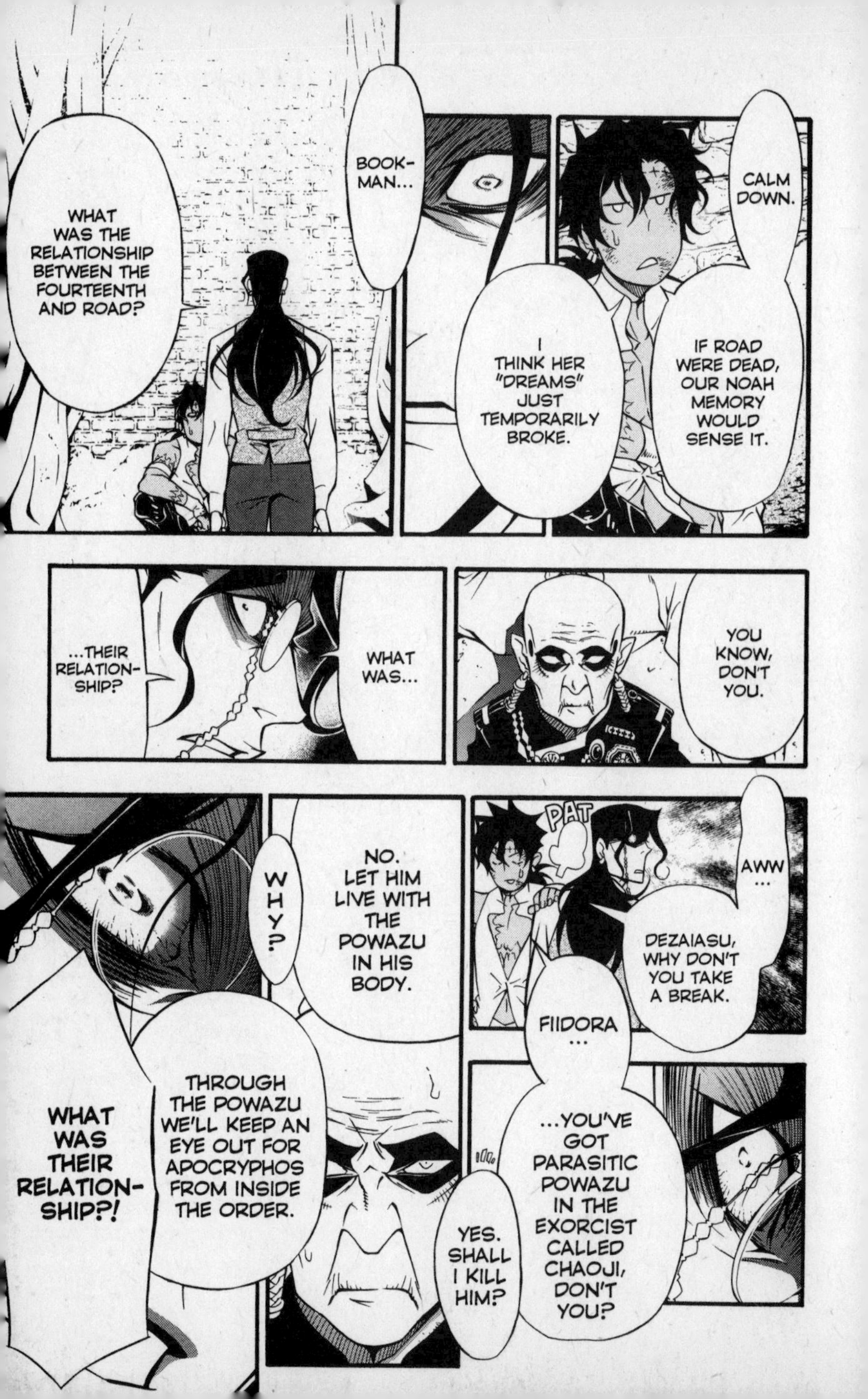
CALM DOWN.
IF ROAD WERE DEAD, OUR NOAH MEMORY WOULD SENSE IT.
I THINK HER "DREAMS" JUST TEMPORARILY BROKE.
BOOK-MAN...
WHAT WAS THE RELATIONSHIP BETWEEN THE FOURTEENTH AND ROAD?
YOU KNOW, DON'T YOU.
WHAT WAS...
...THEIR RELATION-SHIP?
PAT
AWW...
DEZAIASU, WHY DON'T YOU TAKE A BREAK.
FIIDORA...
...YOU'VE GOT PARASITIC POWAZU IN THE EXORCIST CALLED CHAOJI, DON'T YOU?
YES. SHALL I KILL HIM?
NO. LET HIM LIVE WITH THE POWAZU IN HIS BODY.
WHY?
THROUGH THE POWAZU WE'LL KEEP AN EYE OUT FOR APOCRYPHOS FROM INSIDE THE ORDER.
WHAT WAS THEIR RELATION-SHIP?!

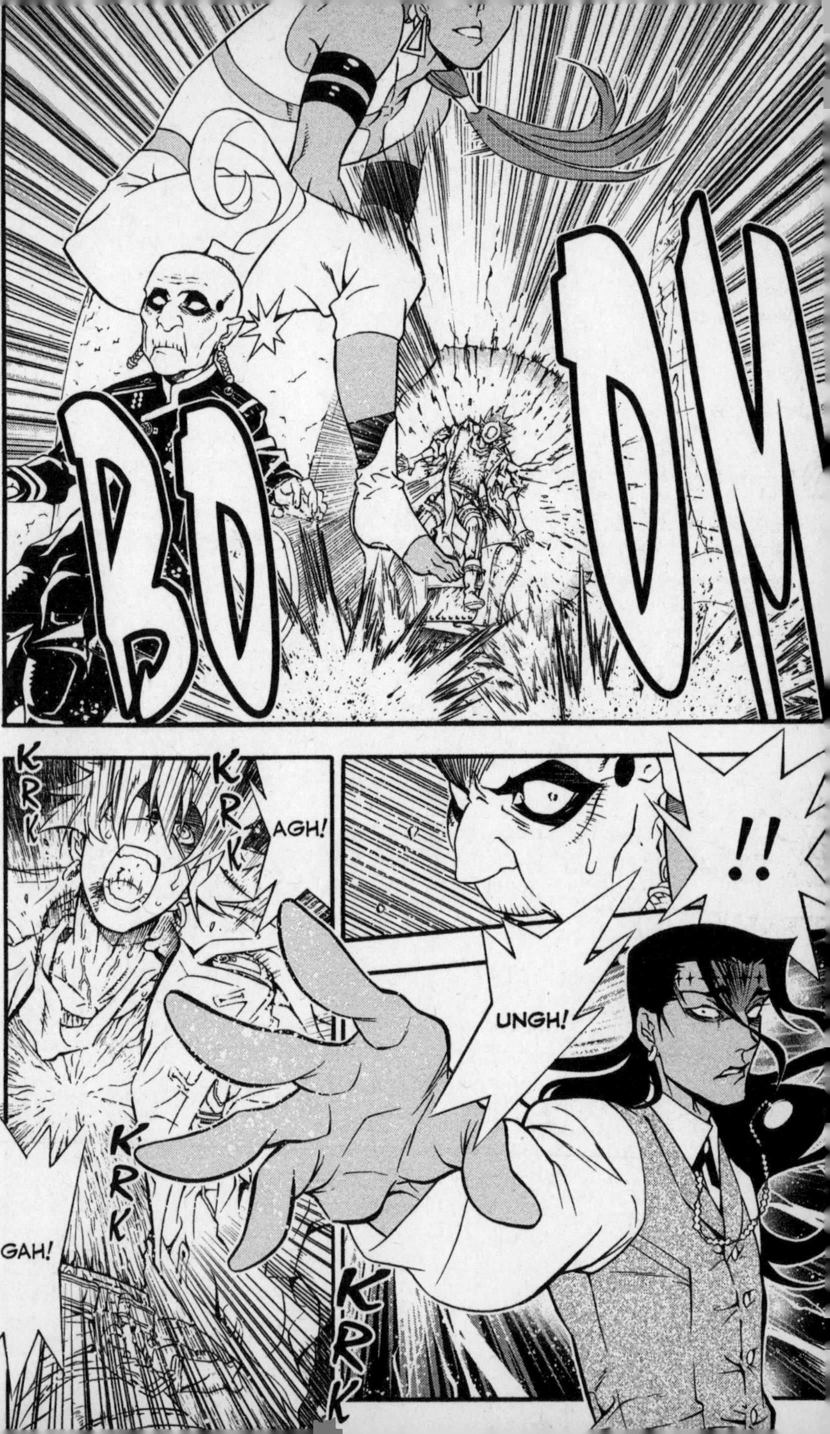
DOM
!!
KRK
KRK
AGH!
UNGH!
KRK
KRK
GAH!

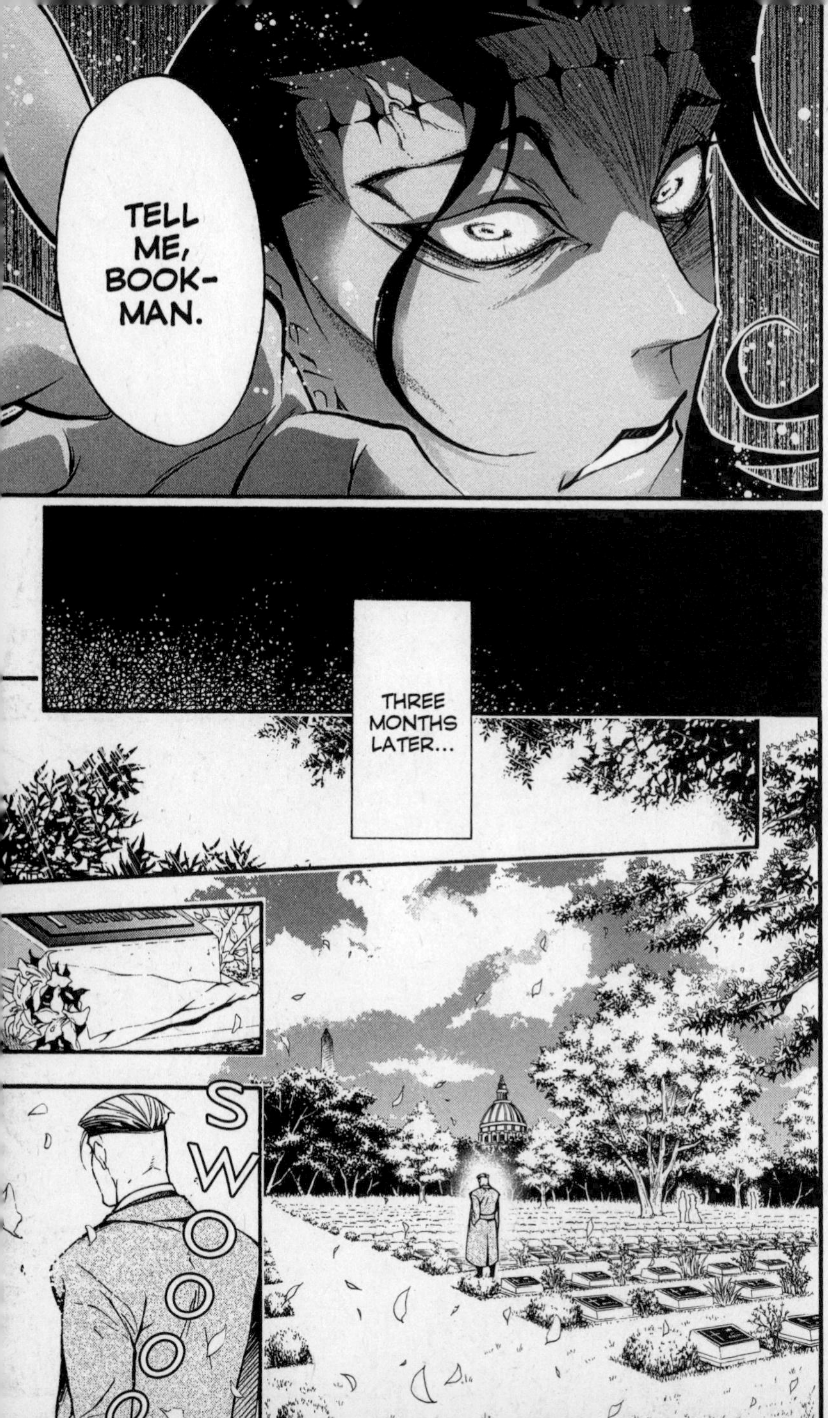
TELL ME, BOOK-MAN.
THREE MONTHS LATER...
SWOOOO

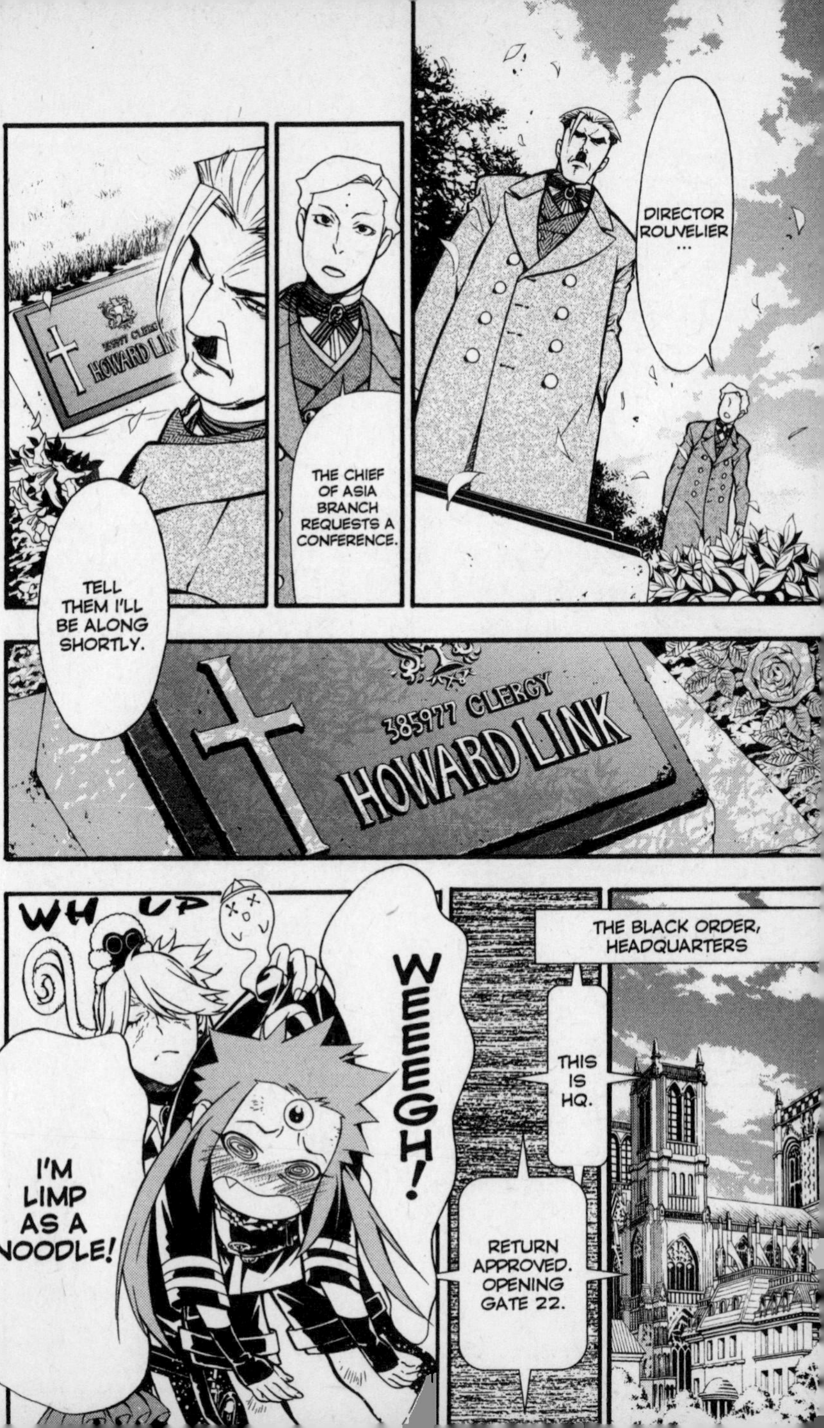
DIRECTOR ROUVELIER ...
THE CHIEF OF ASIA BRANCH REQUESTS A CONFERENCE.
TELL THEM I'LL BE ALONG SHORTLY.
385977 CLERGY
HOWARD LINK
THE BLACK ORDER, HEADQUARTERS
THIS IS HQ.
RETURN APPROVED. OPENING GATE 22.
WH UP
WEEEGH!
I'M LIMP AS A NOODLE!

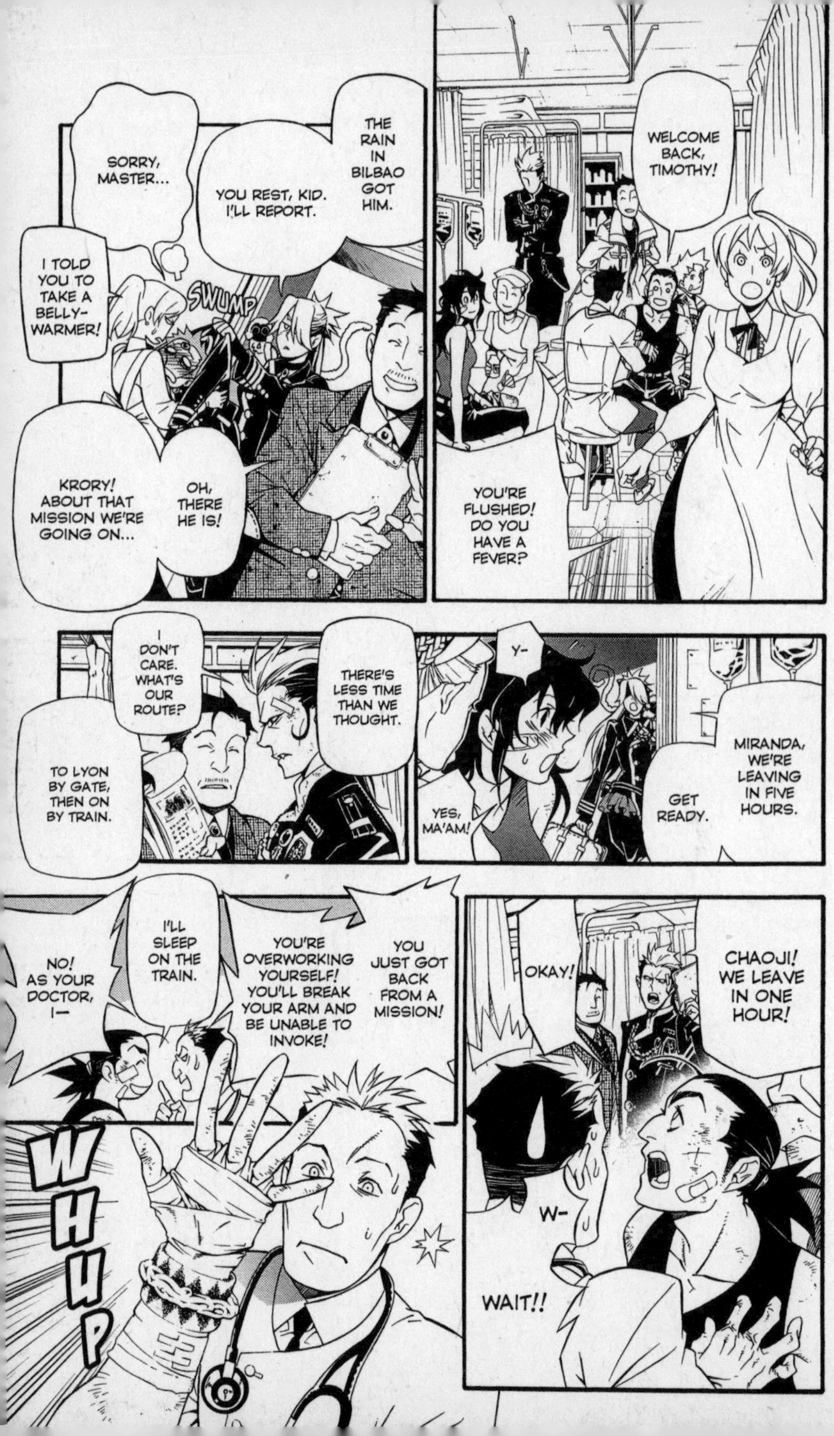
WELCOME BACK, TIMOTHY!
YOU'RE FLUSHED! DO YOU HAVE A FEVER?
THE RAIN IN BILBAO GOT HIM.
YOU REST, KID. I'LL REPORT.
SORRY, MASTER...
I TOLD YOU TO TAKE A BELLY-WARMER!
SWUMP
OH, THERE HE IS!
KRORY! ABOUT THAT MISSION WE'RE GOING ON...
Y-
MIRANDA, WE'RE LEAVING IN FIVE HOURS.
GET READY.
YES, MA'AM!
THERE'S LESS TIME THAN WE THOUGHT.
I DON'T CARE. WHAT'S OUR ROUTE?
TO LYON BY GATE, THEN ON BY TRAIN.
CHAOJI! WE LEAVE IN ONE HOUR!
OKAY!
W-
WAIT!!
YOU JUST GOT BACK FROM A MISSION!
YOU'RE OVERWORKING YOURSELF! YOU'LL BREAK YOUR ARM AND BE UNABLE TO INVOKE!
I'LL SLEEP ON THE TRAIN.
NO! AS YOUR DOCTOR, I—
WHUP

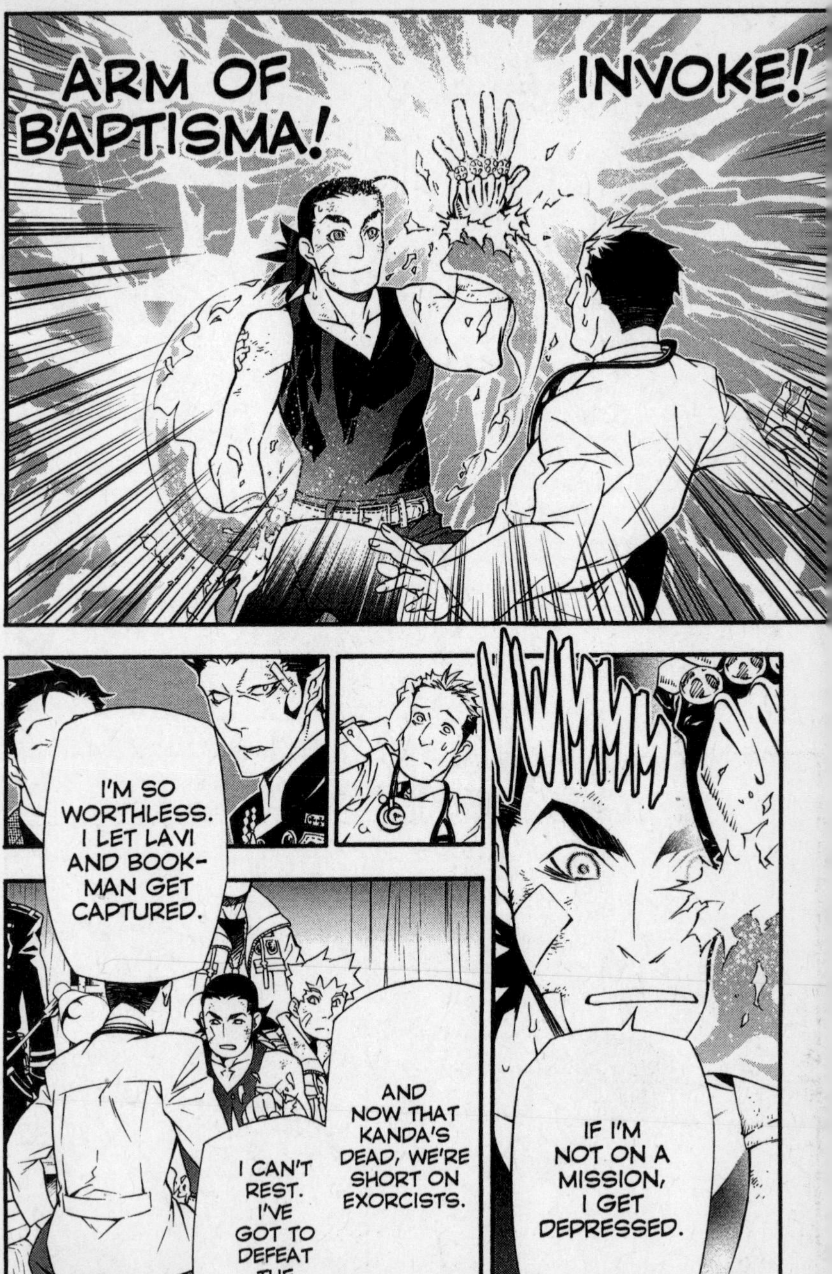
INVOKE!
ARM OF BAPTISMA!
VWMMMM
IF I'M NOT ON A MISSION, I GET DEPRESSED.
I'M SO WORTHLESS. I LET LAVI AND BOOK-MAN GET CAPTURED.
AND NOW THAT KANDA'S DEAD, WE'RE SHORT ON EXORCISTS.
I CAN'T REST. I'VE GOT TO DEFEAT THE AKUMA.

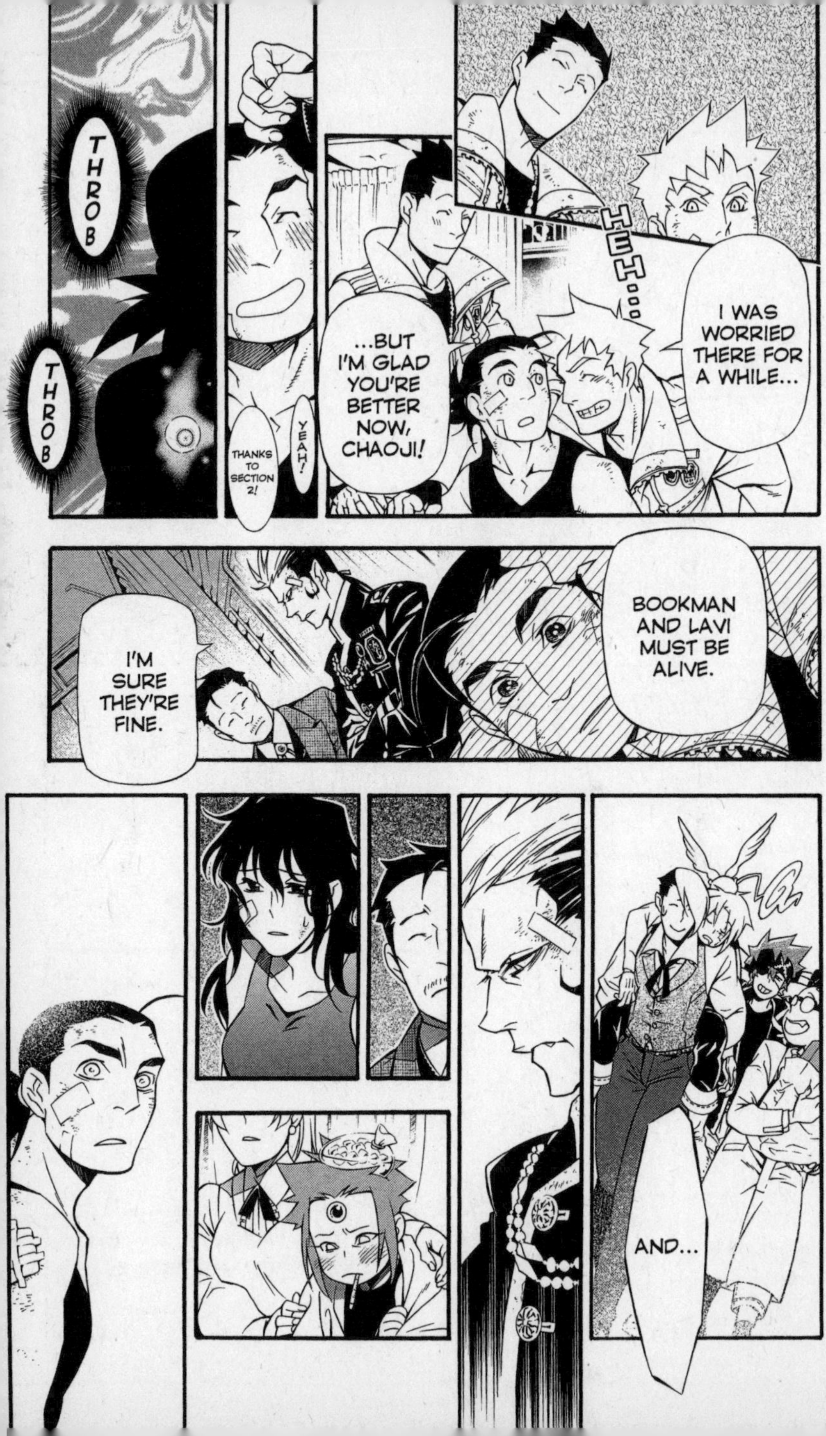
HEH...
I WAS WORRIED THERE FOR A WHILE...
...BUT I'M GLAD YOU'RE BETTER NOW, CHAOJI!
YEAH!
THANKS TO SECTION 2!
THROB
THROB
BOOKMAN AND LAVI MUST BE ALIVE.
I'M SURE THEY'RE FINE.
AND...

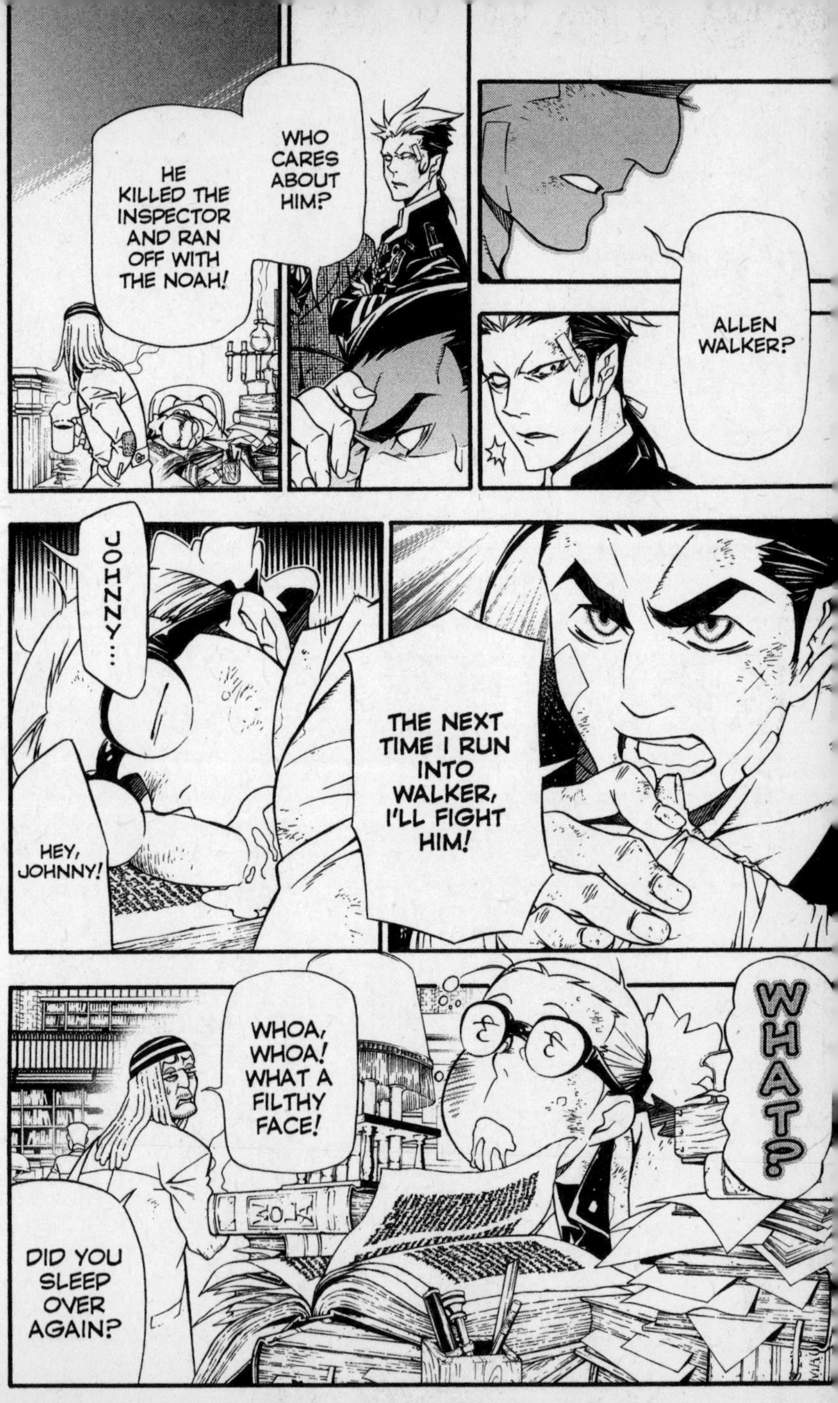
ALLEN WALKER?
WHO CARES ABOUT HIM?
HE KILLED THE INSPECTOR AND RAN OFF WITH THE NOAH!
THE NEXT TIME I RUN INTO WALKER, I'LL FIGHT HIM!
JOHNNY...
HEY, JOHNNY!
WHAT?
WHOA, WHOA! WHAT A FILTHY FACE!
DID YOU SLEEP OVER AGAIN?

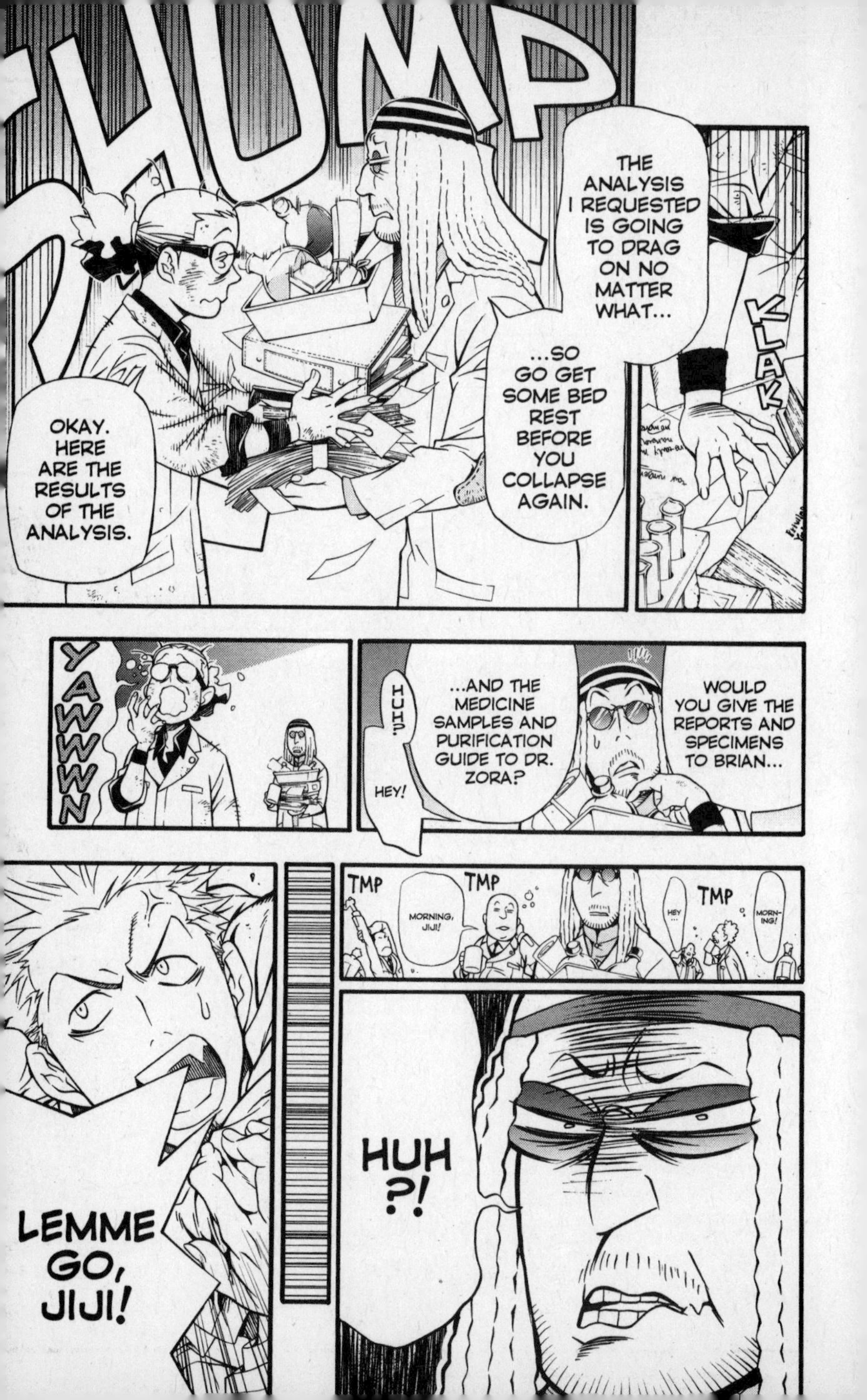
KLAK
THUMP
THE ANALYSIS I REQUESTED IS GOING TO DRAG ON NO MATTER WHAT...
...SO GO GET SOME BED REST BEFORE YOU COLLAPSE AGAIN.
OKAY. HERE ARE THE RESULTS OF THE ANALYSIS.
WOULD YOU GIVE THE REPORTS AND SPECIMENS TO BRIAN...
...AND THE MEDICINE SAMPLES AND PURIFICATION GUIDE TO DR. ZORA?
HUH?
HEY!
YAWWWN
MORN-ING!
TMP
HEY...
TMP
MORNING, JIJI!
TMP
HUH?!
LEMME GO, JIJI!

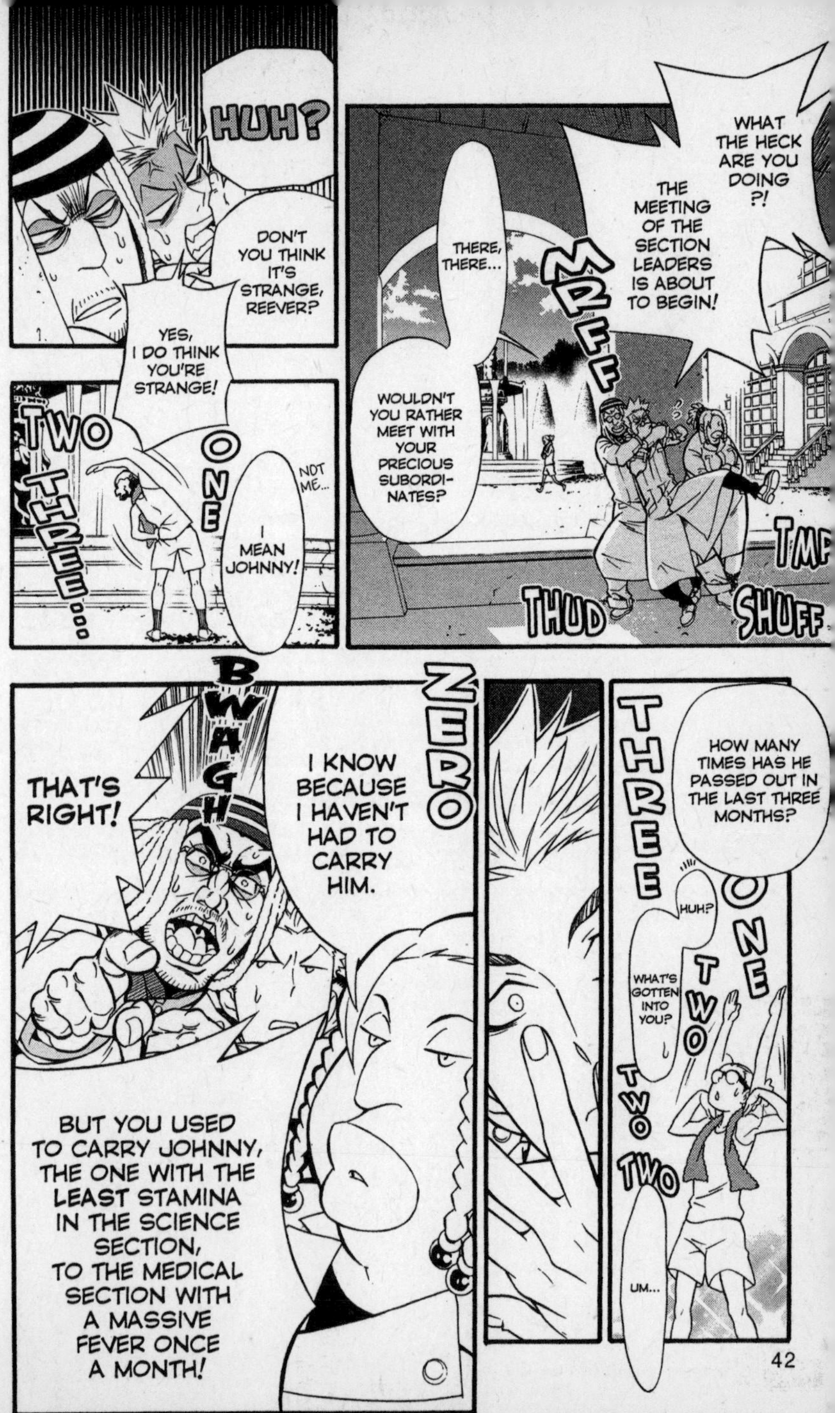
WHAT THE HECK ARE YOU DOING?!
THE MEETING OF THE SECTION LEADERS IS ABOUT TO BEGIN!
MRFF
TMP
SHUFF
THERE, THERE...
WOULDN'T YOU RATHER MEET WITH YOUR PRECIOUS SUBORDINATES?
THUD
HUH?
DON'T YOU THINK IT'S STRANGE, REEVER?
YES, I DO THINK YOU'RE STRANGE!
ONE
NOT ME...
I MEAN JOHNNY!
TWO
THREE...
HOW MANY TIMES HAS HE PASSED OUT IN THE LAST THREE MONTHS?
ONE
THREE
HUH?
WHAT'S GOTTEN INTO YOU?
TWO
TWO
TWO
UM...
ZERO
I KNOW BECAUSE I HAVEN'T HAD TO CARRY HIM.
BWAGH
THAT'S RIGHT!
BUT YOU USED TO CARRY JOHNNY, THE ONE WITH THE LEAST STAMINA IN THE SCIENCE SECTION, TO THE MEDICAL SECTION WITH A MASSIVE FEVER ONCE A MONTH!

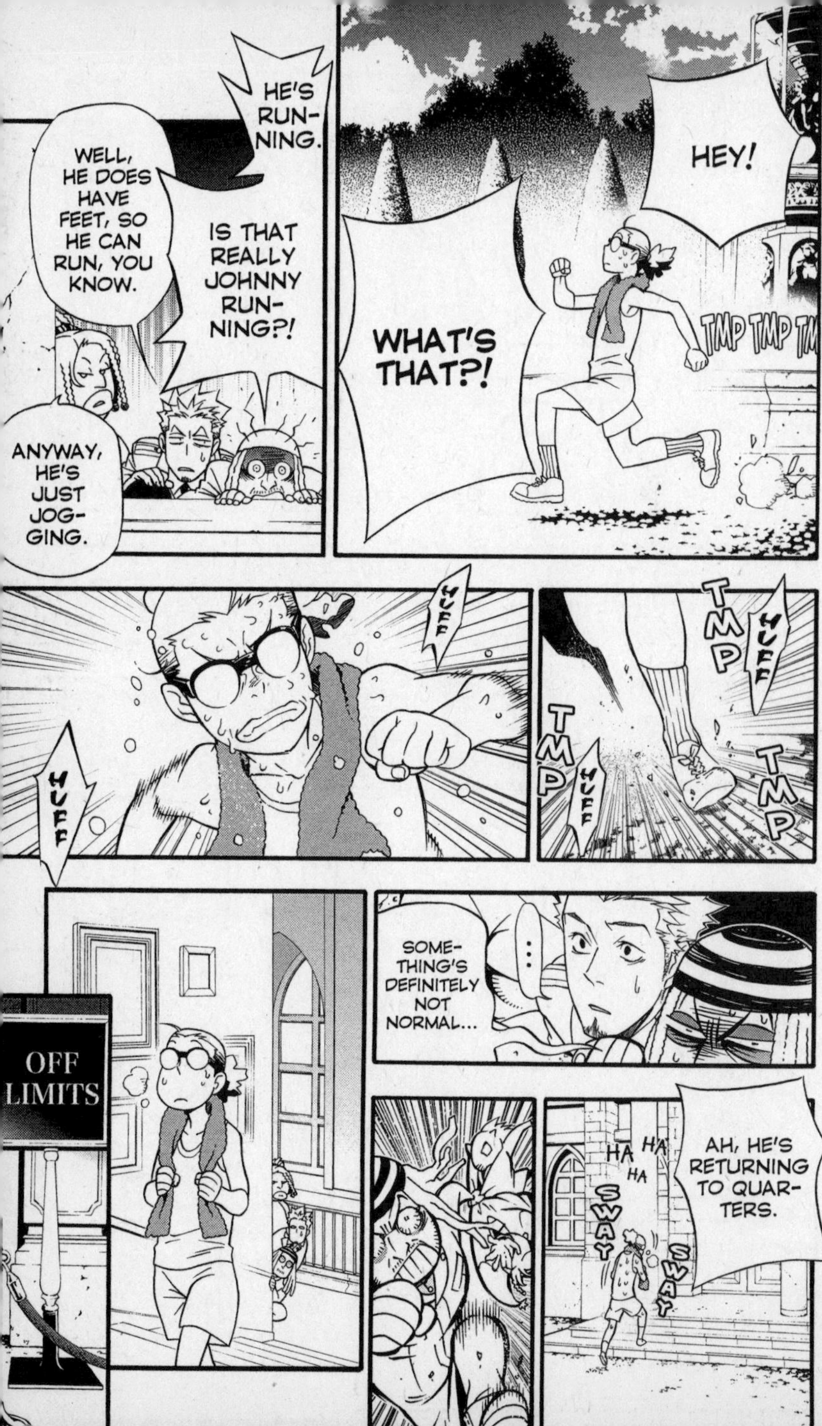

HEY!
TMP TMP TM
WHAT'S THAT?!
HE'S RUN-NING.
IS THAT REALLY JOHNNY RUN-NING?!
WELL, HE DOES HAVE FEET, SO HE CAN RUN, YOU KNOW.
ANYWAY, HE'S JUST JOG-GING.
TMP
HUFF
TMP
TMP
HUFF
HUFF
HUFF
...
SOME-THING'S DEFINITELY NOT NORMAL...
AH, HE'S RETURNING TO QUAR-TERS.
HA HA HA
SWAY
SWAY
OFF LIMITS

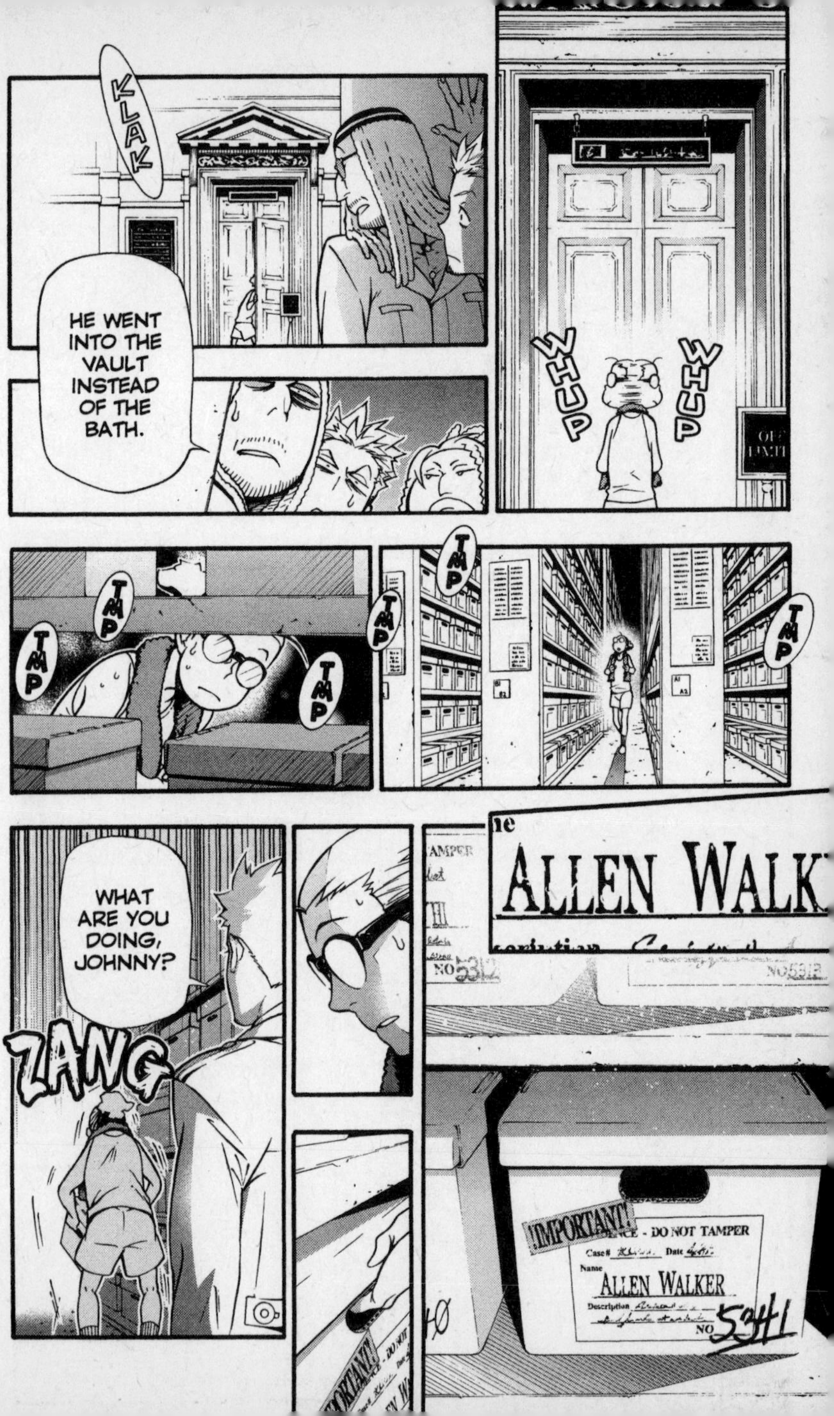
WHUP
WHUP
KLAK
HE WENT INTO THE VAULT INSTEAD OF THE BATH.
TMP
TMP
TMP
TMP
TMP
TMP
ALLEN WALK
NO 5312
IMPORTANT!
- DO NOT TAMPER
Case#
Date
Name
ALLEN WALKER
Description
NO 5341
WHAT ARE YOU DOING, JOHNNY?
ZANG

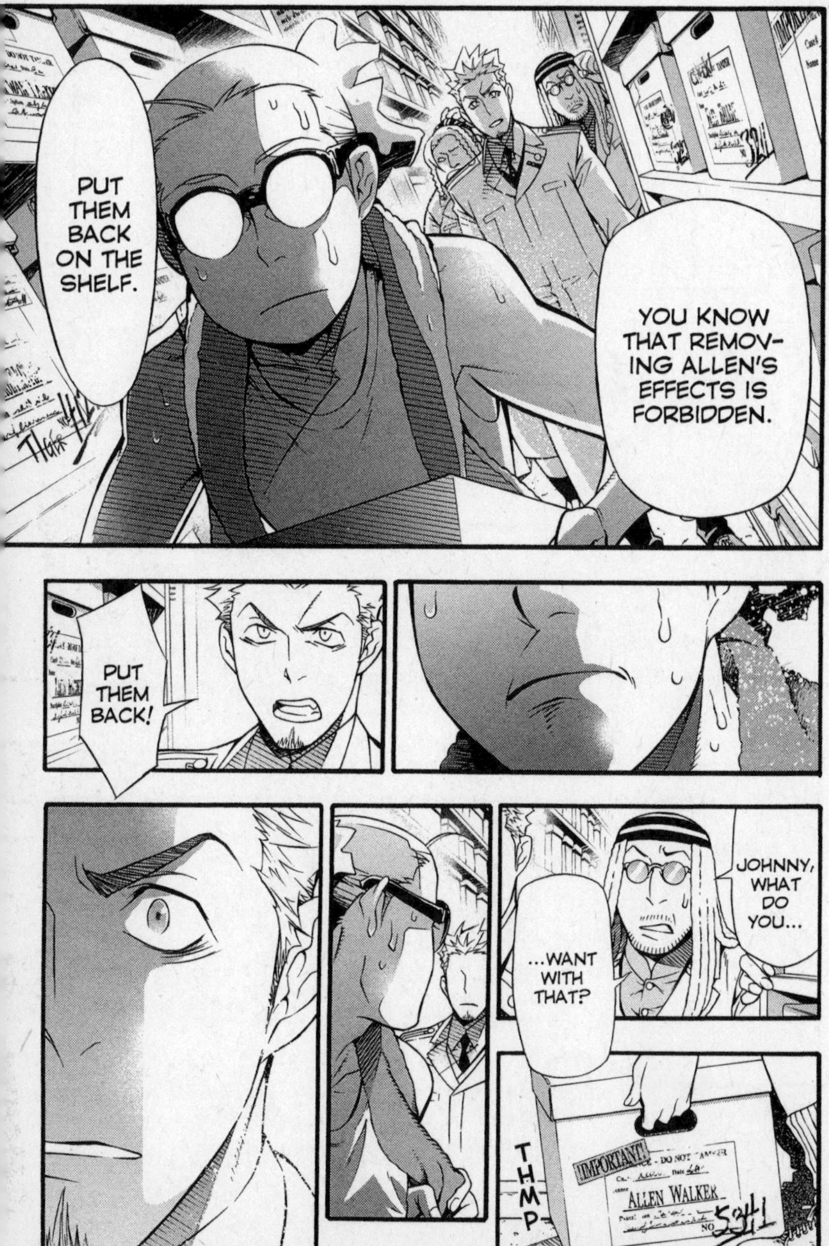
YOU KNOW THAT REMOV-ING ALLEN'S EFFECTS IS FORBIDDEN.
PUT THEM BACK ON THE SHELF.
PUT THEM BACK!
JOHNNY, WHAT DO YOU...
...WANT WITH THAT?
THMP
IMPORTANT
ALLEN WALKER
NO 5341

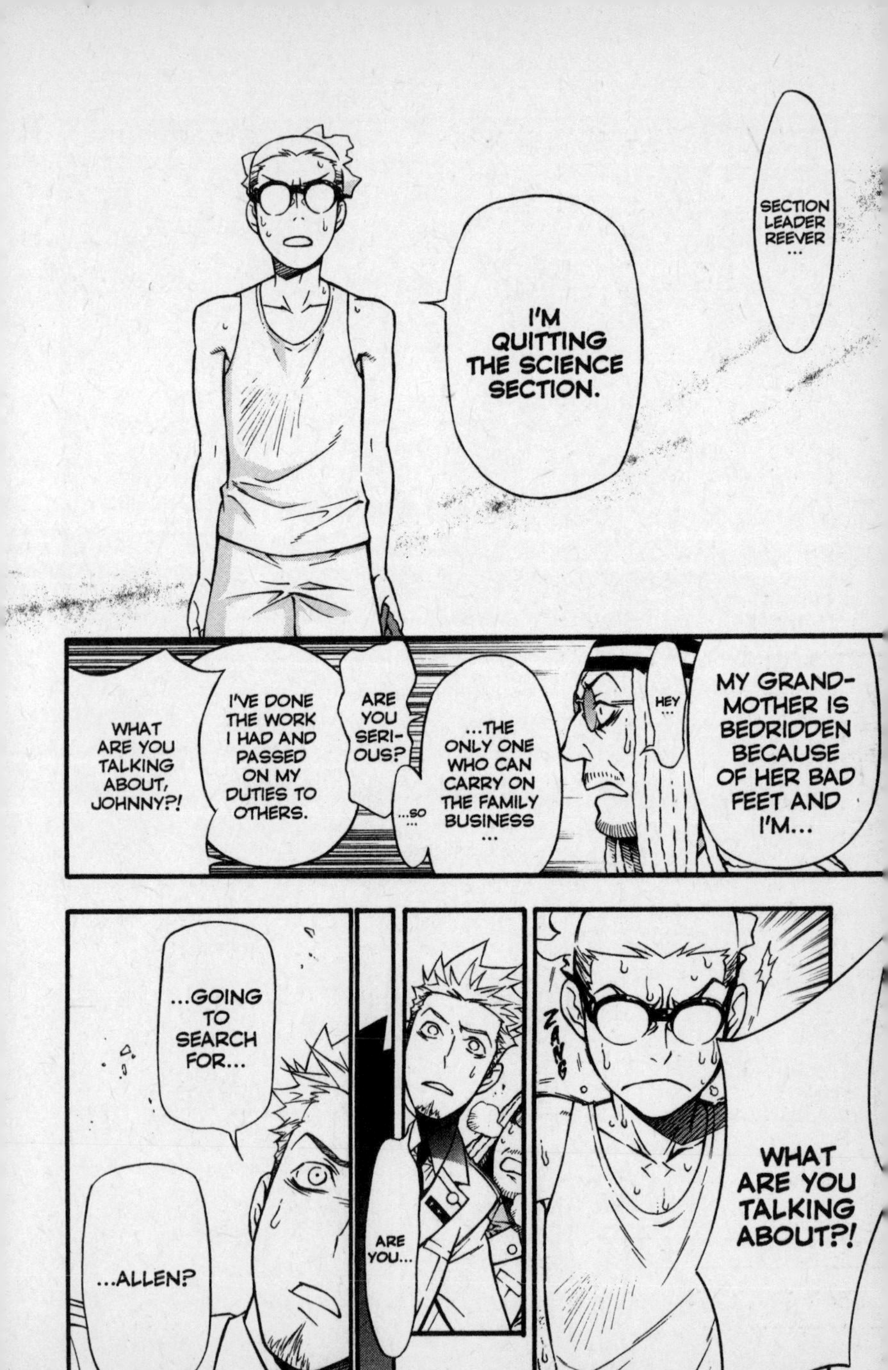
SECTION LEADER REEVER...
I'M QUITTING THE SCIENCE SECTION.
MY GRAND-MOTHER IS BEDRIDDEN BECAUSE OF HER BAD FEET AND I'M...
HEY...
...THE ONLY ONE WHO CAN CARRY ON THE FAMILY BUSINESS...
ARE YOU SERI-OUS?
...SO...
I'VE DONE THE WORK I HAD AND PASSED ON MY DUTIES TO OTHERS.
WHAT ARE YOU TALKING ABOUT, JOHNNY?!
ZANG
WHAT ARE YOU TALKING ABOUT?!
ARE YOU...
...GOING TO SEARCH FOR...
...ALLEN?

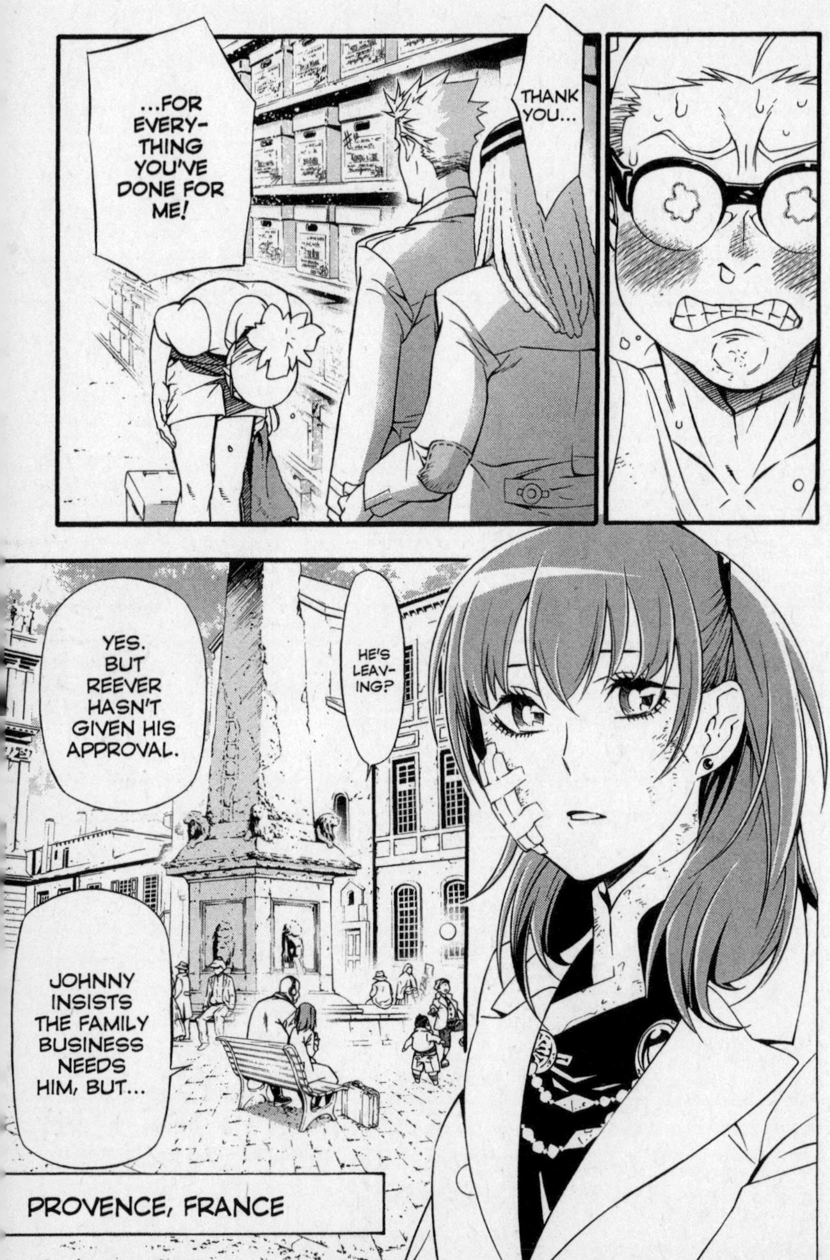
THANK YOU...
...FOR EVERY-THING YOU'VE DONE FOR ME!
HE'S LEAV-ING?
YES. BUT REEVER HASN'T GIVEN HIS APPROVAL.
JOHNNY INSISTS THE FAMILY BUSINESS NEEDS HIM, BUT...
PROVENCE, FRANCE

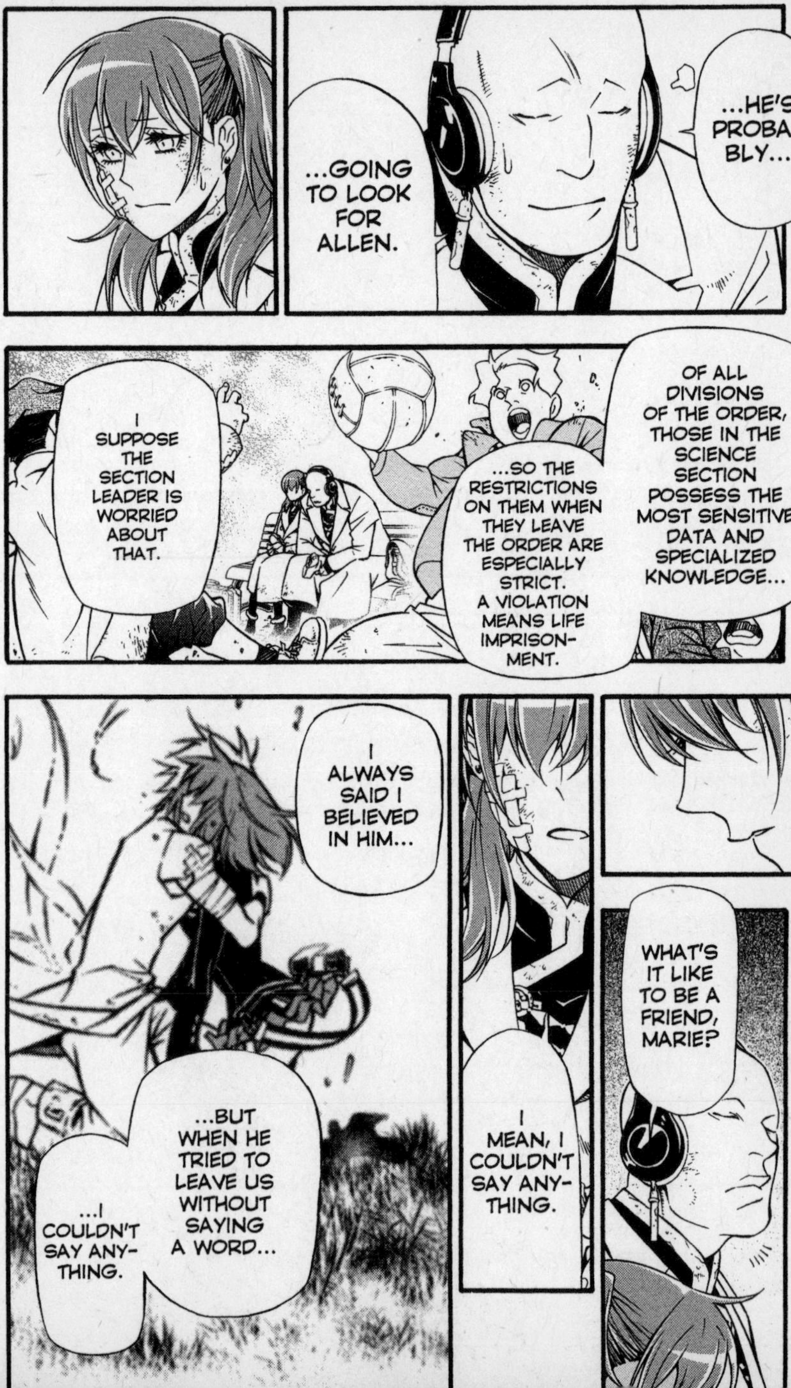
...HE'S PROBABLY...
...GOING TO LOOK FOR ALLEN.
OF ALL DIVISIONS OF THE ORDER, THOSE IN THE SCIENCE SECTION POSSESS THE MOST SENSITIVE DATA AND SPECIALIZED KNOWLEDGE...
...SO THE RESTRICTIONS ON THEM WHEN THEY LEAVE THE ORDER ARE ESPECIALLY STRICT. A VIOLATION MEANS LIFE IMPRISONMENT.
I SUPPOSE THE SECTION LEADER IS WORRIED ABOUT THAT.
WHAT'S IT LIKE TO BE A FRIEND, MARIE?
I MEAN, I COULDN'T SAY ANYTHING.
I ALWAYS SAID I BELIEVED IN HIM...
...BUT WHEN HE TRIED TO LEAVE US WITHOUT SAYING A WORD...
...I COULDN'T SAY ANYTHING.

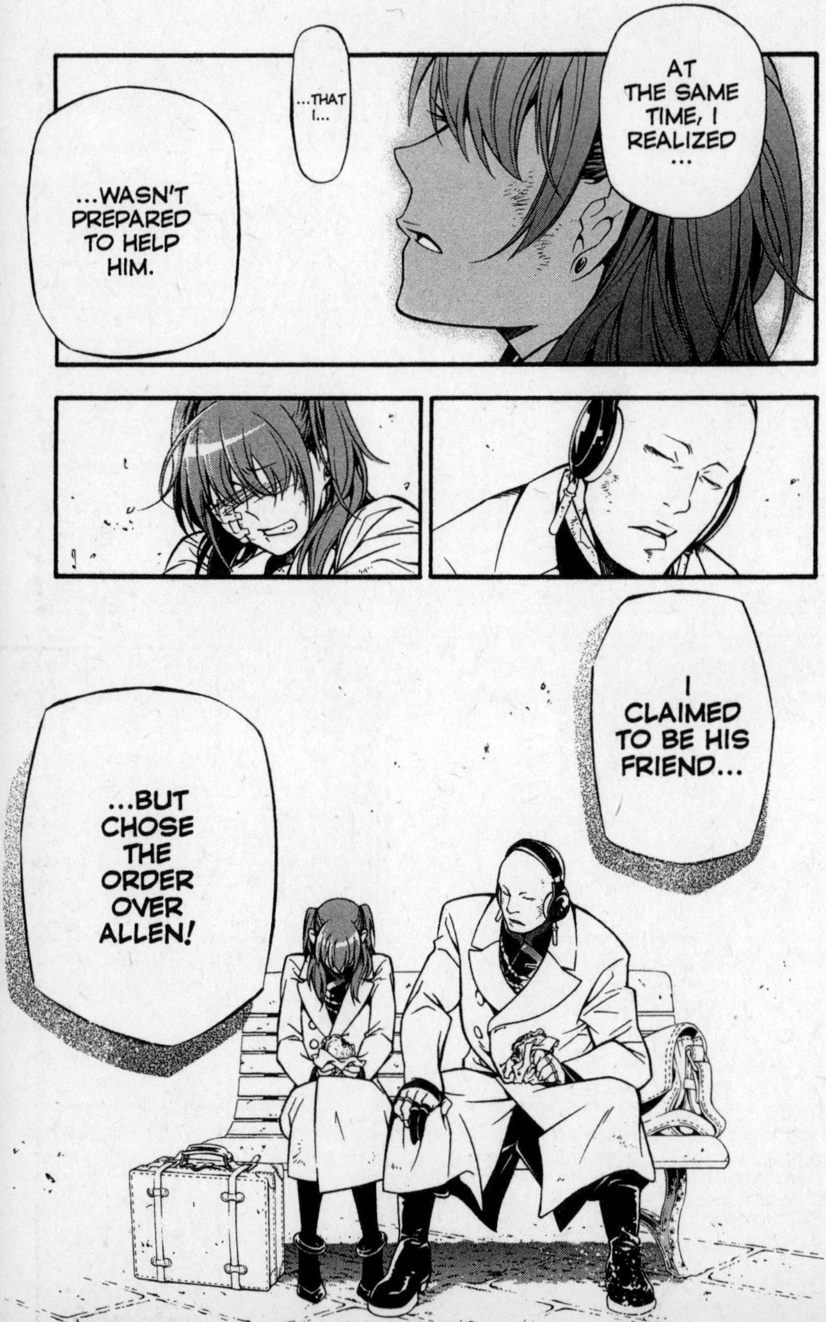
AT THE SAME TIME, I REALIZED...
...THAT I...
...WASN'T PREPARED TO HELP HIM.
I CLAIMED TO BE HIS FRIEND...
...BUT CHOSE THE ORDER OVER ALLEN!

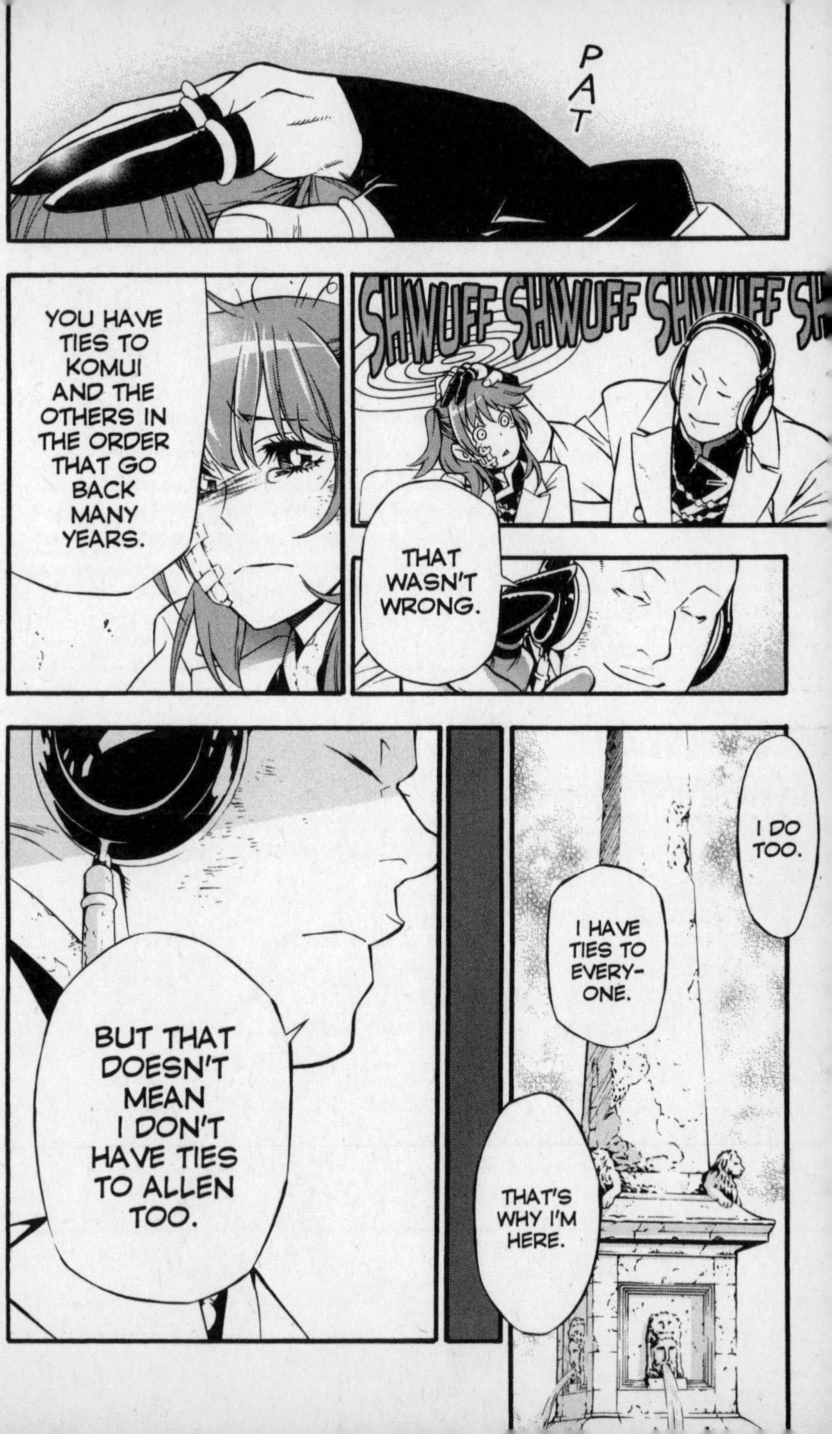
PAT
SHWUFF SHWUFF SHWUFF SH
THAT WASN'T WRONG.
YOU HAVE TIES TO KOMUI AND THE OTHERS IN THE ORDER THAT GO BACK MANY YEARS.
I DO TOO.
I HAVE TIES TO EVERY-ONE.
THAT'S WHY I'M HERE.
BUT THAT DOESN'T MEAN I DON'T HAVE TIES TO ALLEN TOO.

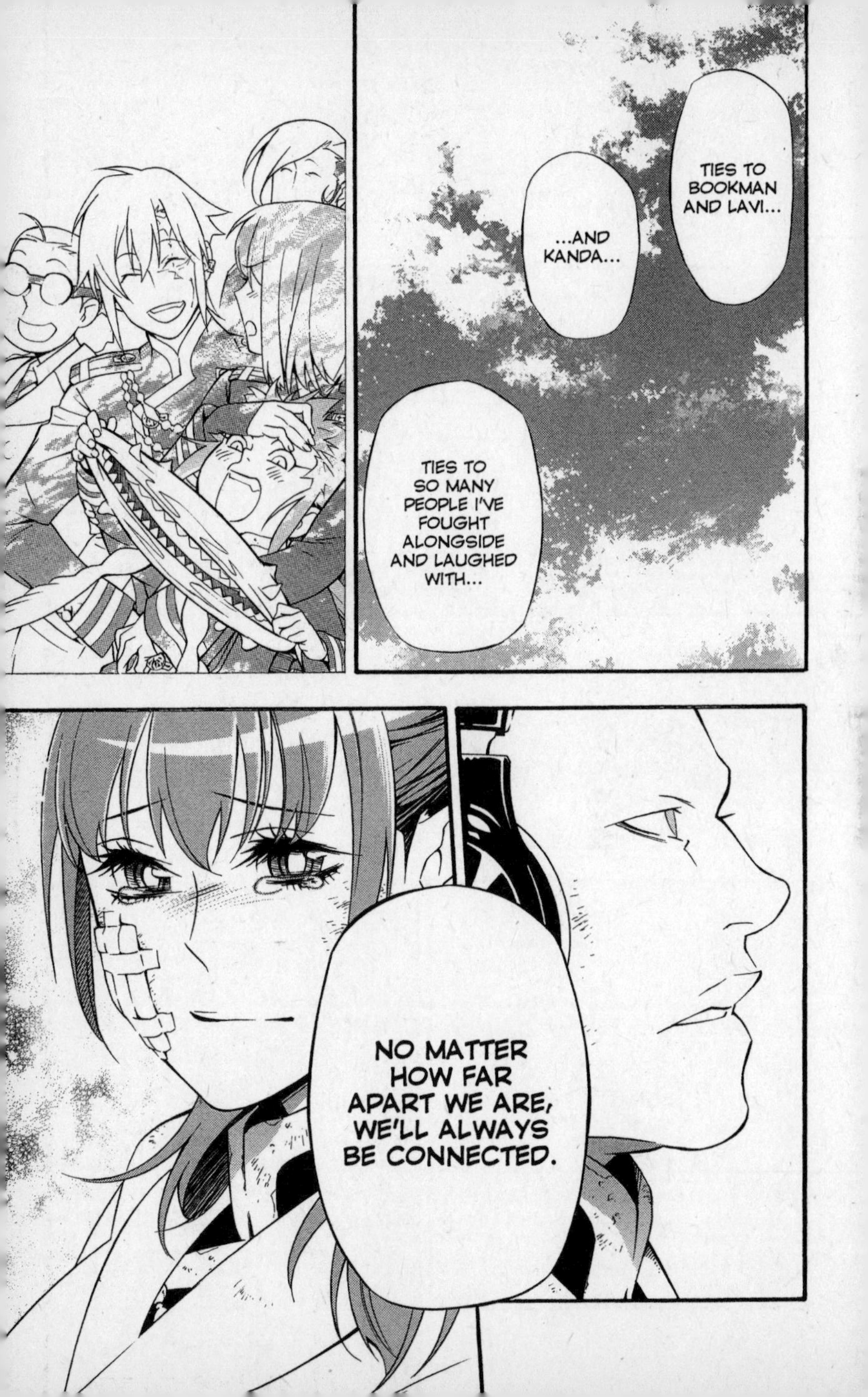
TIES TO BOOKMAN AND LAVI...
...AND KANDA...
TIES TO SO MANY PEOPLE I'VE FOUGHT ALONGSIDE AND LAUGHED WITH...
NO MATTER HOW FAR APART WE ARE, WE'LL ALWAYS BE CONNECTED.

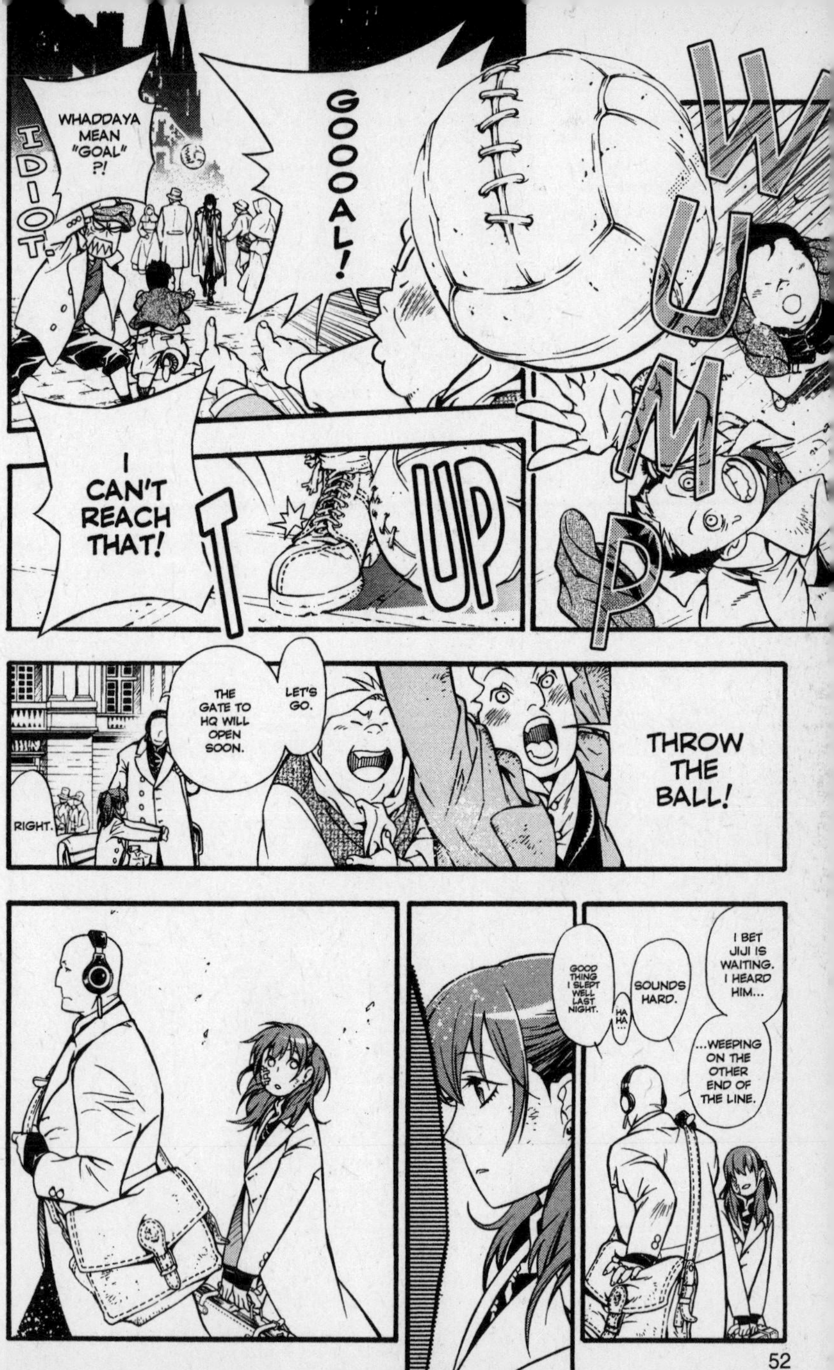
GOOOOAL!
WHADDAYA MEAN "GOAL"?!
IDIOT.
WUMP
T
UP
I CAN'T REACH THAT!
THROW THE BALL!
LET'S GO.
THE GATE TO HQ WILL OPEN SOON.
RIGHT.
I BET JIJI IS WAITING. I HEARD HIM...
...WEEPING ON THE OTHER END OF THE LINE.
SOUNDS HARD.
HA HA...
GOOD THING I SLEPT WELL LAST NIGHT.

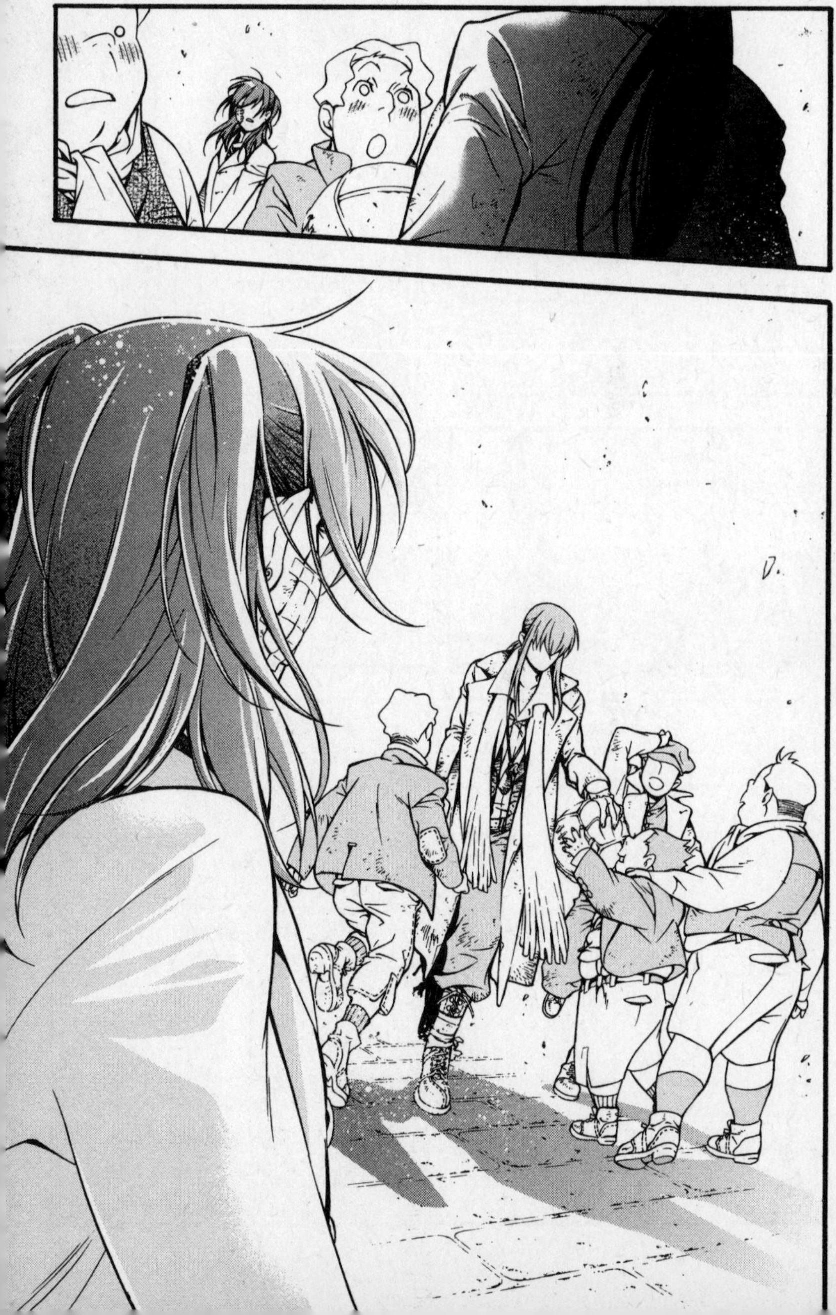

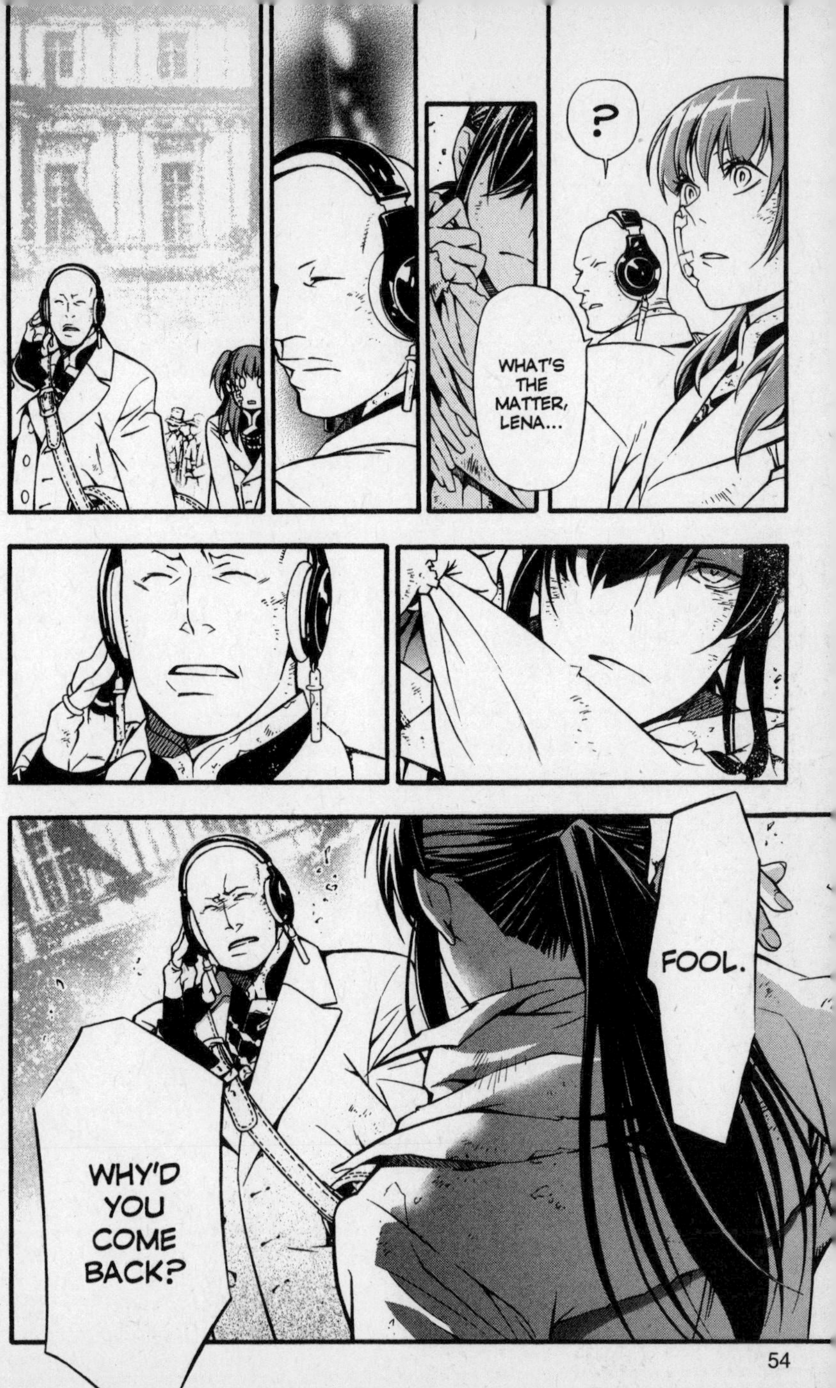
?
WHAT'S THE MATTER, LENA...
FOOL.
WHY'D YOU COME BACK?

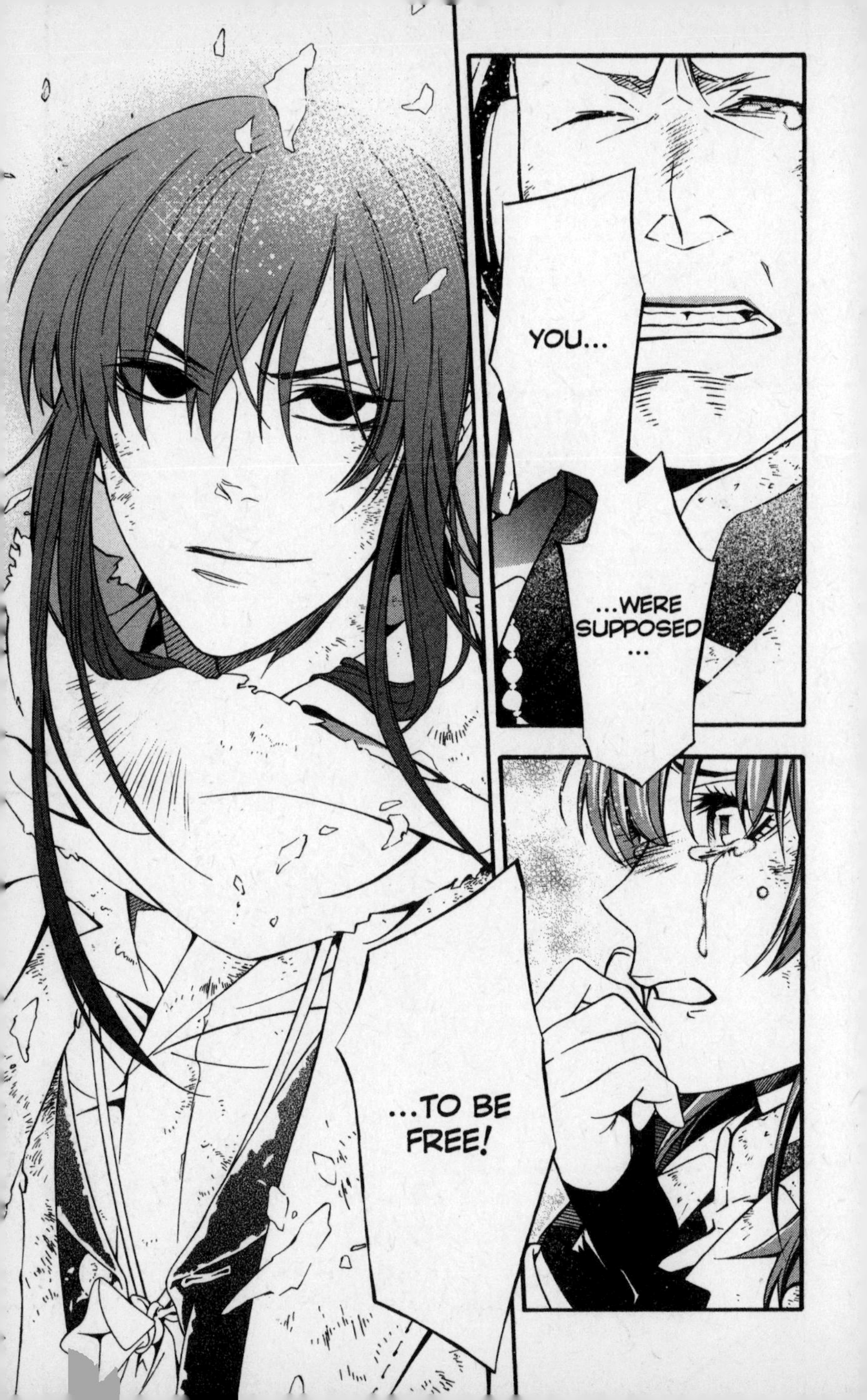
YOU...
...WERE SUPPOSED ...
...TO BE FREE!

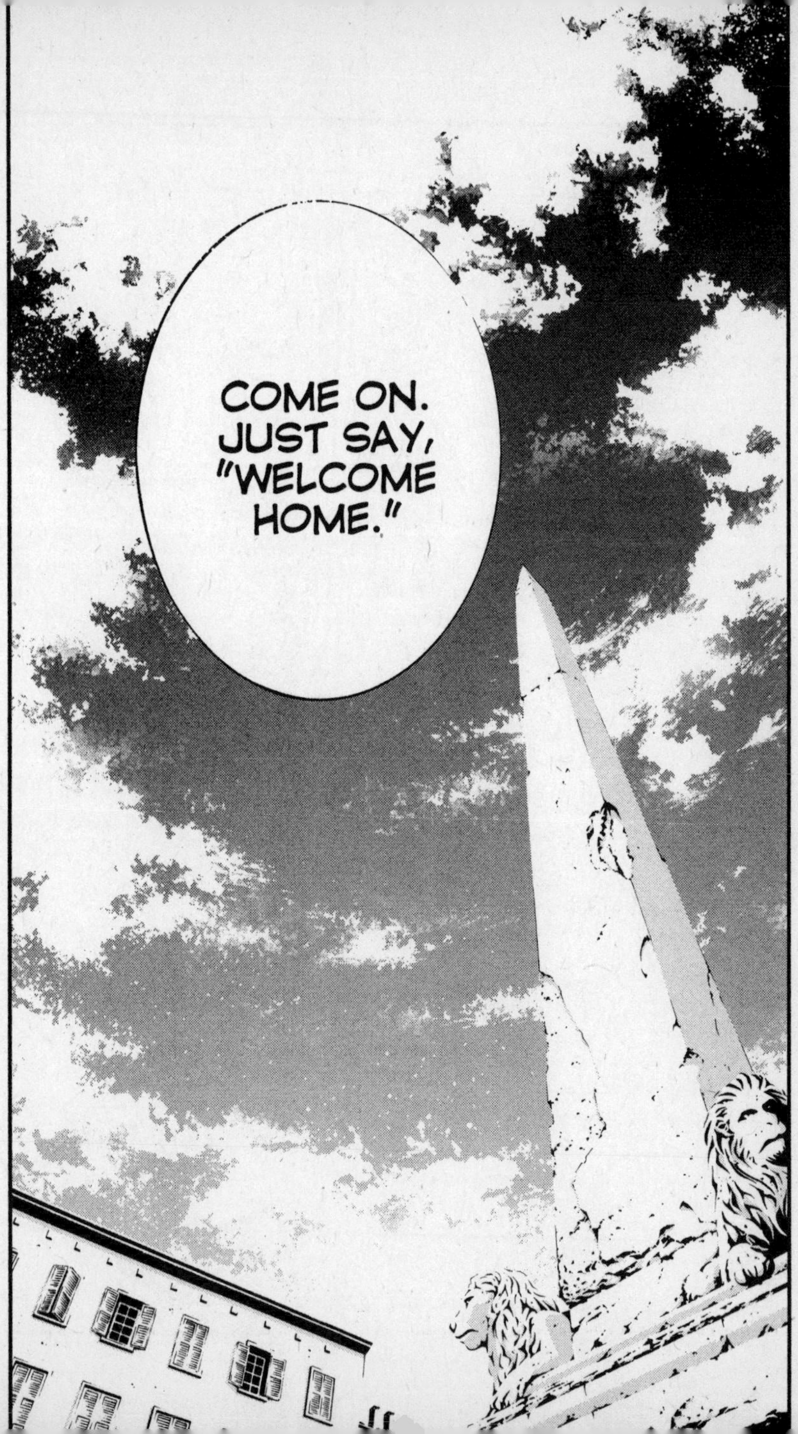
COME ON. JUST SAY, "WELCOME HOME."

208TH NIGHT: WE WHO LIVE IN STRUGGLE

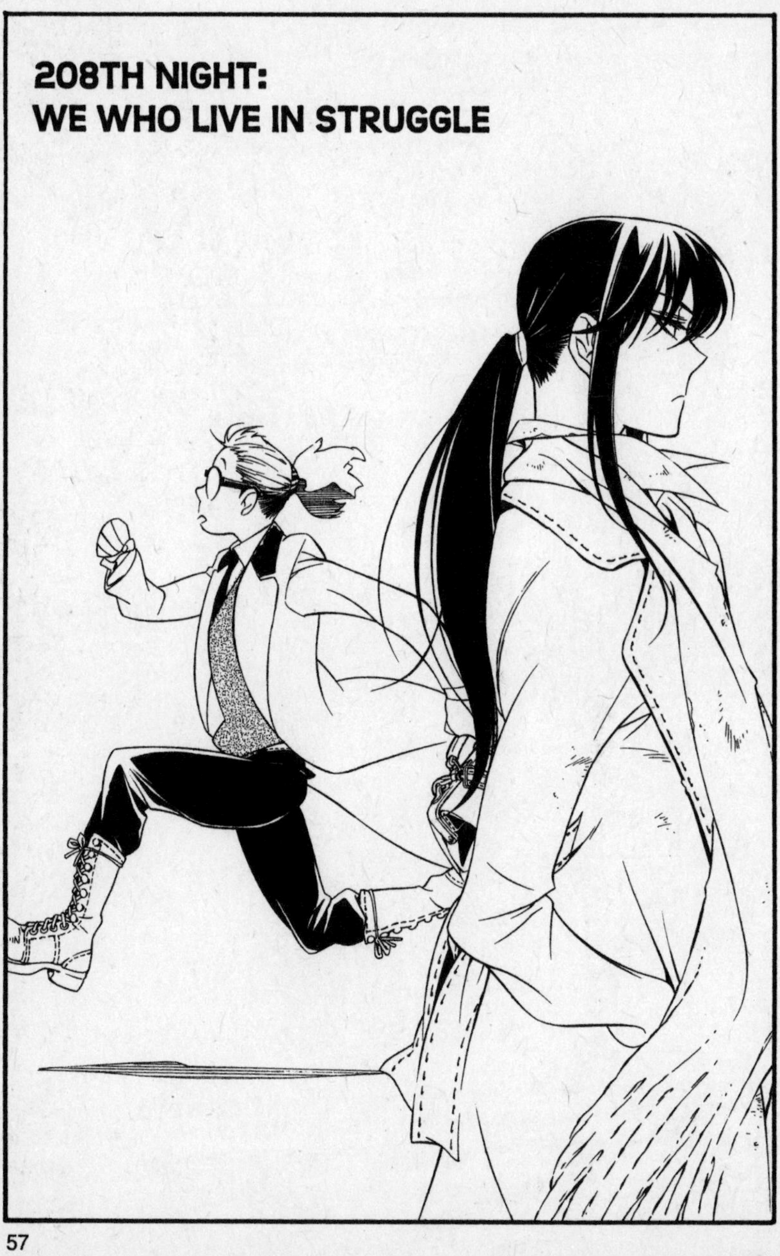

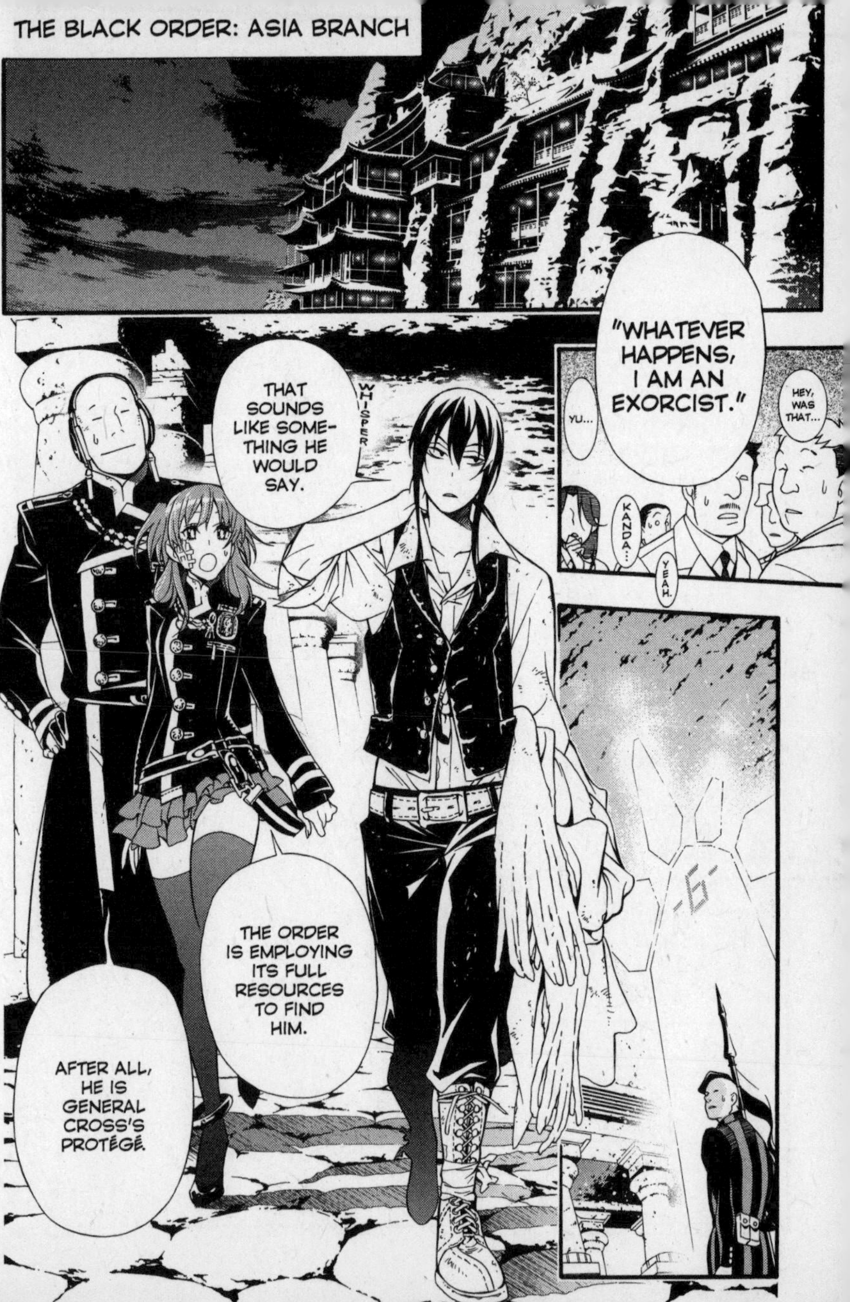
THE BLACK ORDER: ASIA BRANCH
"WHATEVER HAPPENS, I AM AN EXORCIST."
HEY, WAS THAT...
YU...
KANDA...
YEAH.
THAT SOUNDS LIKE SOMETHING HE WOULD SAY.
WHISPER
THE ORDER IS EMPLOYING ITS FULL RESOURCES TO FIND HIM.
AFTER ALL, HE IS GENERAL CROSS'S PROTÉGÉ.

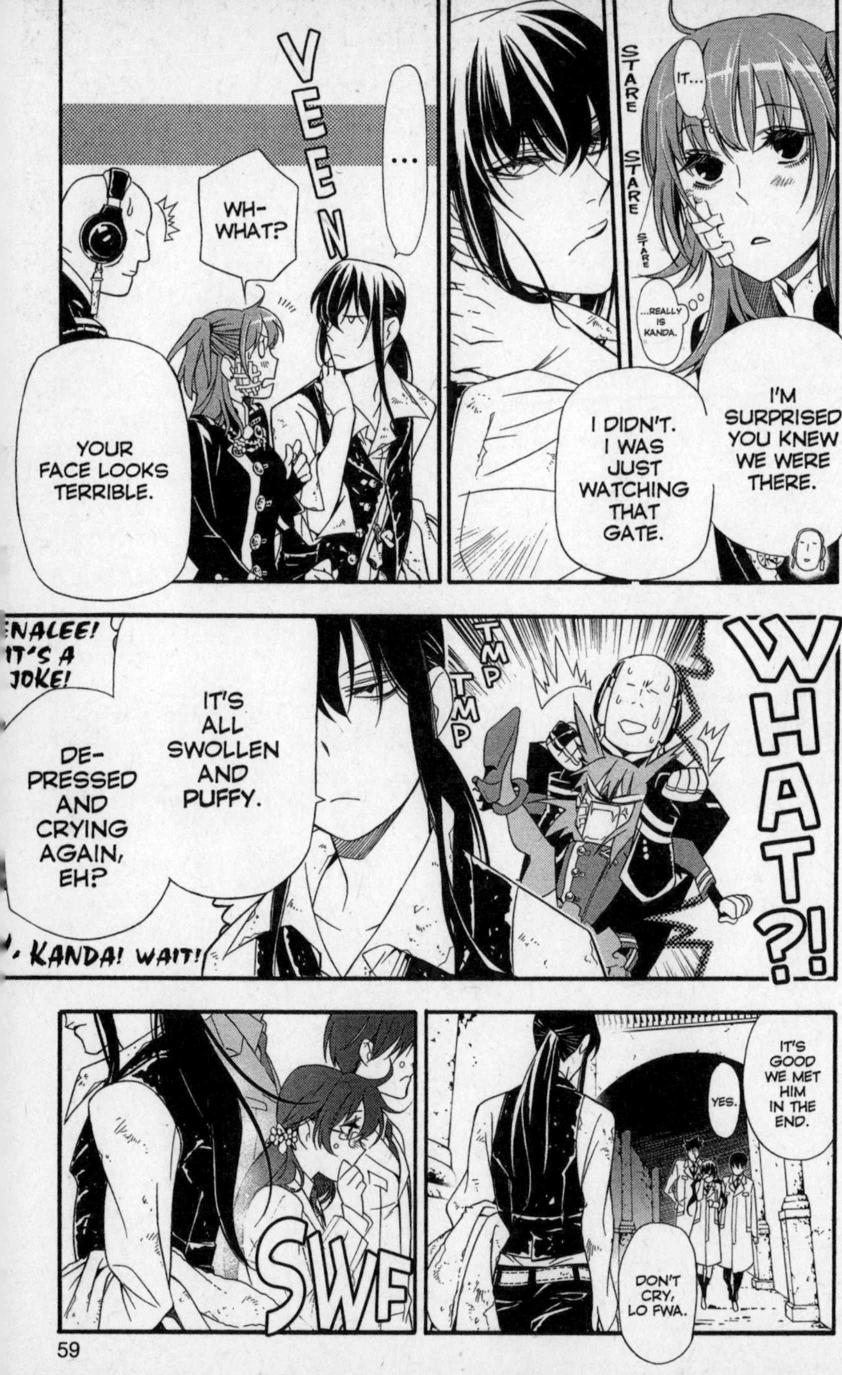
IT...
STARE
STARE
STARE
...REALLY IS KANDA.
I'M SURPRISED YOU KNEW WE WERE THERE.
I DIDN'T. I WAS JUST WATCHING THAT GATE.
VEEN
...
WH- WHAT?
YOUR FACE LOOKS TERRIBLE.
WHAT?!
TMP TMP
TMP TMP
IT'S ALL SWOLLEN AND PUFFY.
DE- PRESSED AND CRYING AGAIN, EH?
ENALEE! IT'S A JOKE!
. KANDA! WAIT!
IT'S GOOD WE MET HIM IN THE END.
YES.
DON'T CRY, LO FWA.
SWF

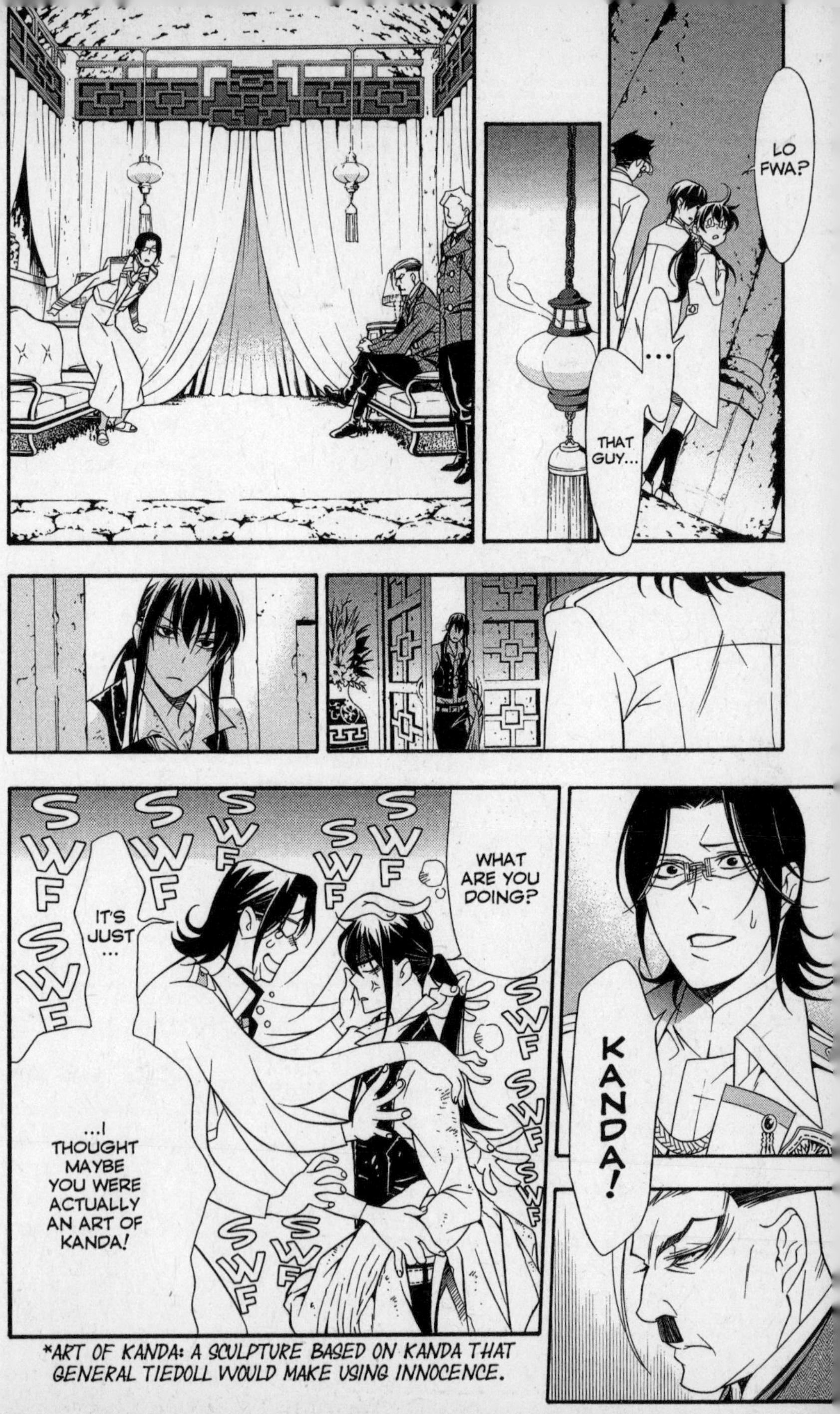
LO FWA?
...
THAT GUY...
KANDA!
WHAT ARE YOU DOING?
SWF SWF SWF SWF
IT'S JUST ...
SWF SWF SWF
SWF SWF SWF SWF
...I THOUGHT MAYBE YOU WERE ACTUALLY AN ART OF KANDA!
SWF SWF

*ART OF KANDA: A SCULPTURE BASED ON KANDA THAT GENERAL TIEDOLL WOULD MAKE USING INNOCENCE.

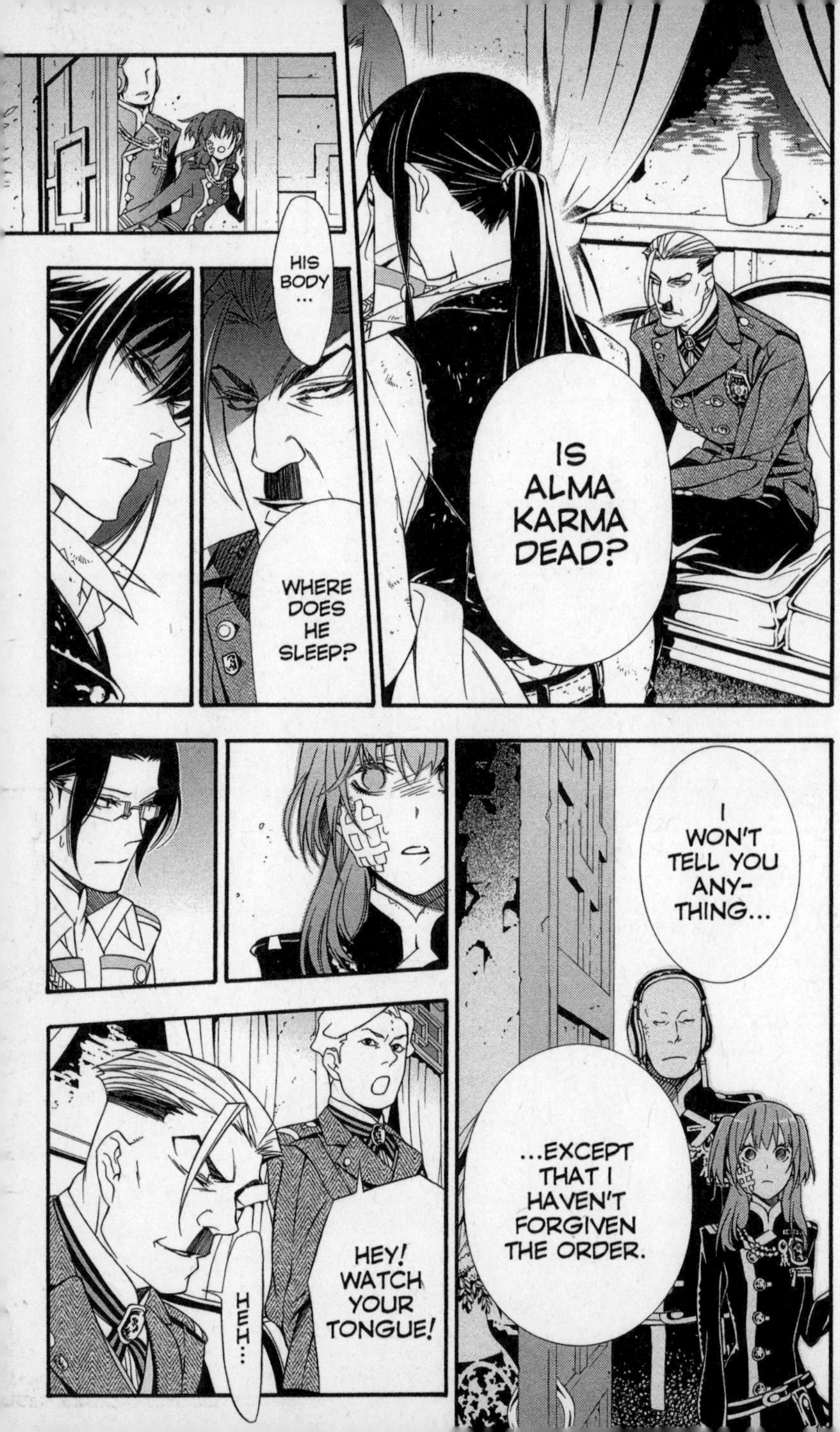
IS ALMA KARMA DEAD?
HIS BODY...
WHERE DOES HE SLEEP?
I WON'T TELL YOU ANY-THING...
...EXCEPT THAT I HAVEN'T FORGIVEN THE ORDER.
HEY! WATCH YOUR TONGUE!
HEH...

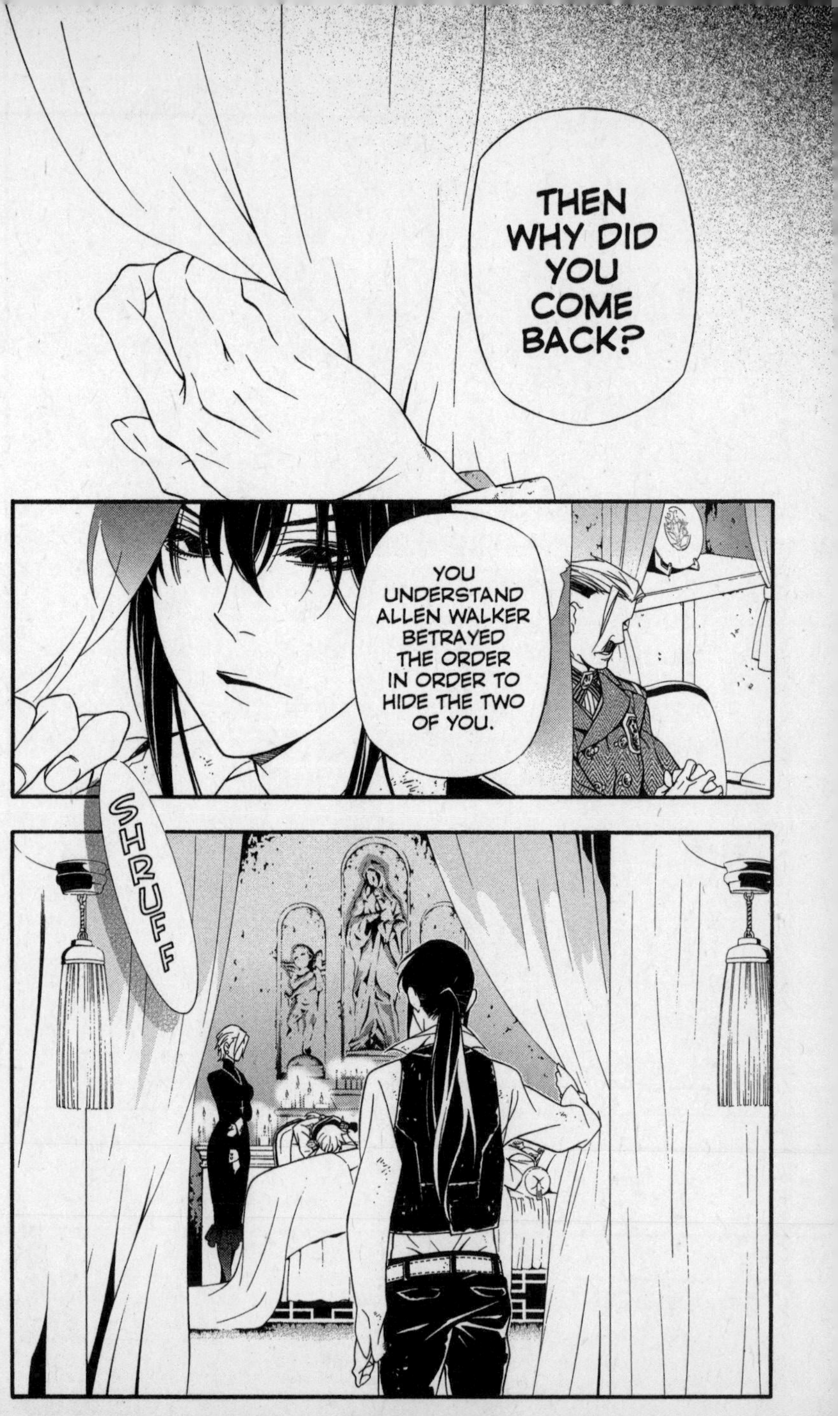
THEN WHY DID YOU COME BACK?
YOU UNDERSTAND ALLEN WALKER BETRAYED THE ORDER IN ORDER TO HIDE THE TWO OF YOU.
SHRUFF

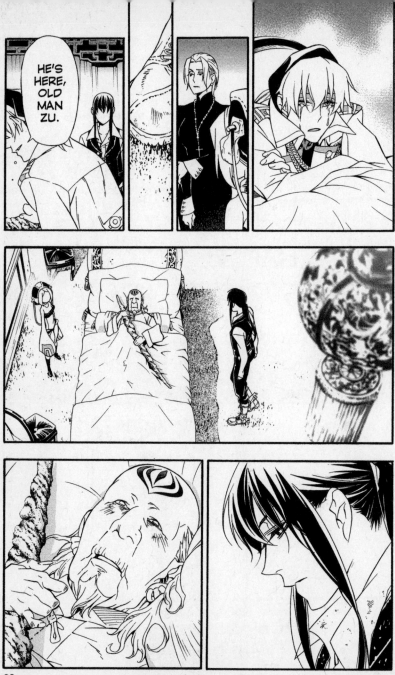

HE'S HERE, OLD MAN ZU.

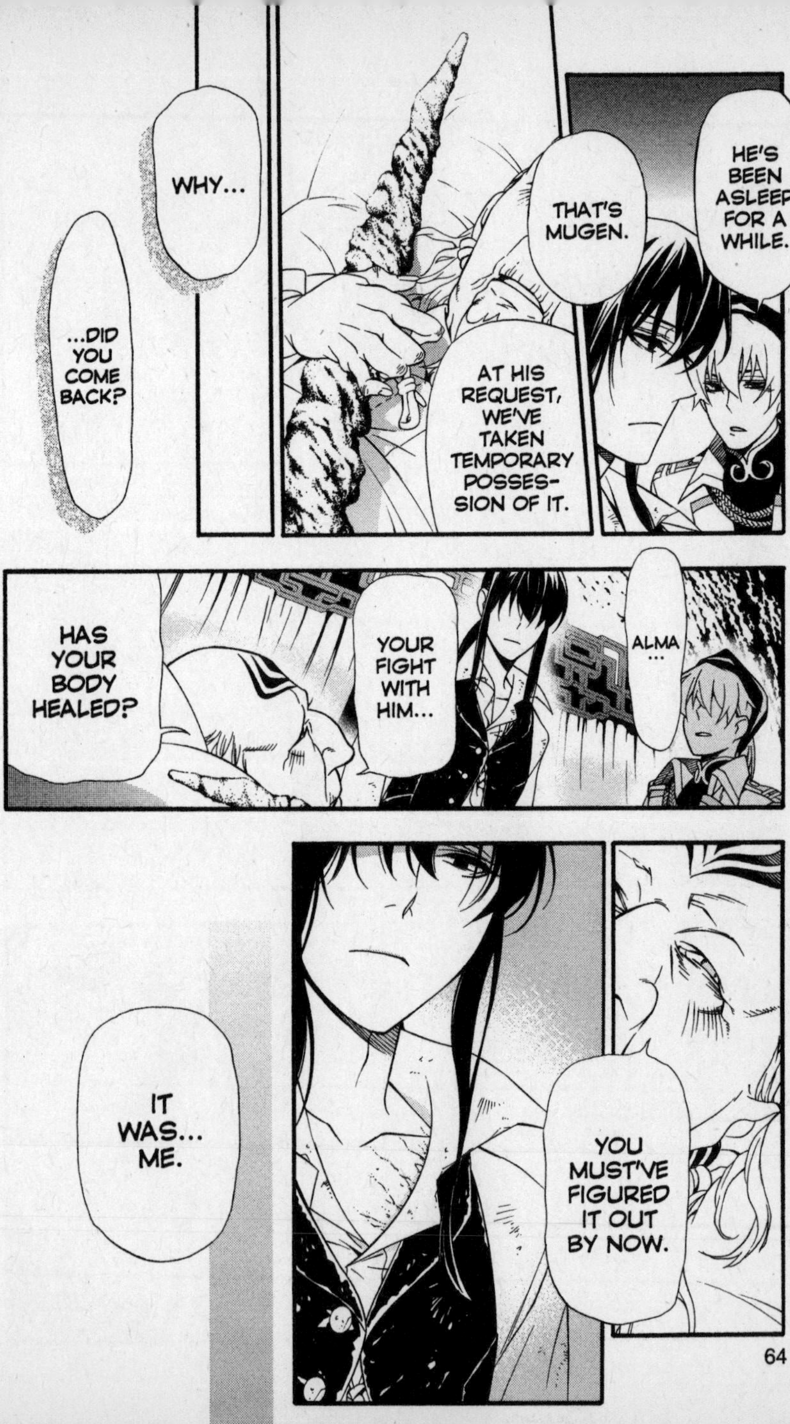
HE'S BEEN ASLEEP FOR A WHILE.
THAT'S MUGEN.
AT HIS REQUEST, WE'VE TAKEN TEMPORARY POSSES-SION OF IT.
WHY...
...DID YOU COME BACK?
ALMA...
YOUR FIGHT WITH HIM...
HAS YOUR BODY HEALED?
YOU MUST'VE FIGURED IT OUT BY NOW.
IT WAS... ME.

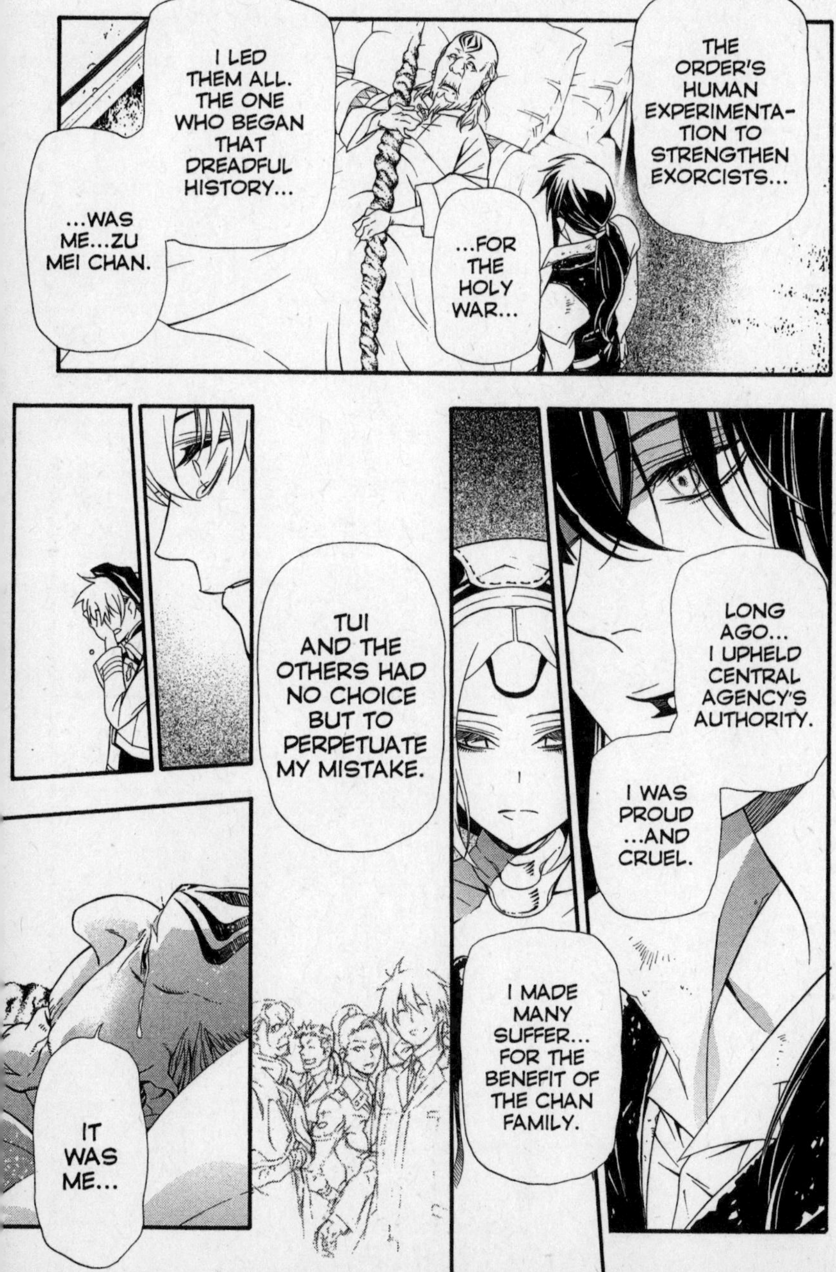
THE ORDER'S HUMAN EXPERIMENTATION TO STRENGTHEN EXORCISTS...
...FOR THE HOLY WAR...
I LED THEM ALL. THE ONE WHO BEGAN THAT DREADFUL HISTORY...
...WAS ME...ZU MEI CHAN.
LONG AGO... I UPHELD CENTRAL AGENCY'S AUTHORITY.
I WAS PROUD ...AND CRUEL.
I MADE MANY SUFFER... FOR THE BENEFIT OF THE CHAN FAMILY.
TUI AND THE OTHERS HAD NO CHOICE BUT TO PERPETUATE MY MISTAKE.
IT WAS ME...

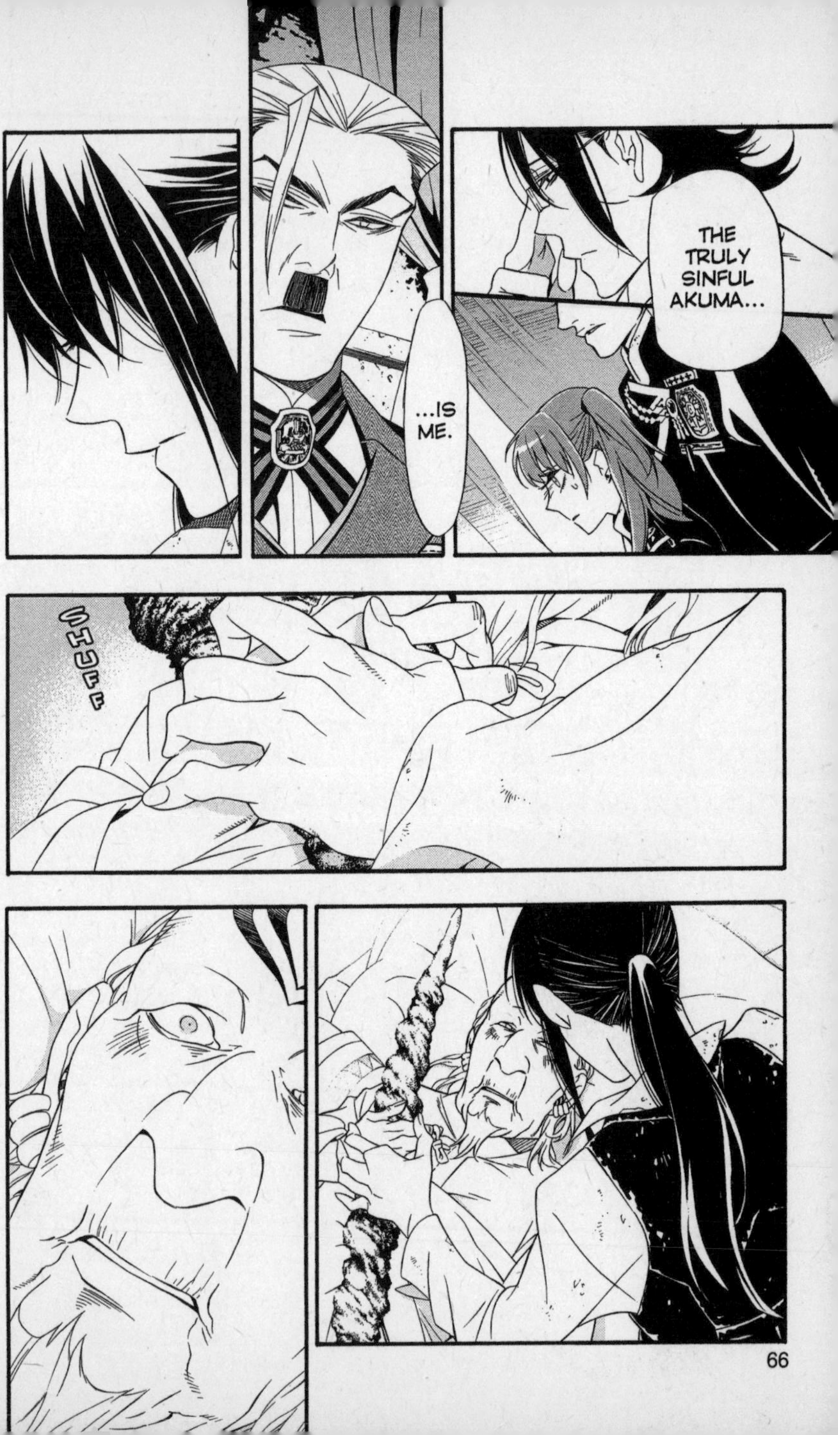
THE TRULY SINFUL AKUMA...
...IS ME.
SHUFF

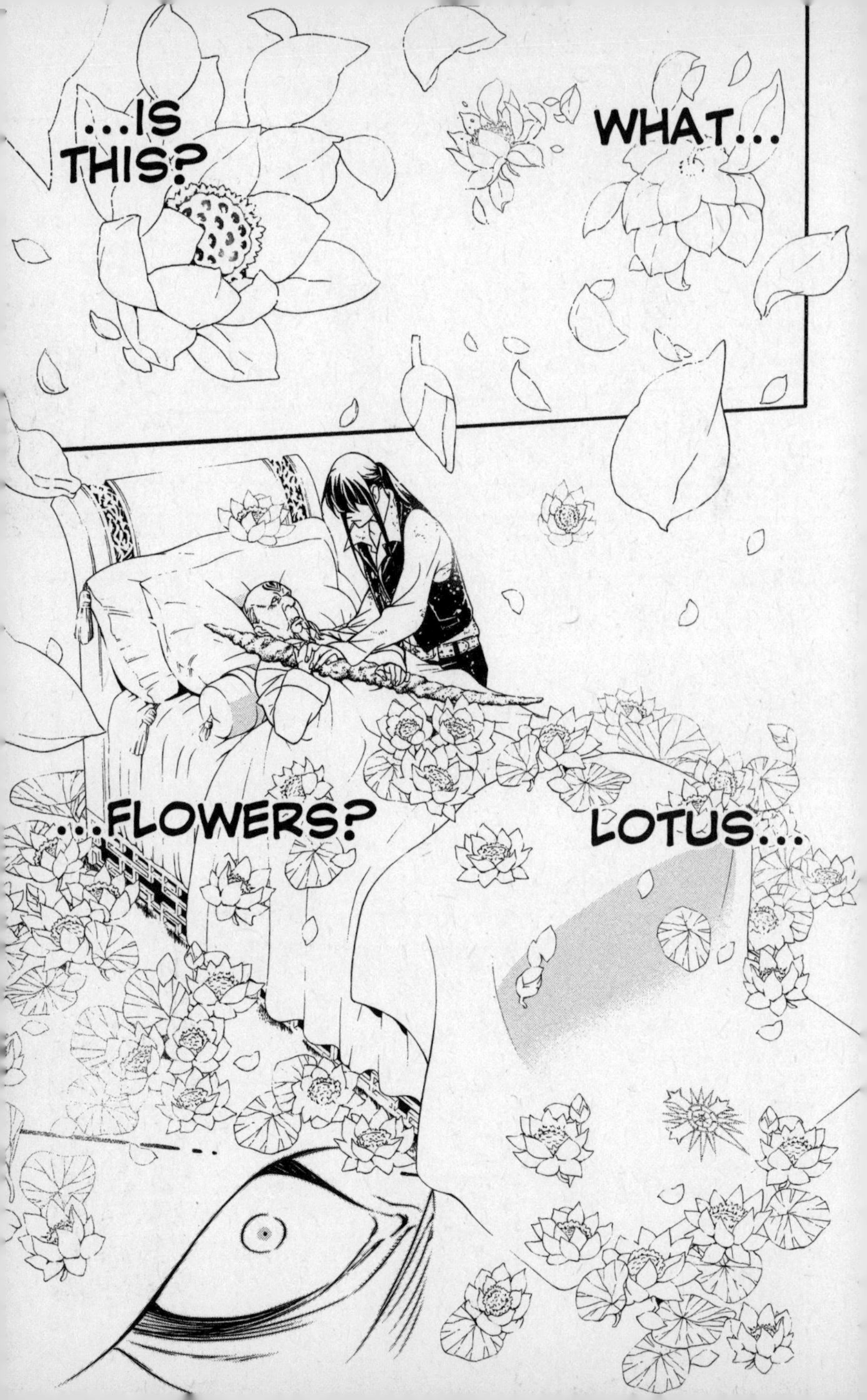
WHAT...
...IS THIS?
LOTUS...
...FLOWERS?

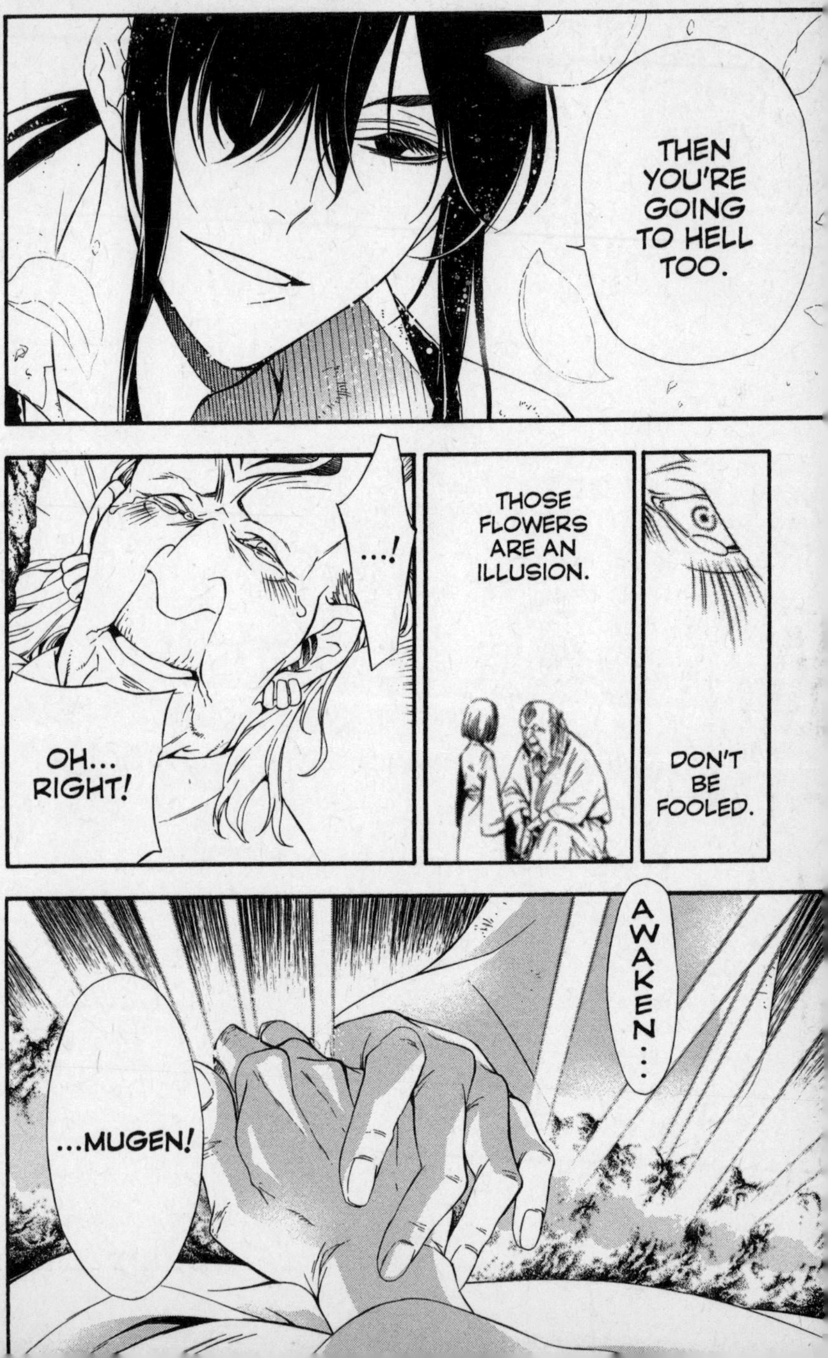
THEN YOU'RE GOING TO HELL TOO.
DON'T BE FOOLED.
THOSE FLOWERS ARE AN ILLUSION.
...!
OH... RIGHT!
AWAKEN...
...MUGEN!

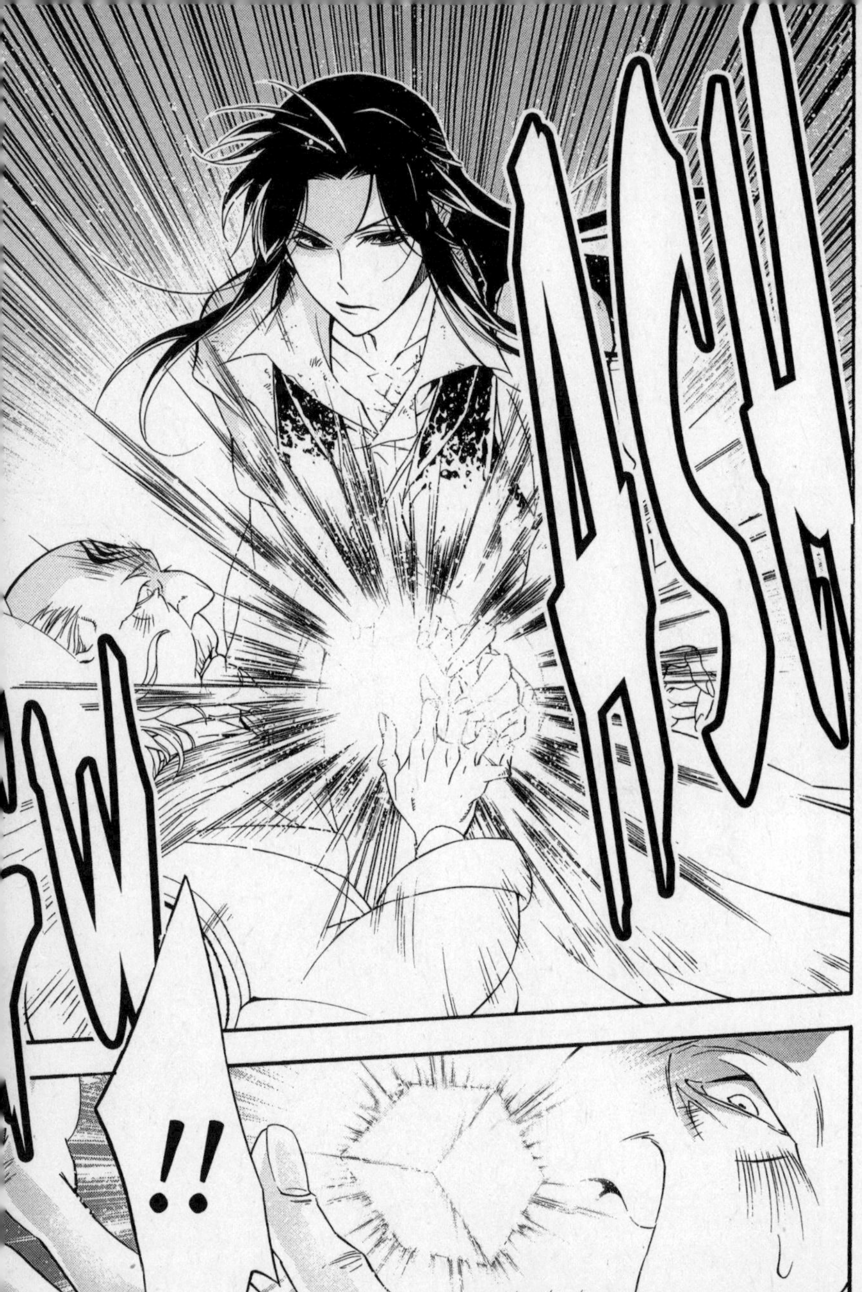
SWASH
!!

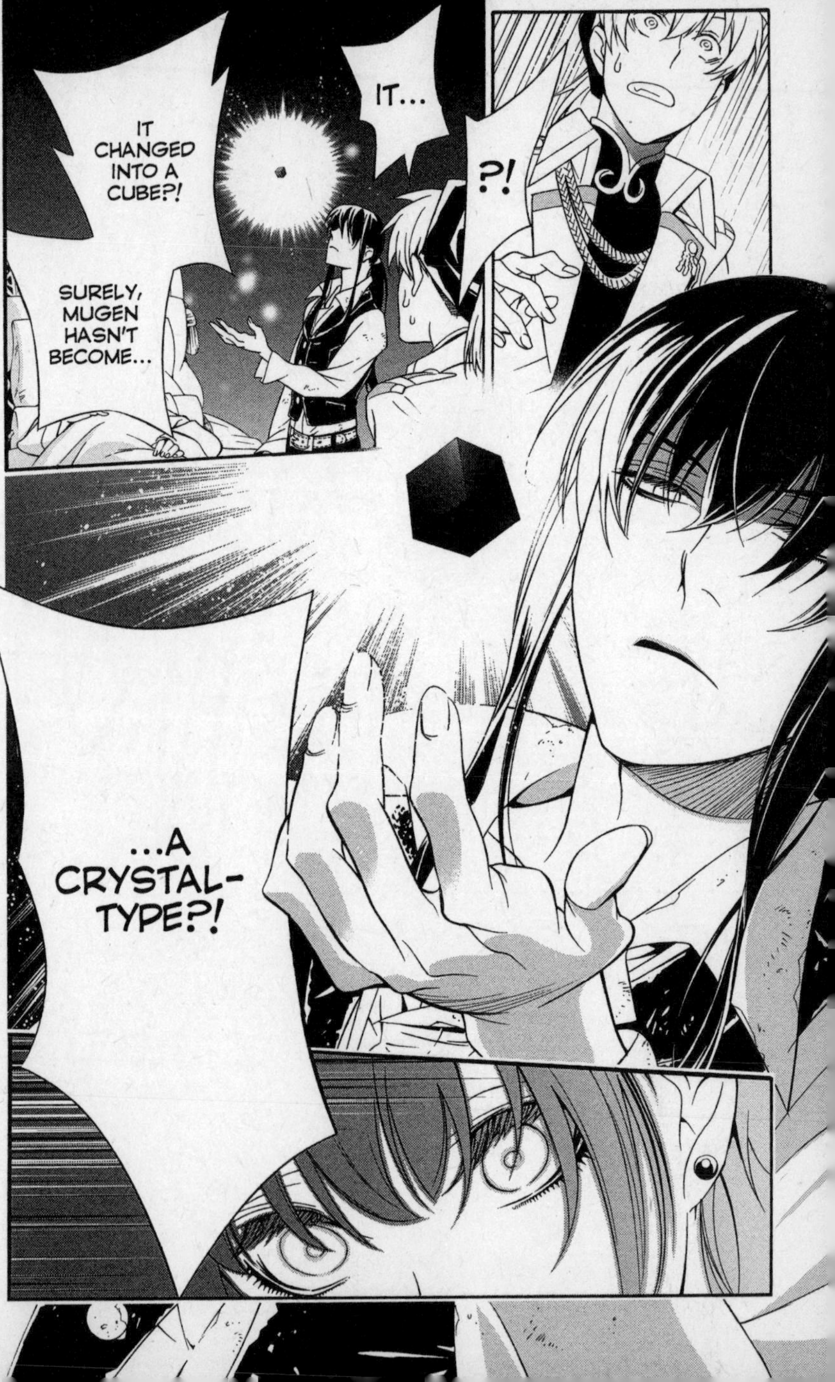
?!
IT...
IT CHANGED INTO A CUBE?!
SURELY, MUGEN HASN'T BECOME...
...A CRYSTAL-TYPE?!

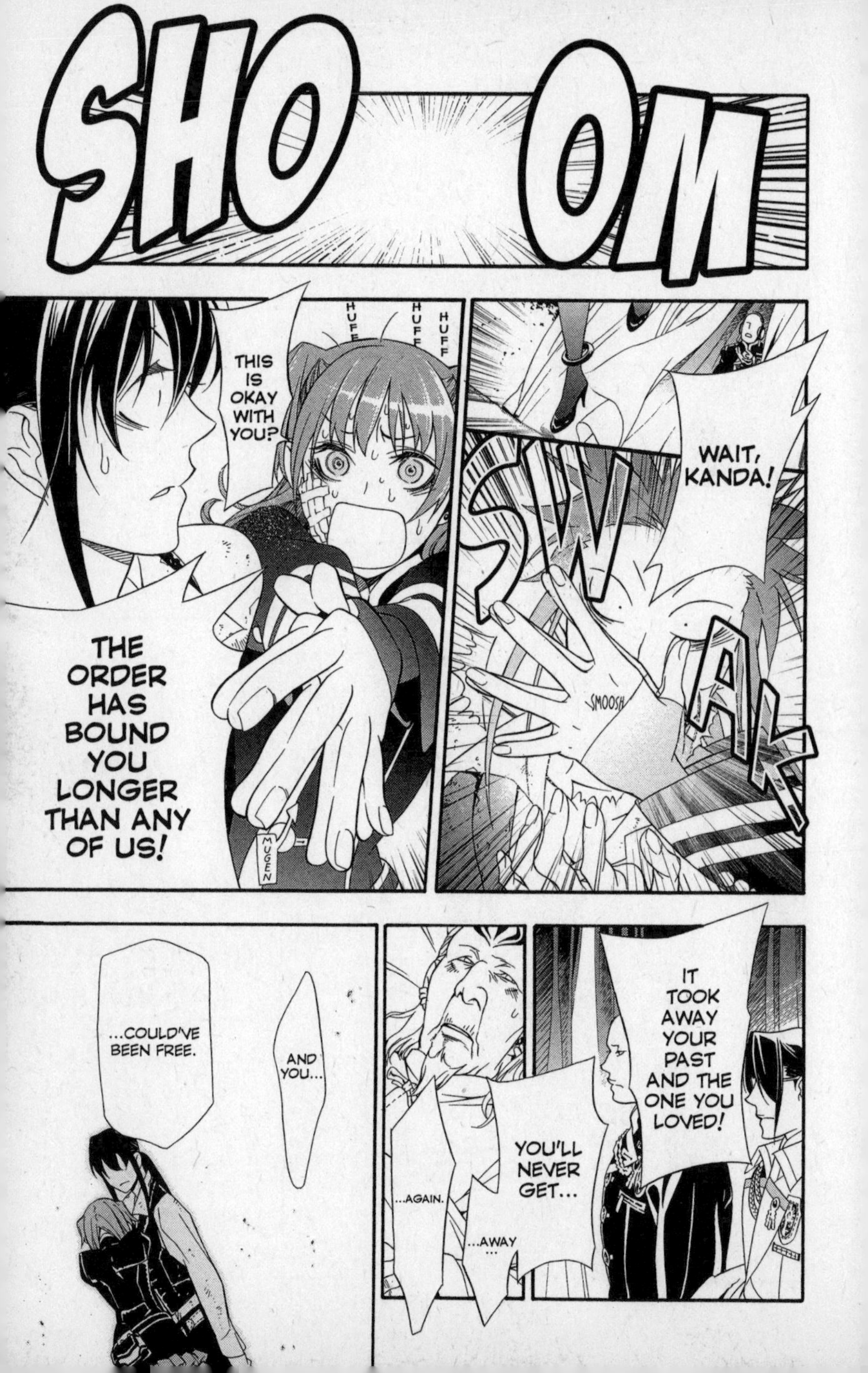
SHO OM
WAIT, KANDA!
SW AK
SMOOSH
HUFF HUFF HUFF
THIS IS OKAY WITH YOU?
THE ORDER HAS BOUND YOU LONGER THAN ANY OF US!
MUGEN
IT TOOK AWAY YOUR PAST AND THE ONE YOU LOVED!
YOU'LL NEVER GET...
...AWAY...
...AGAIN.
AND YOU...
...COULD'VE BEEN FREE.

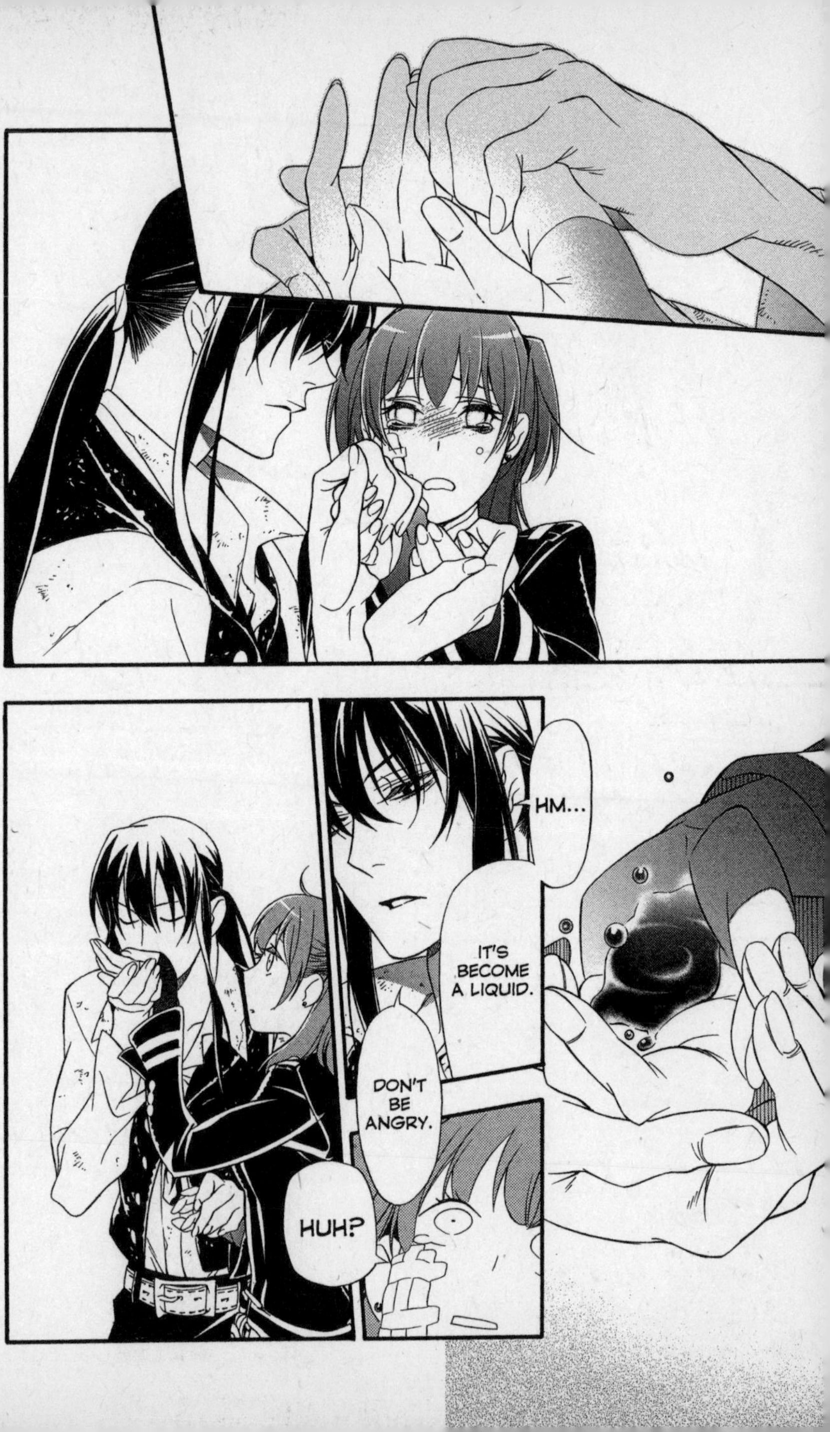
HM...
IT'S BECOME A LIQUID.
DON'T BE ANGRY.
HUH?

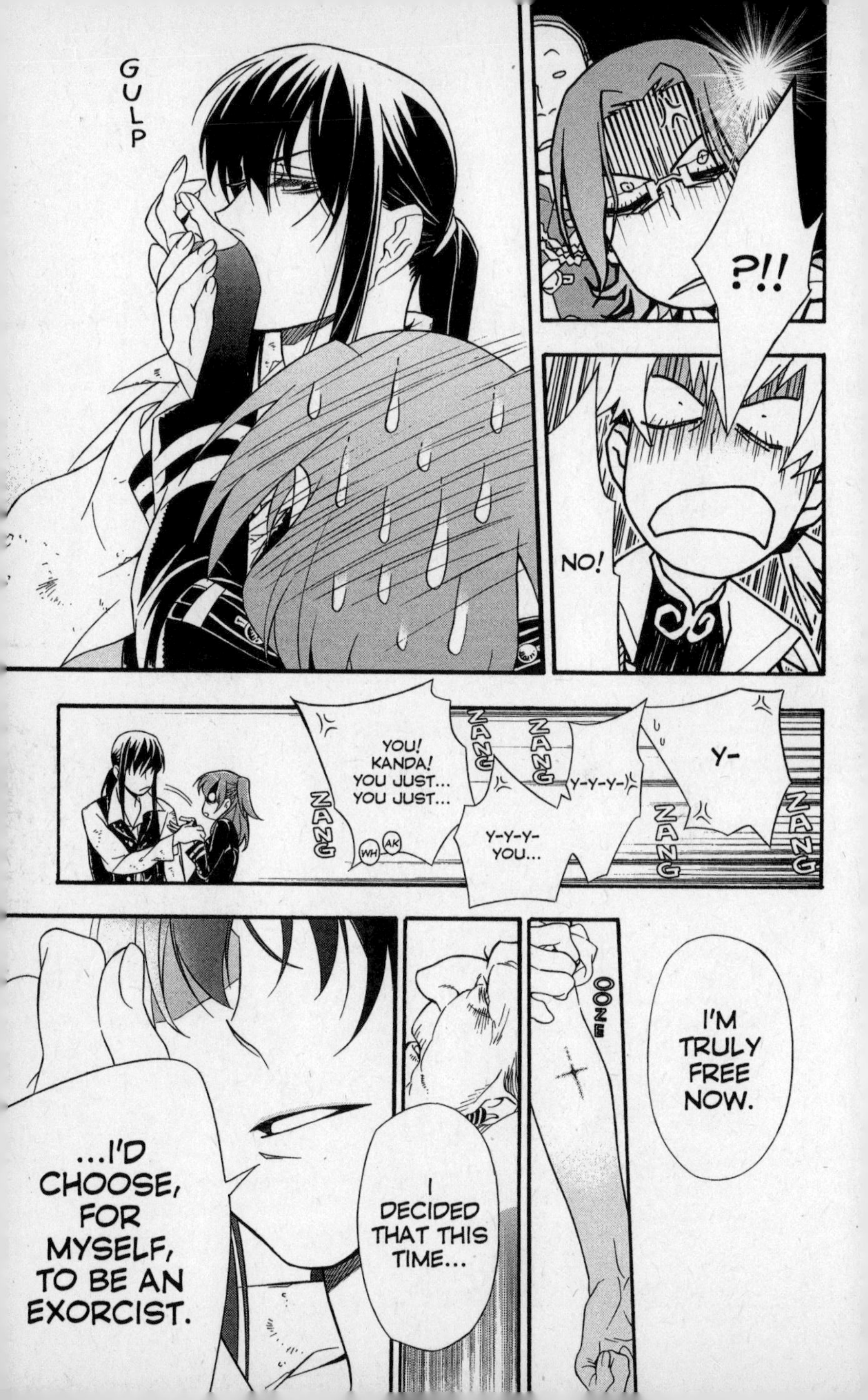

?!!
GULP
NO!
Y-
ZANG
ZANG
Y-Y-Y-
Y-Y-Y-
YOU...
ZANG
ZANG
YOU! KANDA! YOU JUST... YOU JUST...
ZANG
WH
AK
I'M TRULY FREE NOW.
OOZE
I DECIDED THAT THIS TIME...
...I'D CHOOSE, FOR MYSELF, TO BE AN EXORCIST.

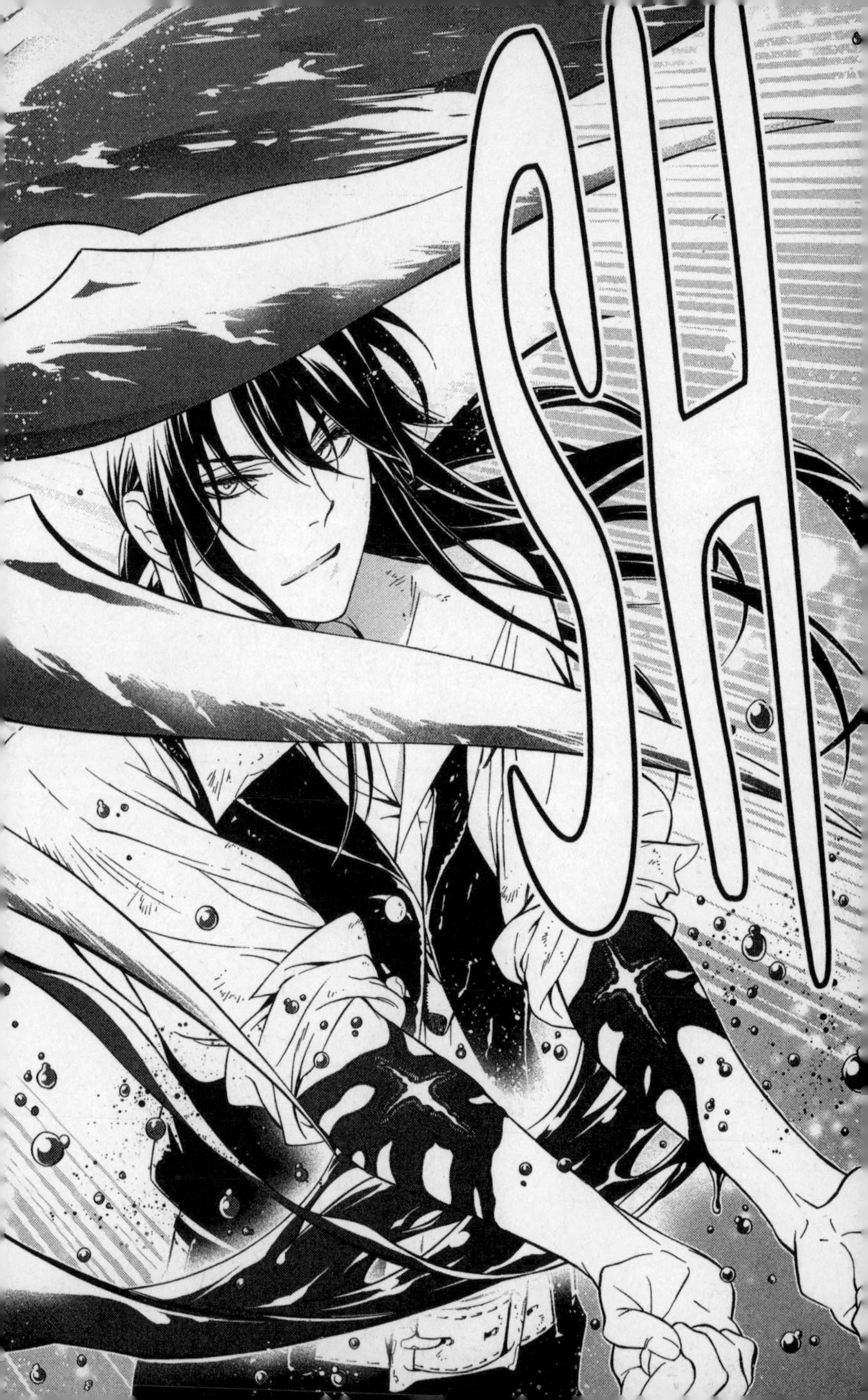
SHA

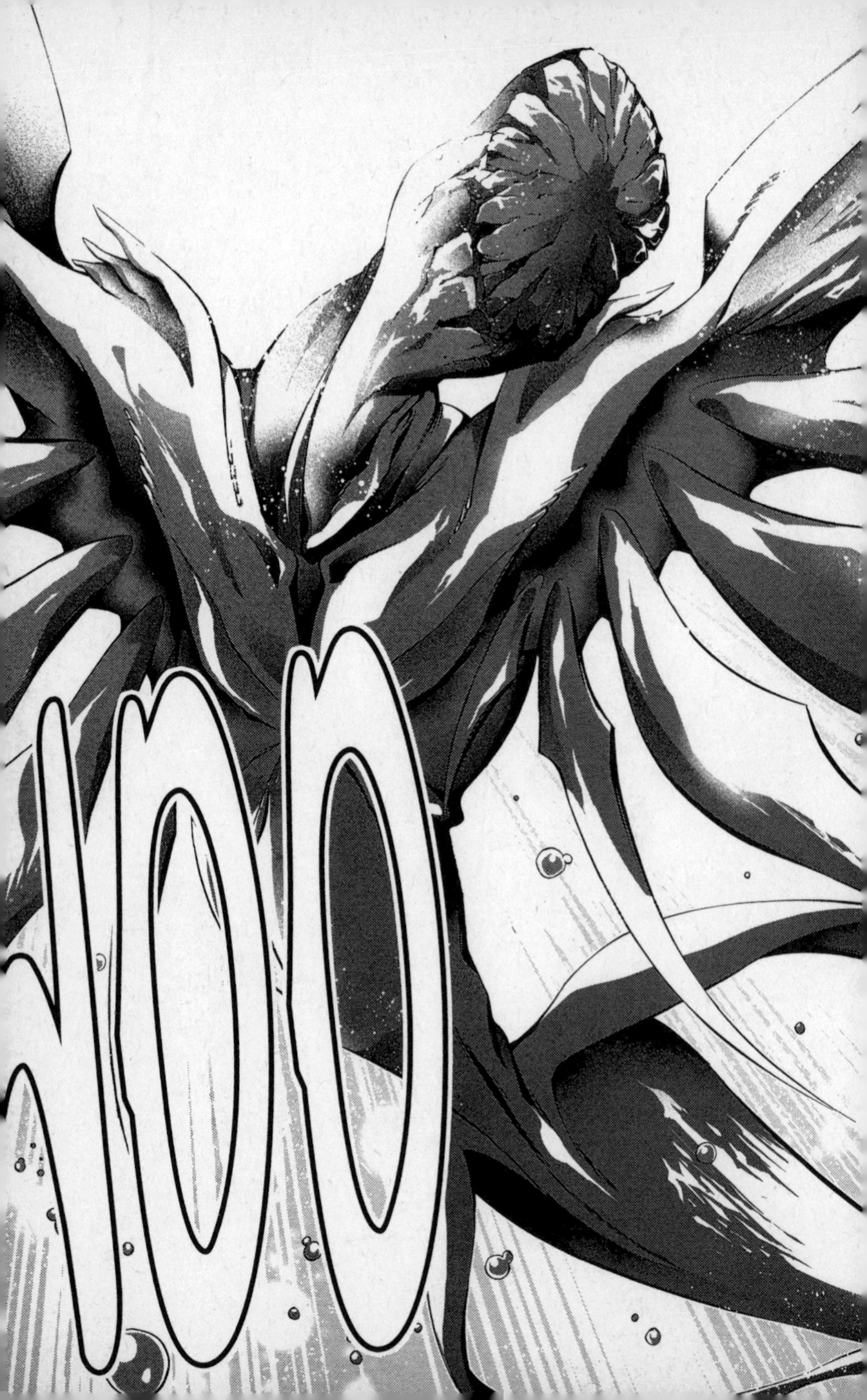

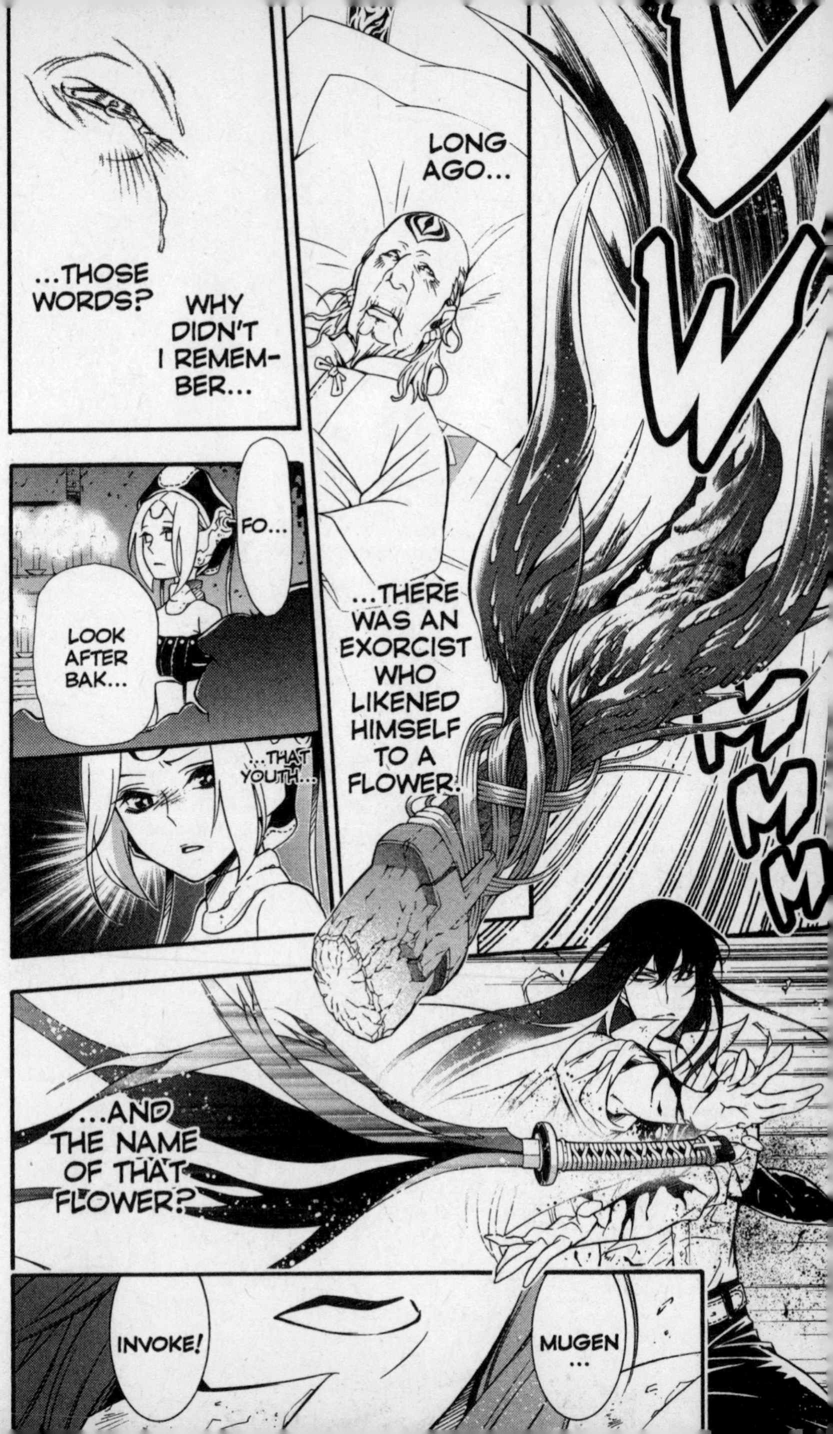

LONG AGO...
...THERE WAS AN EXORCIST WHO LIKENED HIMSELF TO A FLOWER.
WHY DIDN'T I REMEMBER...
...THOSE WORDS?
FO...
LOOK AFTER BAK...
...THAT YOUTH...
...AND THE NAME OF THAT FLOWER?
MUGEN ...
INVOKE!

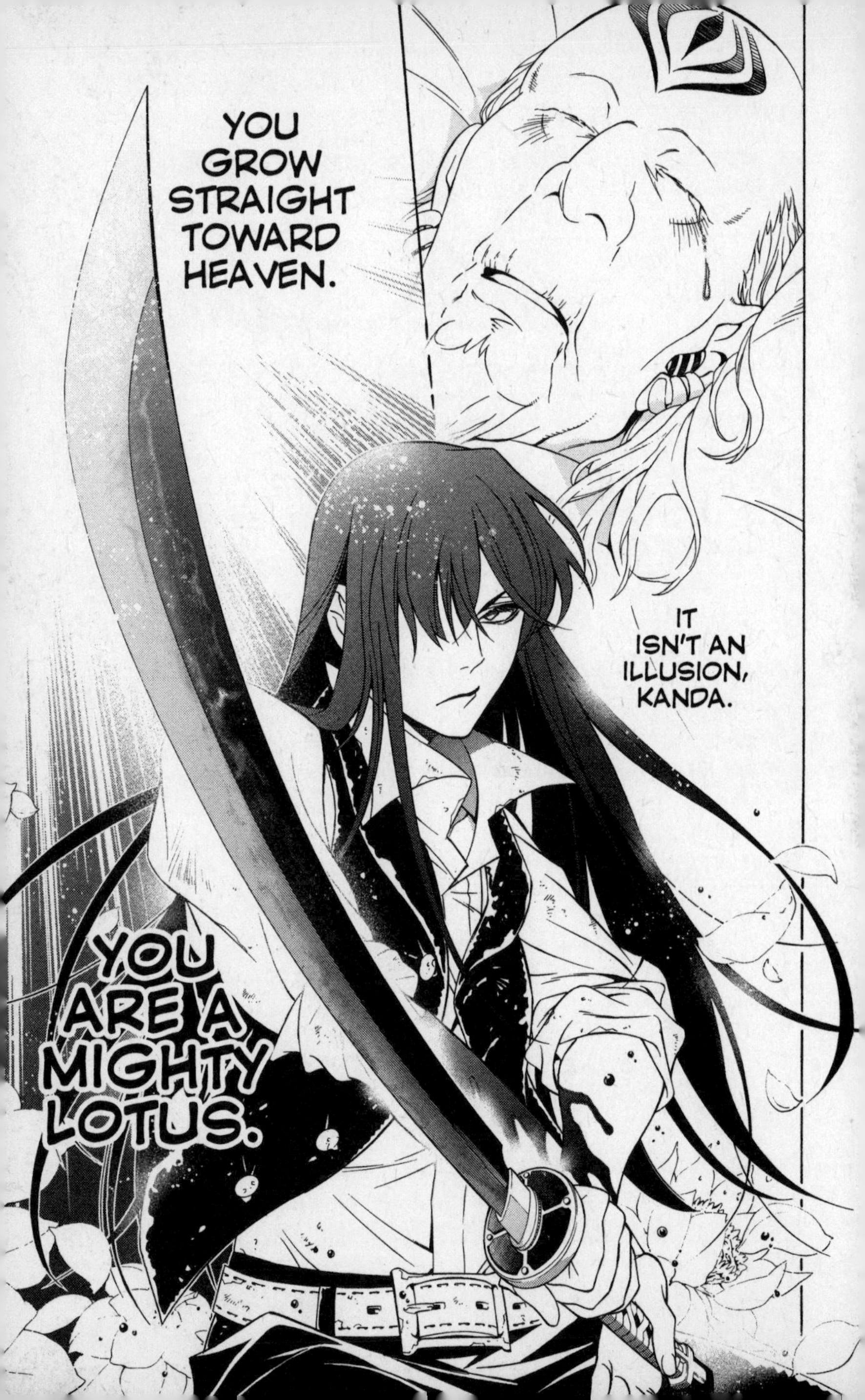
IT ISN'T AN ILLUSION, KANDA.
YOU GROW STRAIGHT TOWARD HEAVEN.
YOU ARE A MIGHTY LOTUS.

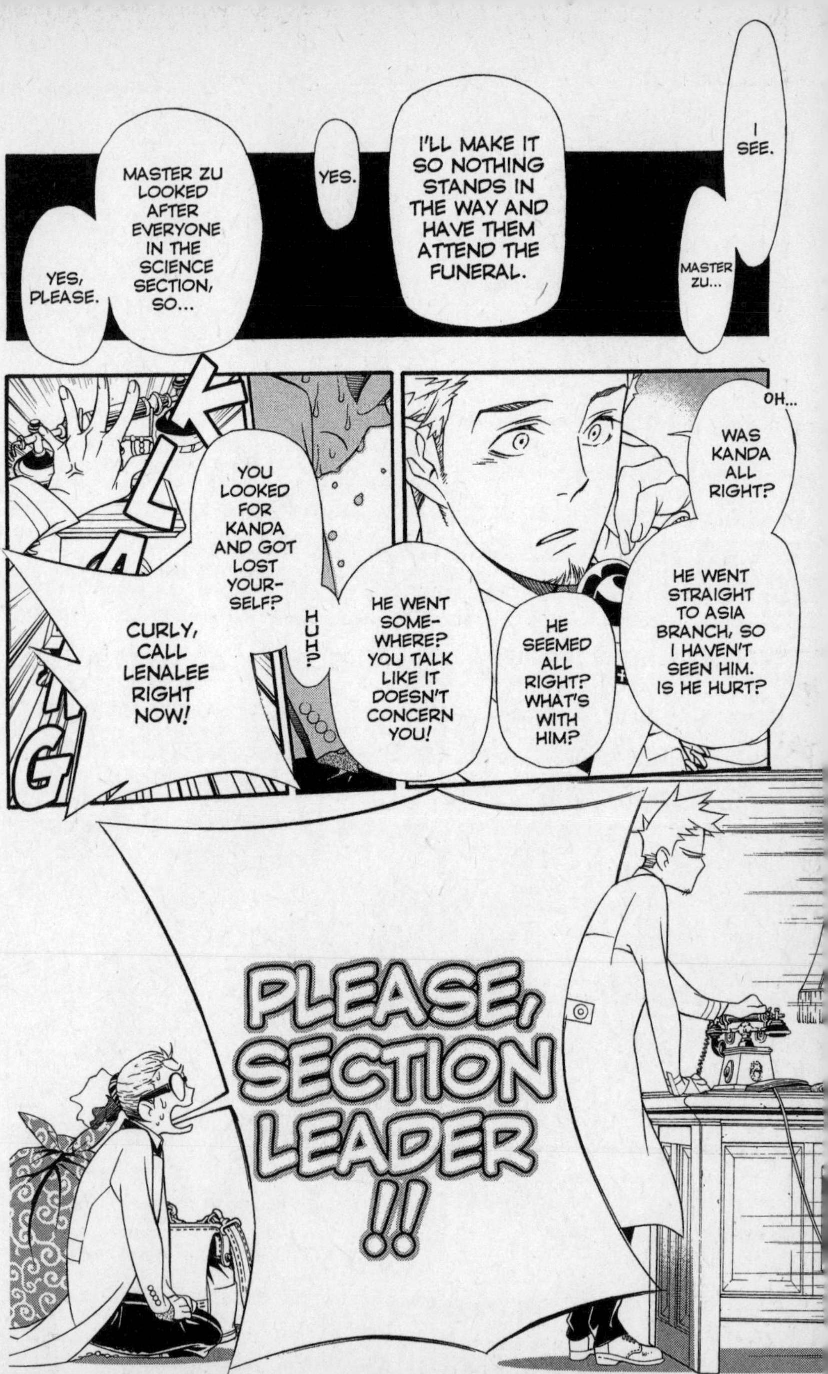
I SEE.
MASTER ZU...
I'LL MAKE IT SO NOTHING STANDS IN THE WAY AND HAVE THEM ATTEND THE FUNERAL.
YES.
MASTER ZU LOOKED AFTER EVERYONE IN THE SCIENCE SECTION, SO...
YES, PLEASE.
OH...
WAS KANDA ALL RIGHT?
HE WENT STRAIGHT TO ASIA BRANCH, SO I HAVEN'T SEEN HIM. IS HE HURT?
HE SEEMED ALL RIGHT? WHAT'S WITH HIM?
HE WENT SOME-WHERE? YOU TALK LIKE IT DOESN'T CONCERN YOU!
HUH?
YOU LOOKED FOR KANDA AND GOT LOST YOUR-SELF?
CURLY, CALL LENALEE RIGHT NOW!
PLEASE, SECTION LEADER!!

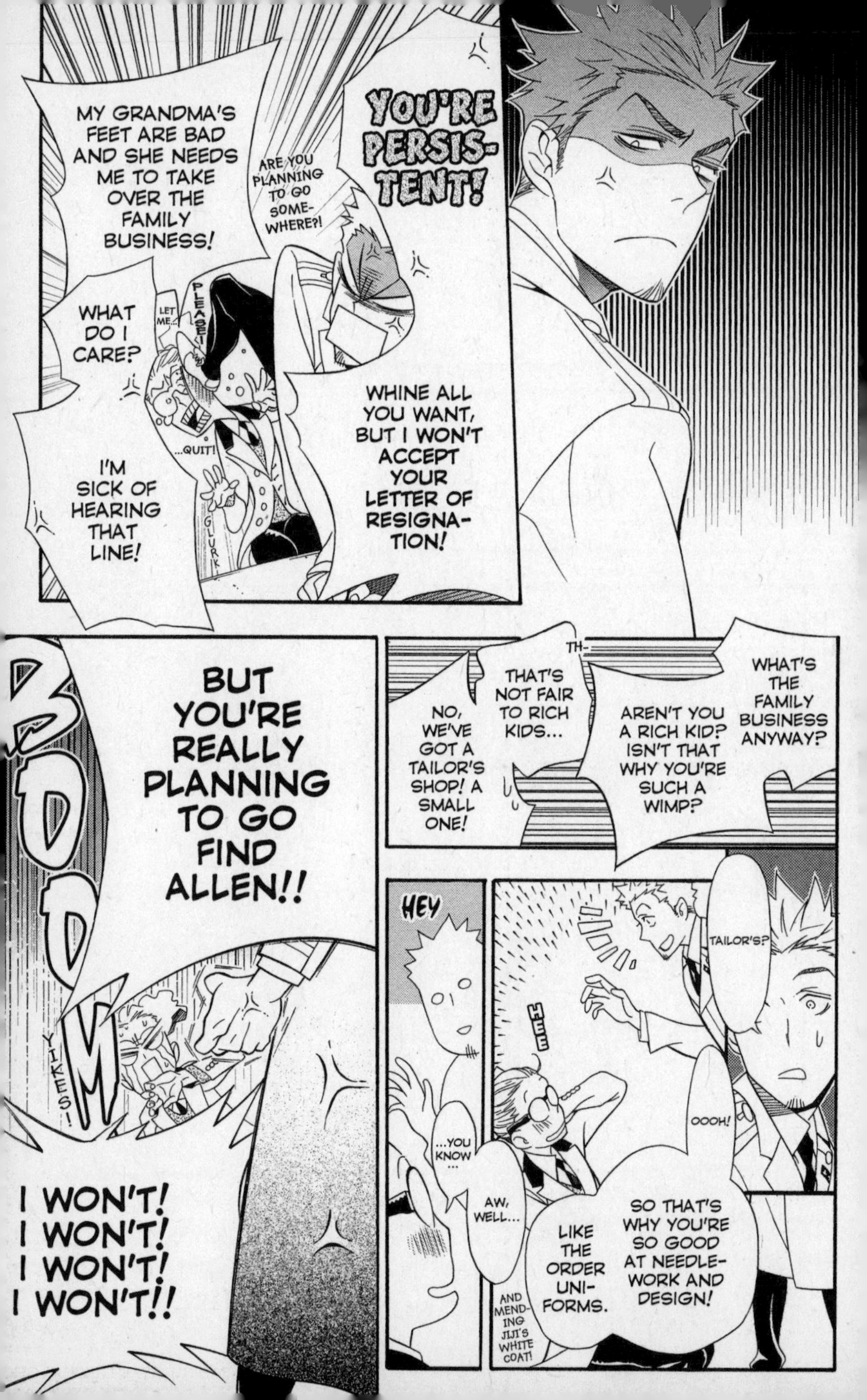

YOU'RE PERSIS-TENT!
ARE YOU PLANNING TO GO SOME-WHERE?!
MY GRANDMA'S FEET ARE BAD AND SHE NEEDS ME TO TAKE OVER THE FAMILY BUSINESS!
PLEASE!
LET ME...
WHAT DO I CARE?
WHINE ALL YOU WANT, BUT I WON'T ACCEPT YOUR LETTER OF RESIGNA-TION!
...QUIT!
GLURK
I'M SICK OF HEARING THAT LINE!
WHAT'S THE FAMILY BUSINESS ANYWAY?
TH-
AREN'T YOU A RICH KID? ISN'T THAT WHY YOU'RE SUCH A WIMP?
THAT'S NOT FAIR TO RICH KIDS...
NO, WE'VE GOT A TAILOR'S SHOP! A SMALL ONE!
TAILOR'S?
HMM
OOOH!
SO THAT'S WHY YOU'RE SO GOOD AT NEEDLE-WORK AND DESIGN!
LIKE THE ORDER UNI-FORMS.
AND MEND-ING JIJI'S WHITE COAT!
HEY
...YOU KNOW...
AW, WELL...
BUT YOU'RE REALLY PLANNING TO GO FIND ALLEN!!
BDOM
YIKES!
I WON'T! I WON'T! I WON'T! I WON'T!!

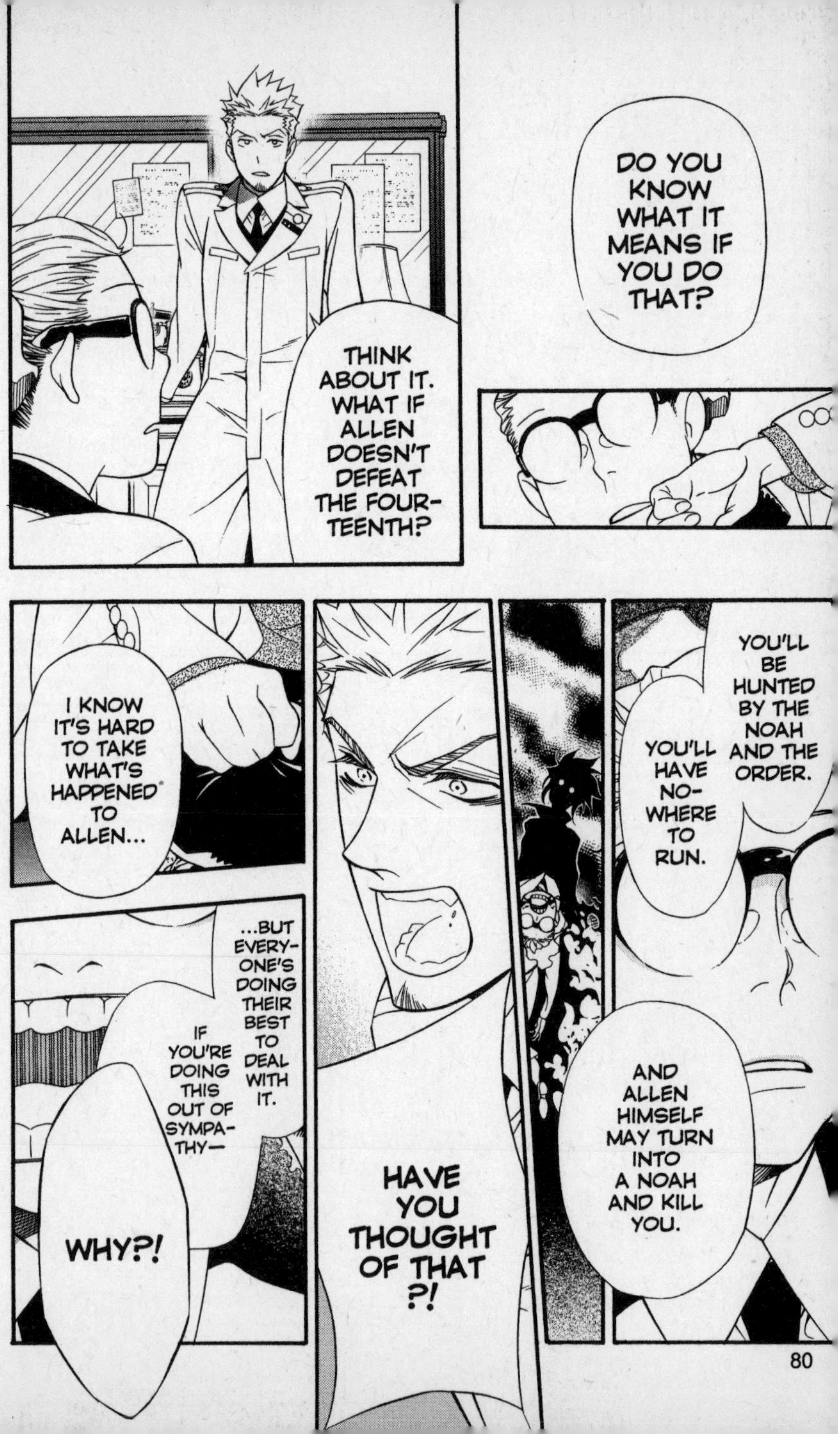
DO YOU KNOW WHAT IT MEANS IF YOU DO THAT?
THINK ABOUT IT. WHAT IF ALLEN DOESN'T DEFEAT THE FOURTEENTH?
YOU'LL BE HUNTED BY THE NOAH AND THE ORDER.
YOU'LL HAVE NOWHERE TO RUN.
AND ALLEN HIMSELF MAY TURN INTO A NOAH AND KILL YOU.
HAVE YOU THOUGHT OF THAT?!
I KNOW IT'S HARD TO TAKE WHAT'S HAPPENED TO ALLEN...
...BUT EVERYONE'S DOING THEIR BEST TO DEAL WITH IT.
IF YOU'RE DOING THIS OUT OF SYMPATHY—
WHY?!

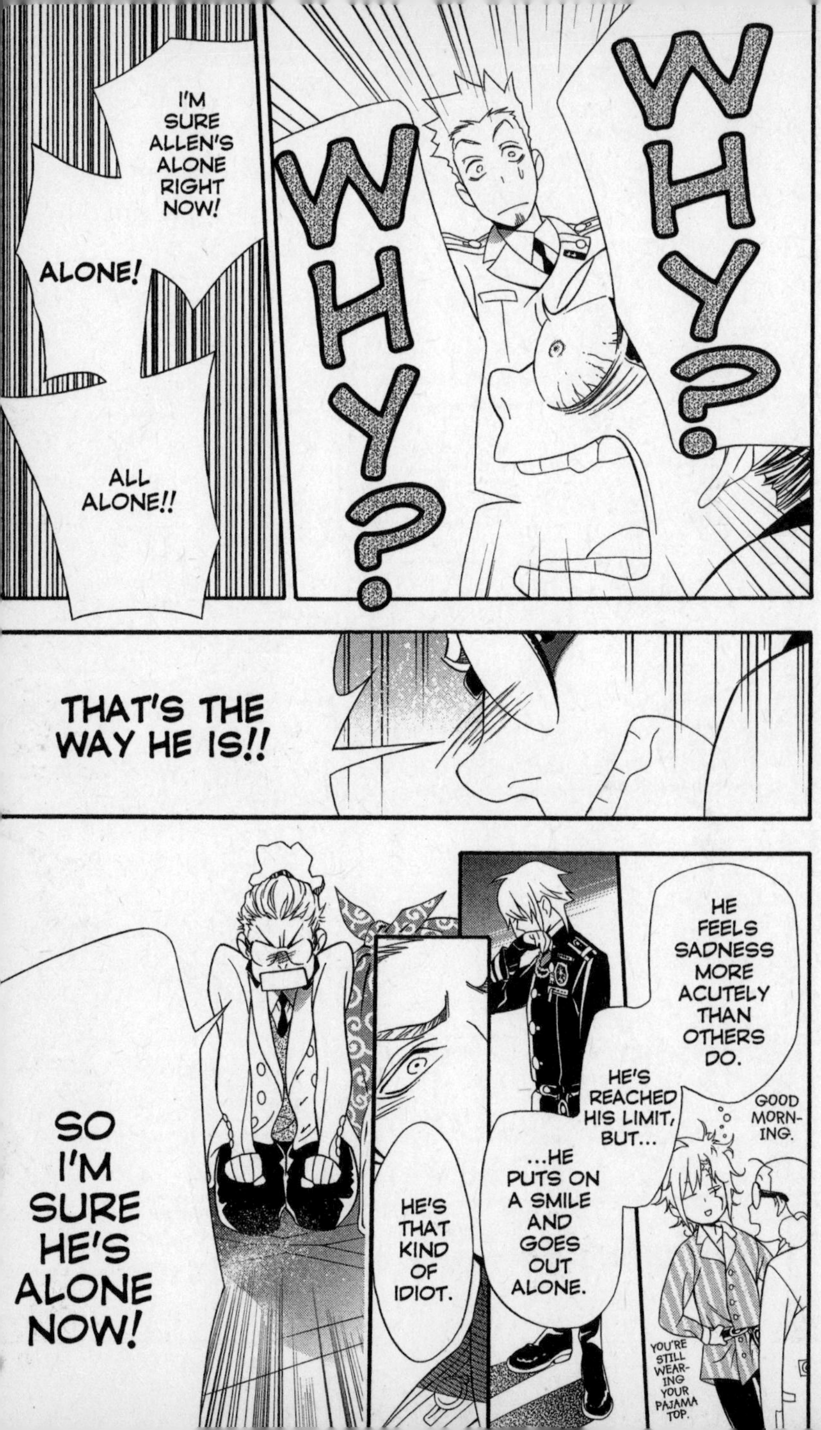
WHY?
WHY?
I'M SURE ALLEN'S ALONE RIGHT NOW!
ALONE!
ALL ALONE!!
THAT'S THE WAY HE IS!!
HE FEELS SADNESS MORE ACUTELY THAN OTHERS DO.
GOOD MORN-ING.
HE'S REACHED HIS LIMIT, BUT...
...HE PUTS ON A SMILE AND GOES OUT ALONE.
YOU'RE STILL WEAR-ING YOUR PAJAMA TOP.
HE'S THAT KIND OF IDIOT.
SO I'M SURE HE'S ALONE NOW!

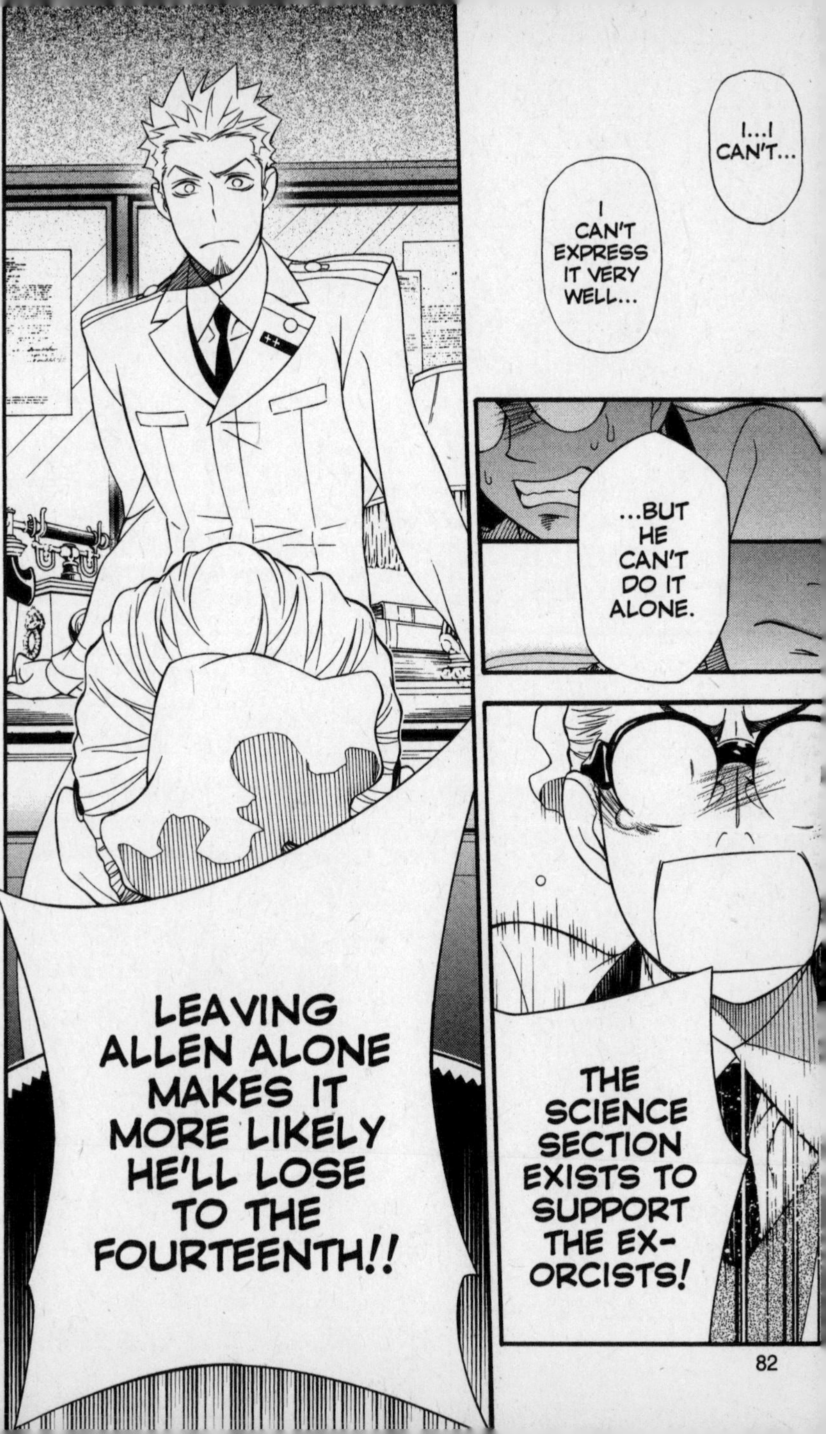
I...I CAN'T...
I CAN'T EXPRESS IT VERY WELL...
...BUT HE CAN'T DO IT ALONE.
THE SCIENCE SECTION EXISTS TO SUPPORT THE EX-ORCISTS!
LEAVING ALLEN ALONE MAKES IT MORE LIKELY HE'LL LOSE TO THE FOURTEENTH!!

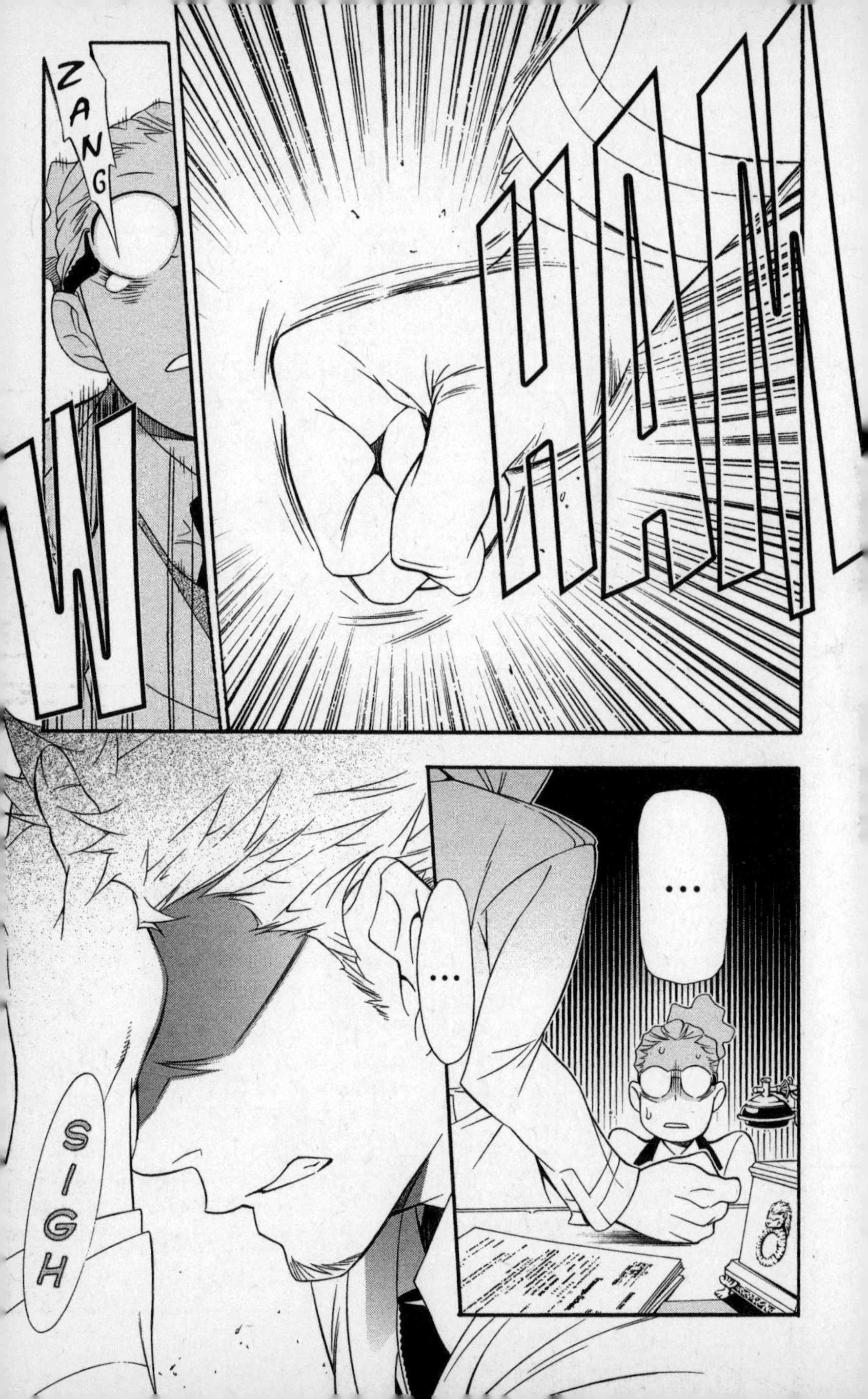
WHAM
ZANG
...
...
SIGH

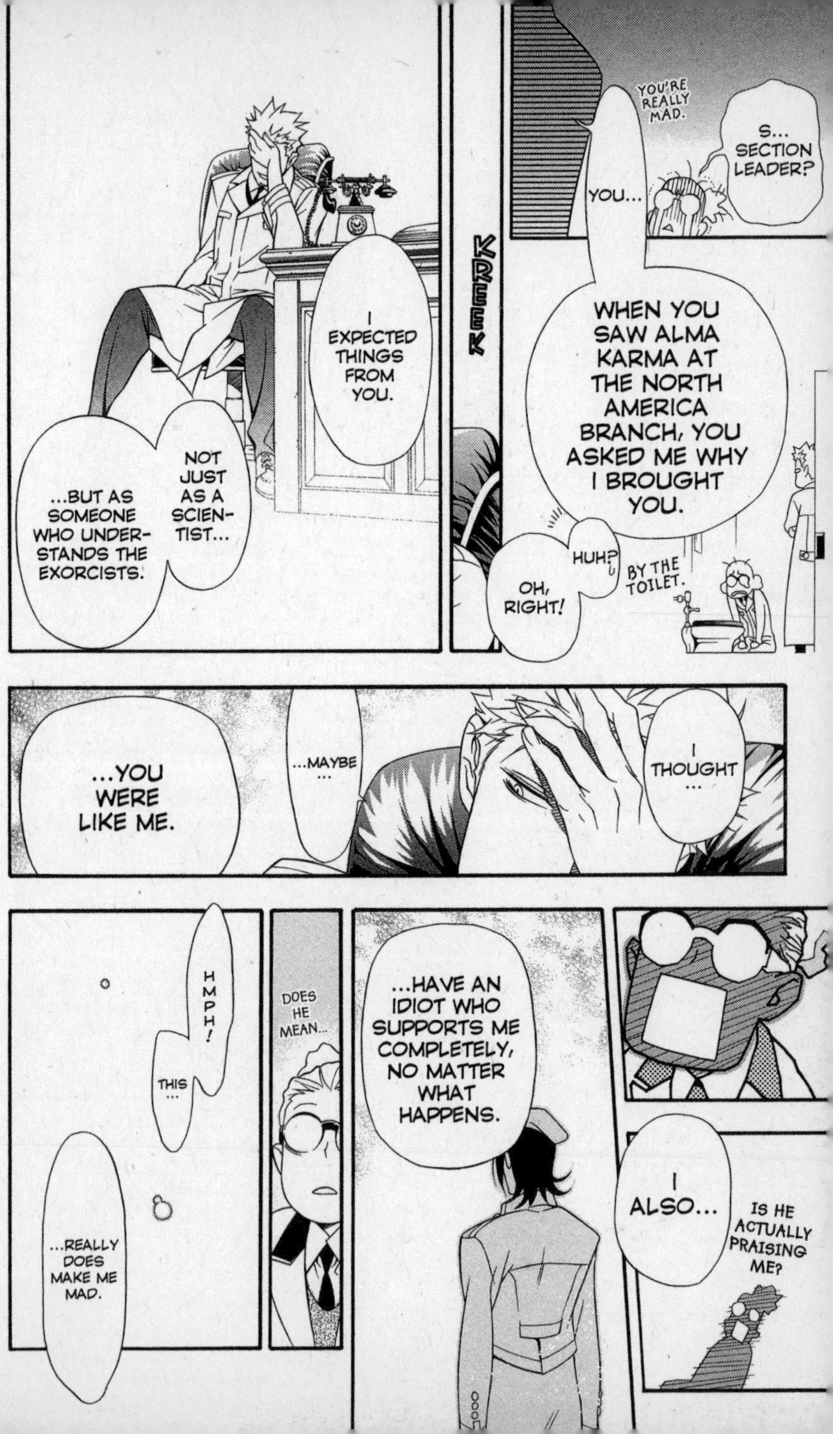

S... SECTION LEADER?
YOU'RE REALLY MAD.
YOU...
WHEN YOU SAW ALMA KARMA AT THE NORTH AMERICA BRANCH, YOU ASKED ME WHY I BROUGHT YOU.
BY THE TOILET.
HUH?
OH, RIGHT!
KREEK
I EXPECTED THINGS FROM YOU.
NOT JUST AS A SCIENTIST...
...BUT AS SOMEONE WHO UNDERSTANDS THE EXORCISTS.
I THOUGHT...
...MAYBE...
...YOU WERE LIKE ME.
I ALSO...
IS HE ACTUALLY PRAISING ME?
...HAVE AN IDIOT WHO SUPPORTS ME COMPLETELY, NO MATTER WHAT HAPPENS.
DOES HE MEAN...
HMPH!
THIS...
...REALLY DOES MAKE ME MAD.

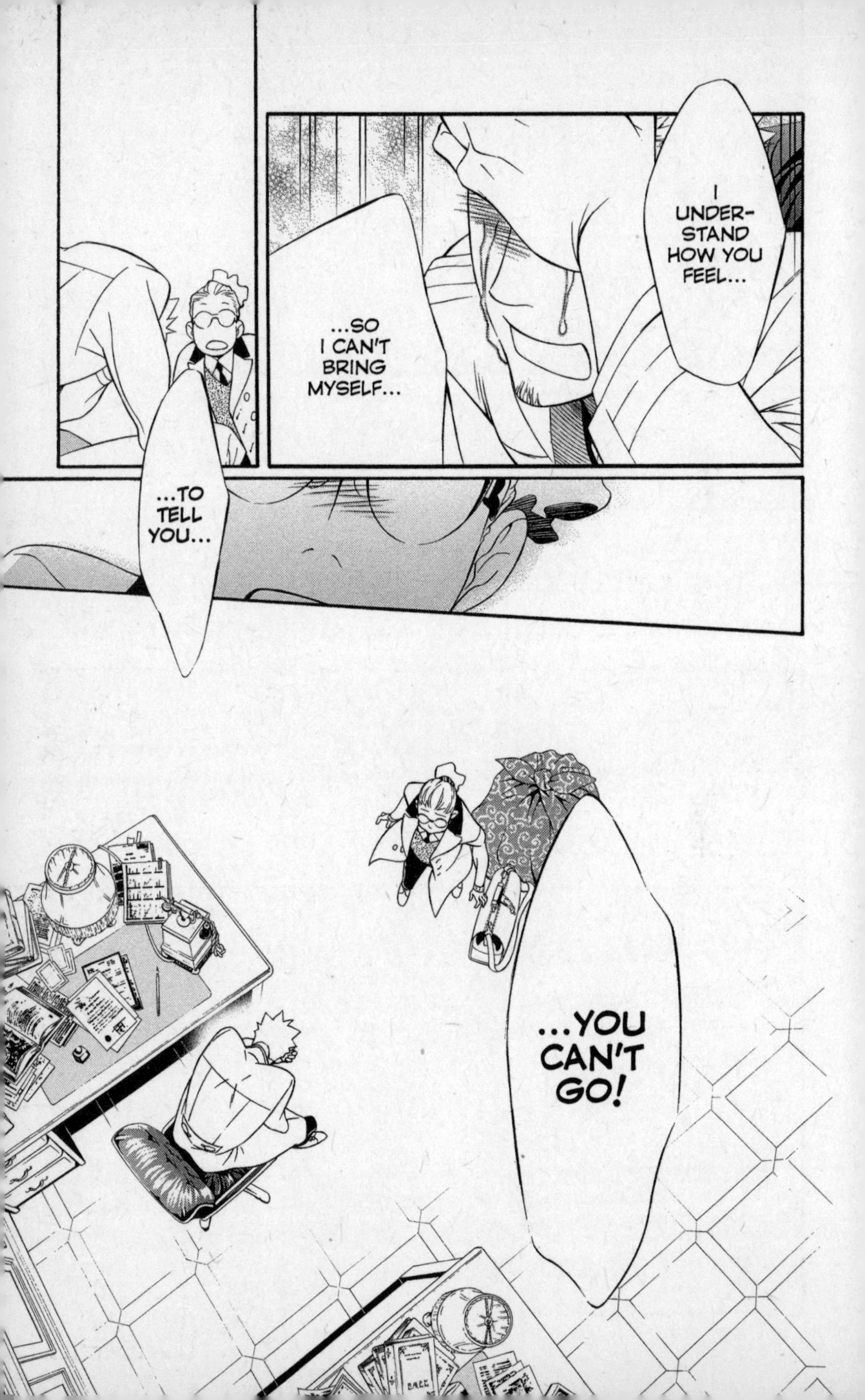
I UNDER-STAND HOW YOU FEEL...
...SO I CAN'T BRING MYSELF...
...TO TELL YOU...
...YOU CAN'T GO!

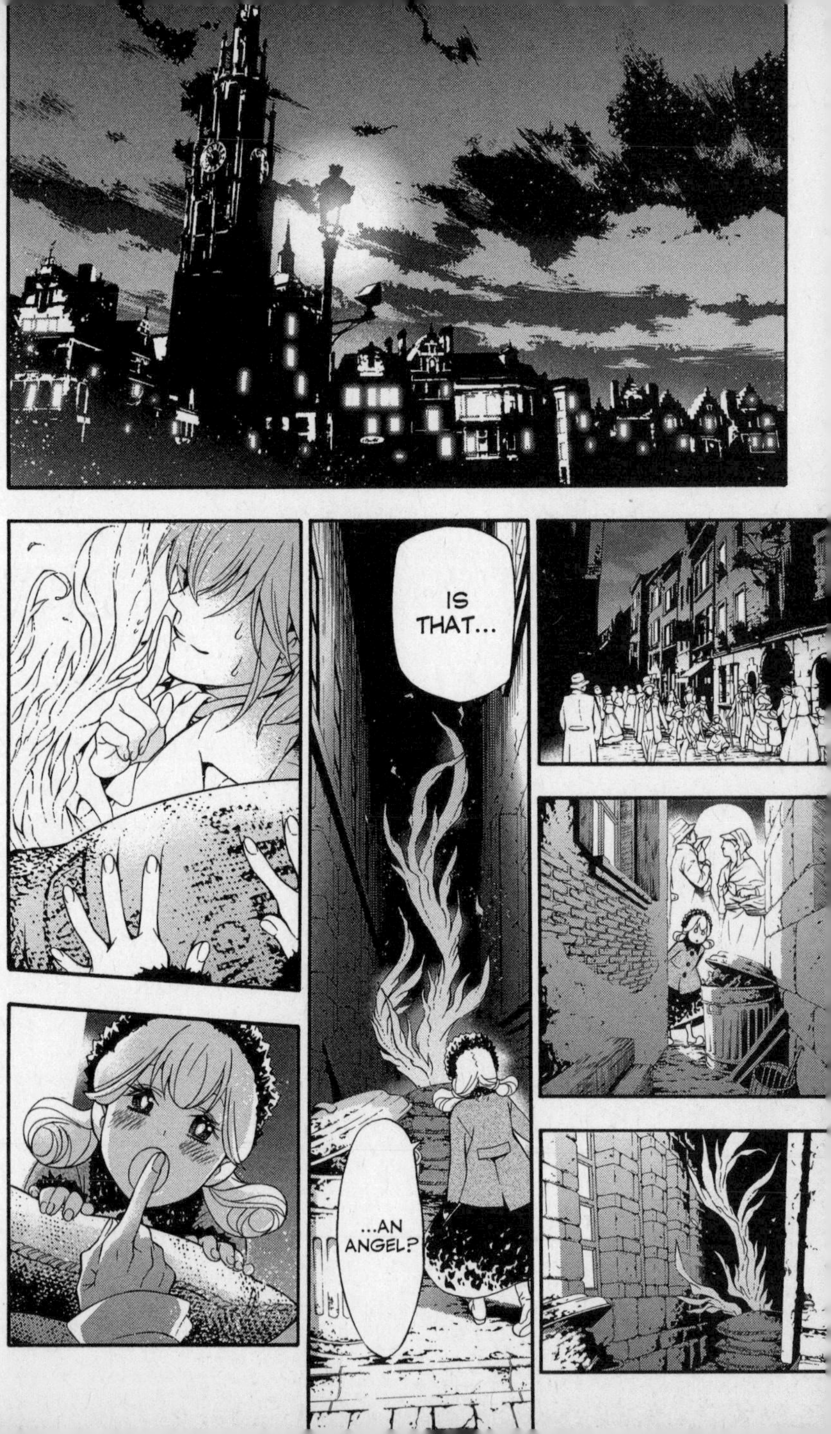
IS THAT...
...AN ANGEL?

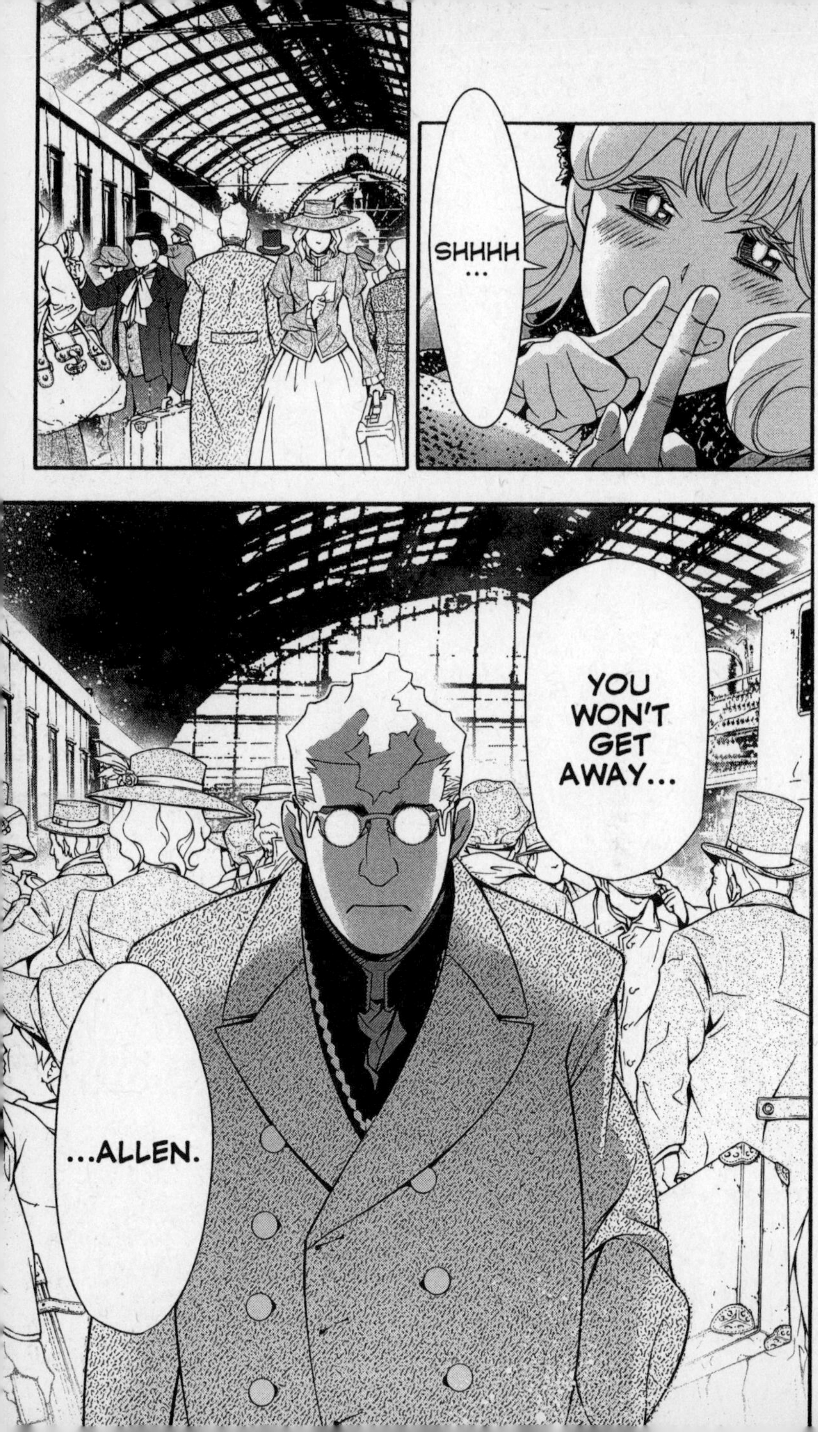
SHHHH...
YOU WON'T GET AWAY...
...ALLEN.

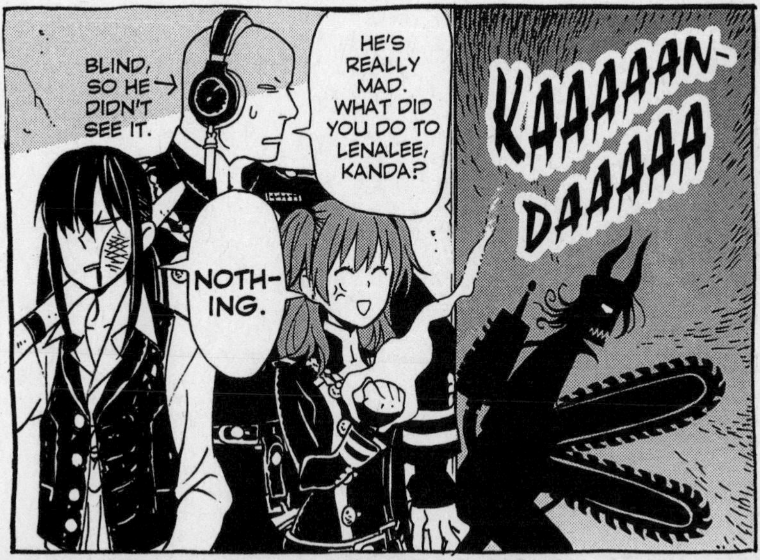
KAAAAAN-DAAAAA
HE'S REALLY MAD. WHAT DID YOU DO TO LENALEE, KANDA?
BLIND, SO HE DIDN'T SEE IT.
NOTH-ING.
SHE DIDN'T KICK HIM, SO HE'LL BE ALL RIGHT.

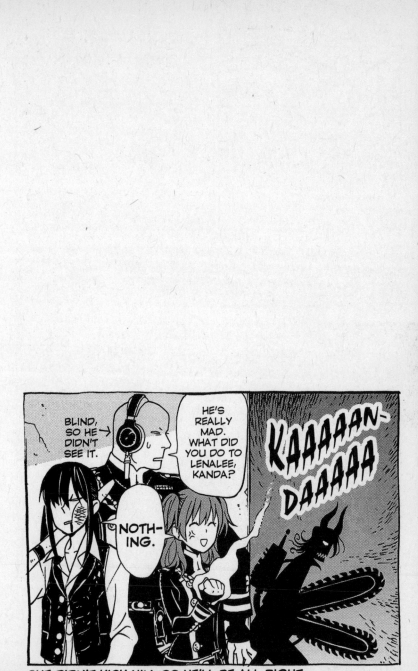

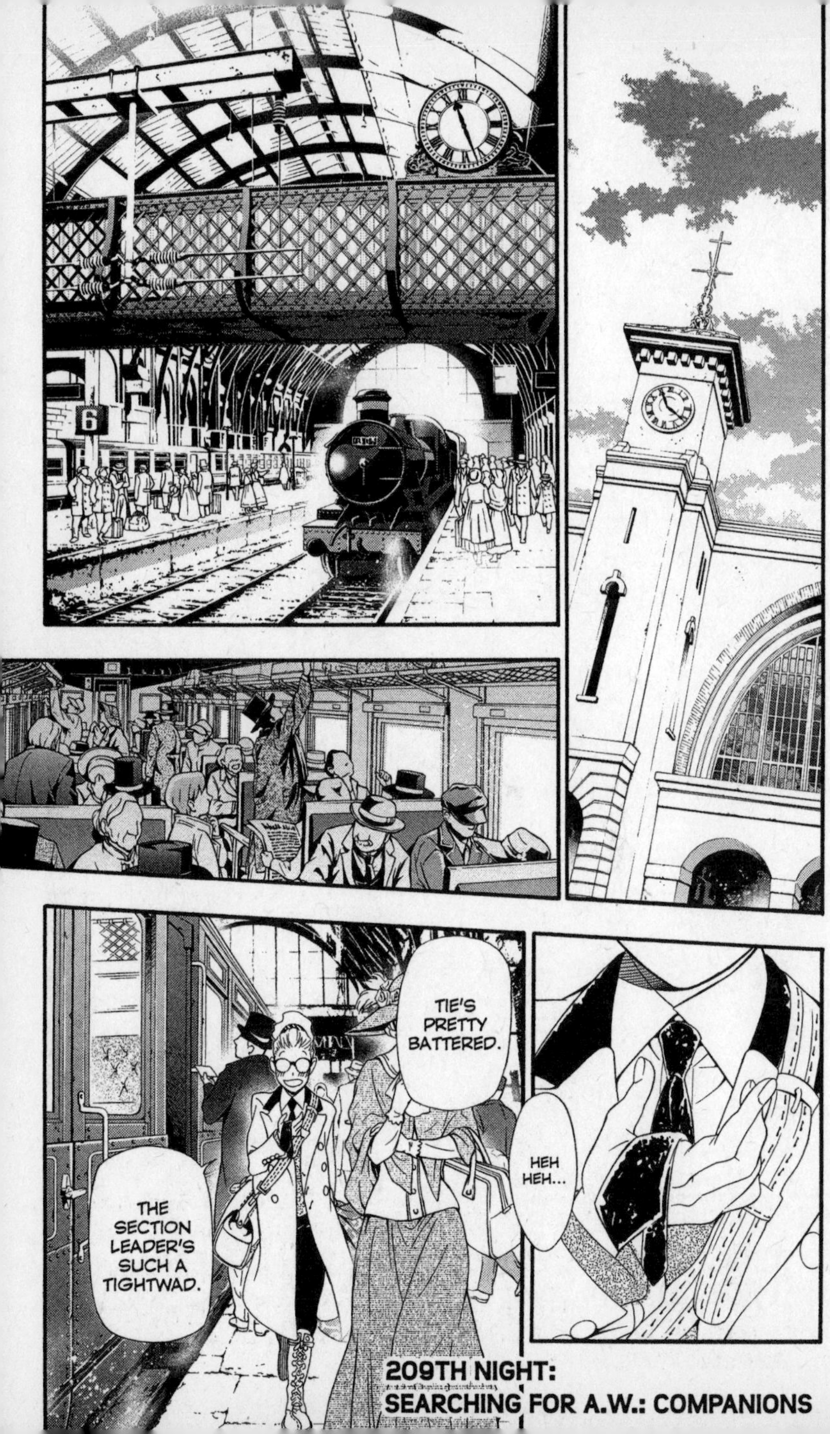
HEH HEH...
TIE'S PRETTY BATTERED.
THE SECTION LEADER'S SUCH A TIGHTWAD.
209TH NIGHT:
SEARCHING FOR A.W.: COMPANIONS

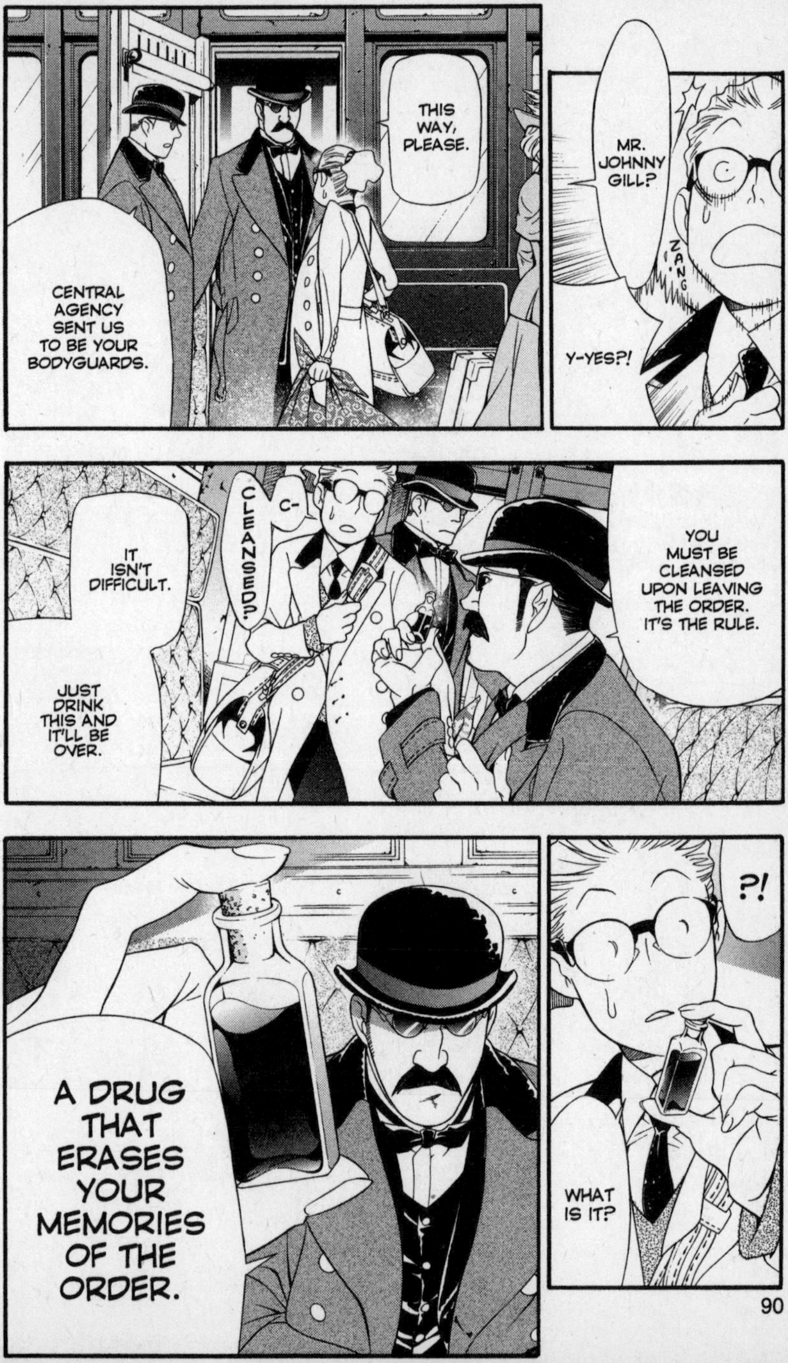
MR. JOHNNY GILL?
ZANG
Y-YES?!
THIS WAY, PLEASE.
CENTRAL AGENCY SENT US TO BE YOUR BODYGUARDS.
YOU MUST BE CLEANSED UPON LEAVING THE ORDER. IT'S THE RULE.
C-
CLEANSED?
IT ISN'T DIFFICULT.
JUST DRINK THIS AND IT'LL BE OVER.
?!
WHAT IS IT?
A DRUG THAT ERASES YOUR MEMORIES OF THE ORDER.

209TH NIGHT: SEARCHING FOR A.W.: COMPANIONS

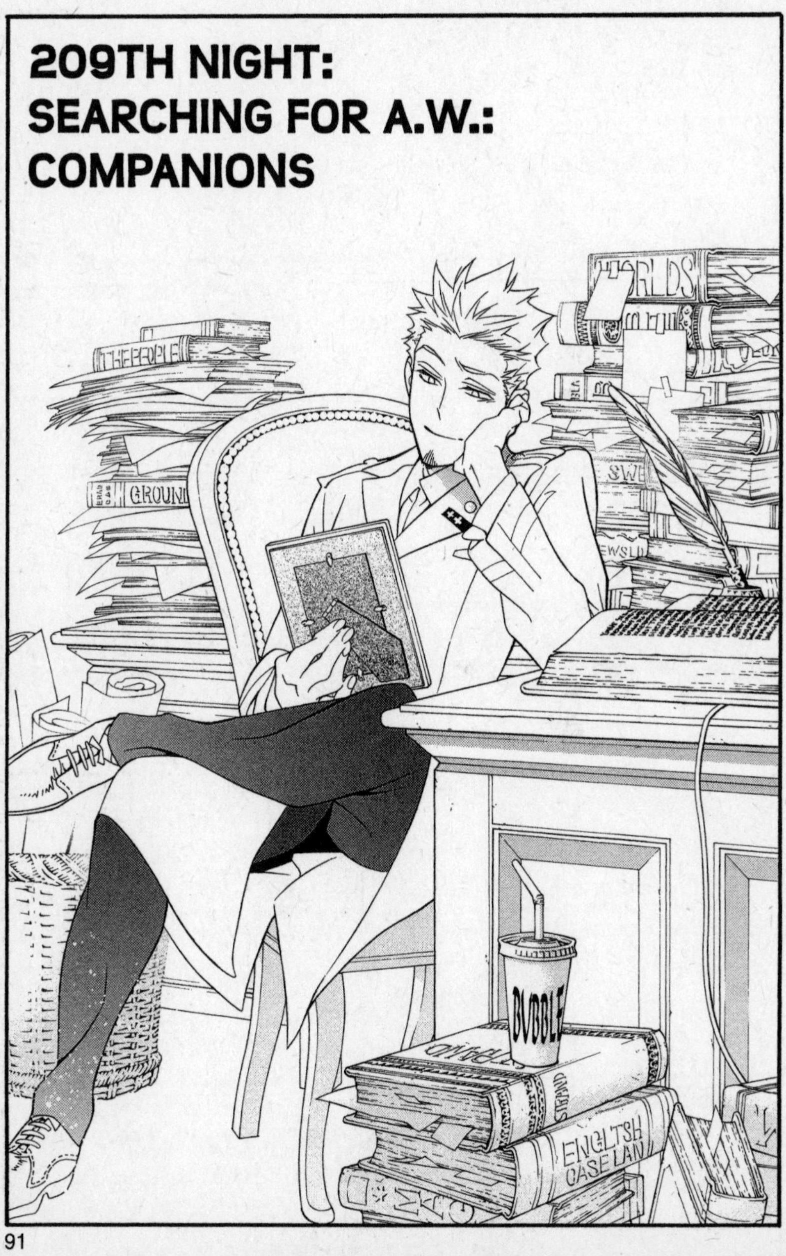
THEPEOPLE
GROUND
BVBBLE
ENGLTSH
CASE LAN

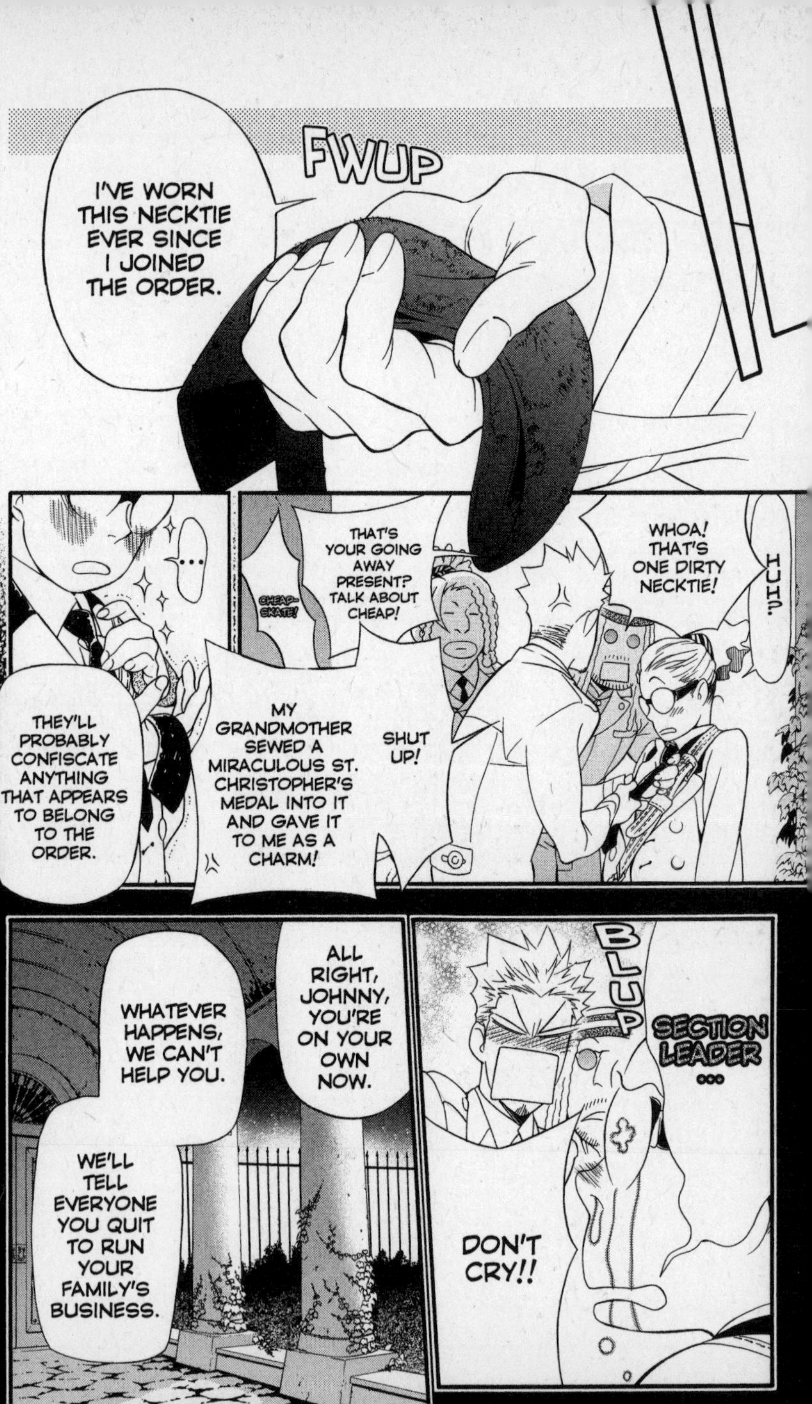
FWUP
I'VE WORN THIS NECKTIE EVER SINCE I JOINED THE ORDER.
HUH?
WHOA! THAT'S ONE DIRTY NECKTIE!
THAT'S YOUR GOING AWAY PRESENT? TALK ABOUT CHEAP!
CHEAPSKATE!
SHUT UP!
MY GRANDMOTHER SEWED A MIRACULOUS ST. CHRISTOPHER'S MEDAL INTO IT AND GAVE IT TO ME AS A CHARM!
...
THEY'LL PROBABLY CONFISCATE ANYTHING THAT APPEARS TO BELONG TO THE ORDER.
BLUP
SECTION LEADER...
DON'T CRY!!
ALL RIGHT, JOHNNY, YOU'RE ON YOUR OWN NOW.
WHATEVER HAPPENS, WE CAN'T HELP YOU.
WE'LL TELL EVERYONE YOU QUIT TO RUN YOUR FAMILY'S BUSINESS.

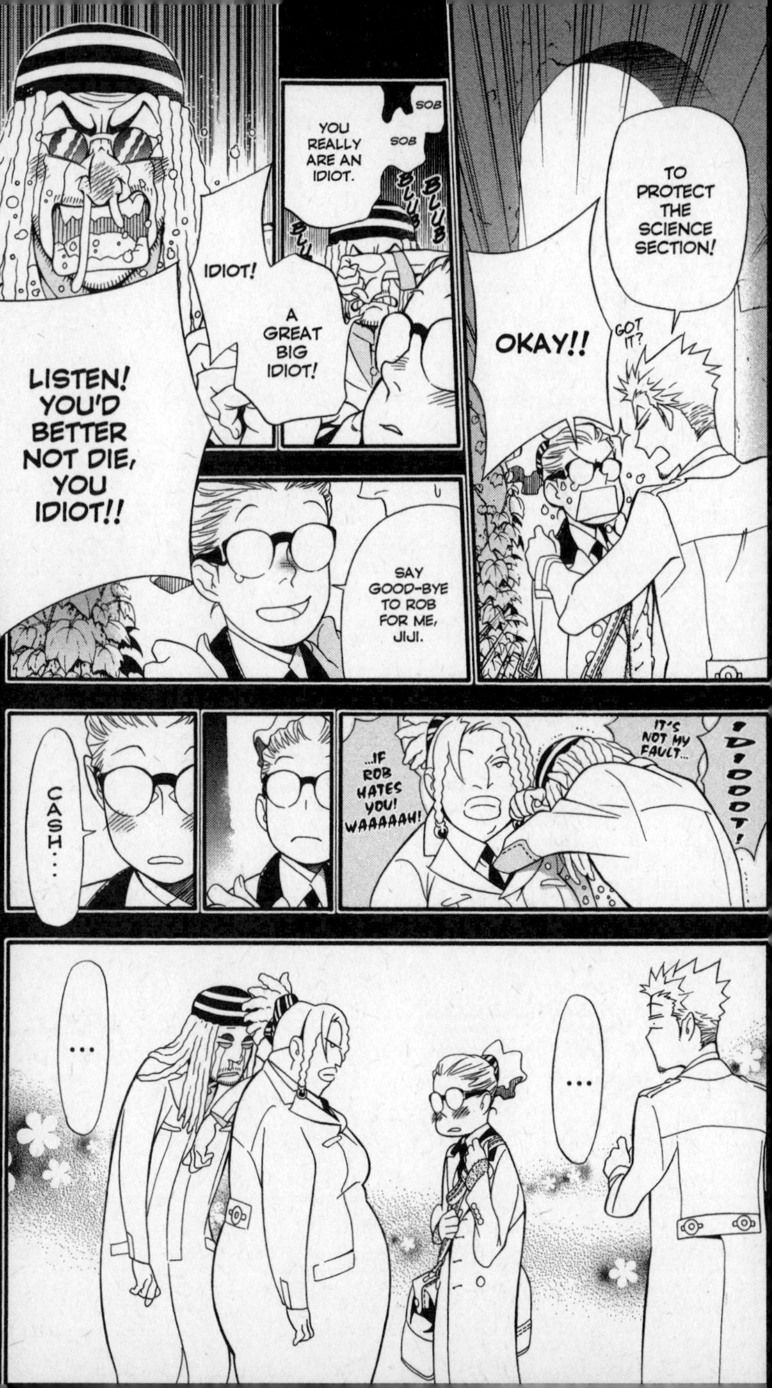

TO PROTECT THE SCIENCE SECTION!
GOT IT?
OKAY!!
YOU REALLY ARE AN IDIOT.
SOB SOB
BLUB BLUB BLUB
IDIOT!
A GREAT BIG IDIOT!
SAY GOOD-BYE TO ROB FOR ME, JIJI.
LISTEN! YOU'D BETTER NOT DIE, YOU IDIOT!!
IDIOOOT!
IT'S NOT MY FAULT...
...IF ROB HATES YOU! WAAAAAH!
CASH...
...
...

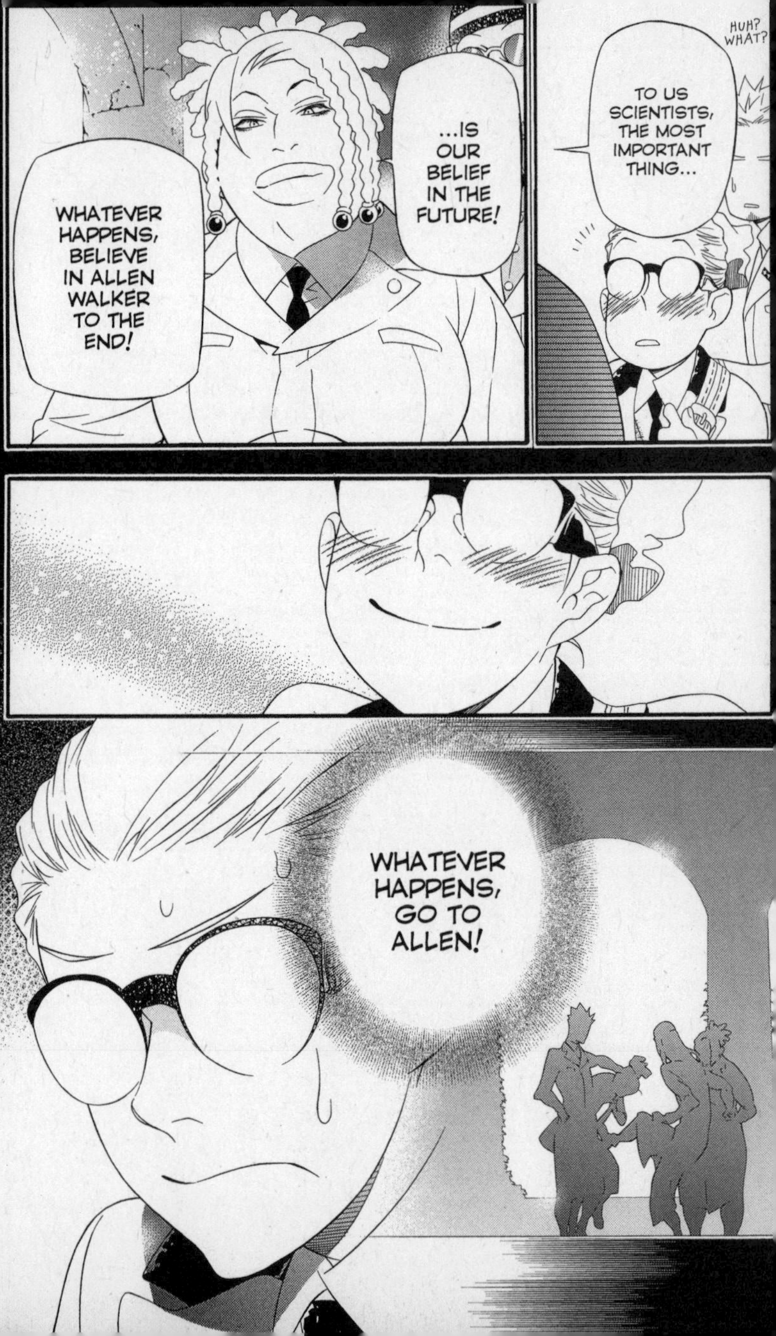
HUH? WHAT?
TO US SCIENTISTS, THE MOST IMPORTANT THING...
...IS OUR BELIEF IN THE FUTURE!
WHATEVER HAPPENS, BELIEVE IN ALLEN WALKER TO THE END!
WHATEVER HAPPENS, GO TO ALLEN!

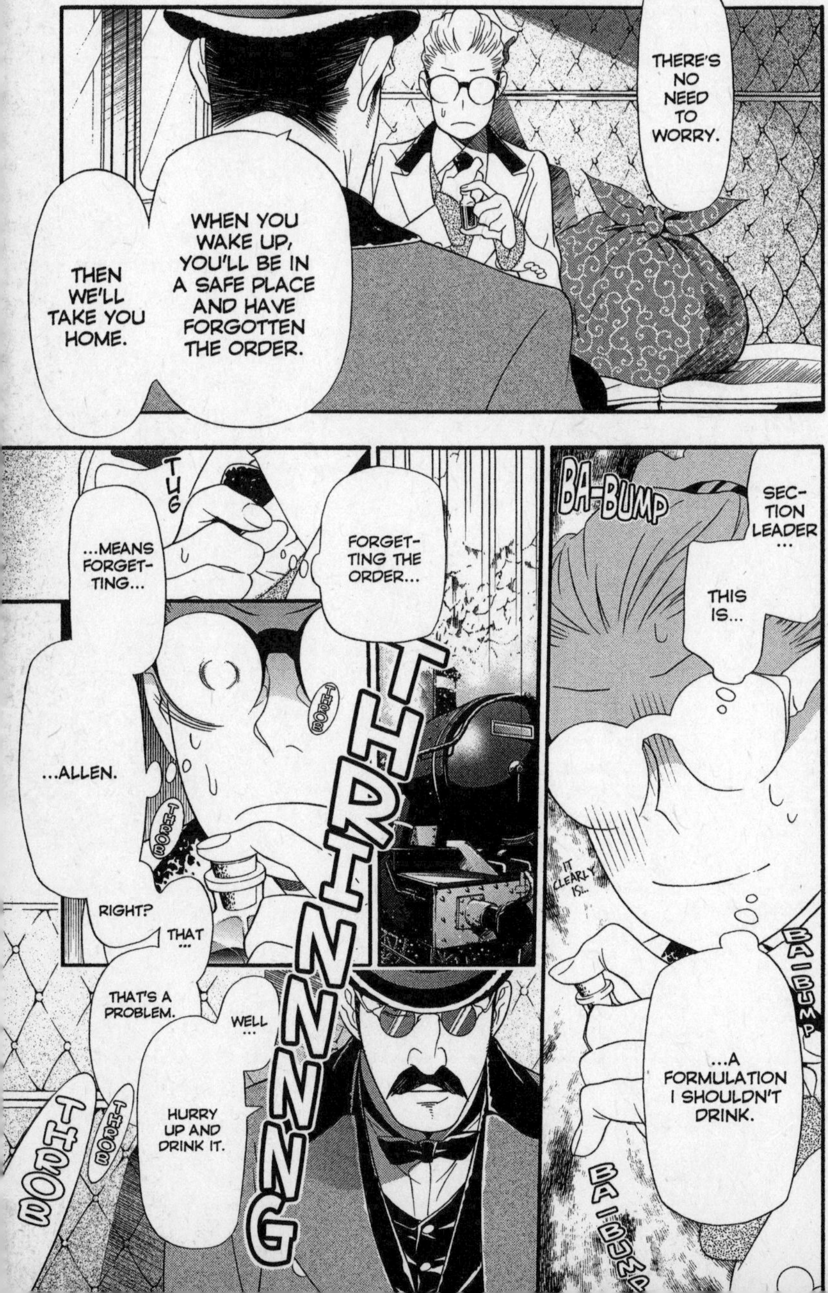
THERE'S NO NEED TO WORRY.
WHEN YOU WAKE UP, YOU'LL BE IN A SAFE PLACE AND HAVE FORGOTTEN THE ORDER.
THEN WE'LL TAKE YOU HOME.
BA-BUMP
SEC-TION LEADER ...
THIS IS...
IT CLEARLY IS...
BA-BUMP
...A FORMULATION I SHOULDN'T DRINK.
BA-BUMP
TUG
FORGET-TING THE ORDER...
...MEANS FORGET-TING...
THROB
THRINNNNG
THROB
...ALLEN.
THAT ...
RIGHT?
WELL ...
THAT'S A PROBLEM.
HURRY UP AND DRINK IT.
THROB
THROB

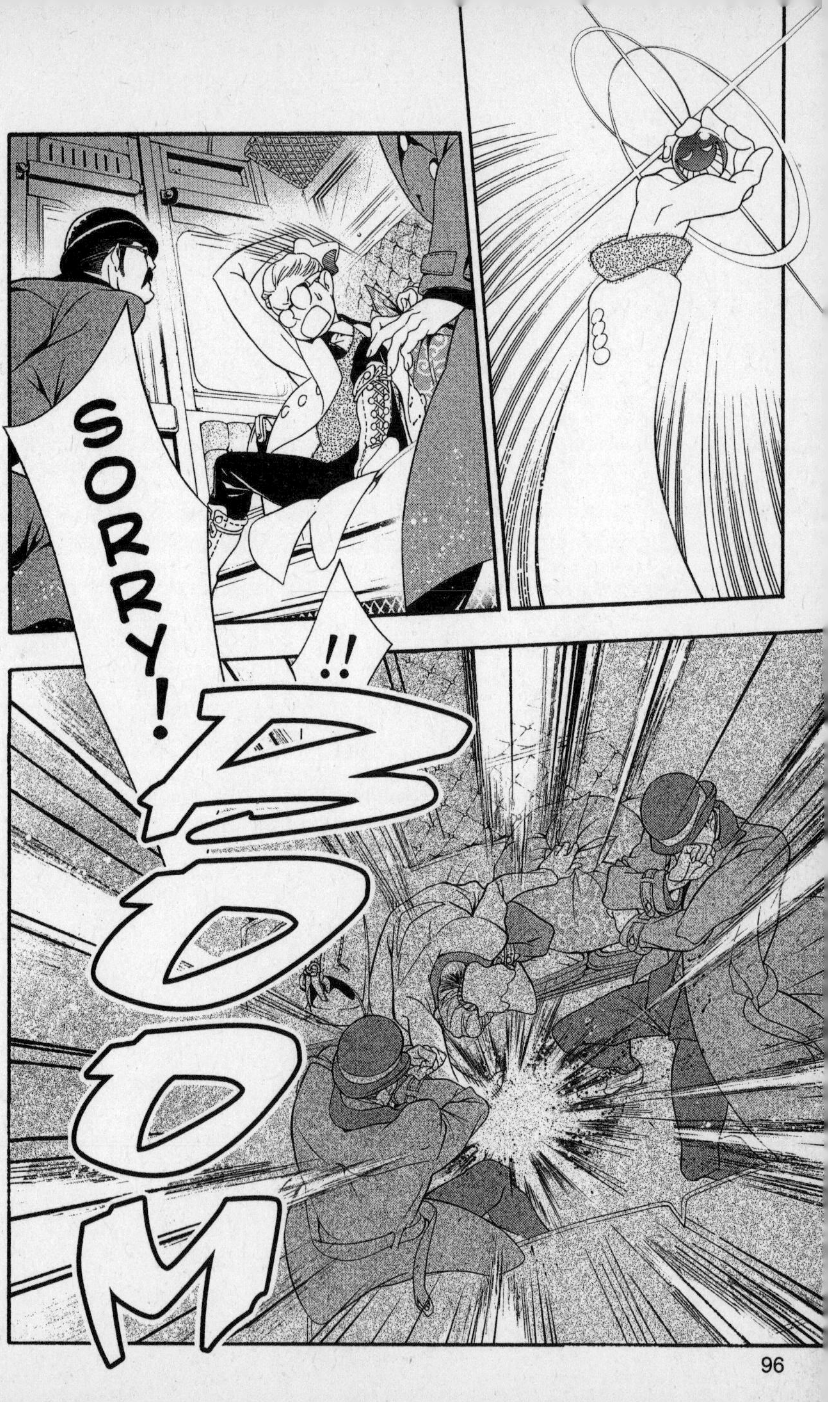
SORRY!
!!
BOOM

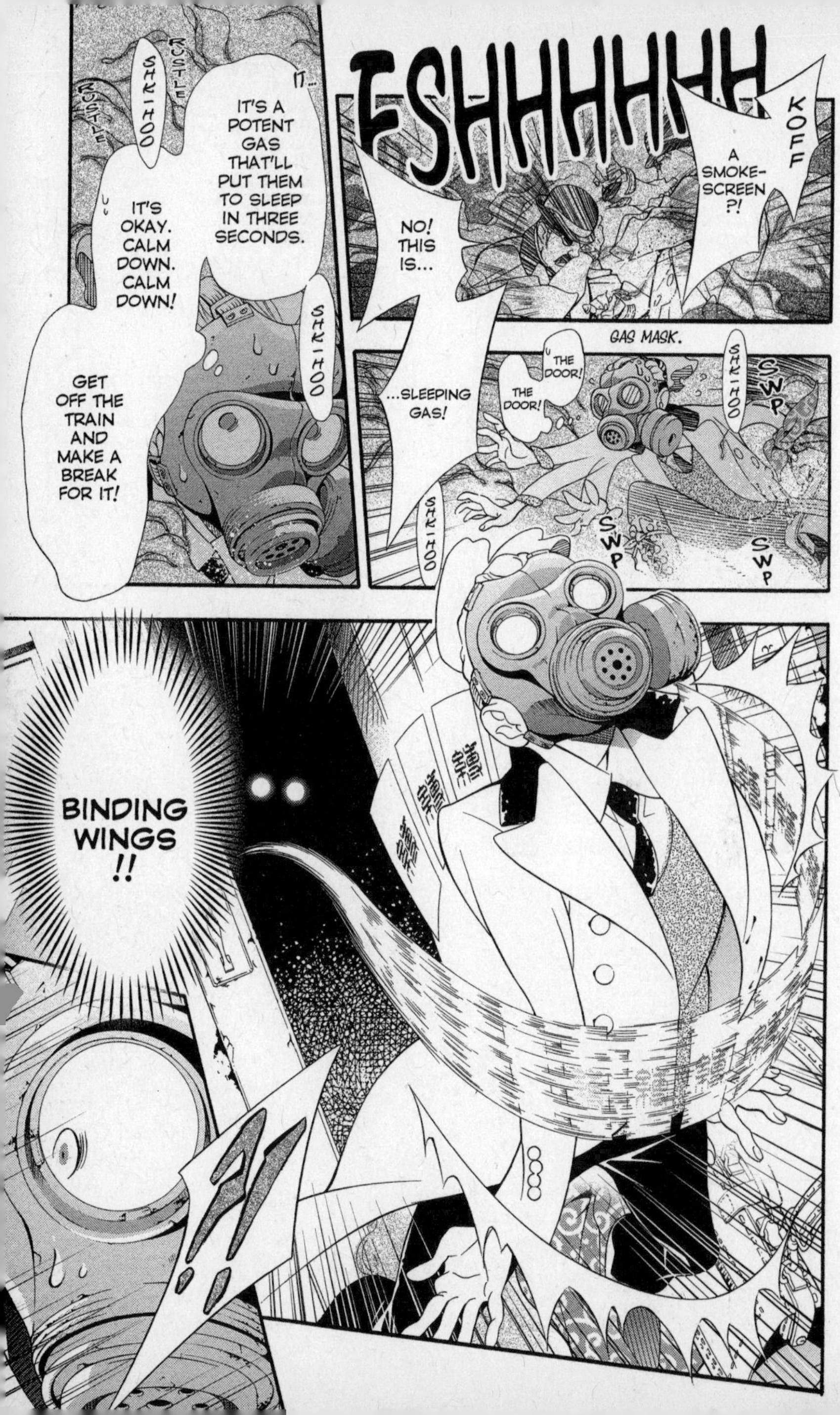
FSHHHHHH
KOFF
A SMOKE-SCREEN?!
NO! THIS IS...
...SLEEPING GAS!
SHK-HOO
SWP
GAS MASK.
THE DOOR!
THE DOOR!
SWP
SWP
SHK-HOO
IT...
IT'S A POTENT GAS THAT'LL PUT THEM TO SLEEP IN THREE SECONDS.
SHK-HOO
RUSTLE
RUSTLE
IT'S OKAY. CALM DOWN. CALM DOWN!
GET OFF THE TRAIN AND MAKE A BREAK FOR IT!
SHK-HOO
BINDING WINGS!!

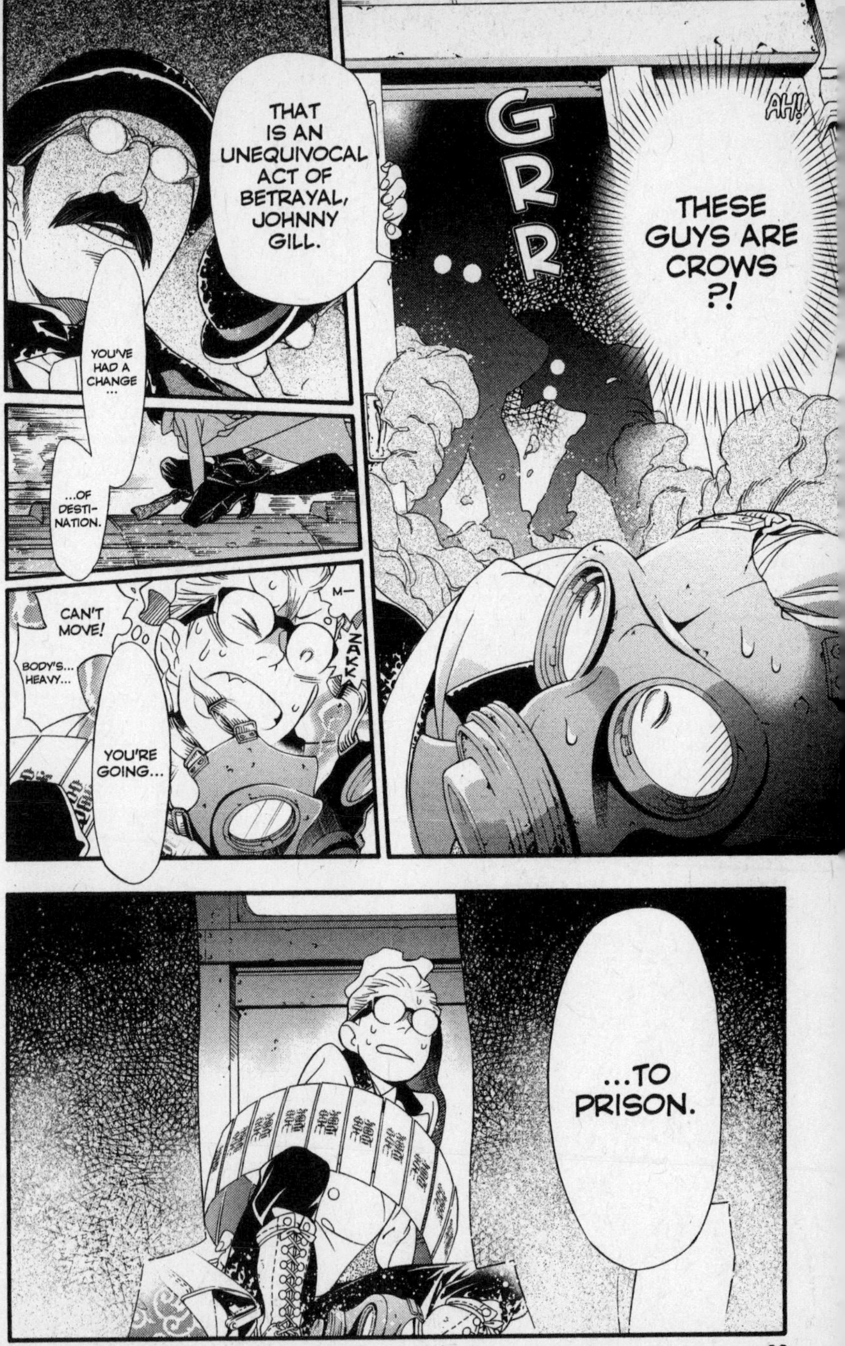
AH!
GRR
THESE GUYS ARE CROWS?!
THAT IS AN UNEQUIVOCAL ACT OF BETRAYAL, JOHNNY GILL.
YOU'VE HAD A CHANGE ...
...OF DESTINATION.
M—
ZAKK
CAN'T MOVE!
BODY'S... HEAVY...
YOU'RE GOING...
...TO PRISON.

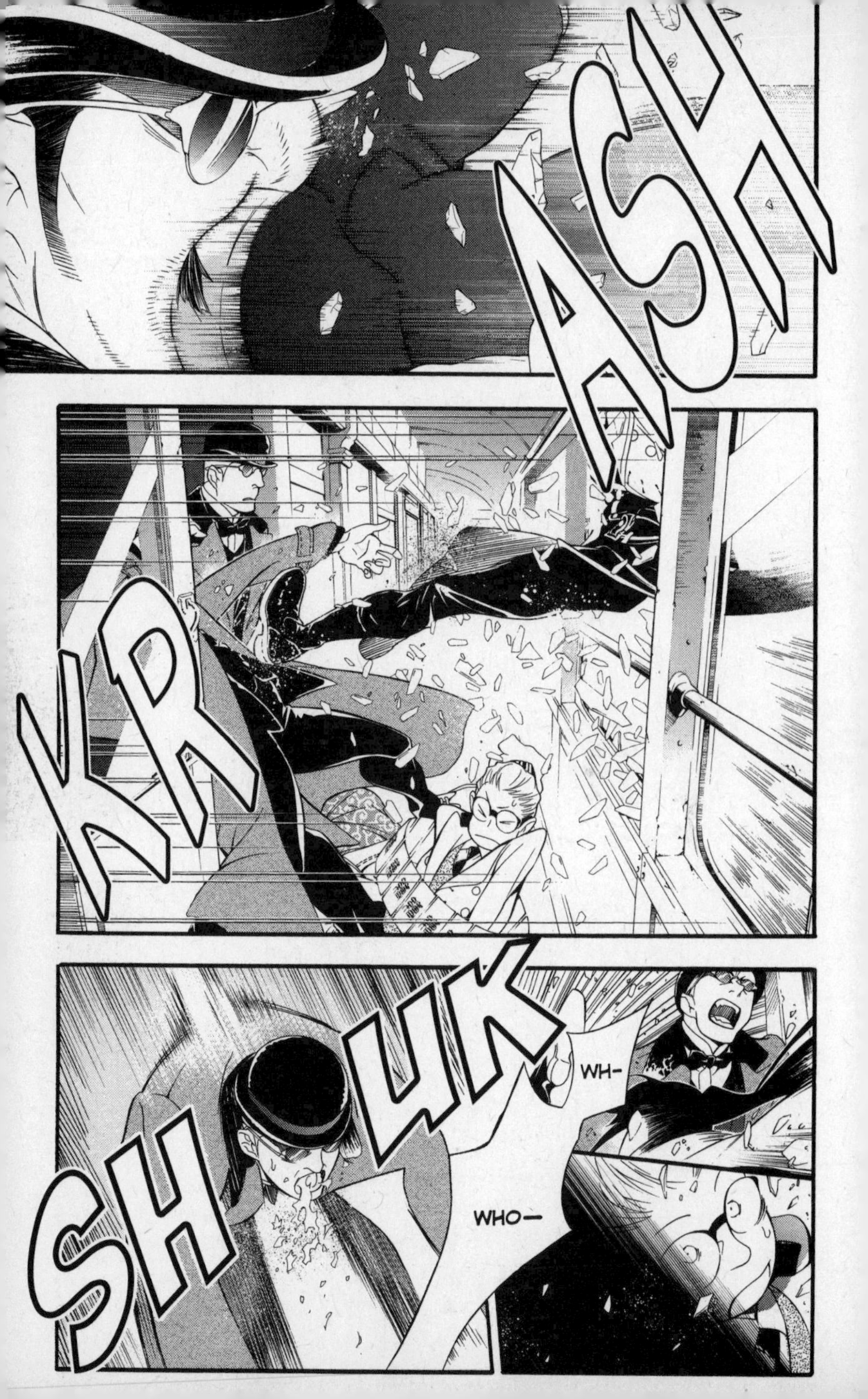

KRASH
SHUNK
WH-
WHO—

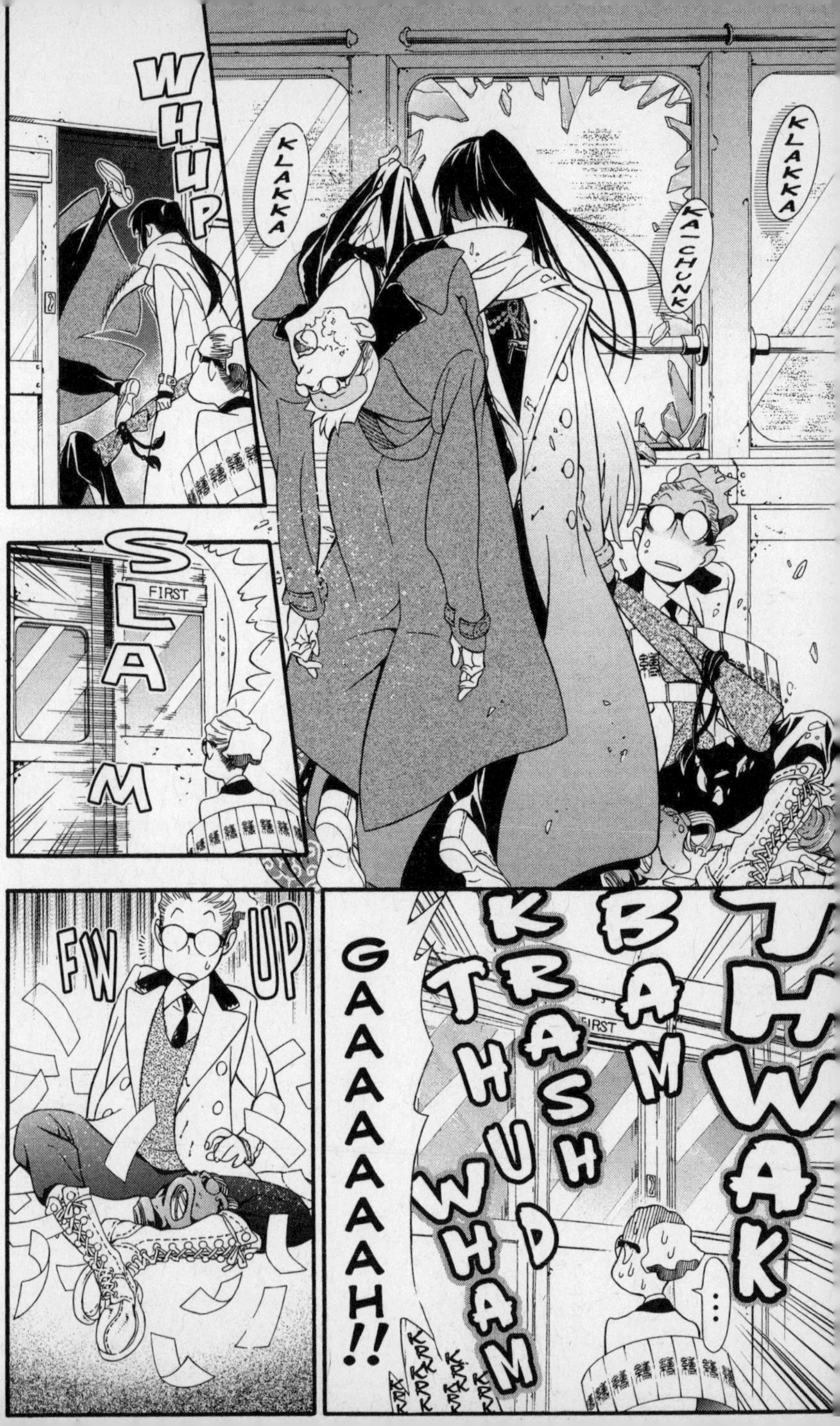
KLAKKA
KA-CHUNK
KLAKKA
WHUP
SLAM
FIRST
THWAK
BAM
KBTRASH
WHUD
WHAM
GAAAAAAAAH!!
KRK KRK KRK KRK KRK KRK KRK
...
FIRST
FWUP

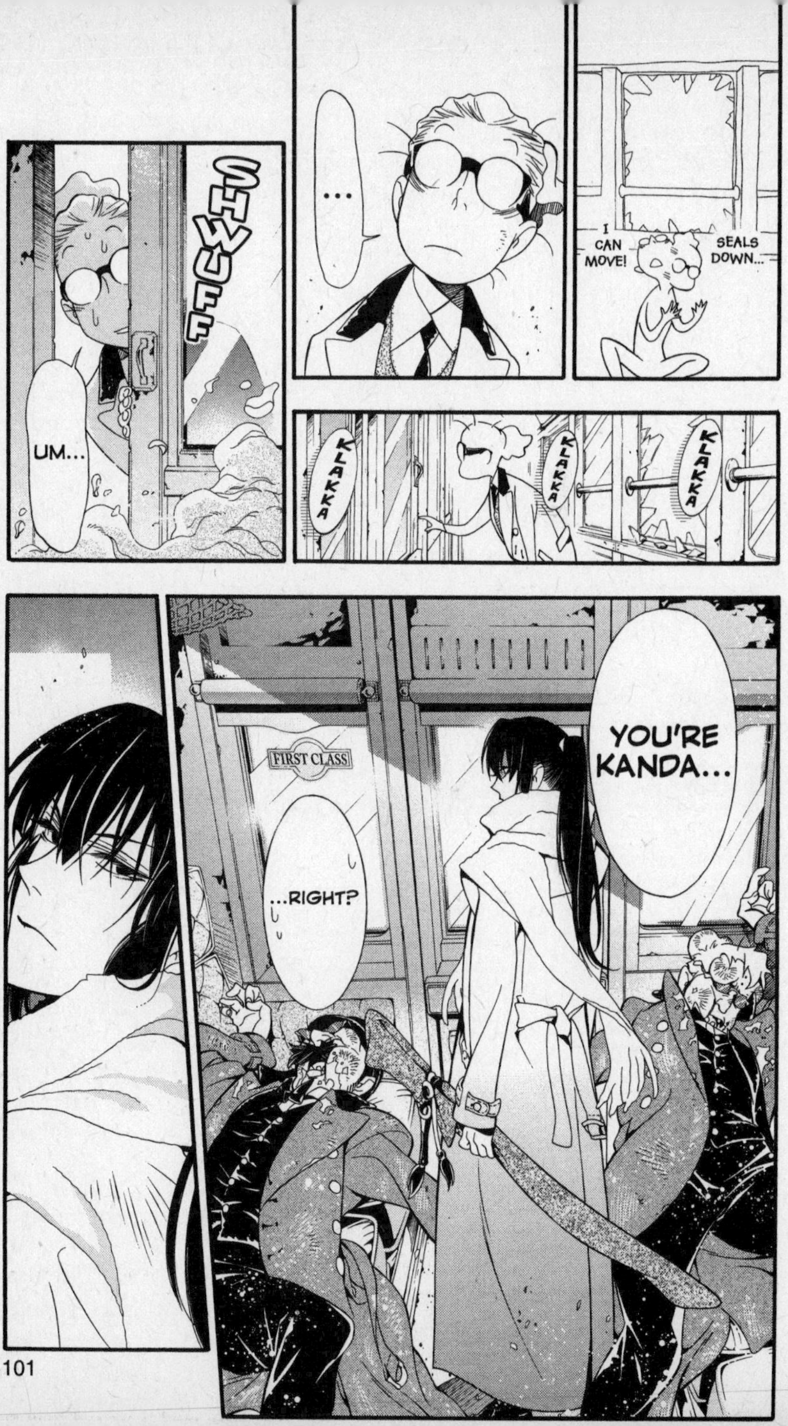
SEALS DOWN...
I CAN MOVE!
...
KLAKKA
KLAKKA
KLAKKA
SHWUFF
UM...
YOU'RE KANDA...
...RIGHT?
FIRST CLASS

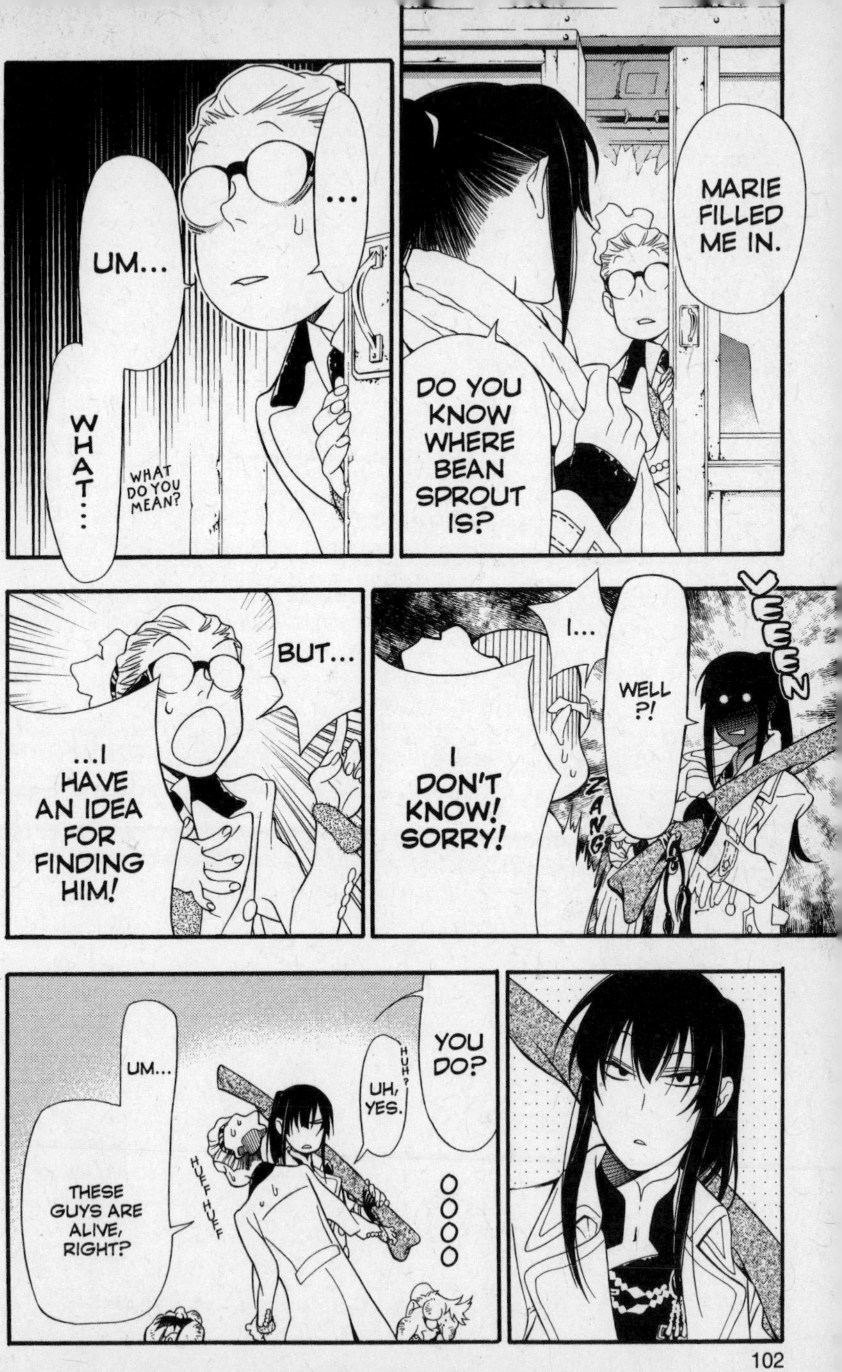
MARIE FILLED ME IN.
DO YOU KNOW WHERE BEAN SPROUT IS?
...
UM...
WHAT...
WHAT DO YOU MEAN?
YEEEN
WELL?!
I...
ZANG
I DON'T KNOW! SORRY!
BUT...
...I HAVE AN IDEA FOR FINDING HIM!
YOU DO?
HUH?
UH, YES.
OOOO
UM...
HUFF HUFF
THESE GUYS ARE ALIVE, RIGHT?

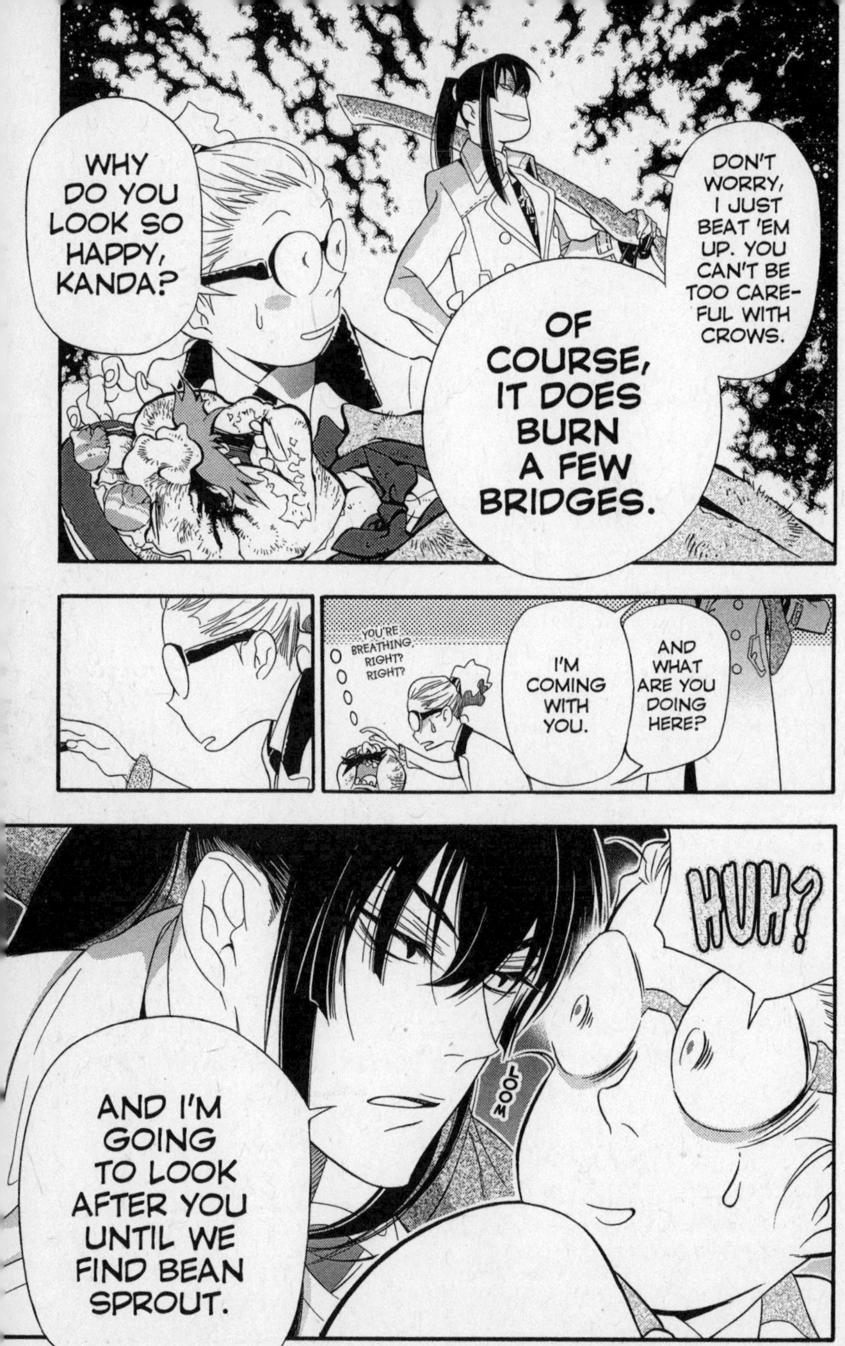
DON'T WORRY, I JUST BEAT 'EM UP. YOU CAN'T BE TOO CAREFUL WITH CROWS.
OF COURSE, IT DOES BURN A FEW BRIDGES.
WHY DO YOU LOOK SO HAPPY, KANDA?
AND WHAT ARE YOU DOING HERE?
I'M COMING WITH YOU.
YOU'RE BREATHING, RIGHT? RIGHT?
HUH?
LOOM
AND I'M GOING TO LOOK AFTER YOU UNTIL WE FIND BEAN SPROUT.

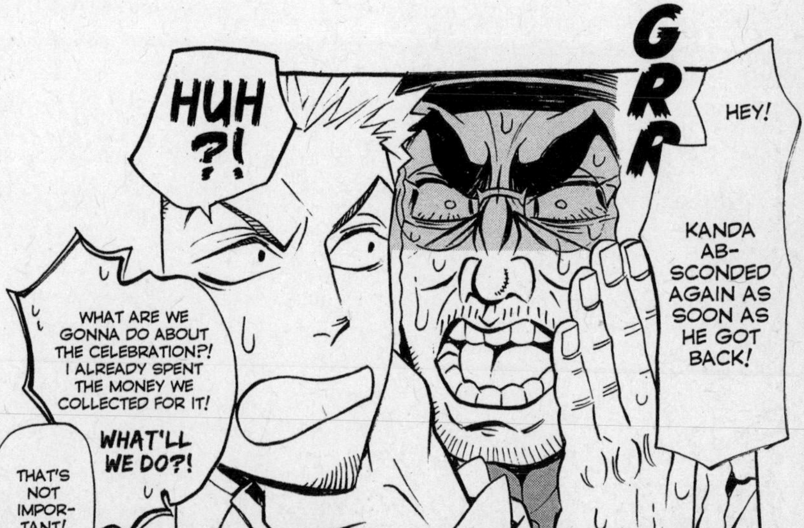
GRR
HEY!
KANDA AB-SCONDED AGAIN AS SOON AS HE GOT BACK!
HUH?!
WHAT ARE WE GONNA DO ABOUT THE CELEBRATION?! I ALREADY SPENT THE MONEY WE COLLECTED FOR IT!
WHAT'LL WE DO?!
THAT'S NOT IMPOR-TANT!

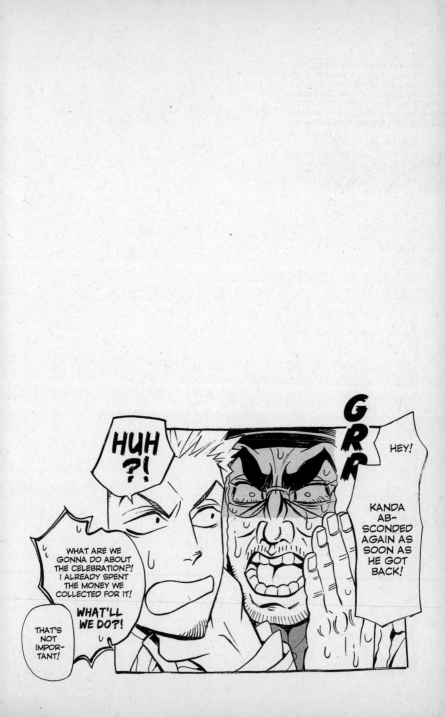

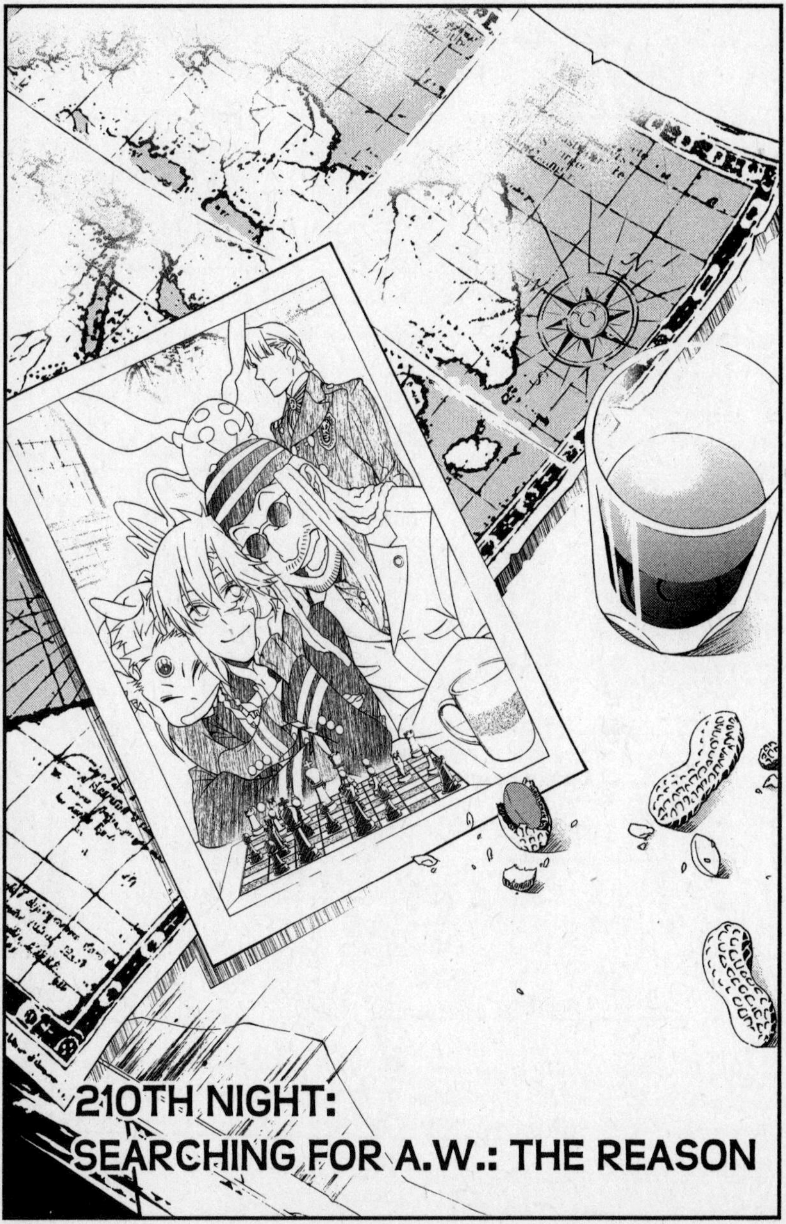

210TH NIGHT: SEARCHING FOR A.W.: THE REASON

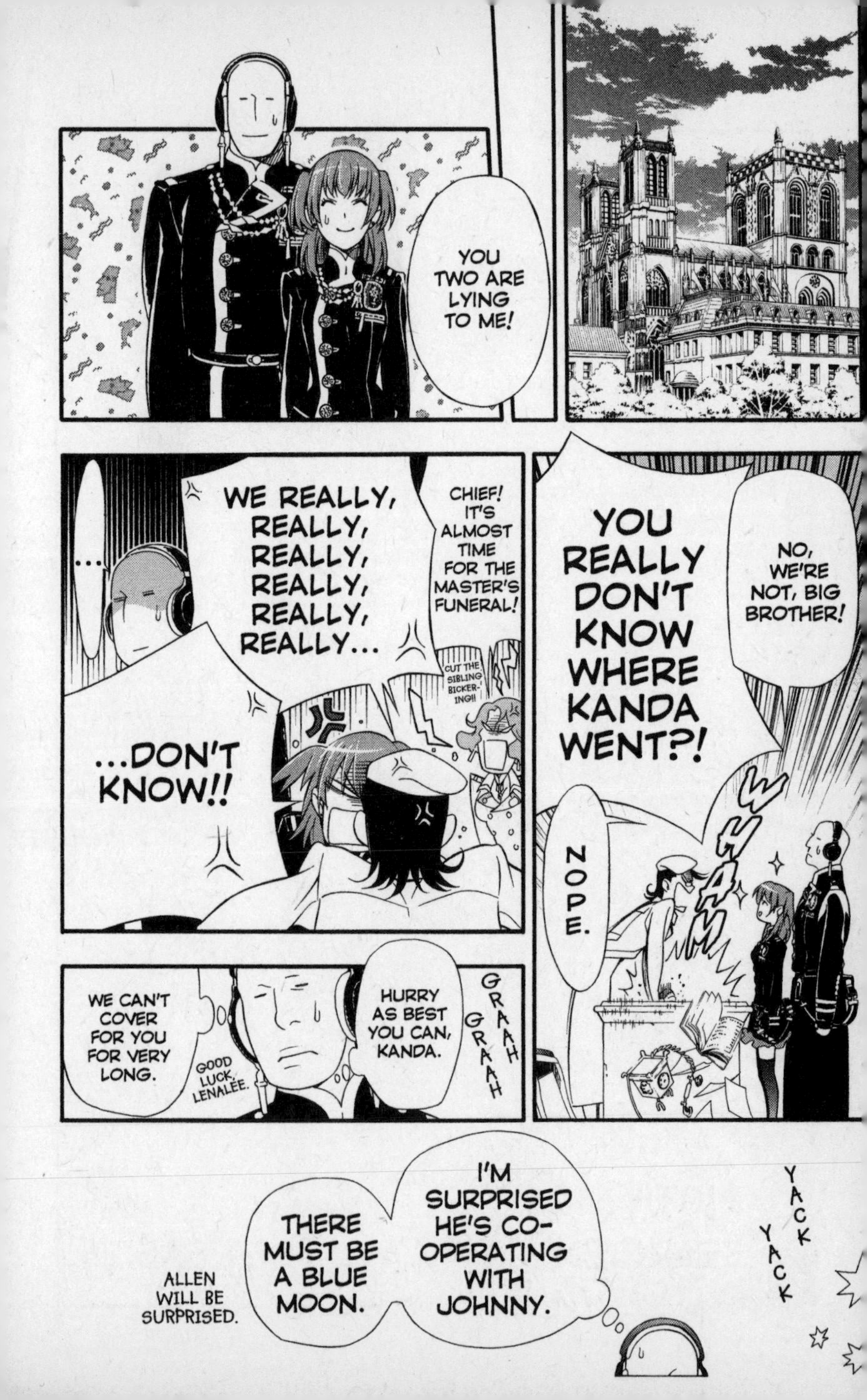
YOU TWO ARE LYING TO ME!
NO, WE'RE NOT, BIG BROTHER!
YOU REALLY DON'T KNOW WHERE KANDA WENT?!
NOPE.
WHAM
CHIEF! IT'S ALMOST TIME FOR THE MASTER'S FUNERAL!
WE REALLY, REALLY, REALLY, REALLY, REALLY, REALLY...
...
CUT THE SIBLING BICKERING!!
...DON'T KNOW!!
GRAAH GRAAH
HURRY AS BEST YOU CAN, KANDA.
GOOD LUCK, LENALEE.
WE CAN'T COVER FOR YOU FOR VERY LONG.
YACK YACK
I'M SURPRISED HE'S CO-OPERATING WITH JOHNNY.
THERE MUST BE A BLUE MOON.
ALLEN WILL BE SURPRISED.

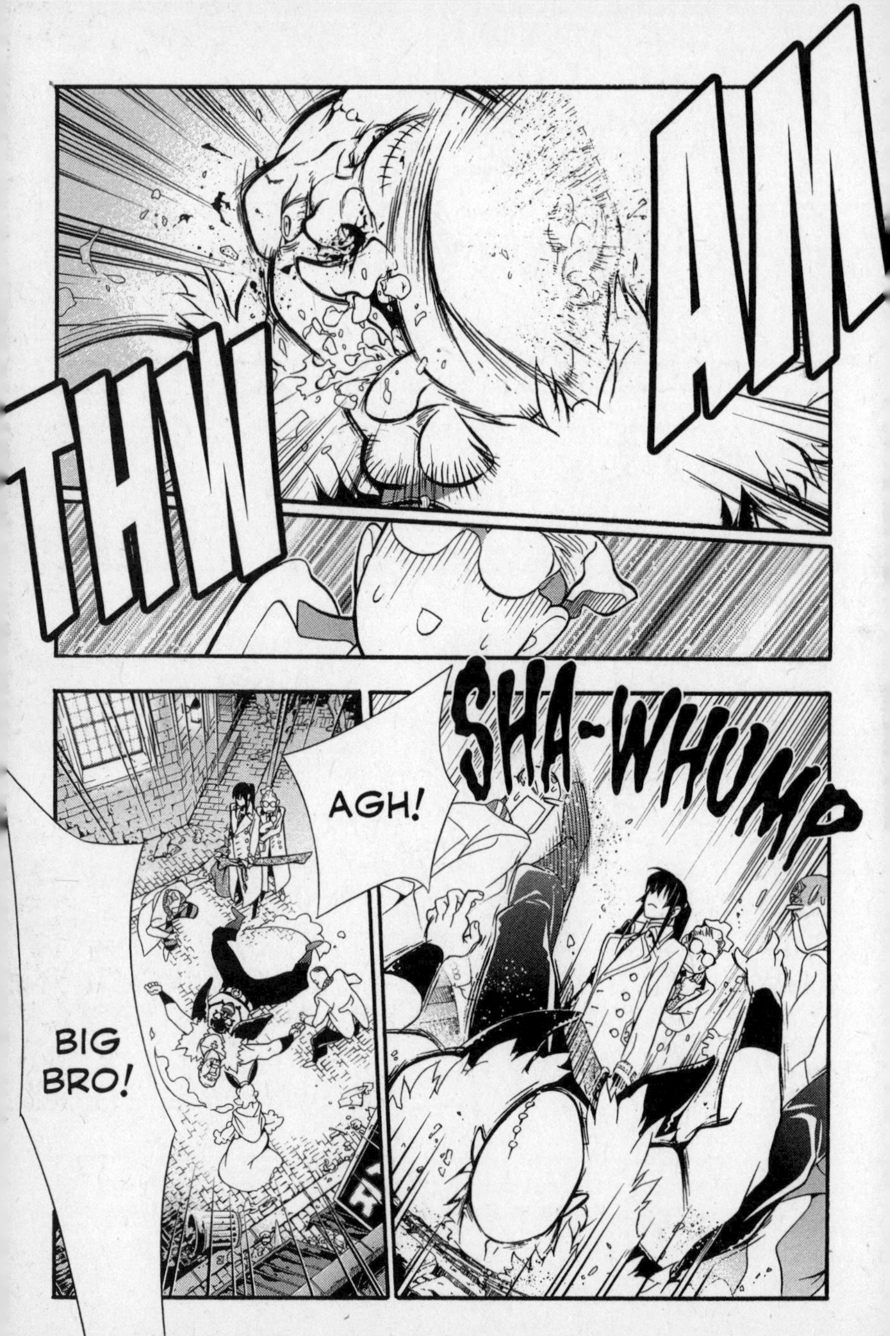
THWAM
SHA-WHUMP
AGH!
BIG BRO!

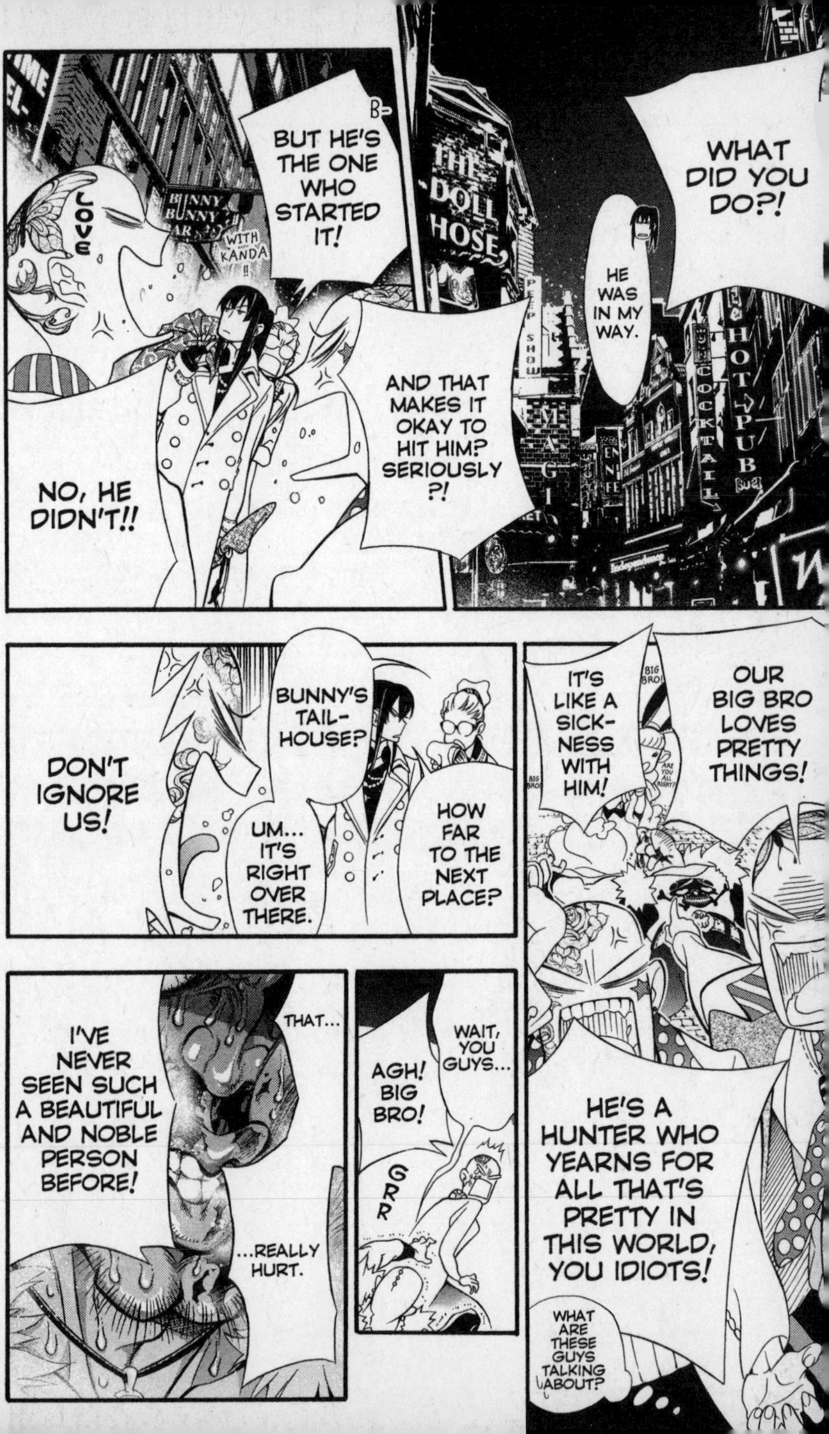
WHAT DID YOU DO?!
HE WAS IN MY WAY.
THE DOLL HOSE
HOT PUB
COCKTAIL
B-
BUT HE'S THE ONE WHO STARTED IT!
AND THAT MAKES IT OKAY TO HIT HIM? SERIOUSLY?!
LOVE
WITH KANDA!!
NO, HE DIDN'T!!
OUR BIG BRO LOVES PRETTY THINGS!
BIG BRO!
IT'S LIKE A SICKNESS WITH HIM!
ARE YOU ALL RIGHT?
BIG BRO
HE'S A HUNTER WHO YEARNS FOR ALL THAT'S PRETTY IN THIS WORLD, YOU IDIOTS!
WHAT ARE THESE GUYS TALKING ABOUT?
BUNNY'S TAIL-HOUSE?
HOW FAR TO THE NEXT PLACE?
UM... IT'S RIGHT OVER THERE.
DON'T IGNORE US!
WAIT, YOU GUYS...
AGH! BIG BRO!
GRR
THAT...
I'VE NEVER SEEN SUCH A BEAUTIFUL AND NOBLE PERSON BEFORE!
...REALLY HURT.

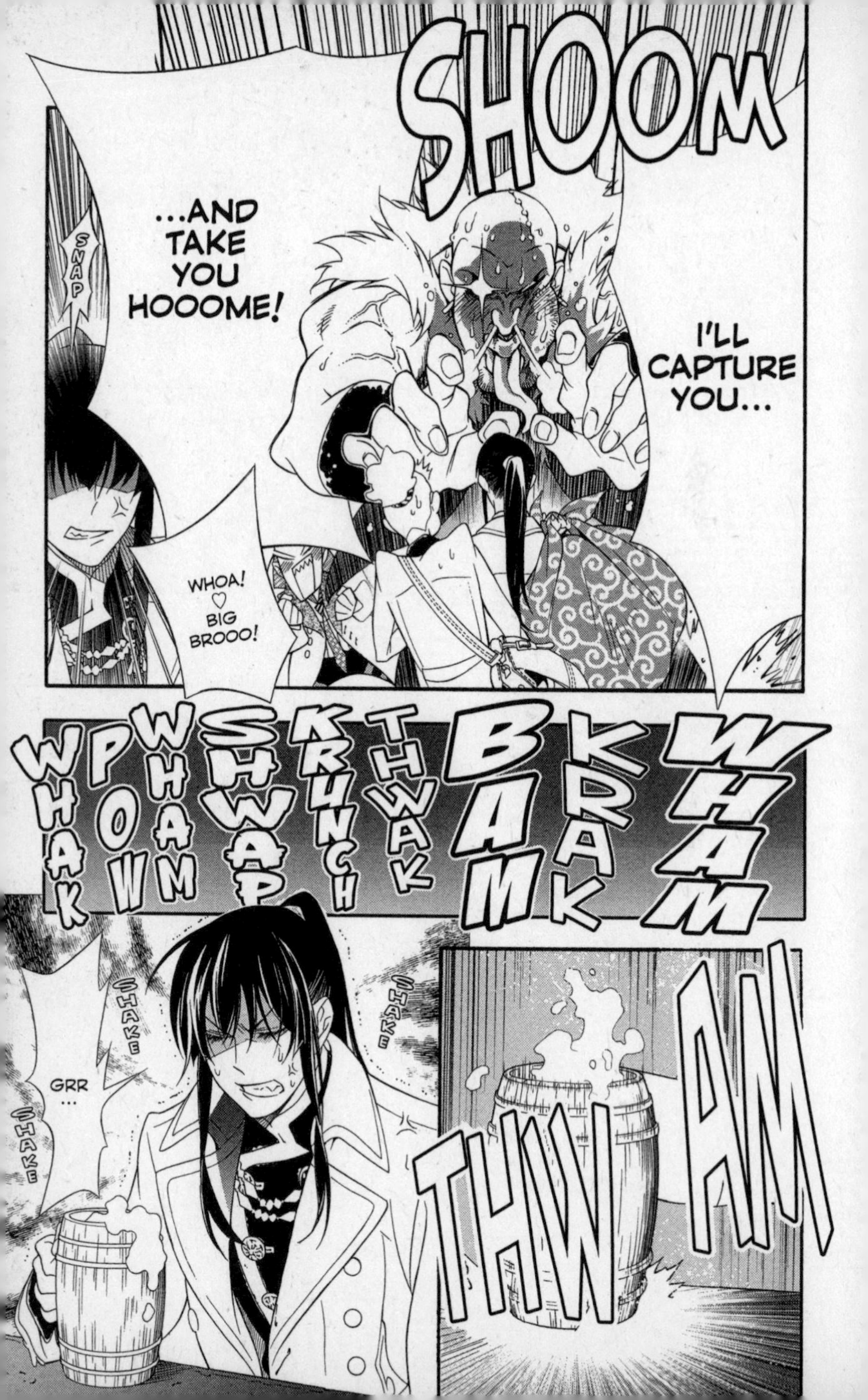

SHOOM
I'LL CAPTURE YOU...
...AND TAKE YOU HOOOME!
SNAP
WHOA! ♡ BIG BROOO!
WHAM
KRAMK
BAMM
THWAK
KRUNCH
SHWAP
WHAM
POW
WHAK
THWAM
SHAKE
SHAKE
GRR...
SHAKE

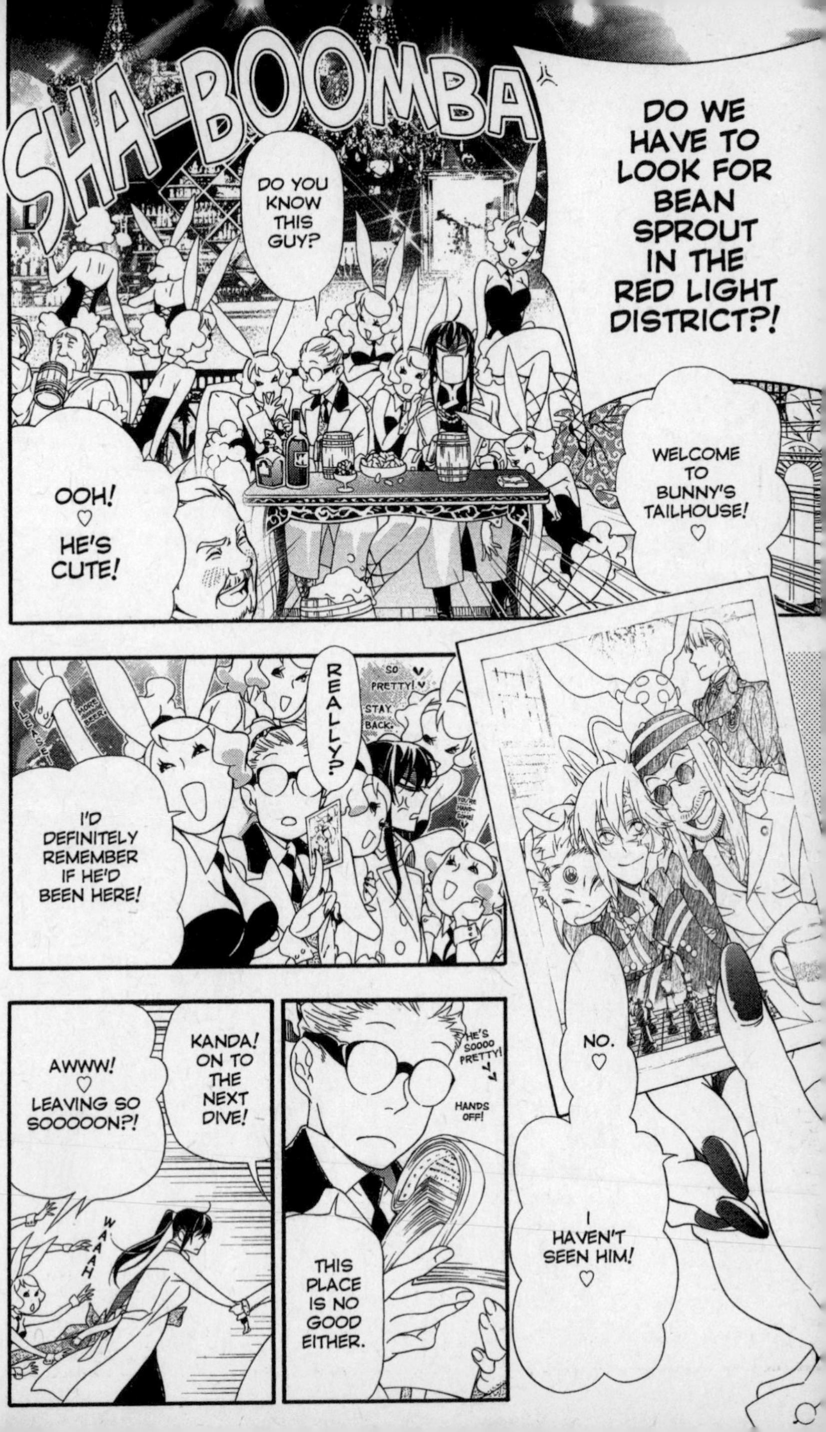
SHA-BOOMBA
DO WE HAVE TO LOOK FOR BEAN SPROUT IN THE RED LIGHT DISTRICT?!
DO YOU KNOW THIS GUY?
WELCOME TO BUNNY'S TAILHOUSE! ♡
OOH! ♡ HE'S CUTE!
NO. ♡
I HAVEN'T SEEN HIM! ♡
REALLY?
SO PRETTY! ♡
STAY BACK.
YOU'RE HAND-SOME!
MORE BEER.
PLEASE!
I'D DEFINITELY REMEMBER IF HE'D BEEN HERE!
HE'S SOOOO PRETTY! ♡
HANDS OFF!
THIS PLACE IS NO GOOD EITHER.
KANDA! ON TO THE NEXT DIVE!
AWWW! ♡ LEAVING SO SOOOOON?!
WAAAH

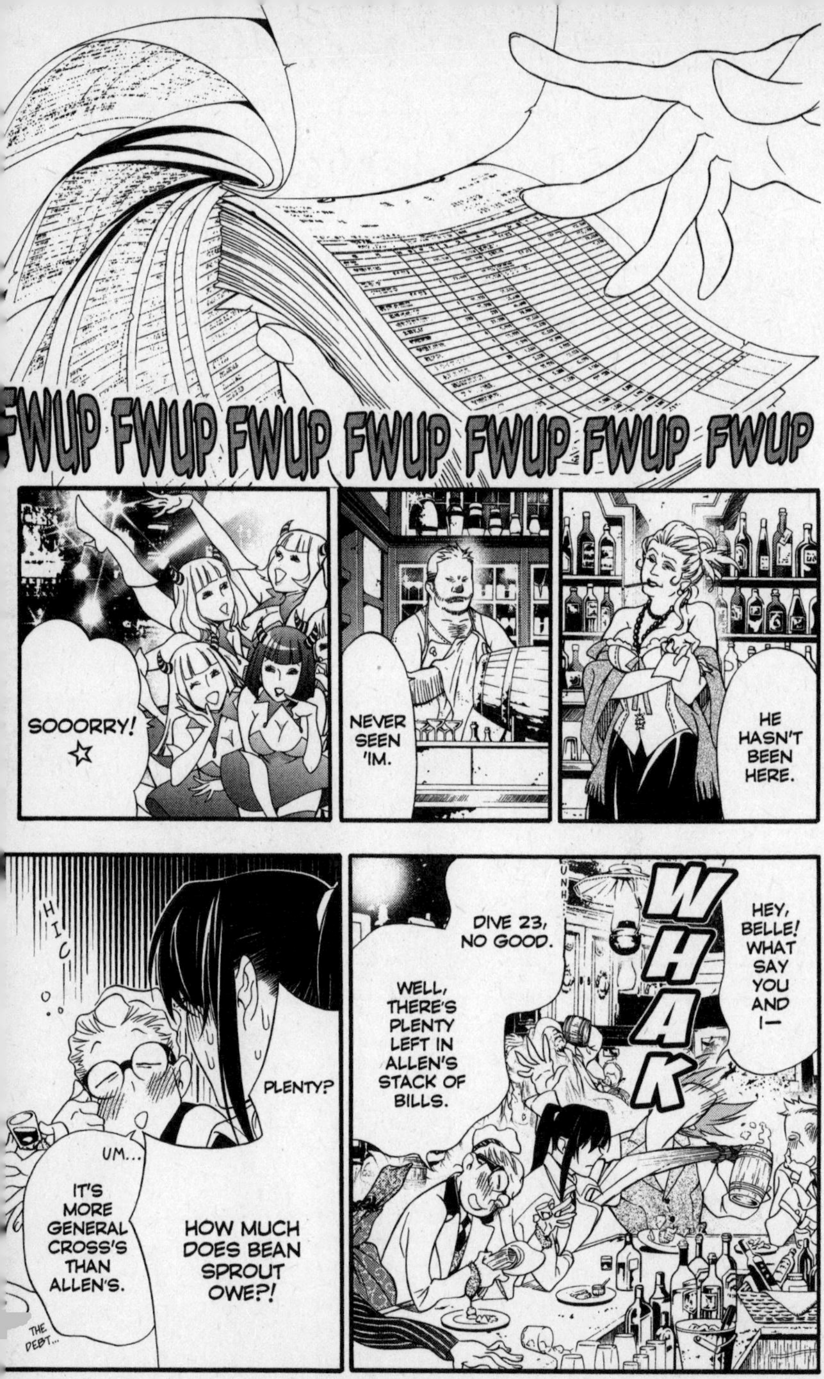
FWUP FWUP FWUP FWUP FWUP FWUP FWUP
HE HASN'T BEEN HERE.
NEVER SEEN 'IM.
SOOORRY! ☆
HEY, BELLE! WHAT SAY YOU AND I—
WHAK
UNH
DIVE 23, NO GOOD.
WELL, THERE'S PLENTY LEFT IN ALLEN'S STACK OF BILLS.
PLENTY?
HIC
UM...
HOW MUCH DOES BEAN SPROUT OWE?!
IT'S MORE GENERAL CROSS'S THAN ALLEN'S.
THE DEBT...

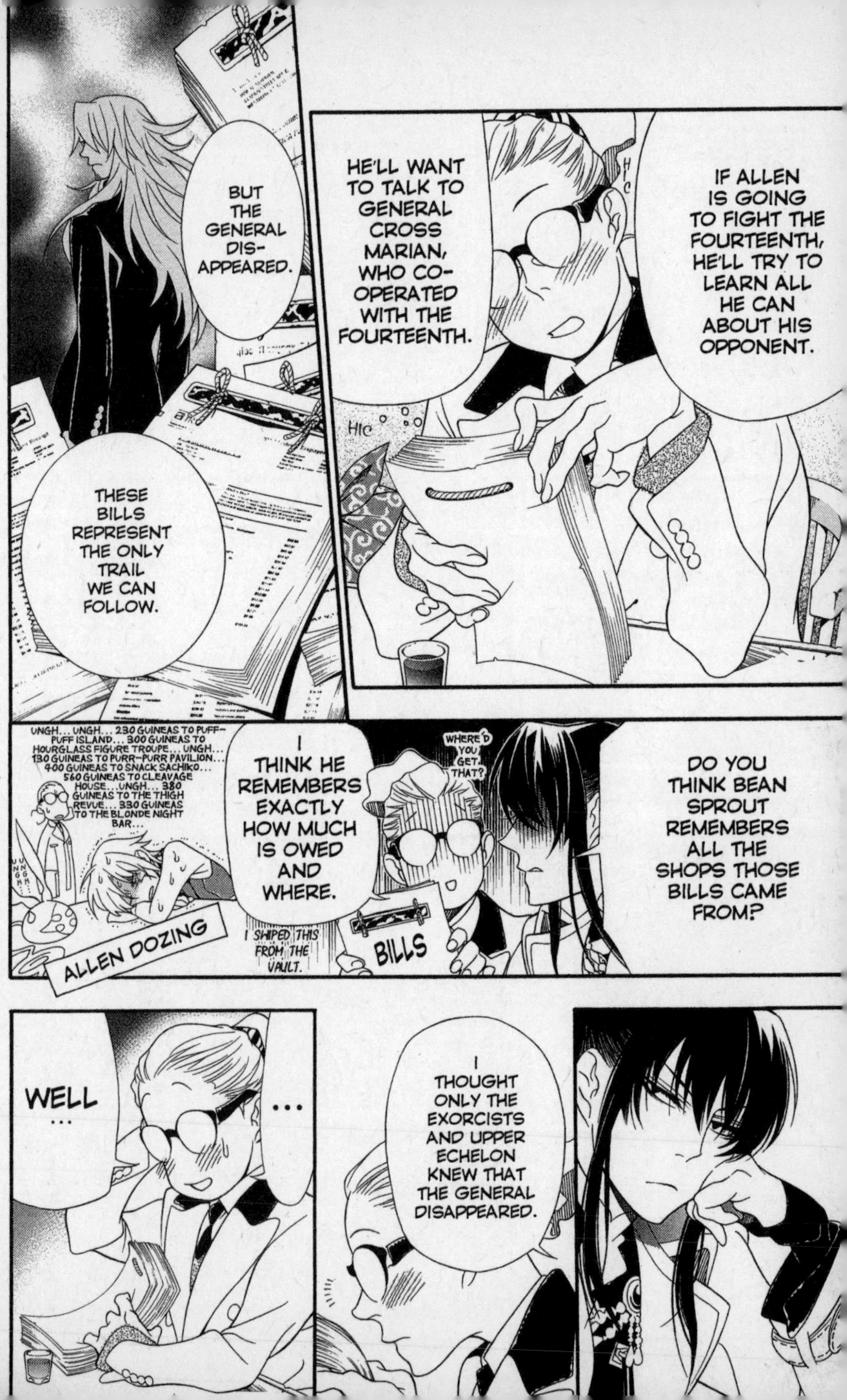

IF ALLEN IS GOING TO FIGHT THE FOURTEENTH, HE'LL TRY TO LEARN ALL HE CAN ABOUT HIS OPPONENT.
HIC
HE'LL WANT TO TALK TO GENERAL CROSS MARIAN, WHO CO-OPERATED WITH THE FOURTEENTH.
HIC
BUT THE GENERAL DIS-APPEARED.
THESE BILLS REPRESENT THE ONLY TRAIL WE CAN FOLLOW.
DO YOU THINK BEAN SPROUT REMEMBERS ALL THE SHOPS THOSE BILLS CAME FROM?
WHERE'D YOU GET THAT?
I THINK HE REMEMBERS EXACTLY HOW MUCH IS OWED AND WHERE.
I SWIPED THIS FROM THE VAULT.
BILLS
UNGH... UNGH... 230 GUINEAS TO PUFF-PUFF ISLAND... 300 GUINEAS TO HOURGLASS FIGURE TROUPE... UNGH... 130 GUINEAS TO PURR-PURR PAVILION... 400 GUINEAS TO SNACK SACHIKO... 560 GUINEAS TO CLEAVAGE HOUSE... UNGH... 380 GUINEAS TO THE THIGH REVUE... 330 GUINEAS TO THE BLONDE NIGHT BAR...
UNNGH
ALLEN DOZING
I THOUGHT ONLY THE EXORCISTS AND UPPER ECHELON KNEW THAT THE GENERAL DISAPPEARED.
...
WELL ...

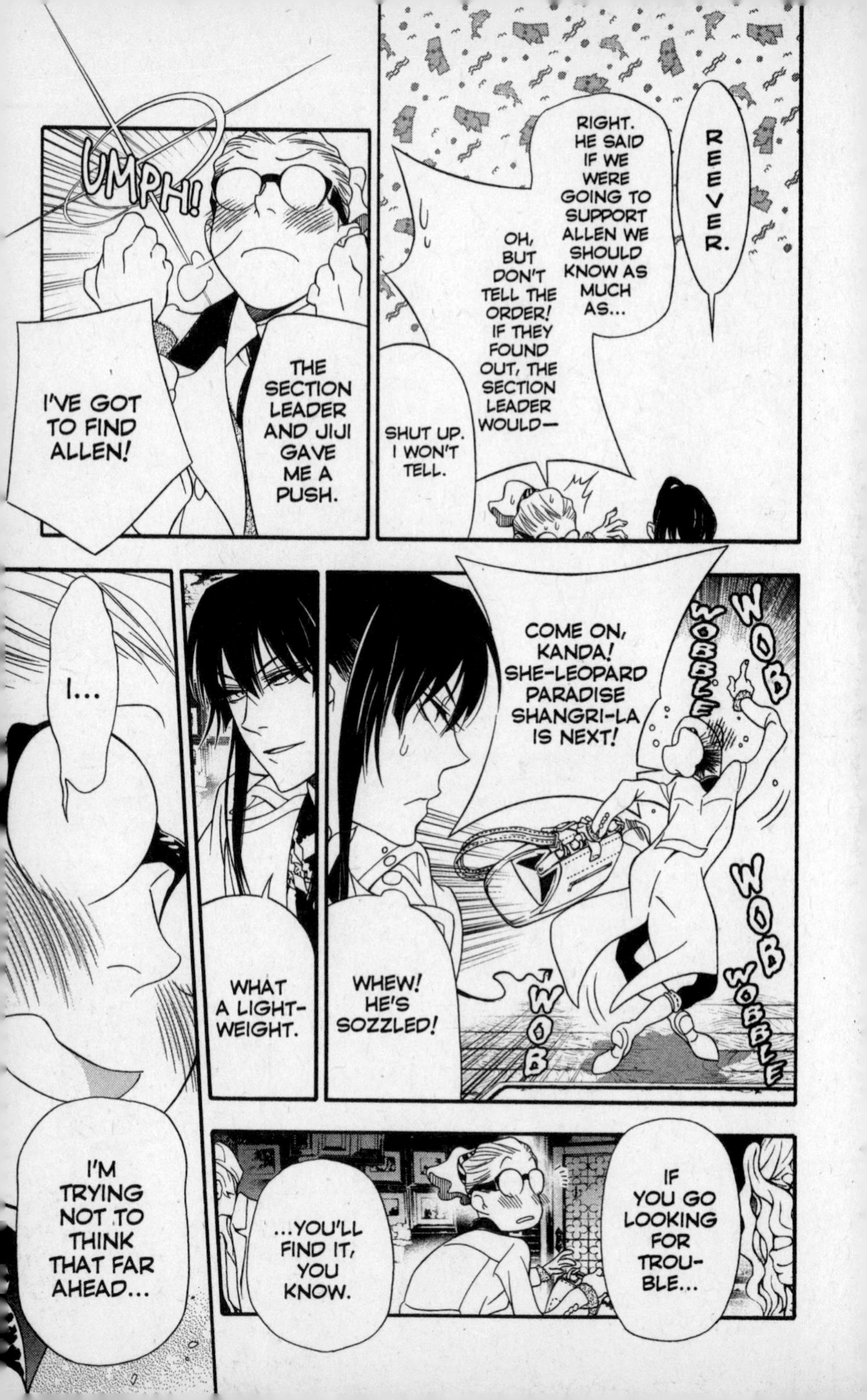
REEVER.
RIGHT. HE SAID IF WE WERE GOING TO SUPPORT ALLEN WE SHOULD KNOW AS MUCH AS...
OH, BUT DON'T TELL THE ORDER! IF THEY FOUND OUT, THE SECTION LEADER WOULD—
SHUT UP. I WON'T TELL.
UMPH!
THE SECTION LEADER AND JIJI GAVE ME A PUSH.
I'VE GOT TO FIND ALLEN!
WOB WOBBLE
COME ON, KANDA! SHE-LEOPARD PARADISE SHANGRI-LA IS NEXT!
WOB WOBBLE
WOB
WHEW! HE'S SOZZLED!
WHAT A LIGHT-WEIGHT.
IF YOU GO LOOKING FOR TROU-BLE...
...YOU'LL FIND IT, YOU KNOW.
I...
I'M TRYING NOT TO THINK THAT FAR AHEAD...

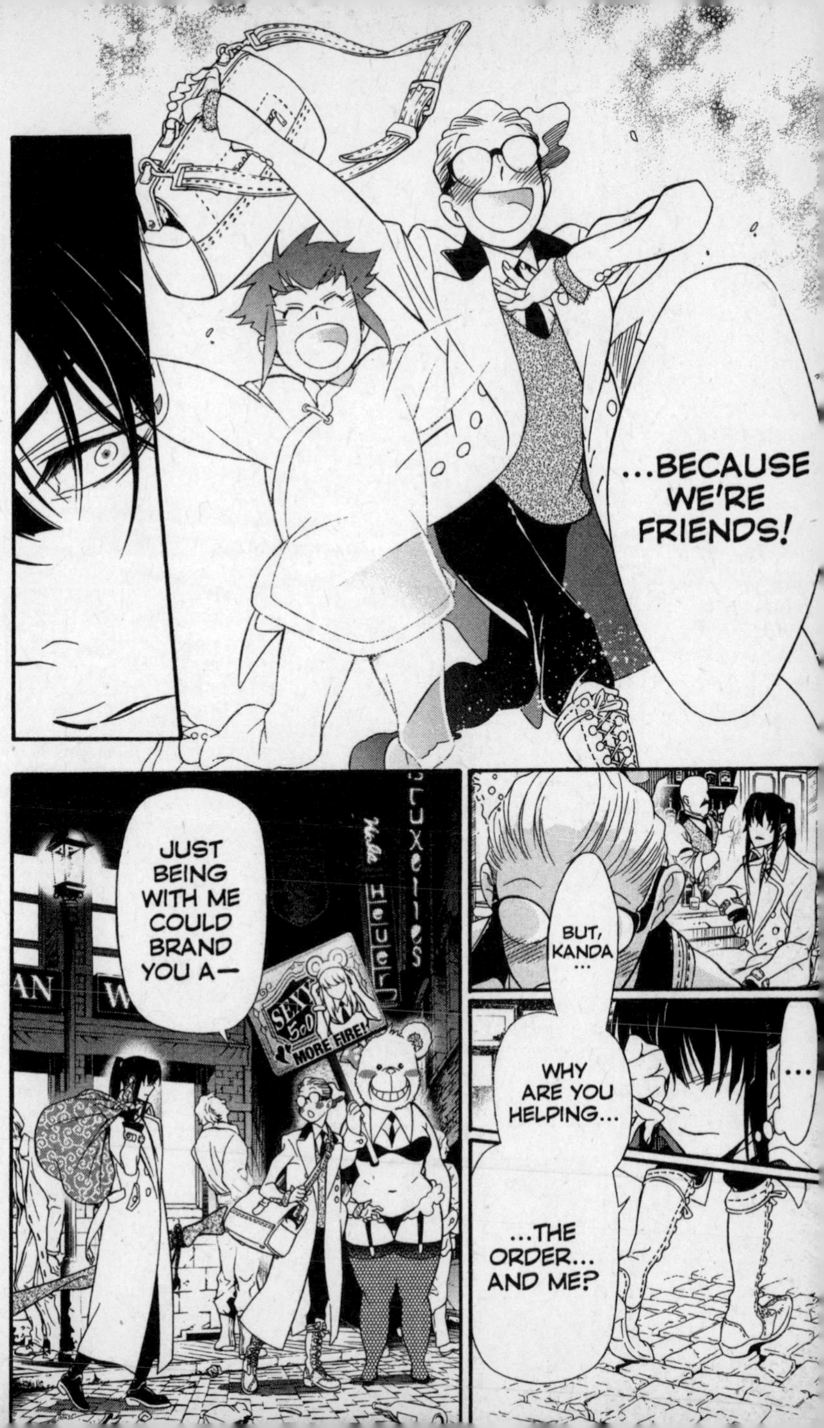
...BECAUSE WE'RE FRIENDS!
BUT, KANDA...
...
WHY ARE YOU HELPING...
...THE ORDER... AND ME?
JUST BEING WITH ME COULD BRAND YOU A—
SEXY 500 MORE FIRE!

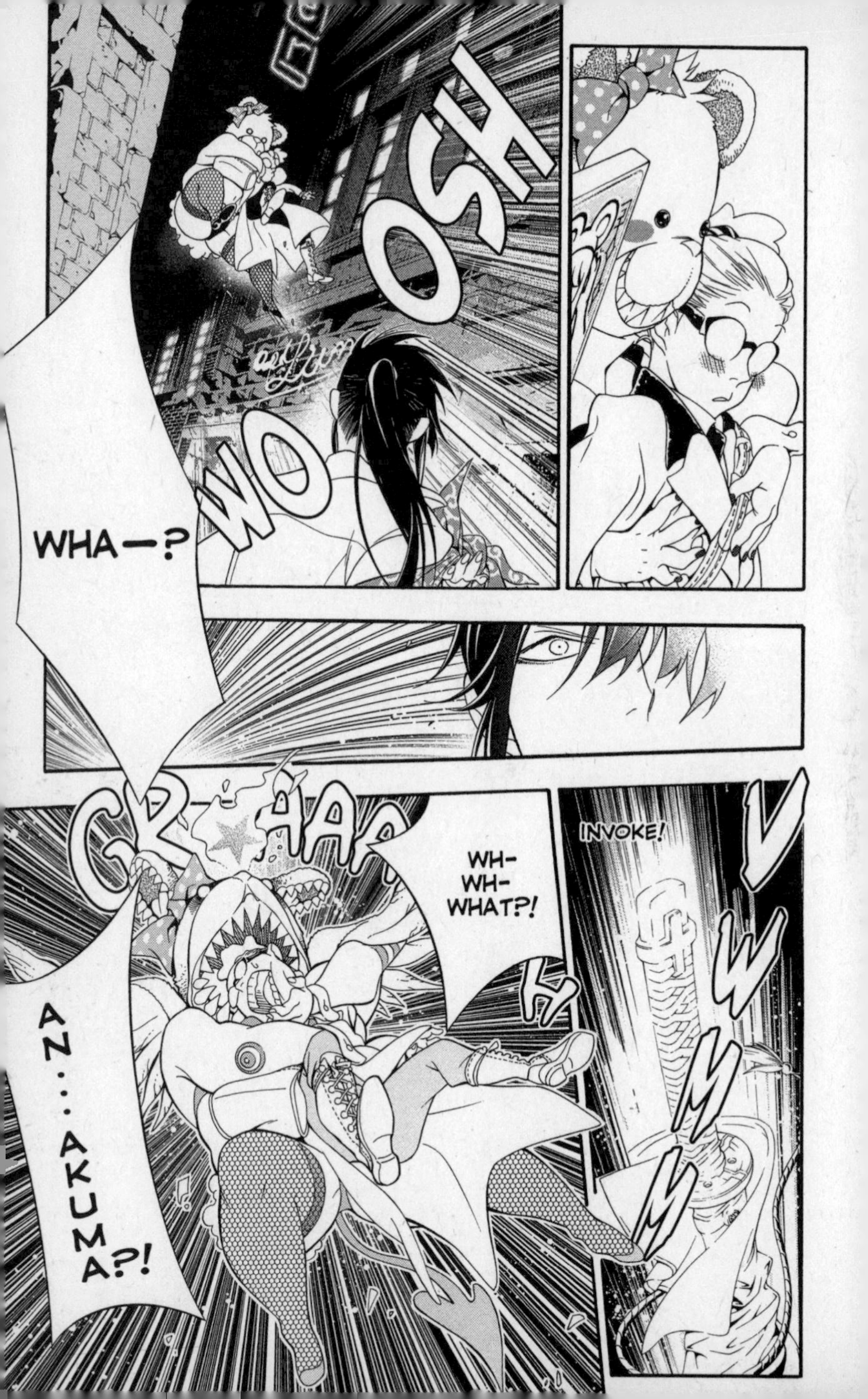
WOOSH
WHA—?
INVOKE!
WH-
WH-
WHAT?!
AN...AKUMA?!

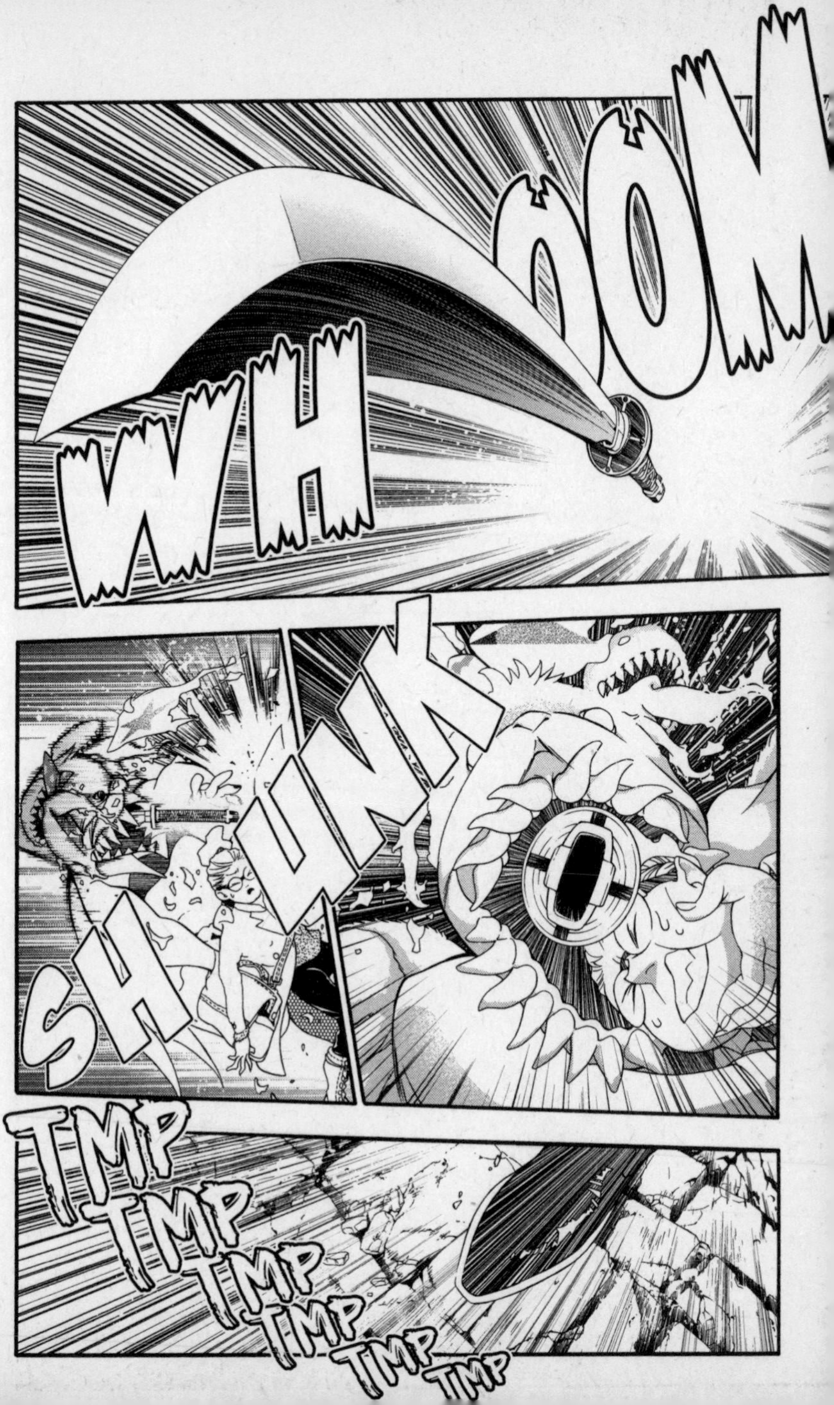
WHOOM
SHUNK
TMP TMP TMP TMP TMP TMP

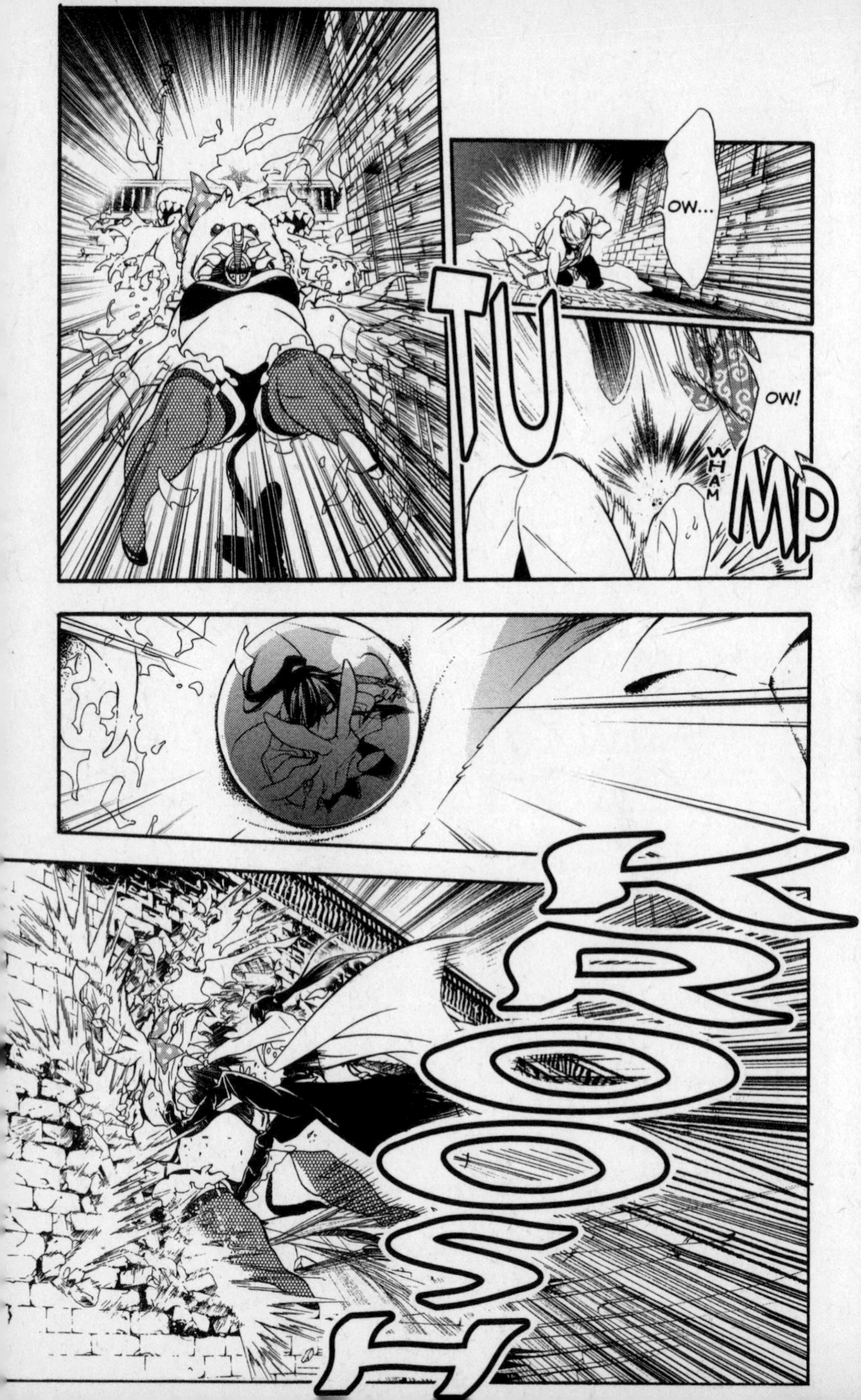
OW...
TUMP
OW!
WHAM
KROOSH

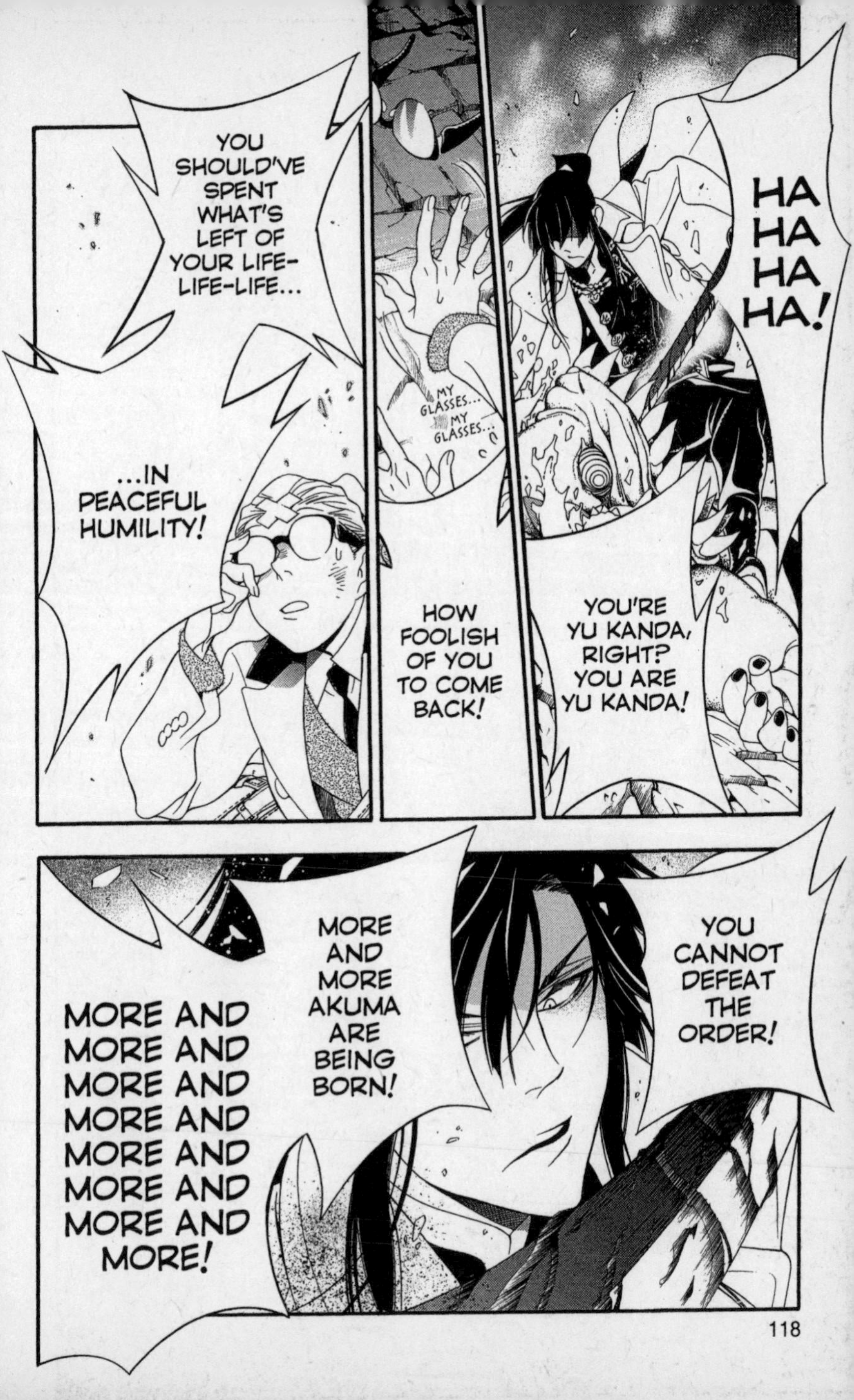
HA HA HA HA!
YOU'RE YU KANDA, RIGHT? YOU ARE YU KANDA!
MY GLASSES... MY GLASSES...
HOW FOOLISH OF YOU TO COME BACK!
YOU SHOULD'VE SPENT WHAT'S LEFT OF YOUR LIFE-LIFE-LIFE...
...IN PEACEFUL HUMILITY!
YOU CANNOT DEFEAT THE ORDER!
MORE AND MORE AKUMA ARE BEING BORN!
MORE AND MORE AND MORE AND MORE AND MORE AND MORE AND MORE AND MORE!

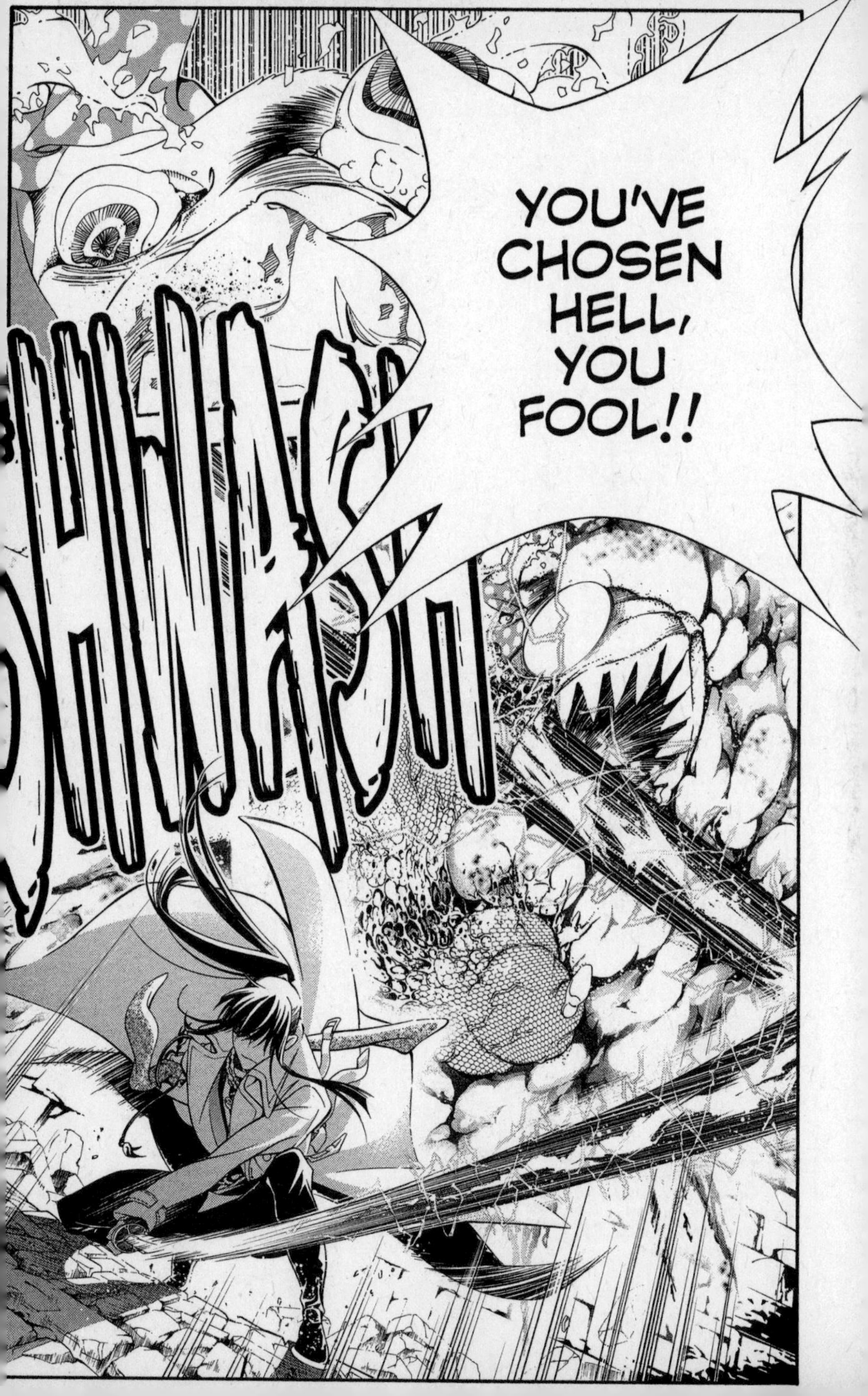
YOU'VE CHOSEN HELL, YOU FOOL!!

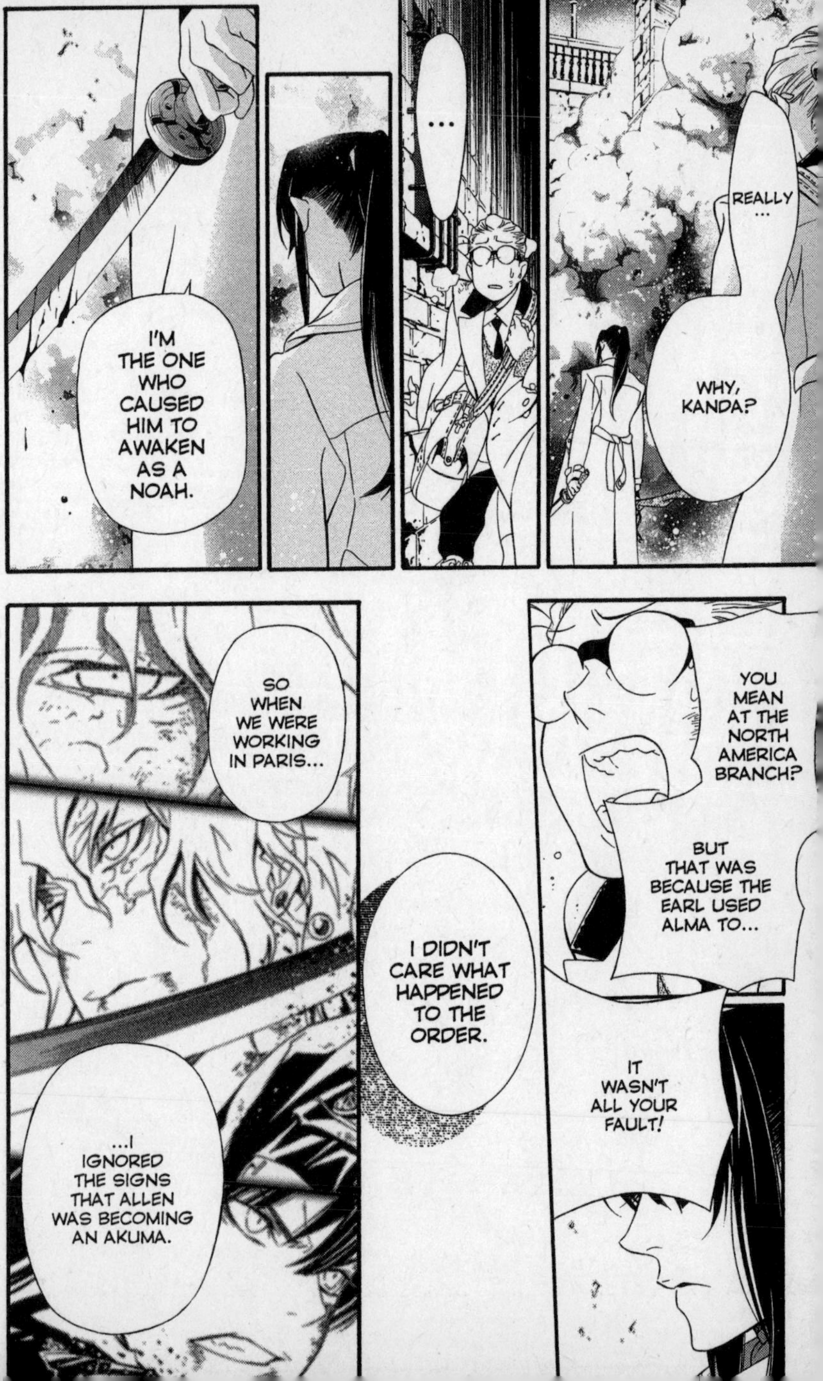

REALLY...
WHY, KANDA?
...
I'M THE ONE WHO CAUSED HIM TO AWAKEN AS A NOAH.
YOU MEAN AT THE NORTH AMERICA BRANCH?
BUT THAT WAS BECAUSE THE EARL USED ALMA TO...
IT WASN'T ALL YOUR FAULT!
SO WHEN WE WERE WORKING IN PARIS...
I DIDN'T CARE WHAT HAPPENED TO THE ORDER.
...I IGNORED THE SIGNS THAT ALLEN WAS BECOMING AN AKUMA.

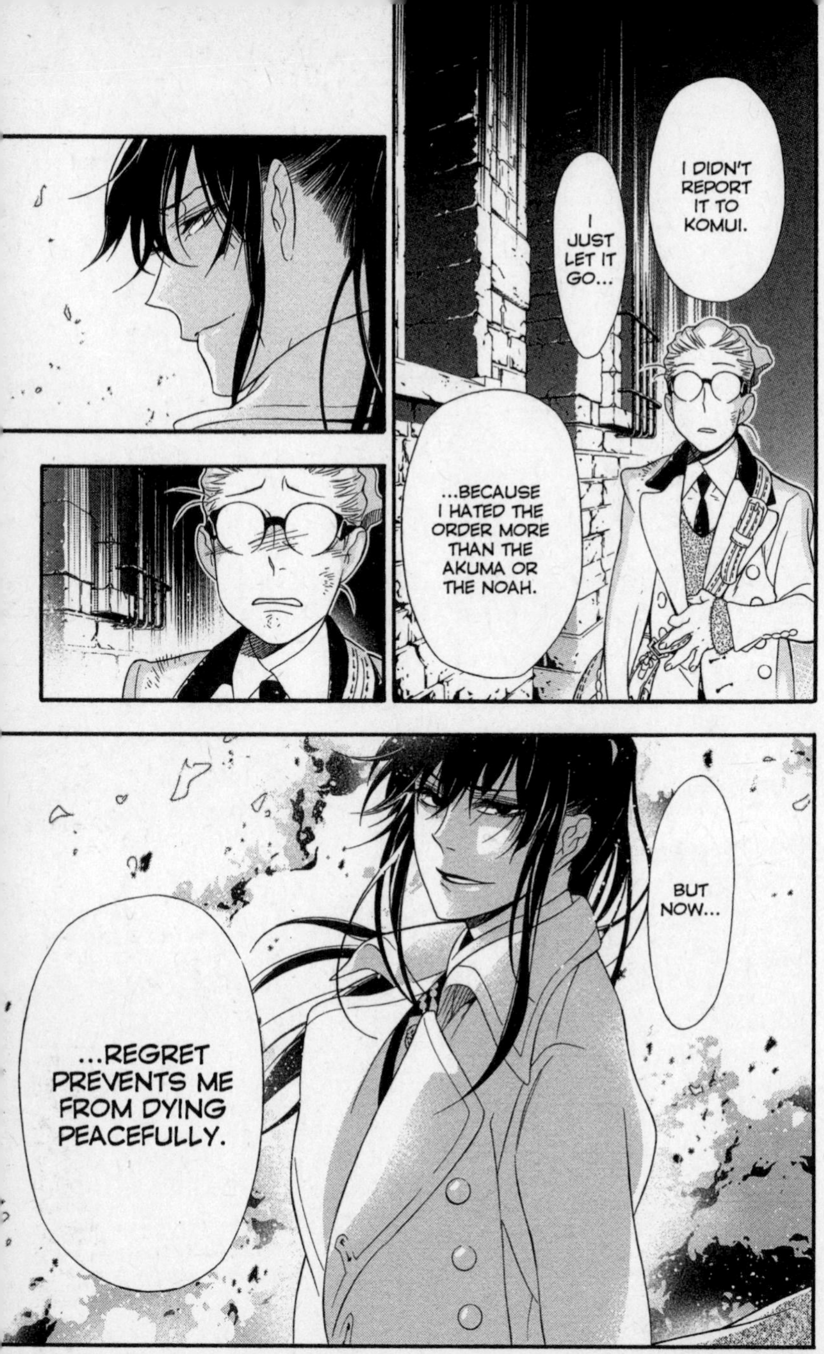
I DIDN'T REPORT IT TO KOMUI.
I JUST LET IT GO...
...BECAUSE I HATED THE ORDER MORE THAN THE AKUMA OR THE NOAH.
BUT NOW...
...REGRET PREVENTS ME FROM DYING PEACEFULLY.

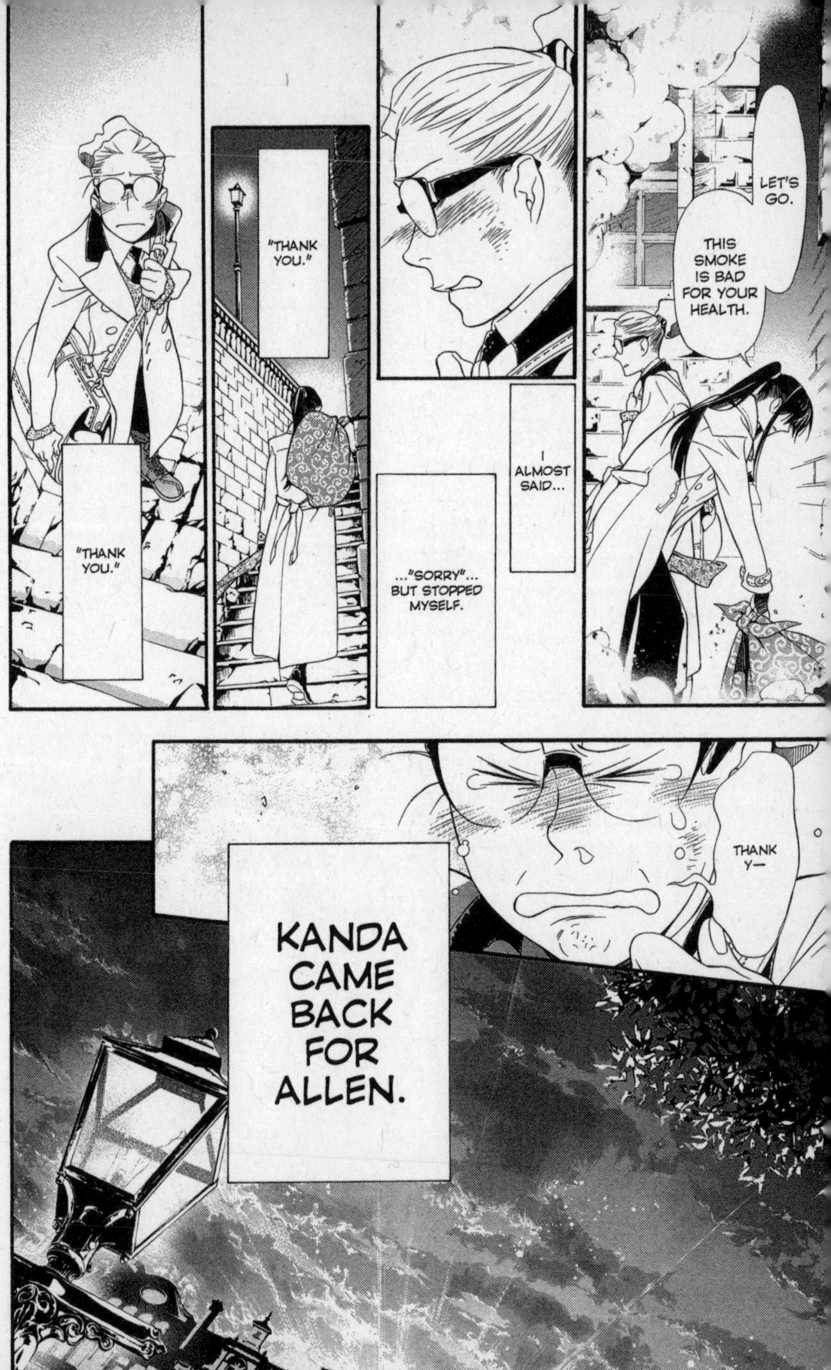
LET'S GO.
THIS SMOKE IS BAD FOR YOUR HEALTH.
I ALMOST SAID...
..."SORRY"... BUT STOPPED MYSELF.
"THANK YOU."
"THANK YOU."
THANK Y—
KANDA CAME BACK FOR ALLEN.

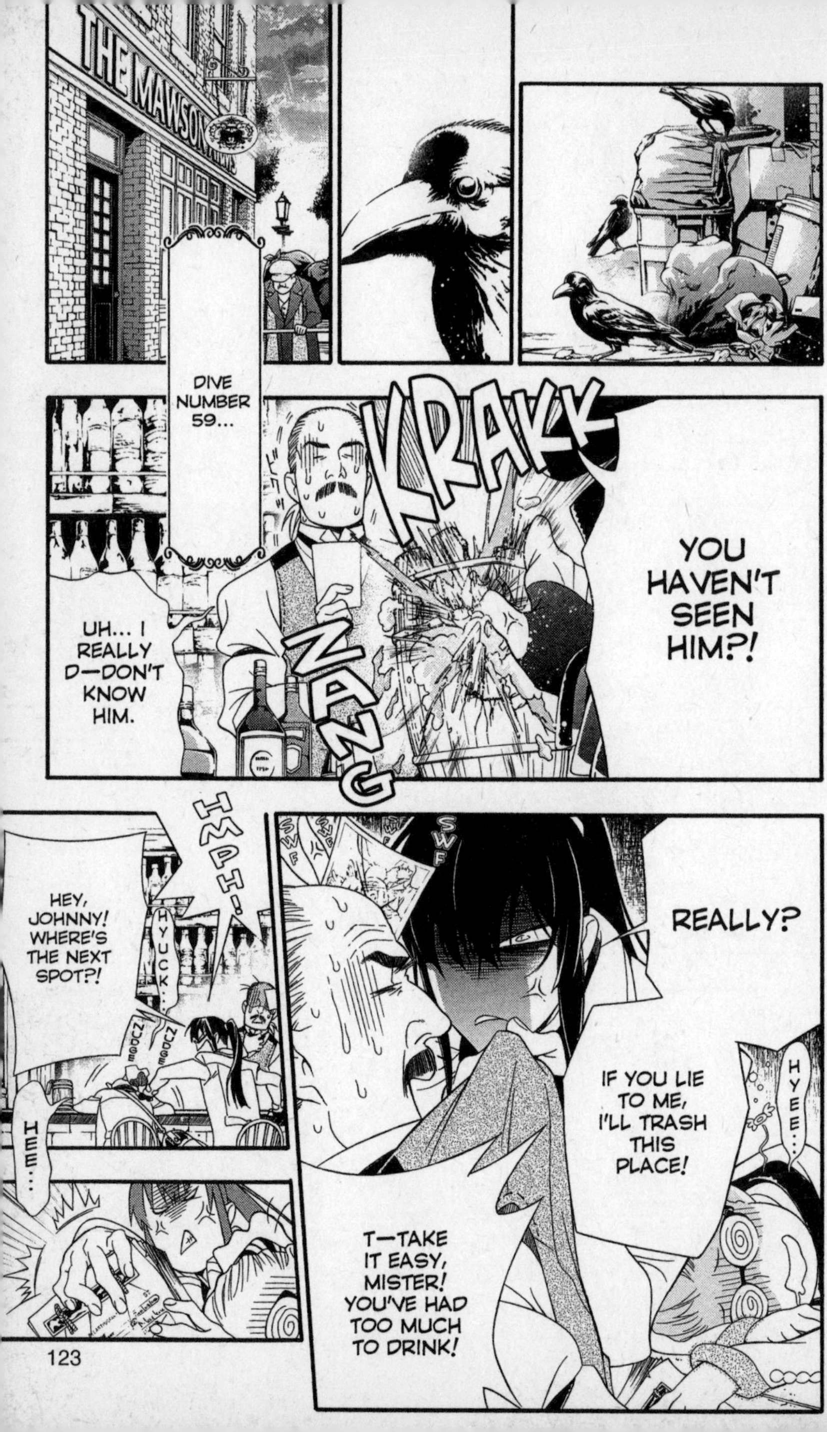
THE MAWSON
DIVE NUMBER 59...
YOU HAVEN'T SEEN HIM?!
KRAKK
ZANG
UH... I REALLY D—DON'T KNOW HIM.
SWF
SWF
SWF
REALLY?
IF YOU LIE TO ME, I'LL TRASH THIS PLACE!
HYEE...
T—TAKE IT EASY, MISTER! YOU'VE HAD TOO MUCH TO DRINK!
HMPH!
HEY, JOHNNY! WHERE'S THE NEXT SPOT?!
HYUCK...
NUDGE
NUDGE
HEE...

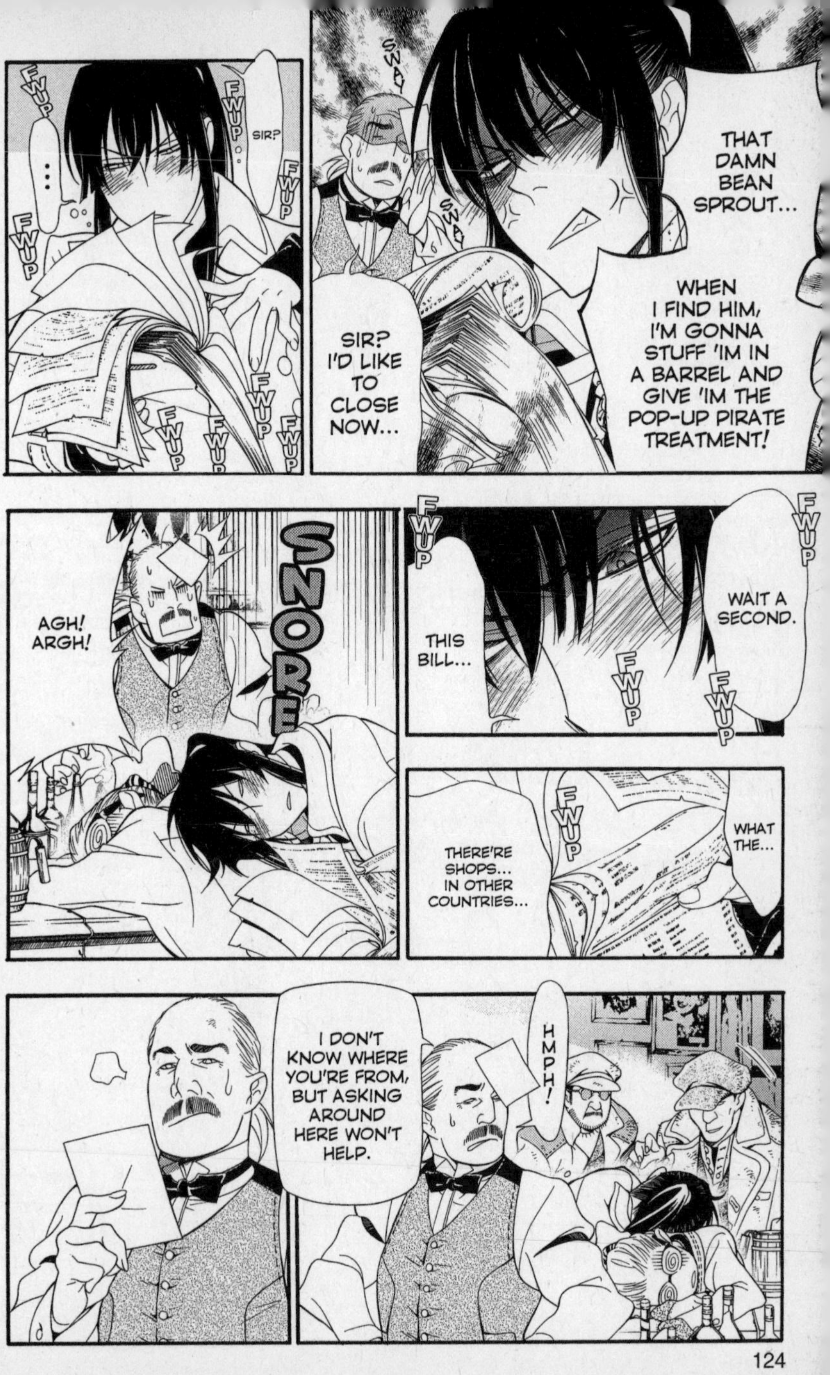
THAT DAMN BEAN SPROUT...
WHEN I FIND HIM, I'M GONNA STUFF 'IM IN A BARREL AND GIVE 'IM THE POP-UP PIRATE TREATMENT!
SWAY
SWAY
SIR? I'D LIKE TO CLOSE NOW...
FWUP
FWUP
SIR?
...
FWUP
FWUP
FWUP
FWUP
FWUP
FWUP
FWUP
WAIT A SECOND.
FWUP
FWUP
THIS BILL...
FWUP
WHAT THE...
FWUP
THERE'RE SHOPS... IN OTHER COUNTRIES...
SNORE
AGH! ARGH!
HMPH!
I DON'T KNOW WHERE YOU'RE FROM, BUT ASKING AROUND HERE WON'T HELP.

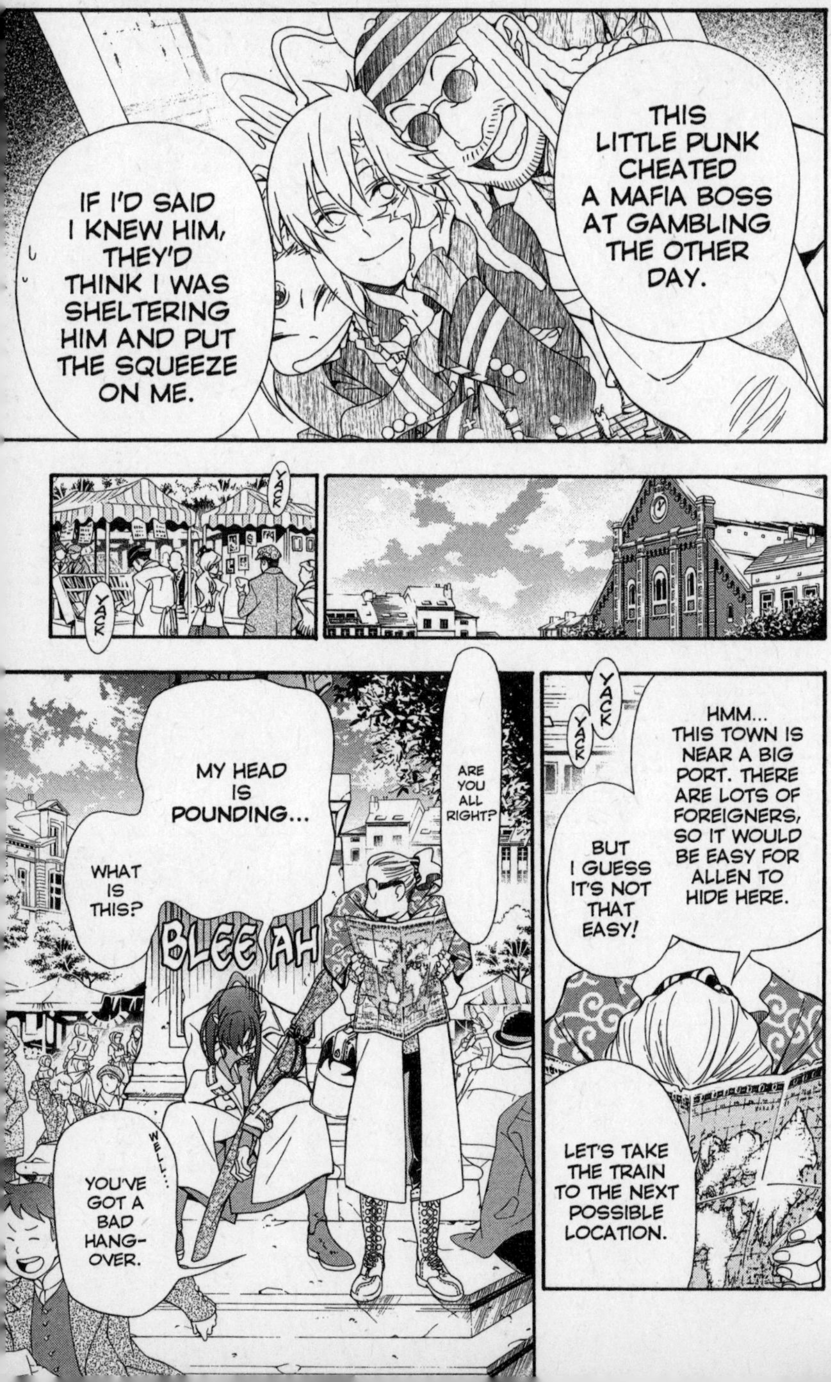
THIS LITTLE PUNK CHEATED A MAFIA BOSS AT GAMBLING THE OTHER DAY.
IF I'D SAID I KNEW HIM, THEY'D THINK I WAS SHELTERING HIM AND PUT THE SQUEEZE ON ME.
YACK
YACK
YACK
YACK
HMM... THIS TOWN IS NEAR A BIG PORT. THERE ARE LOTS OF FOREIGNERS, SO IT WOULD BE EASY FOR ALLEN TO HIDE HERE.
BUT I GUESS IT'S NOT THAT EASY!
LET'S TAKE THE TRAIN TO THE NEXT POSSIBLE LOCATION.
ARE YOU ALL RIGHT?
MY HEAD IS POUNDING...
WHAT IS THIS?
BLEEAH
WELL...
YOU'VE GOT A BAD HANG-OVER.

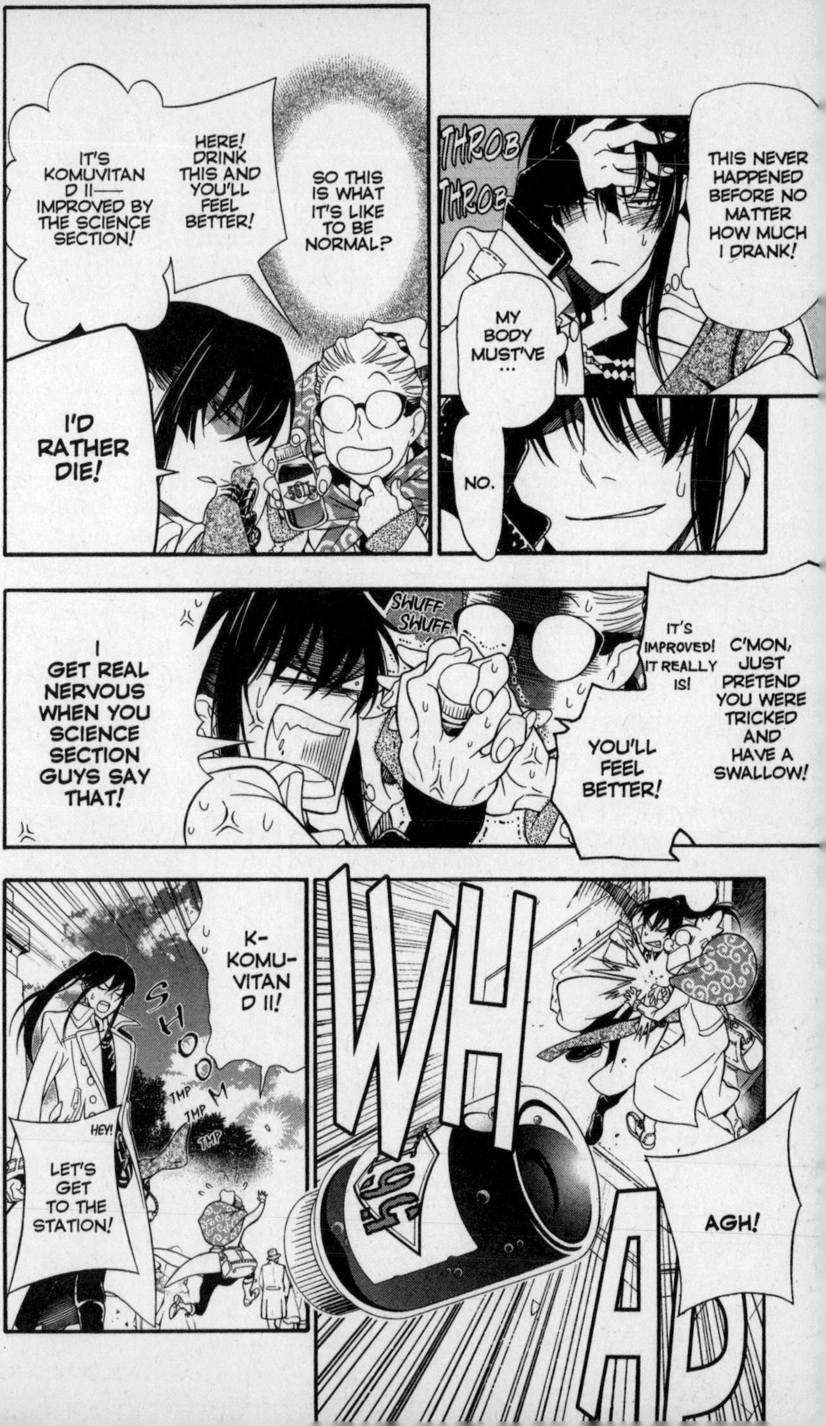
THROB
THROB
THIS NEVER HAPPENED BEFORE NO MATTER HOW MUCH I DRANK!
MY BODY MUST'VE ...
NO.
SO THIS IS WHAT IT'S LIKE TO BE NORMAL?
HERE! DRINK THIS AND YOU'LL FEEL BETTER!
IT'S KOMUVITAN D II—IMPROVED BY THE SCIENCE SECTION!
I'D RATHER DIE!
C'MON, JUST PRETEND YOU WERE TRICKED AND HAVE A SWALLOW!
IT'S IMPROVED! IT REALLY IS!
SWUFF SWUFF
YOU'LL FEEL BETTER!
I GET REAL NERVOUS WHEN YOU SCIENCE SECTION GUYS SAY THAT!
WHAP
AGH!
K-KOMUVITAN D II!
SHOOM
TMP TMP TMP
HEY!
LET'S GET TO THE STATION!

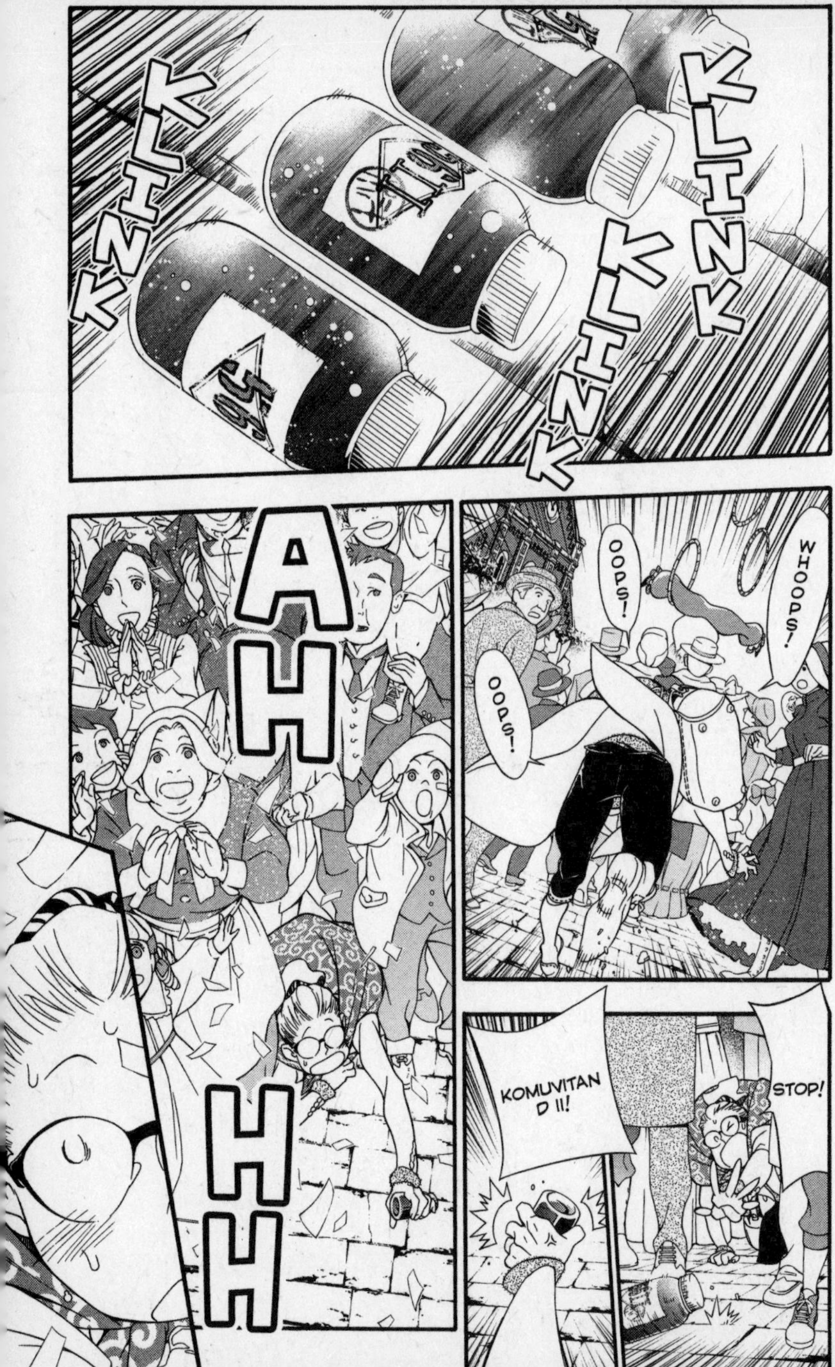
KLINK
KLINK
KLINK
WHOOPS!
OOPS!
OOPS!
STOP!
KOMUVITAN D II!
AHHHHH

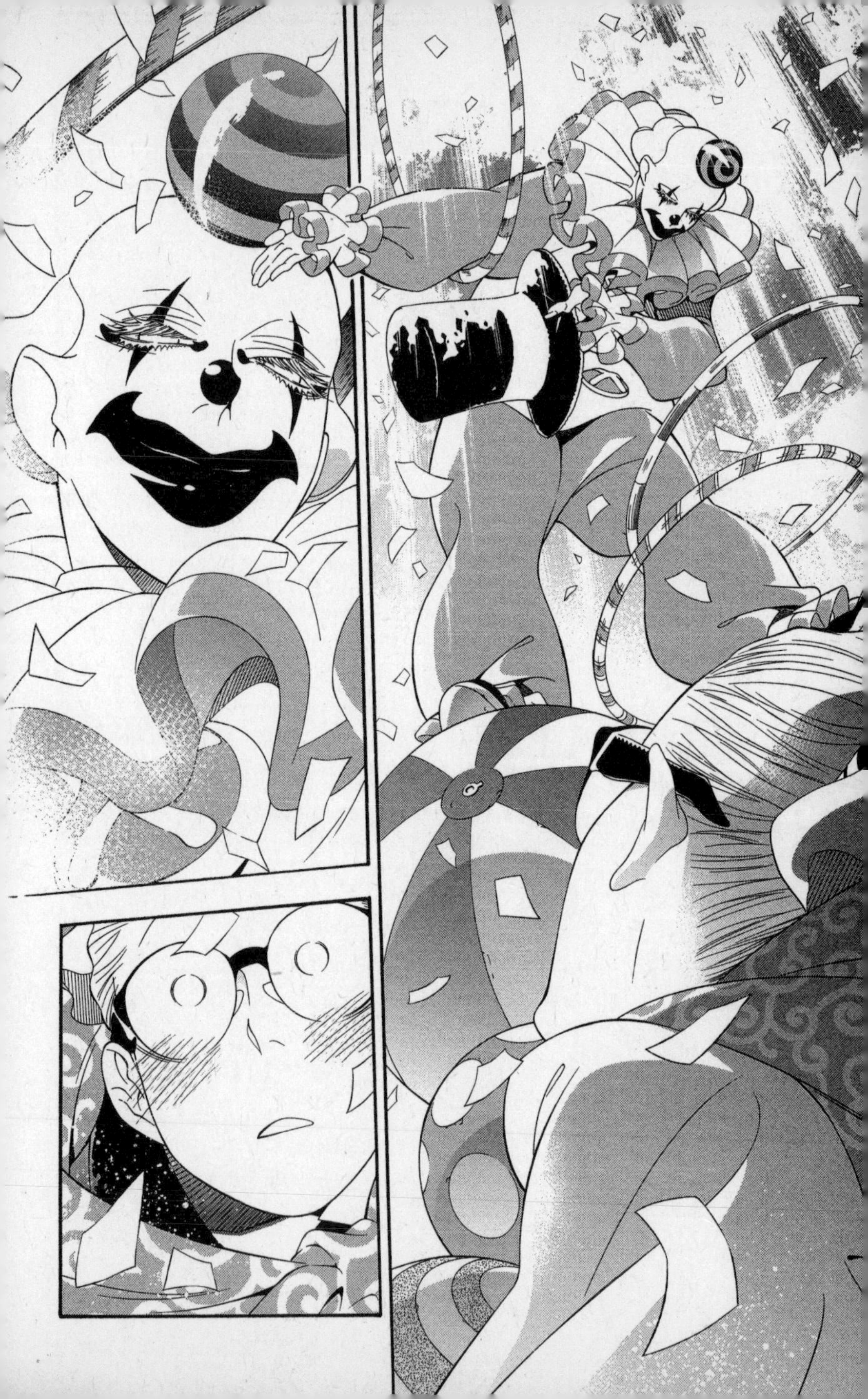

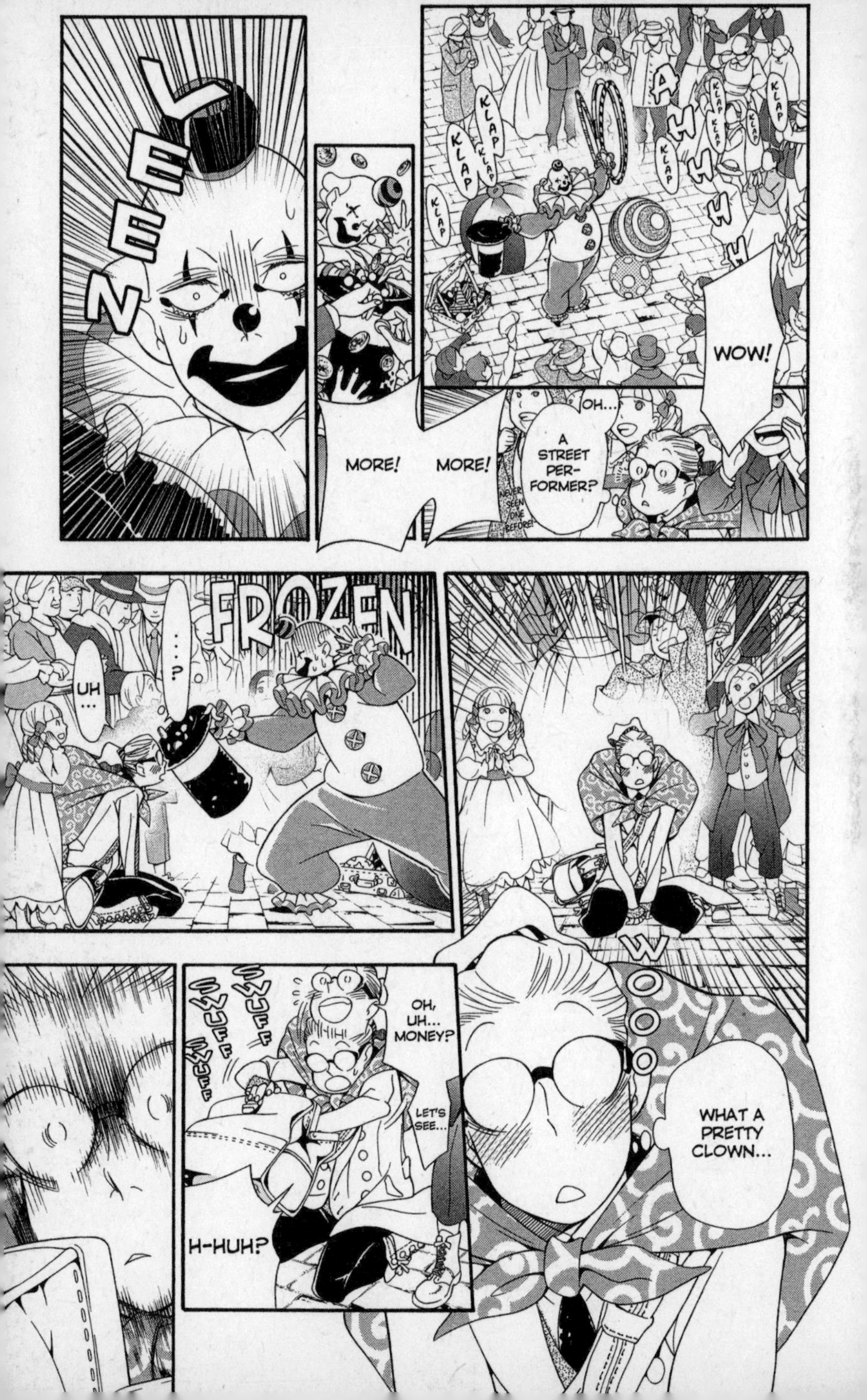
KLAP KLAP KLAP KLAP KLAP KLAP KLAP KLAP KLAP
AHHHH
WOW!
OH...
A STREET PER-FORMER?
NEVER SEEN ONE BEFORE!
MORE! MORE!
VEEN
WOOO
FROZEN
...?
UH...
WHAT A PRETTY CLOWN...
OH, UH... MONEY?
LET'S SEE...
SWUFF SWUFF SWUFF
H-HUH?

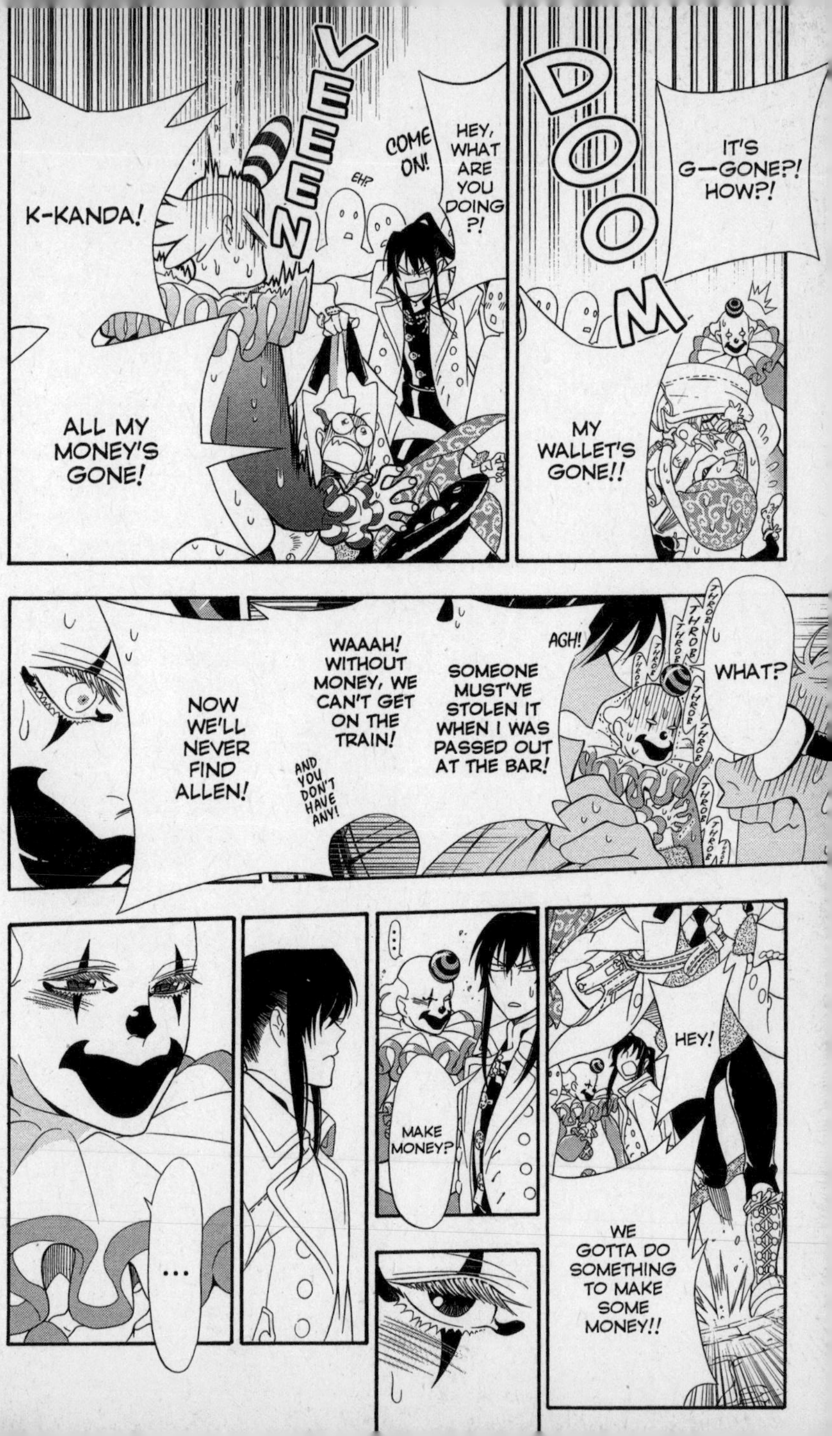
DOOM
IT'S G—GONE?! HOW?!
MY WALLET'S GONE!!
VEEEN
HEY, WHAT ARE YOU DOING?!
COME ON!
EH?
K-KANDA!
ALL MY MONEY'S GONE!
WHAT?
THROB THROB THROB THROB THROB
AGH!
SOMEONE MUST'VE STOLEN IT WHEN I WAS PASSED OUT AT THE BAR!
WAAAH! WITHOUT MONEY, WE CAN'T GET ON THE TRAIN!
AND YOU DON'T HAVE ANY!
NOW WE'LL NEVER FIND ALLEN!
HEY!
WE GOTTA DO SOMETHING TO MAKE SOME MONEY!!
...
MAKE MONEY?
...

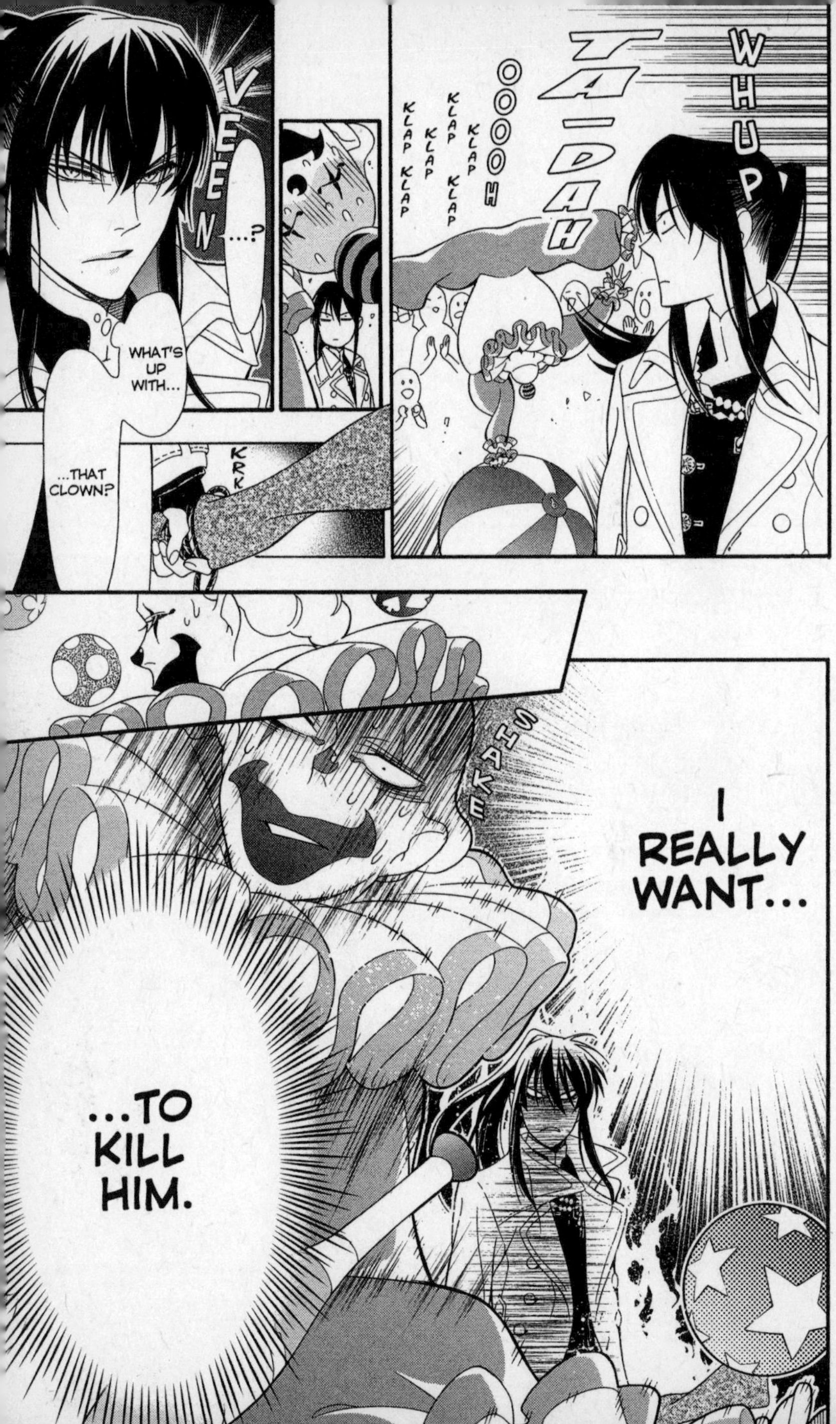

WHUP
TA-DAH
OOOOOH
KLAP KLAP KLAP
KLAP KLAP KLAP
KLAP KLAP
VEEN
...?
WHAT'S UP WITH...
KRK
...THAT CLOWN?
SHAKE
I REALLY WANT...
...TO KILL HIM.

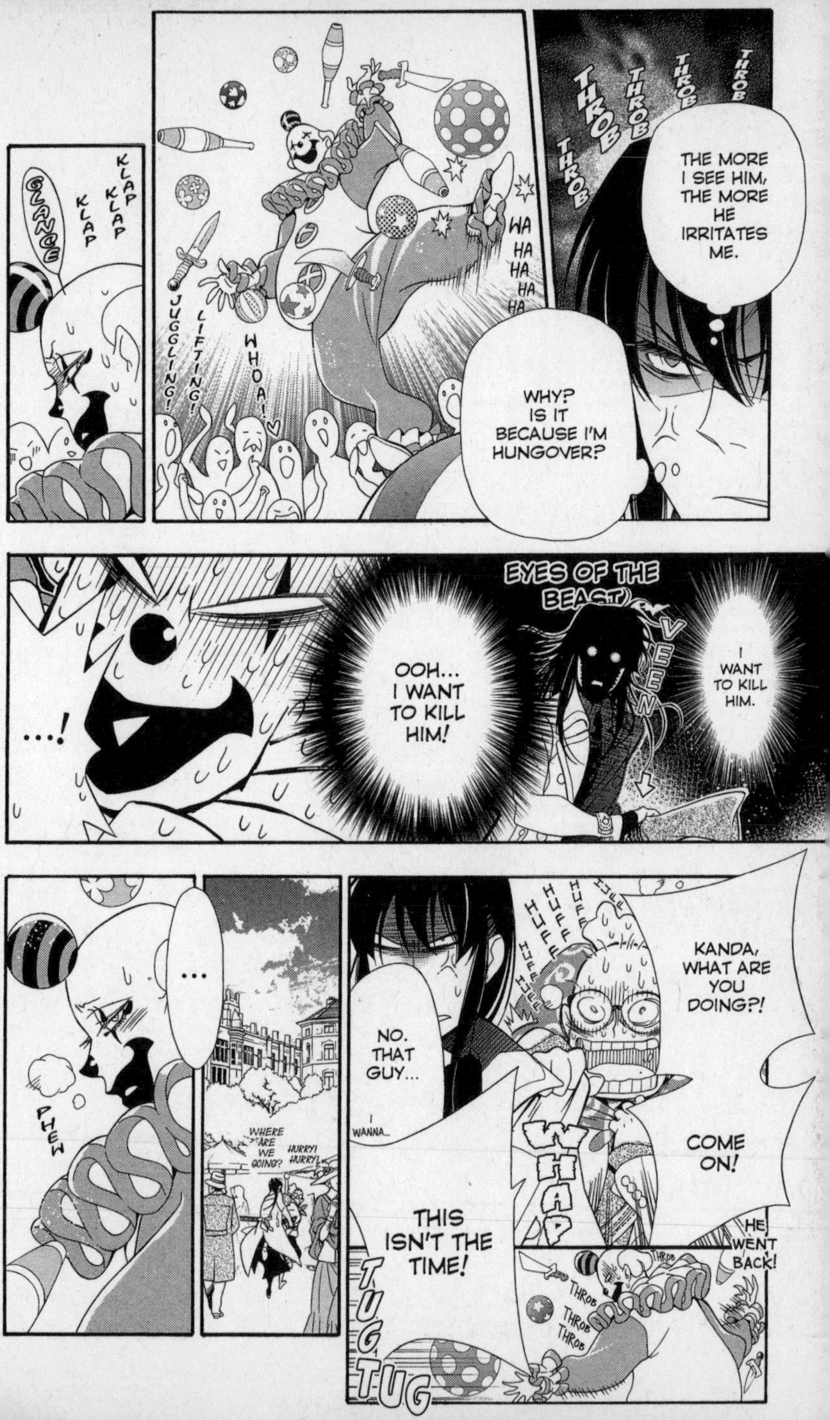
THROB THROB THROB THROB THROB
THE MORE I SEE HIM, THE MORE HE IRRITATES ME.
WHY? IS IT BECAUSE I'M HUNGOVER?
WA HA HA HA HA HA
WHOA!
LIFTING!
JUGGLING!
KLAP KLAP KLAP
GLANCE
EYES OF THE BEAST)
VEEN
I WANT TO KILL HIM.
OOH... I WANT TO KILL HIM!
...!
KANDA, WHAT ARE YOU DOING?!
HUFF HUFF HUFF HUFF HUFF
NO. THAT GUY...
I WANNA...
WHAP
COME ON!
THIS ISN'T THE TIME!
HE WENT BACK!
THROB THROB THROB THROB
TUG TUG
WHERE ARE WE GOING?
HURRY! HURRY!
...
PHEW

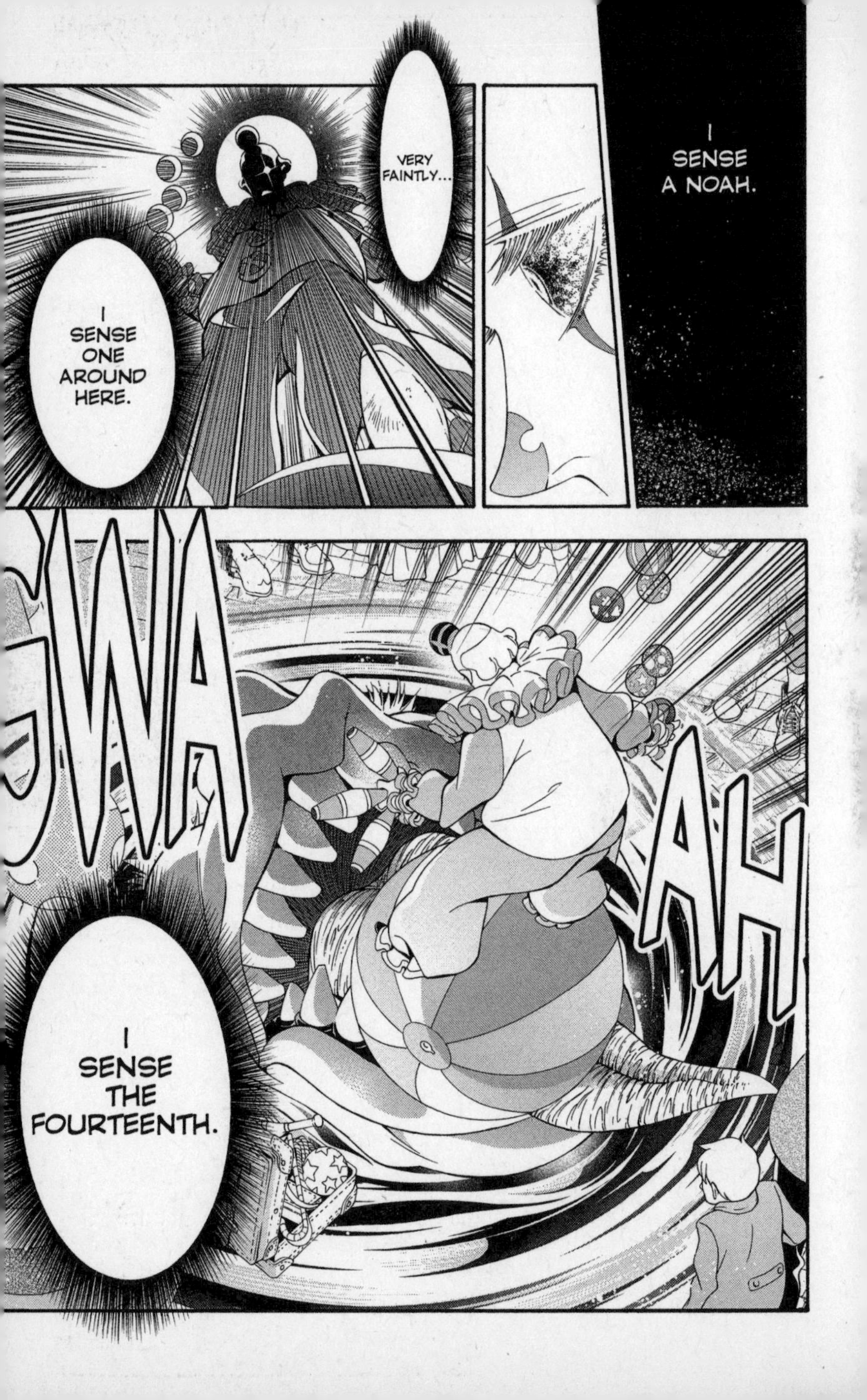
I SENSE A NOAH.
VERY FAINTLY...
I SENSE ONE AROUND HERE.
GWA
AH
I SENSE THE FOURTEENTH.

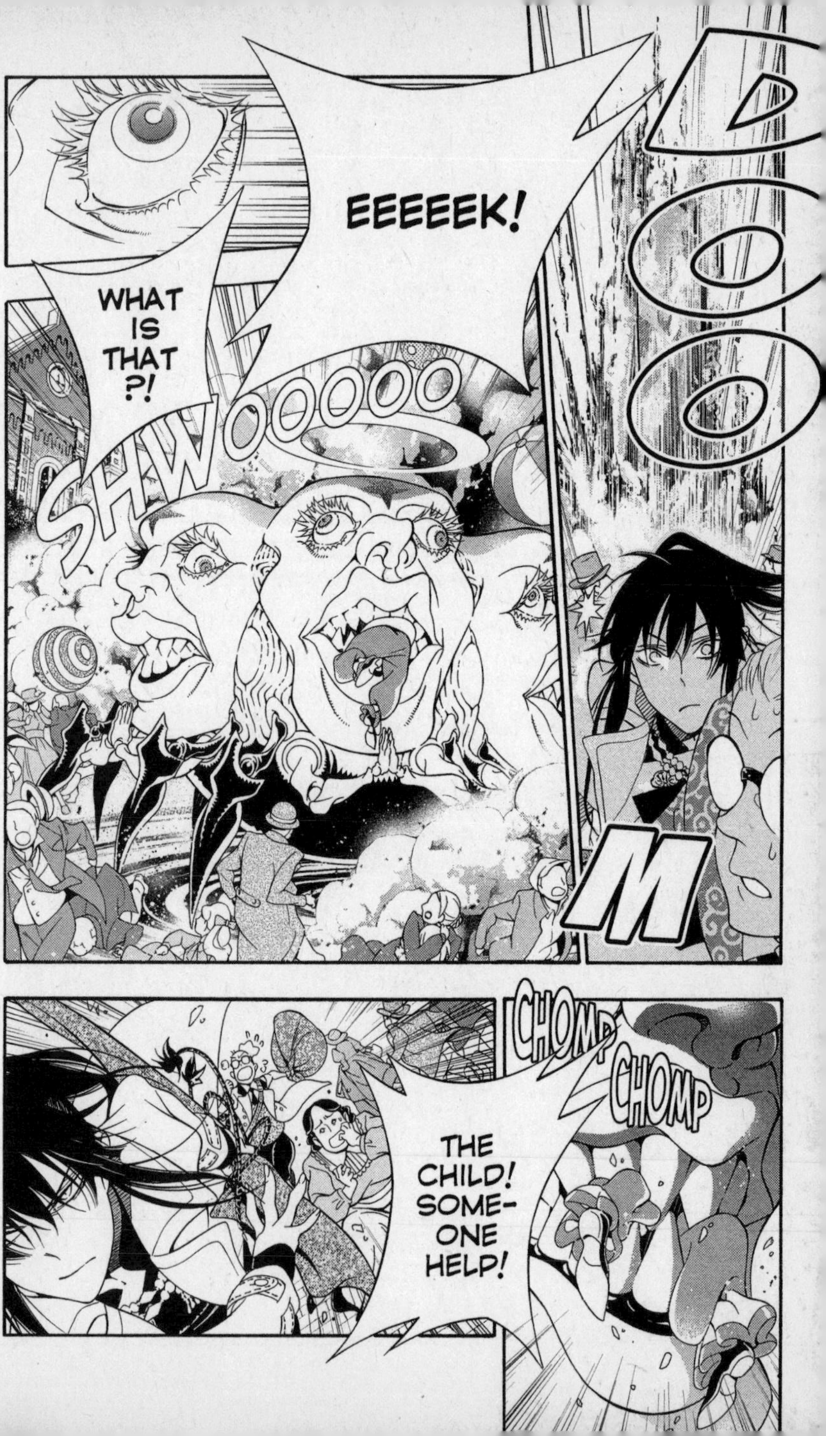
DOOOM
EEEEEK!
WHAT IS THAT?!
SHWOOOOO
CHOMP CHOMP
THE CHILD! SOME-ONE HELP!

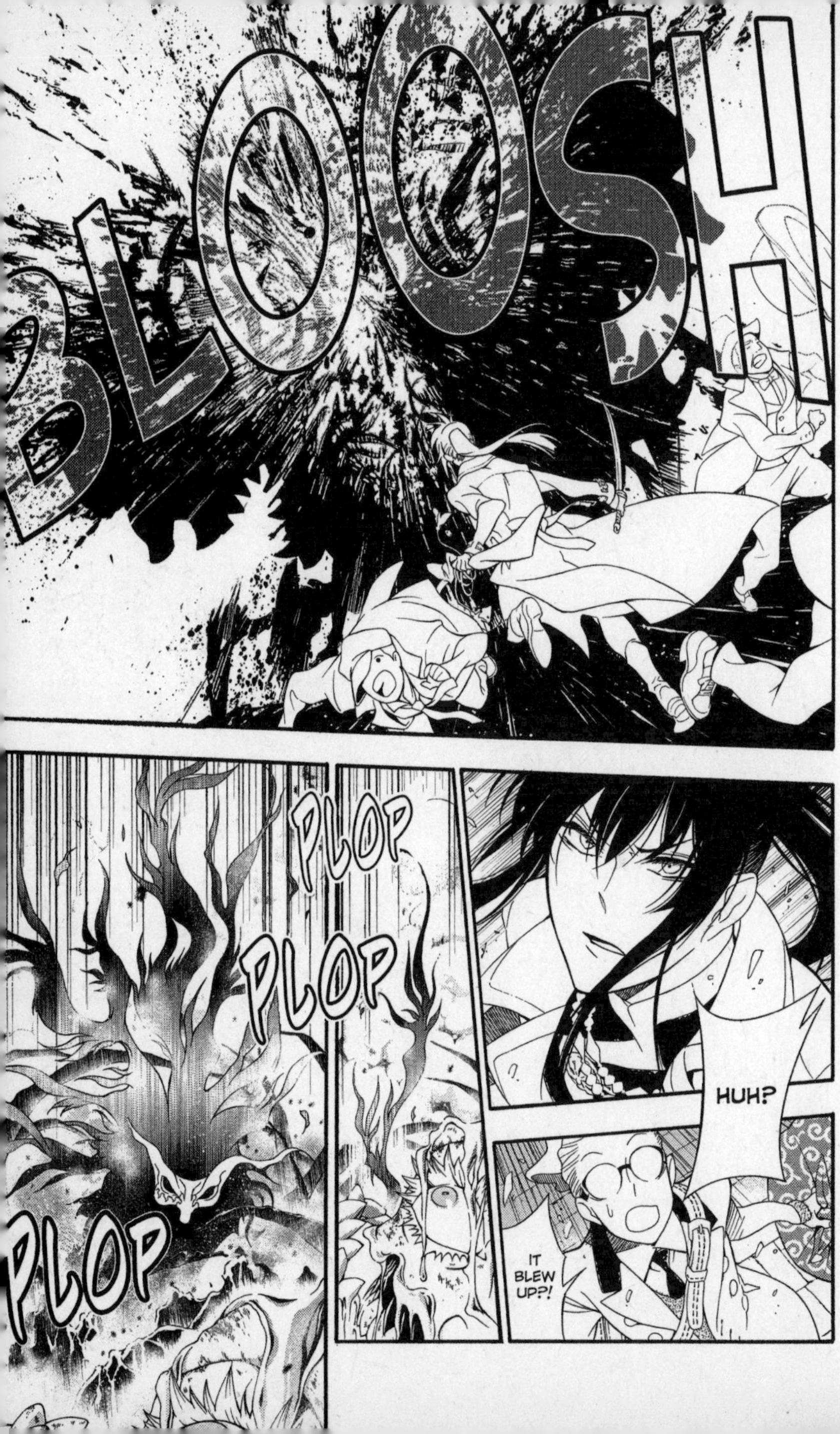
BLOOOSH!
HUH?
IT BLEW UP?!
PLOP
PLOP
PLOP

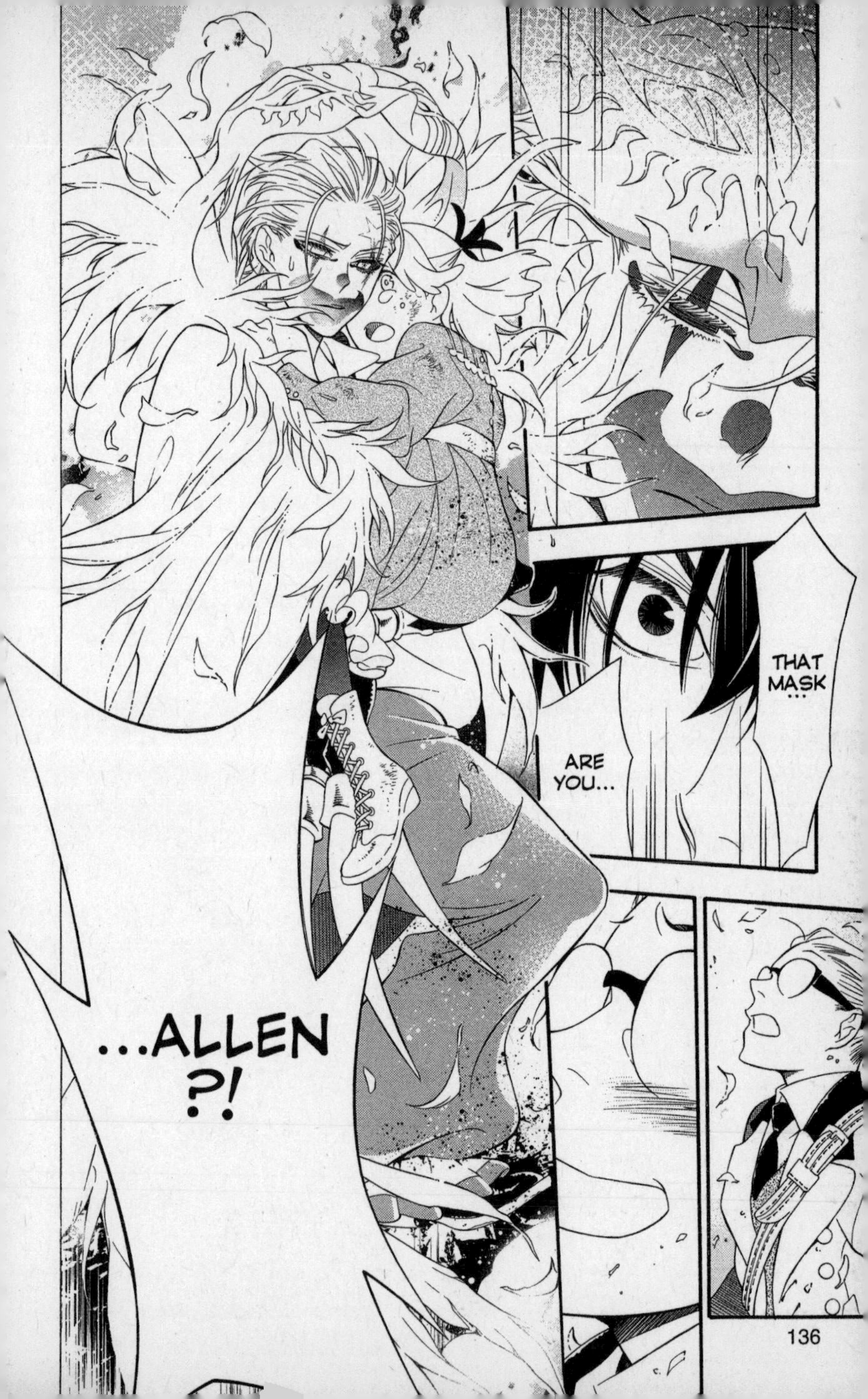
THAT MASK ...
ARE YOU...
...ALLEN ?!

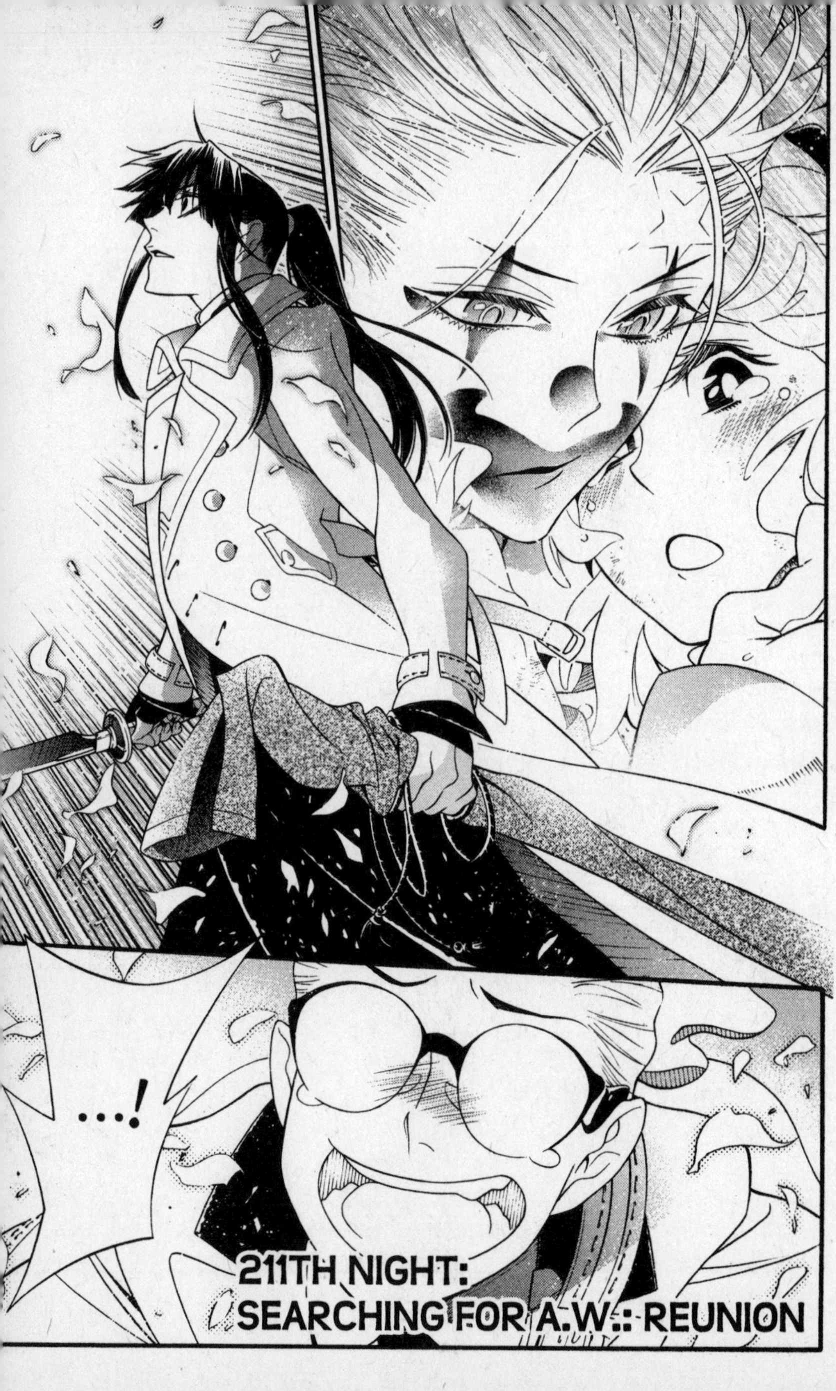
...!
211TH NIGHT:
SEARCHING FOR A.W.: REUNION

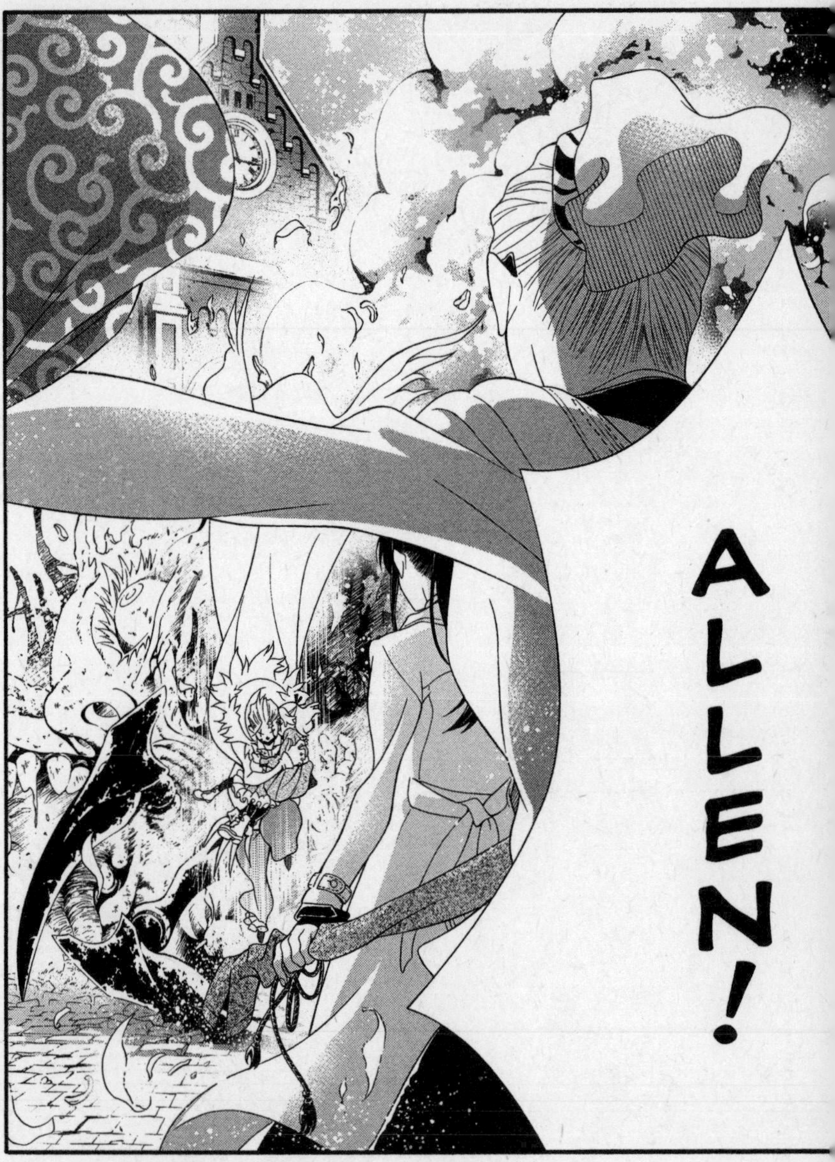
ALLEN!

211TH NIGHT: SEARCHING FOR A.W.: REUNION

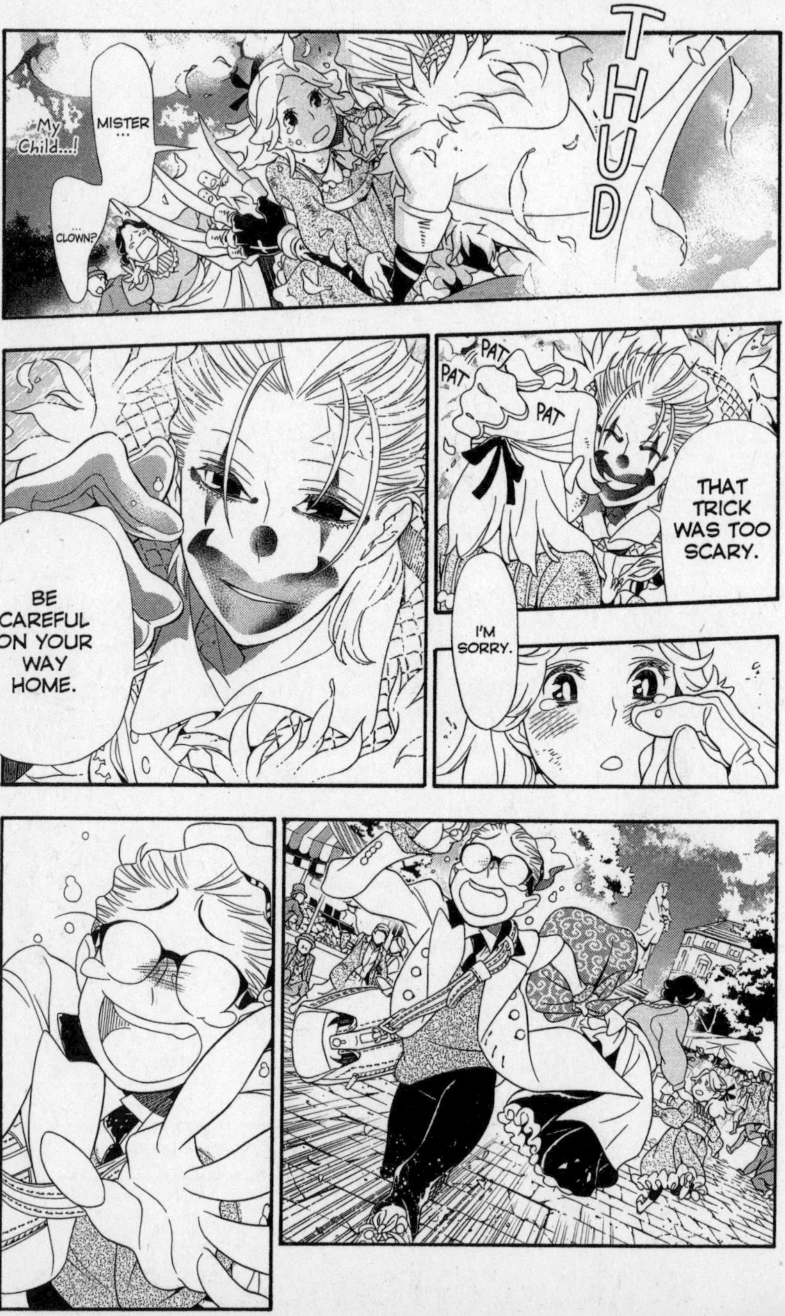
THUD
MISTER ... ... CLOWN?
My Child...!
PAT PAT PAT
THAT TRICK WAS TOO SCARY.
I'M SORRY.
BE CAREFUL ON YOUR WAY HOME.

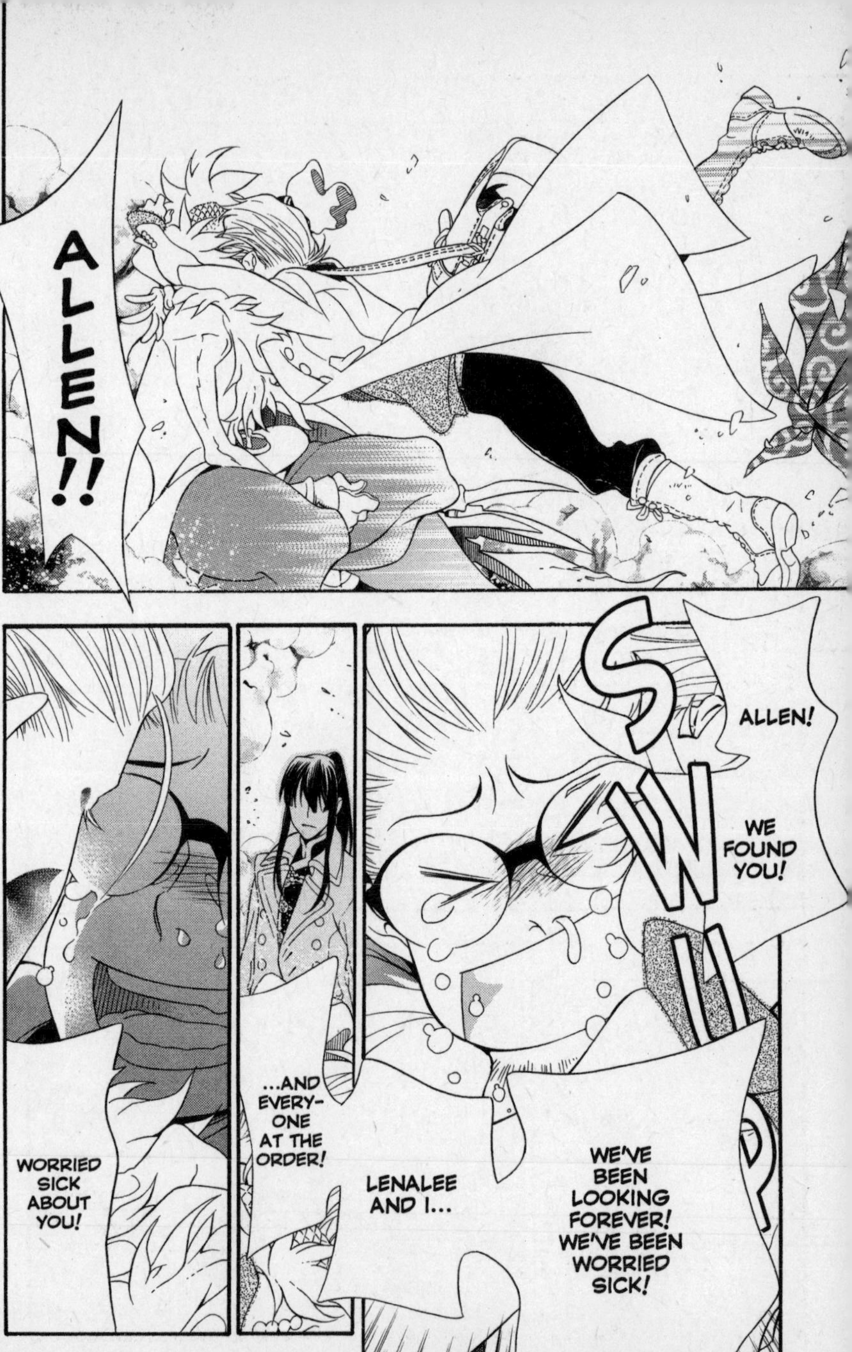
ALLEN!!
ALLEN!
WE FOUND YOU!
WE'VE BEEN LOOKING FOREVER! WE'VE BEEN WORRIED SICK!
LENALEE AND I...
...AND EVERYONE AT THE ORDER!
WORRIED SICK ABOUT YOU!

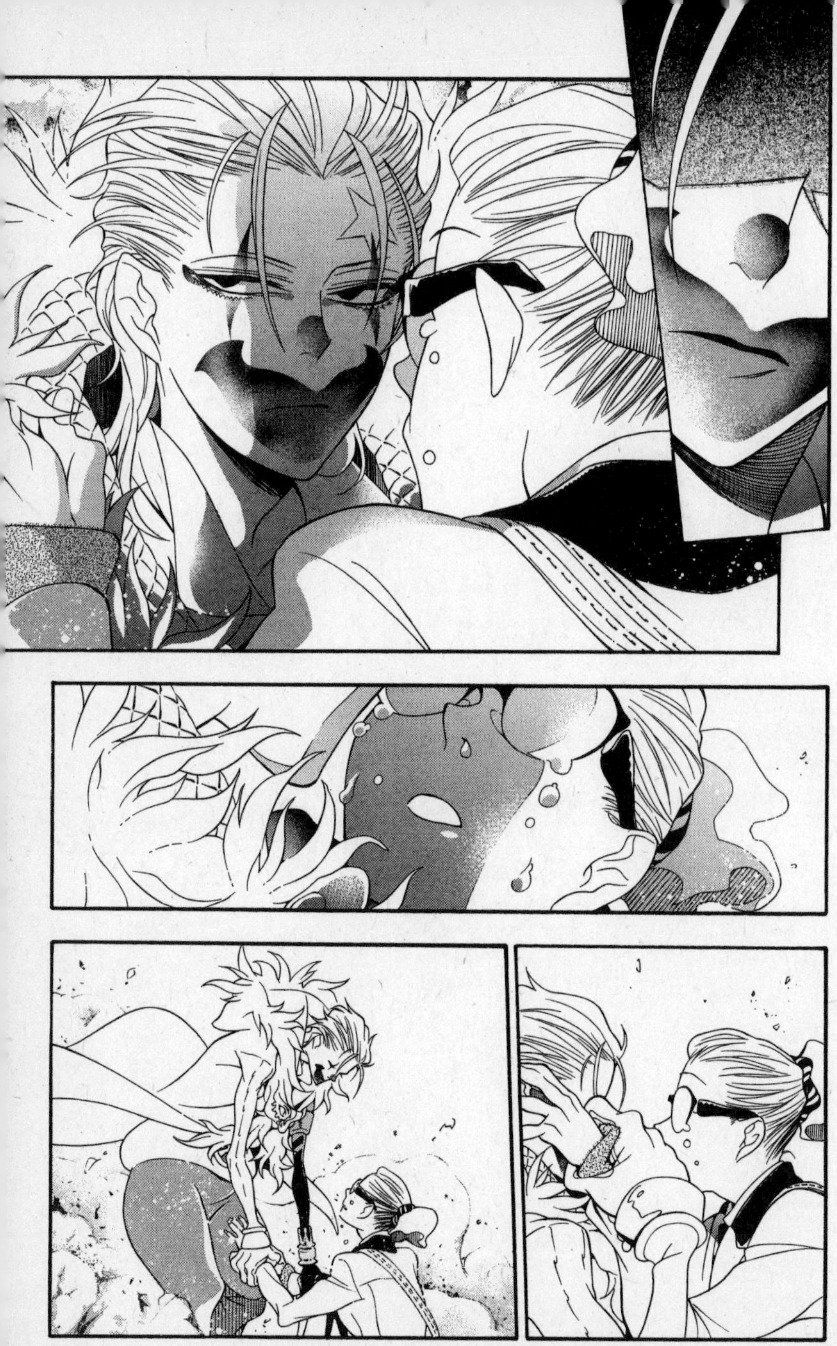

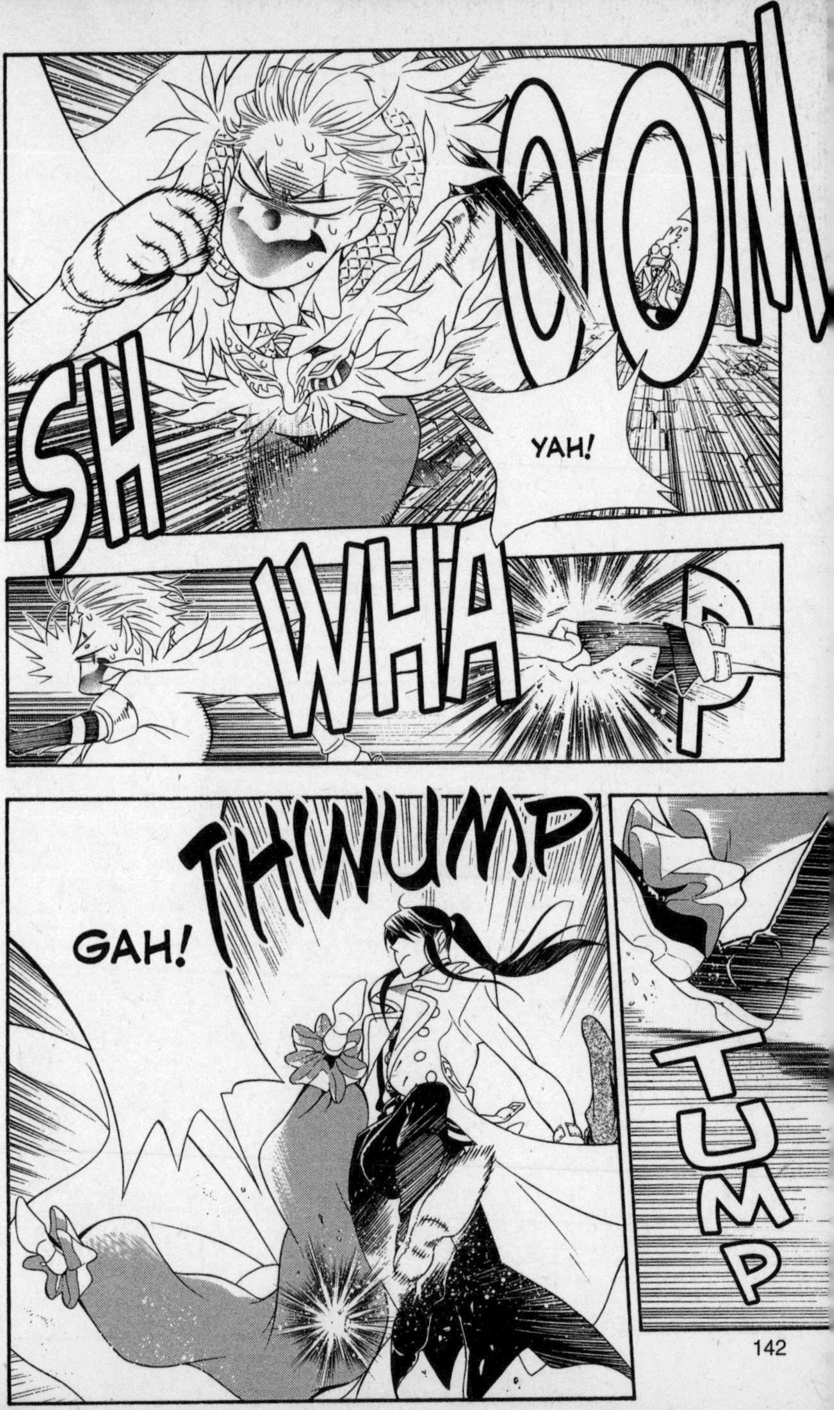
SHOOM
YAH!
WHAP
TUMP
THWUMP
GAH!

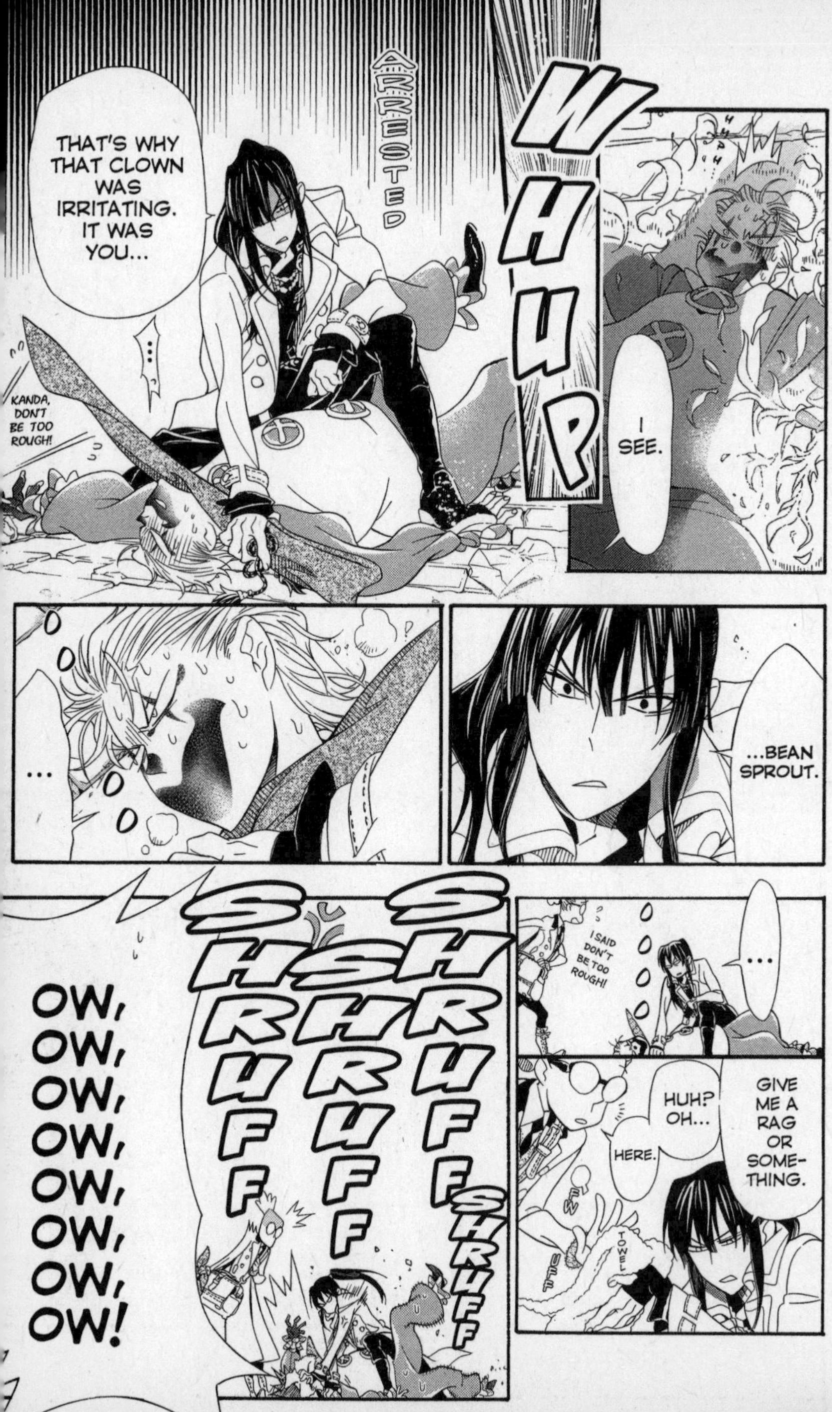
WHUP
I SEE.
ARRESTED
THAT'S WHY THAT CLOWN WAS IRRITATING. IT WAS YOU...
...
KANDA, DON'T BE TOO ROUGH!
...BEAN SPROUT.
...
...
I SAID DON'T BE TOO ROUGH!
GIVE ME A RAG OR SOMETHING.
HUH? OH...
HERE.
FWUFF
TOWEL
SHRUFF
SHRUFF
SHRUFF
SHRUFF
OW, OW, OW, OW, OW, OW, OW, OW!

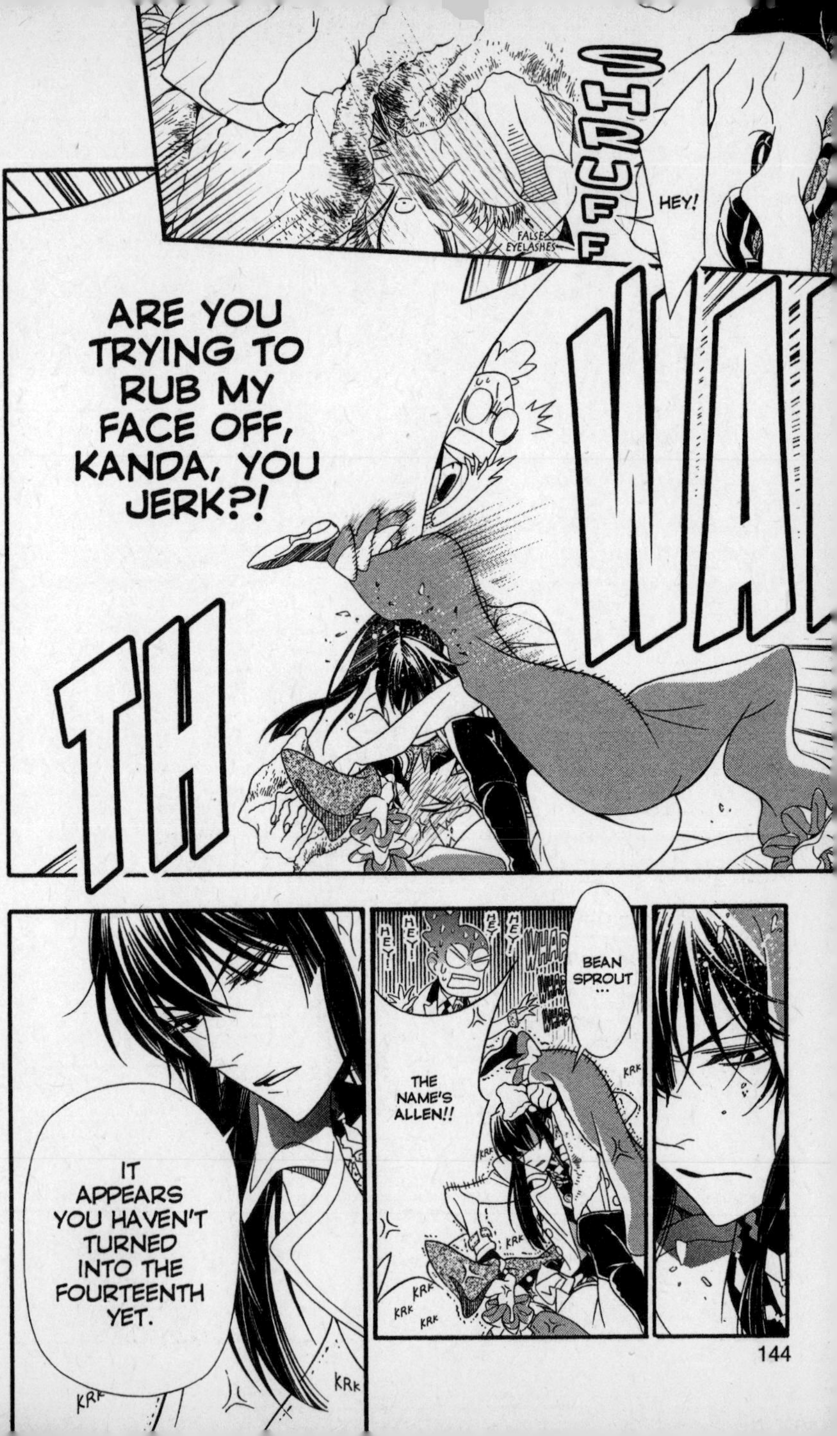
HEY!
SHRUFF
FALSE EYELASHES
WHA
ARE YOU TRYING TO RUB MY FACE OFF, KANDA, YOU JERK?!
TH
BEAN SPROUT...
WHAP WHAP WHAP
HEY! HEY! HEY! HEY!
THE NAME'S ALLEN!!
KRK KRK KRK KRK KRK KRK
IT APPEARS YOU HAVEN'T TURNED INTO THE FOURTEENTH YET.
KRK KRK

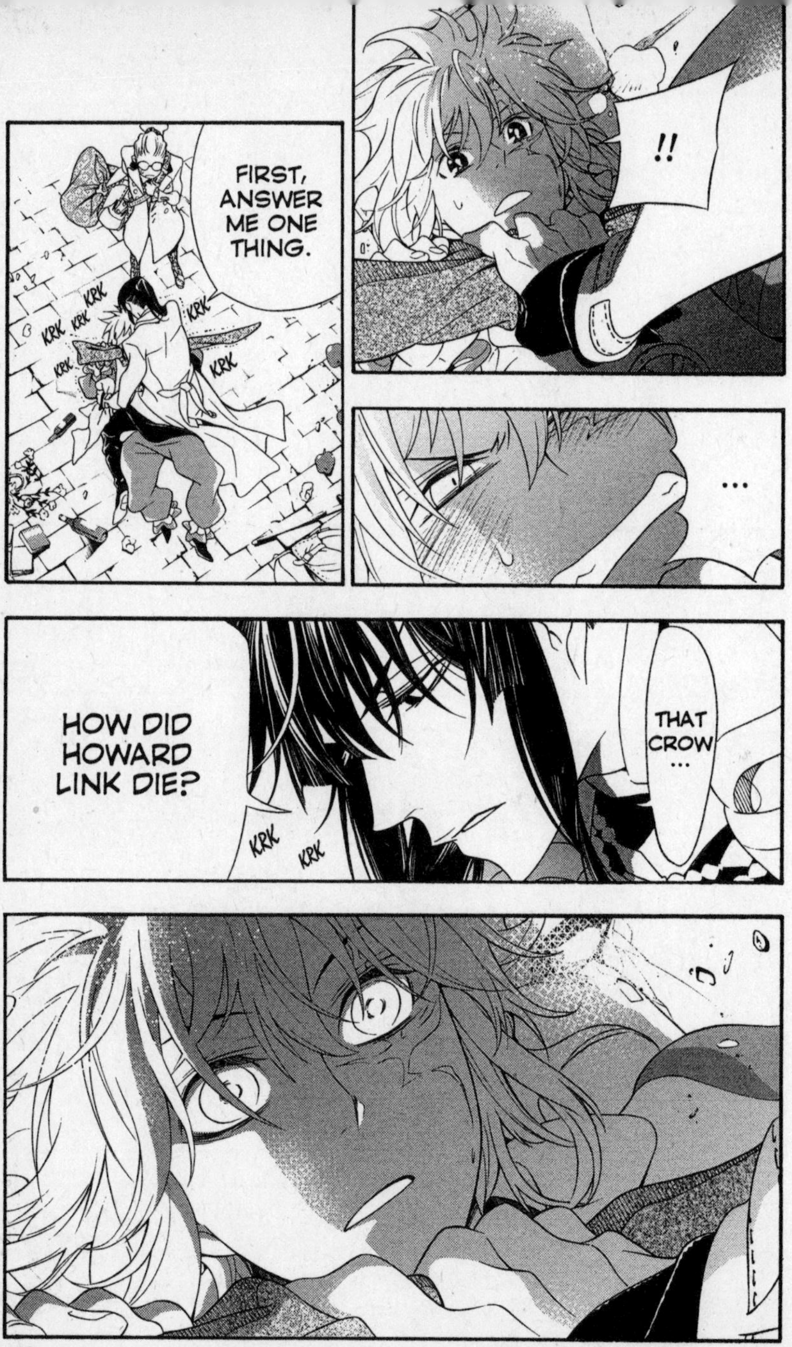
!!
...
FIRST, ANSWER ME ONE THING.
KRK KRK KRK KRK KRK KRK
THAT CROW ...
HOW DID HOWARD LINK DIE?
KRK KRK

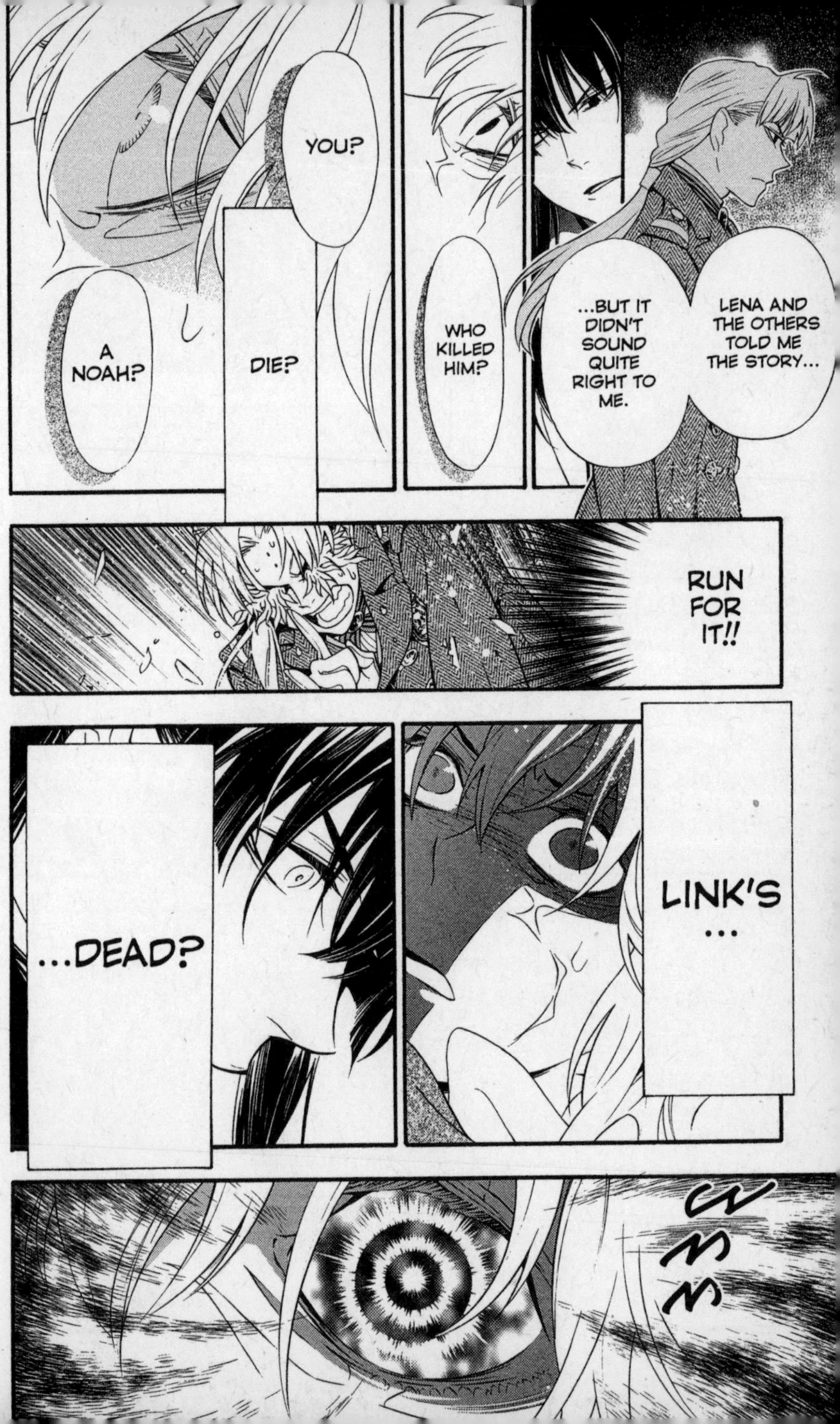
LENA AND THE OTHERS TOLD ME THE STORY...
...BUT IT DIDN'T SOUND QUITE RIGHT TO ME.
WHO KILLED HIM?
YOU?
DIE?
A NOAH?
RUN FOR IT!!
LINK'S ...
...DEAD?

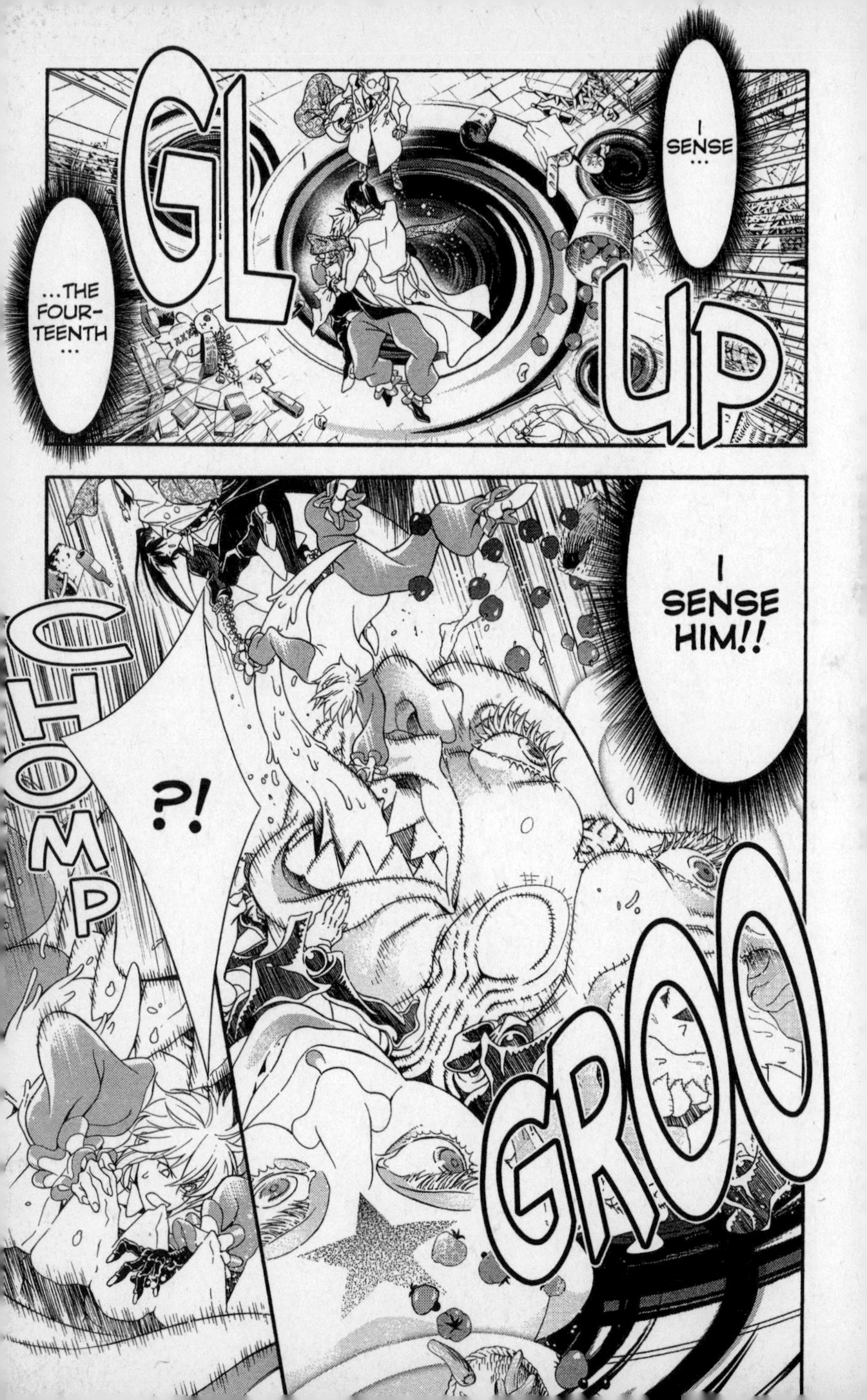
I SENSE ...
...THE FOUR-TEENTH ...
GL UP
I SENSE HIM!!
?!
CHOMP
GROO

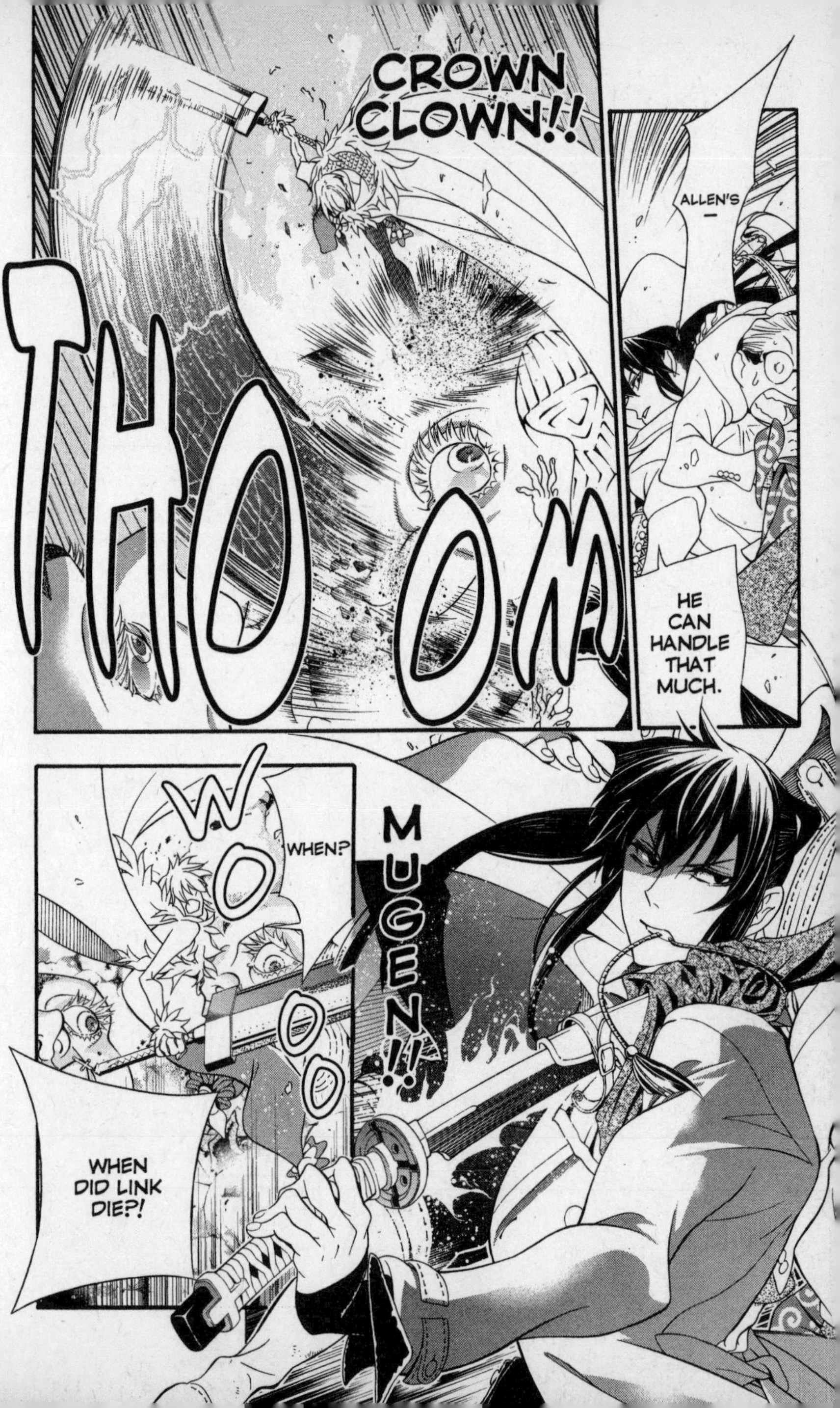
ALLEN'S —
HE CAN HANDLE THAT MUCH.
CROWN CLOWN!!
THOOM
MUGEN!!
WOOOO
WHEN?
WHEN DID LINK DIE?!

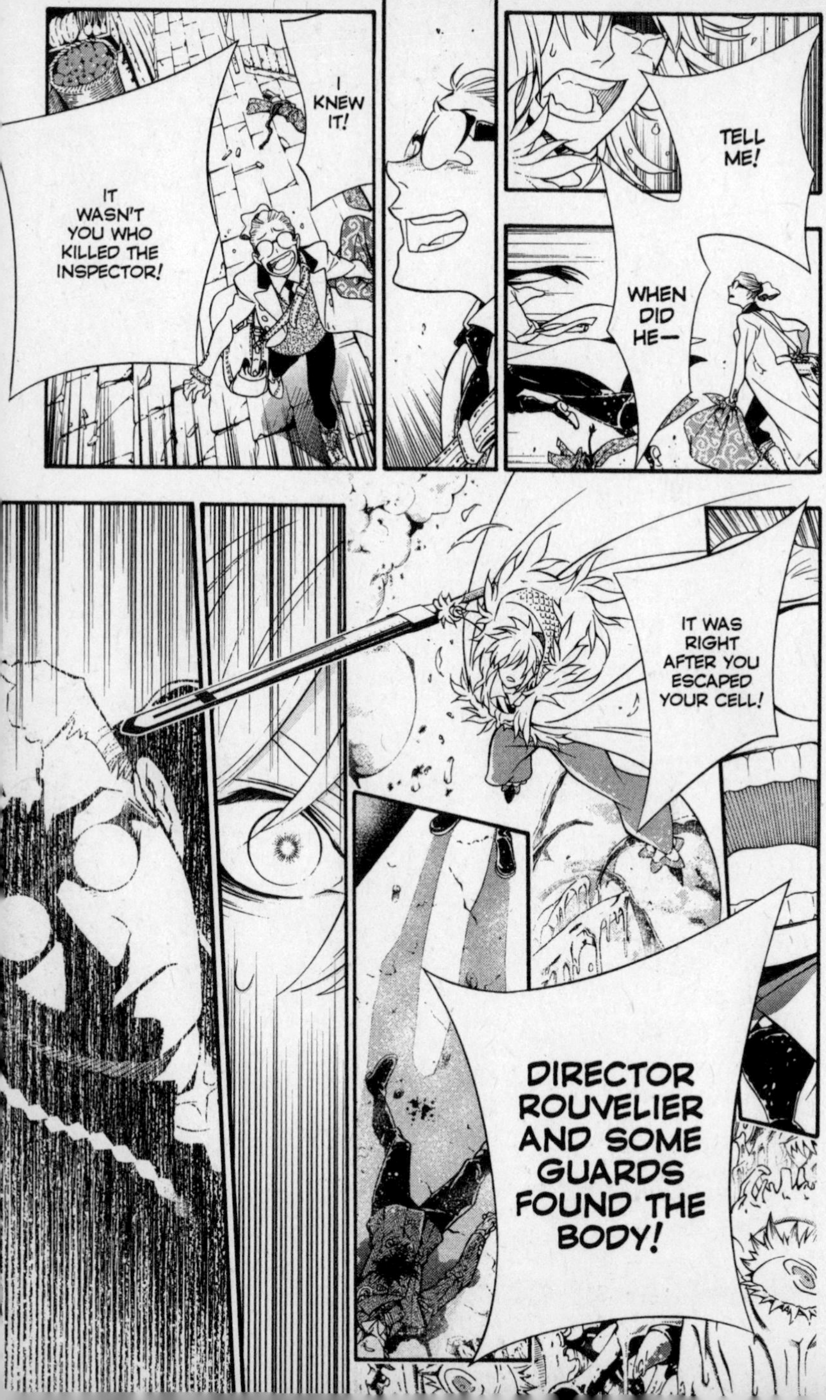
TELL ME!
WHEN DID HE—
I KNEW IT!
IT WASN'T YOU WHO KILLED THE INSPECTOR!
IT WAS RIGHT AFTER YOU ESCAPED YOUR CELL!
DIRECTOR ROUVELIER AND SOME GUARDS FOUND THE BODY!

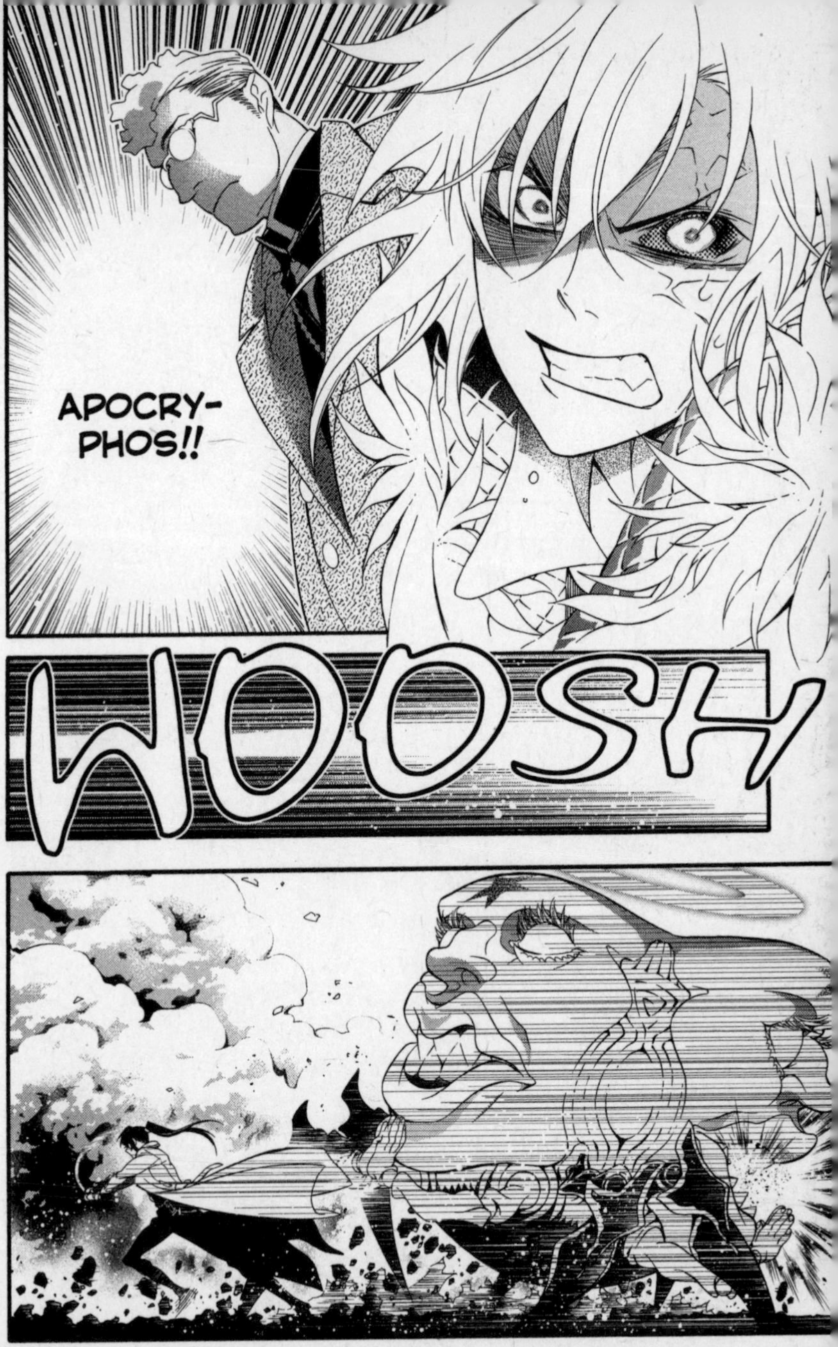
APOCRY-PHOS!!
WOOSH

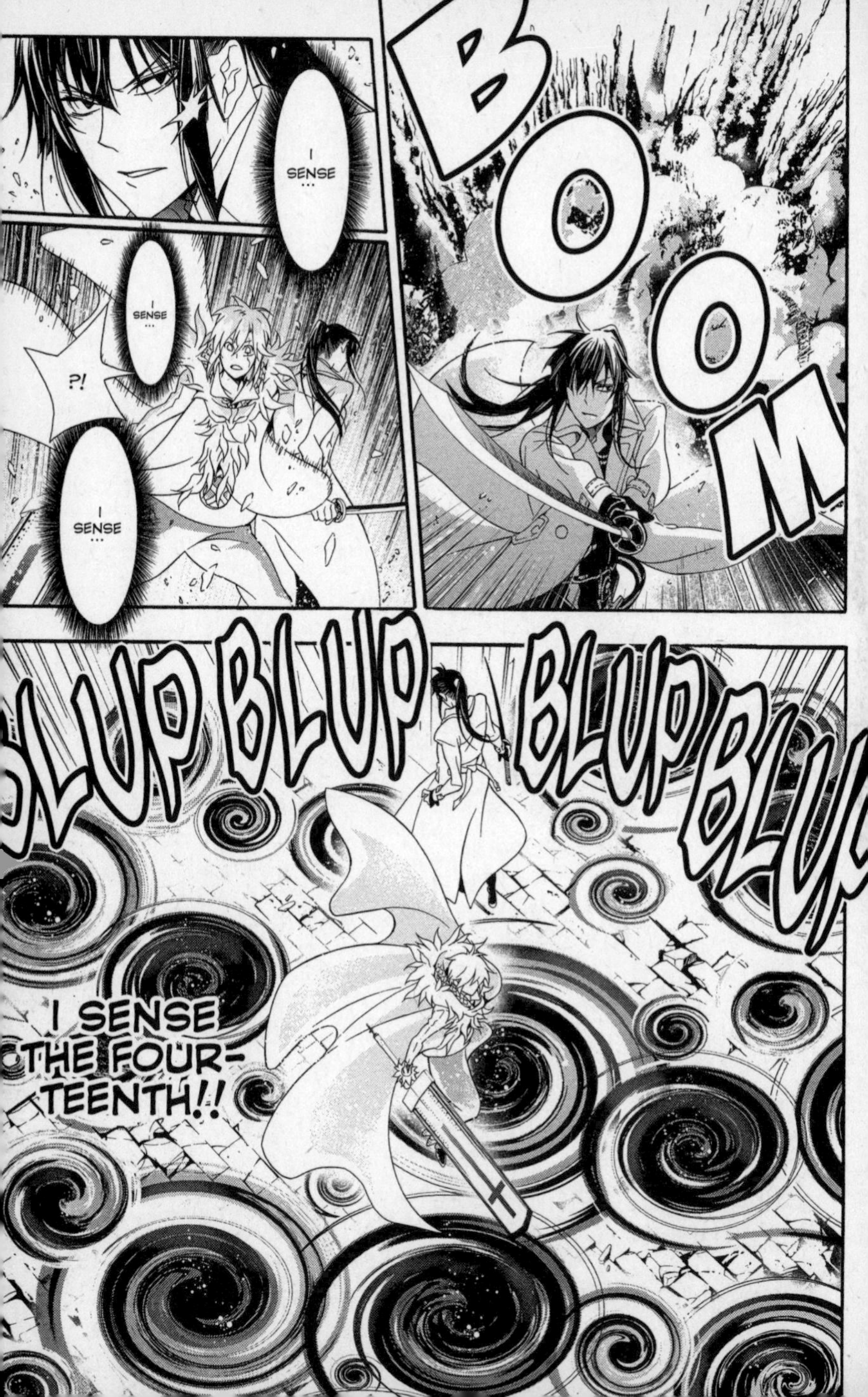
BOOM
I SENSE...
I SENSE...
?!
I SENSE...
BLUP BLUP BLUP BLUP
I SENSE THE FOUR-TEENTH!!

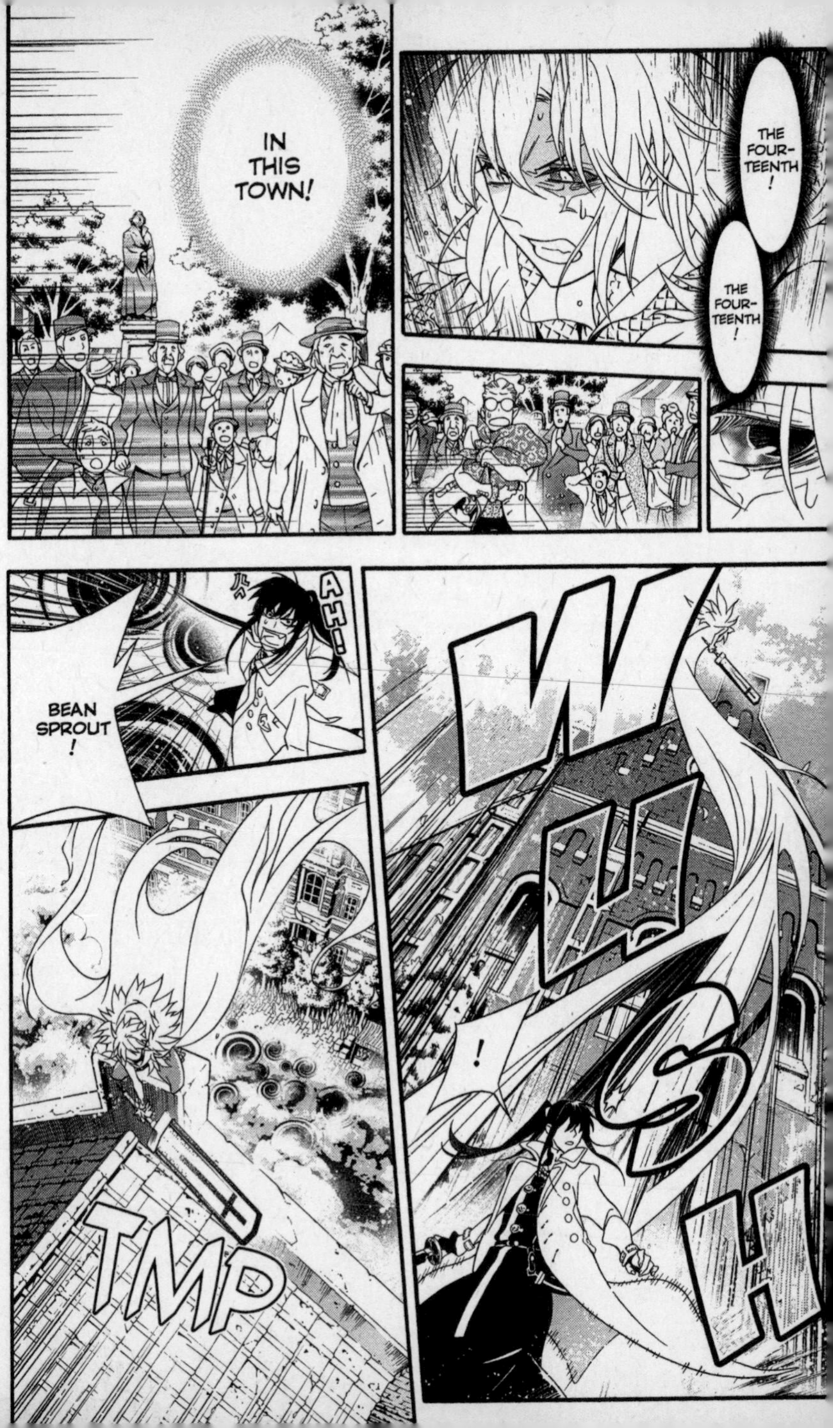
THE FOURTEENTH!
THE FOURTEENTH!
IN THIS TOWN!
WHUSH
!
AH!
BEAN SPROUT!
TMP

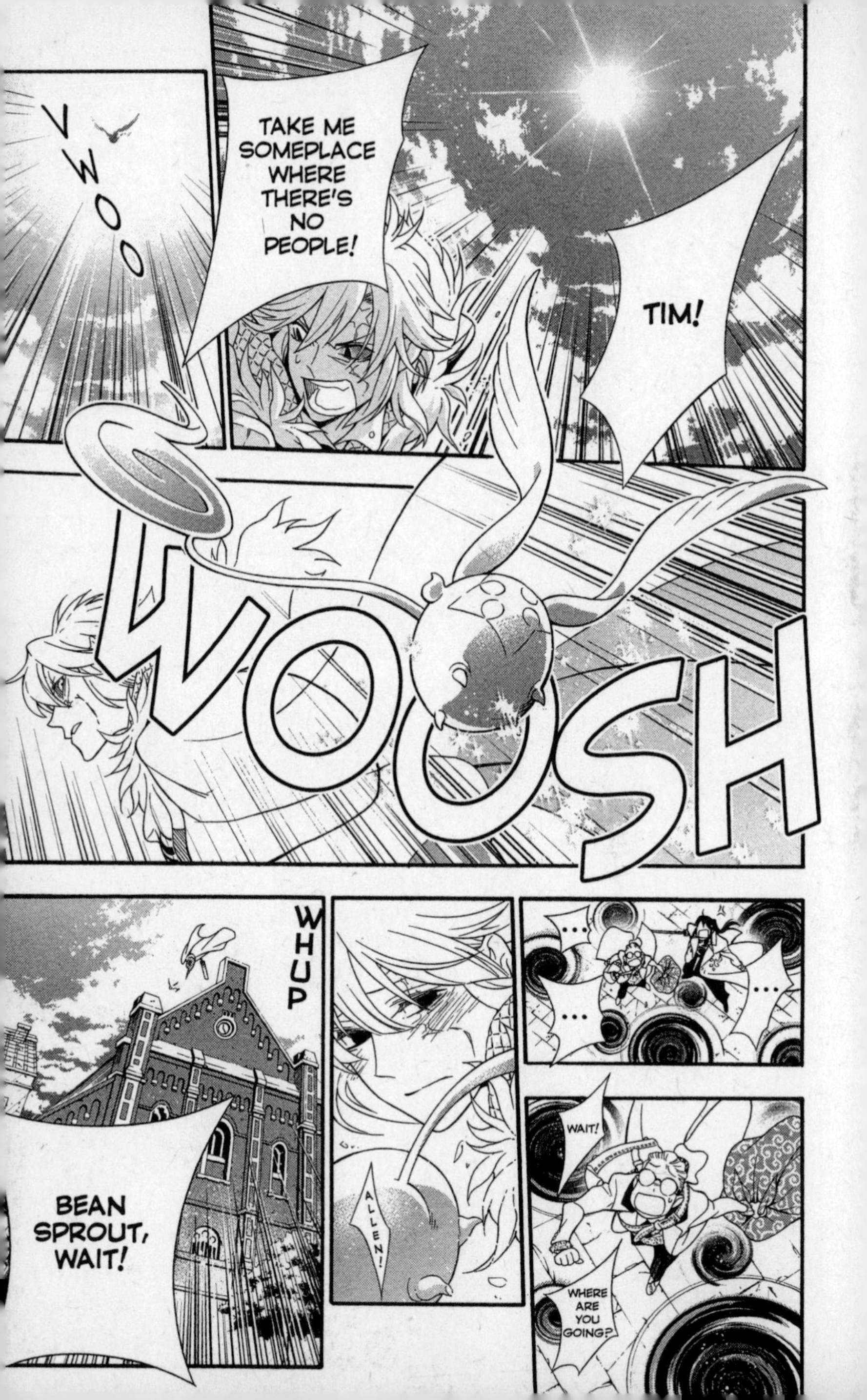
TIM!
TAKE ME SOMEPLACE WHERE THERE'S NO PEOPLE!
VWOO
WOOSH
...
...
...
WAIT!
WHERE ARE YOU GOING?
ALLEN!
WHUP
BEAN SPROUT, WAIT!

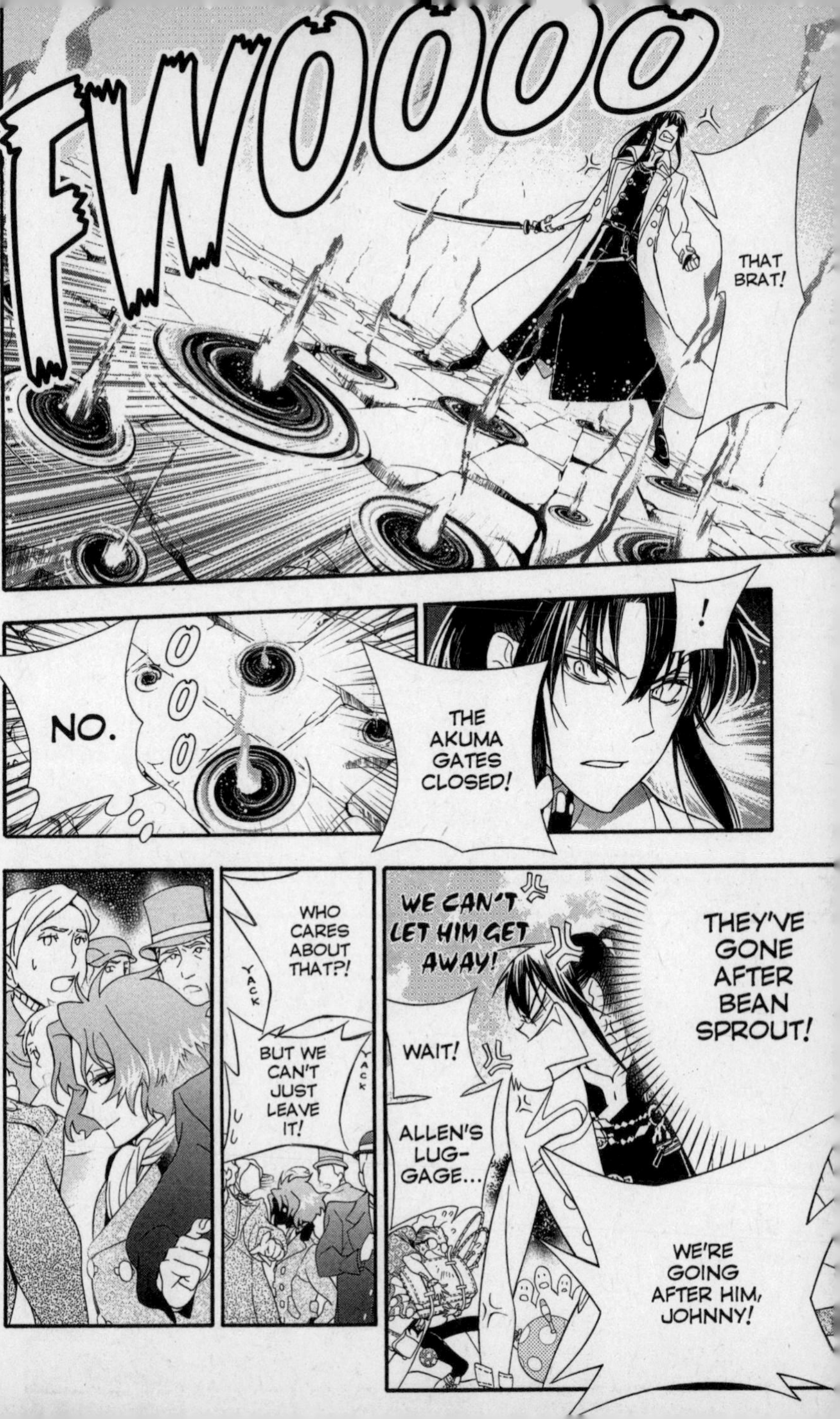
FWOOOO
THAT BRAT!
!
THE AKUMA GATES CLOSED!
NO.
THEY'VE GONE AFTER BEAN SPROUT!
WE CAN'T LET HIM GET AWAY!
WAIT!
ALLEN'S LUG-GAGE...
WE'RE GOING AFTER HIM, JOHNNY!
WHO CARES ABOUT THAT?!
YACK
BUT WE CAN'T JUST LEAVE IT!
YACK

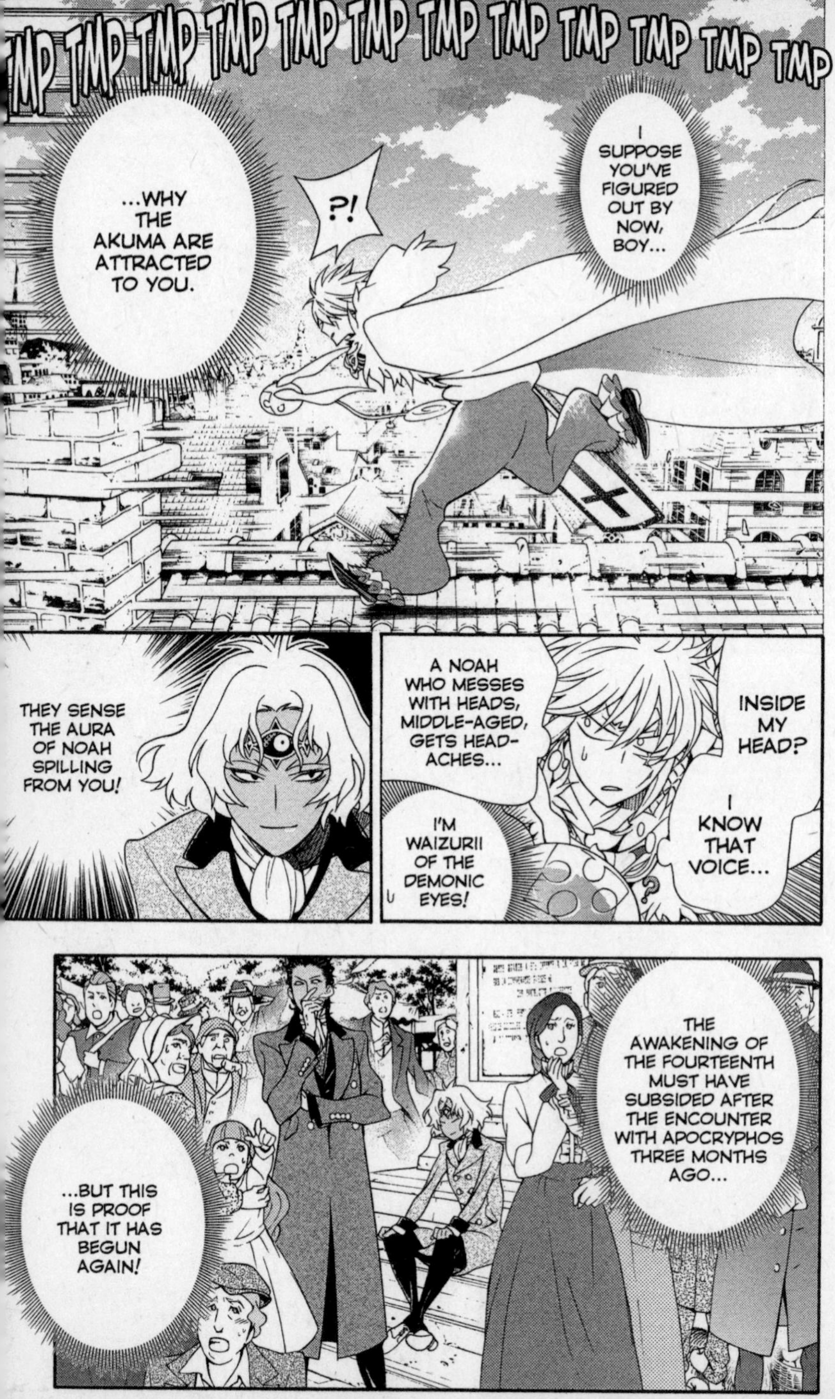
TMP TMP TMP TMP TMP TMP TMP TMP TMP TMP TMP
I SUPPOSE YOU'VE FIGURED OUT BY NOW, BOY...
?!
...WHY THE AKUMA ARE ATTRACTED TO YOU.
INSIDE MY HEAD?
I KNOW THAT VOICE...
A NOAH WHO MESSES WITH HEADS, MIDDLE-AGED, GETS HEAD-ACHES...
I'M WAIZURII OF THE DEMONIC EYES!
THEY SENSE THE AURA OF NOAH SPILLING FROM YOU!
THE AWAKENING OF THE FOURTEENTH MUST HAVE SUBSIDED AFTER THE ENCOUNTER WITH APOCRYPHOS THREE MONTHS AGO...
...BUT THIS IS PROOF THAT IT HAS BEGUN AGAIN!

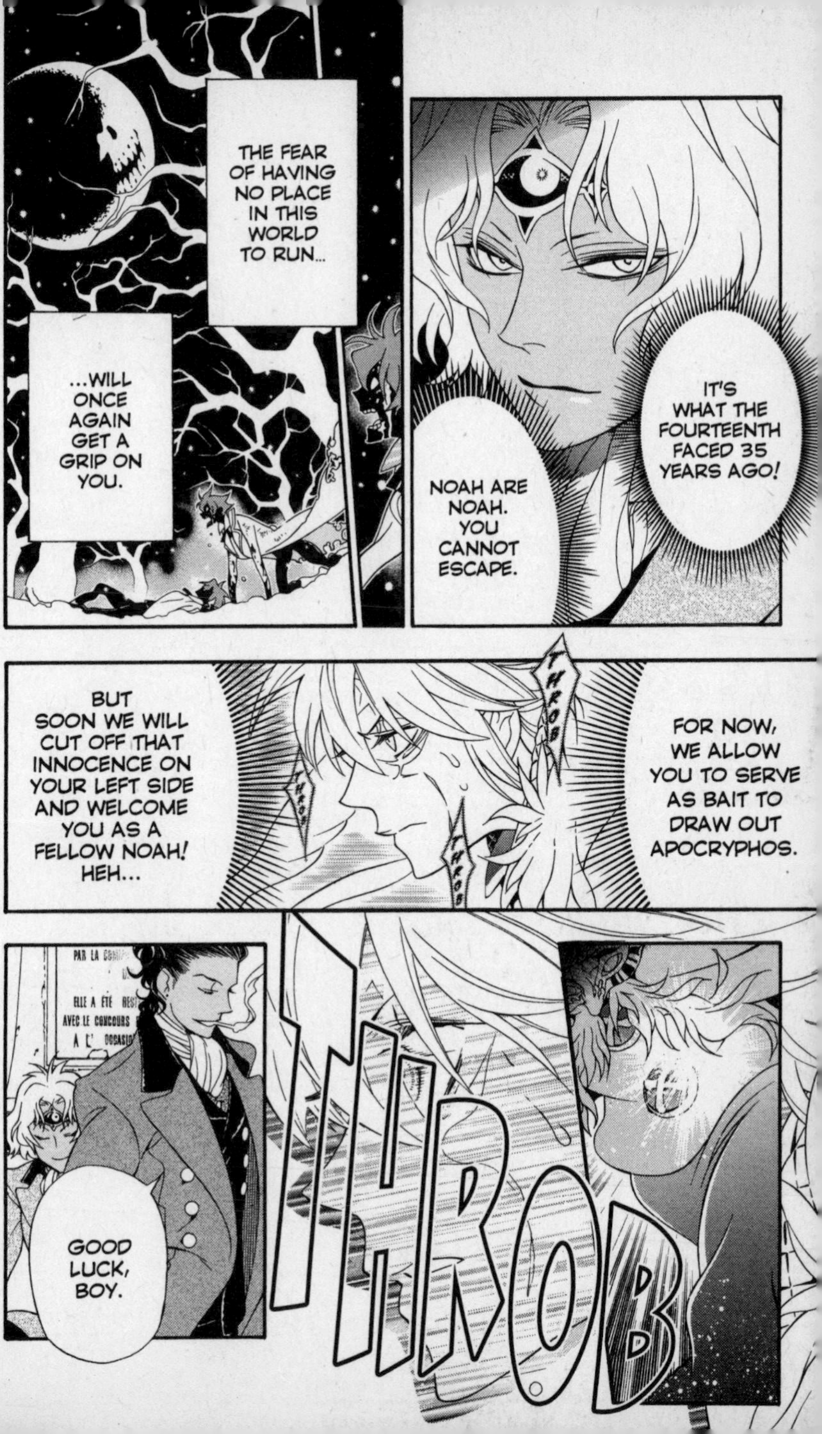
IT'S WHAT THE FOURTEENTH FACED 35 YEARS AGO!
NOAH ARE NOAH. YOU CANNOT ESCAPE.
THE FEAR OF HAVING NO PLACE IN THIS WORLD TO RUN...
...WILL ONCE AGAIN GET A GRIP ON YOU.
FOR NOW, WE ALLOW YOU TO SERVE AS BAIT TO DRAW OUT APOCRYPHOS.
THROB
THROB
THROB
BUT SOON WE WILL CUT OFF THAT INNOCENCE ON YOUR LEFT SIDE AND WELCOME YOU AS A FELLOW NOAH! HEH...
THROB
GOOD LUCK, BOY.

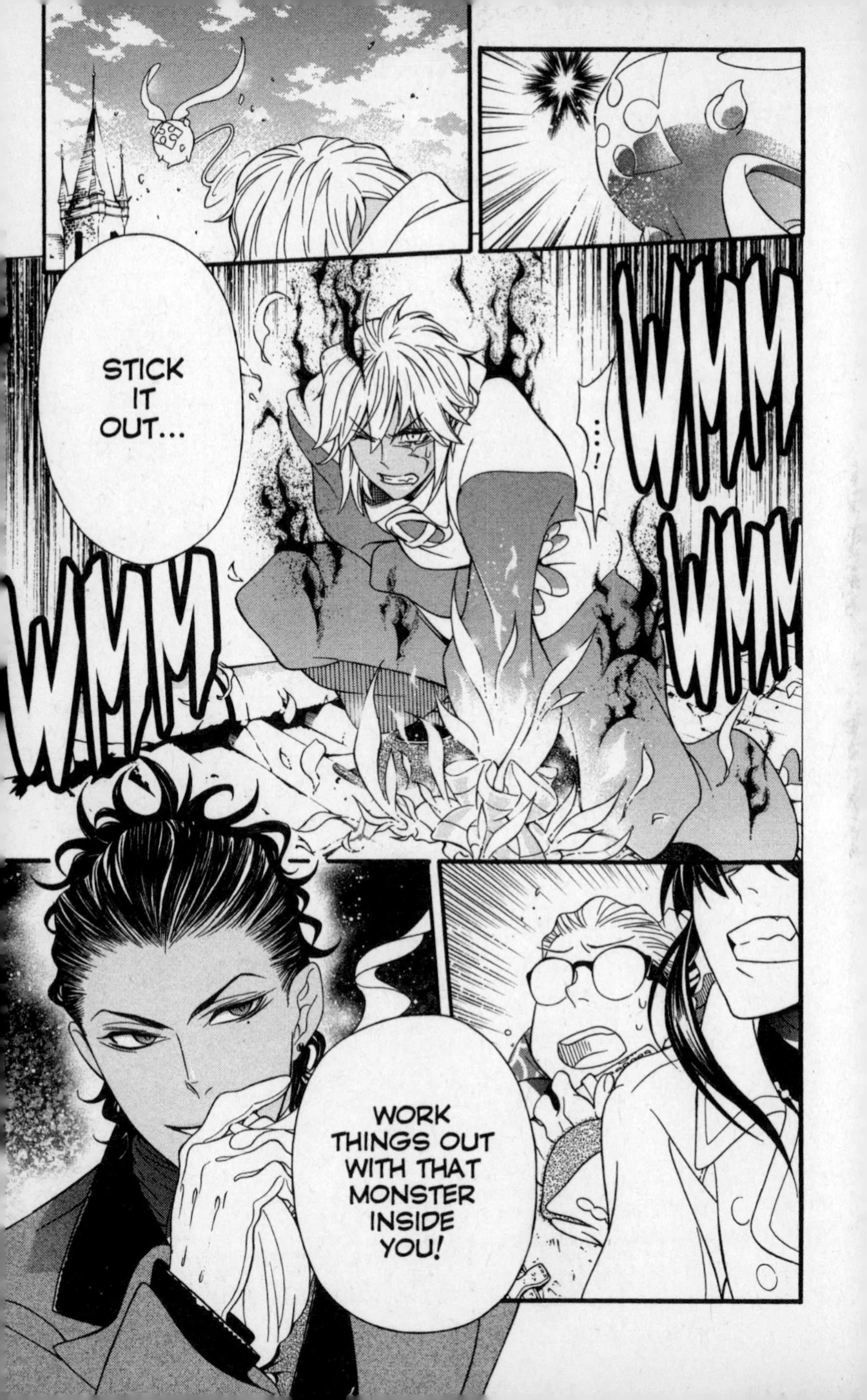
WMM
WMM
...!
STICK IT OUT...
WMMM
WORK THINGS OUT WITH THAT MONSTER INSIDE YOU!

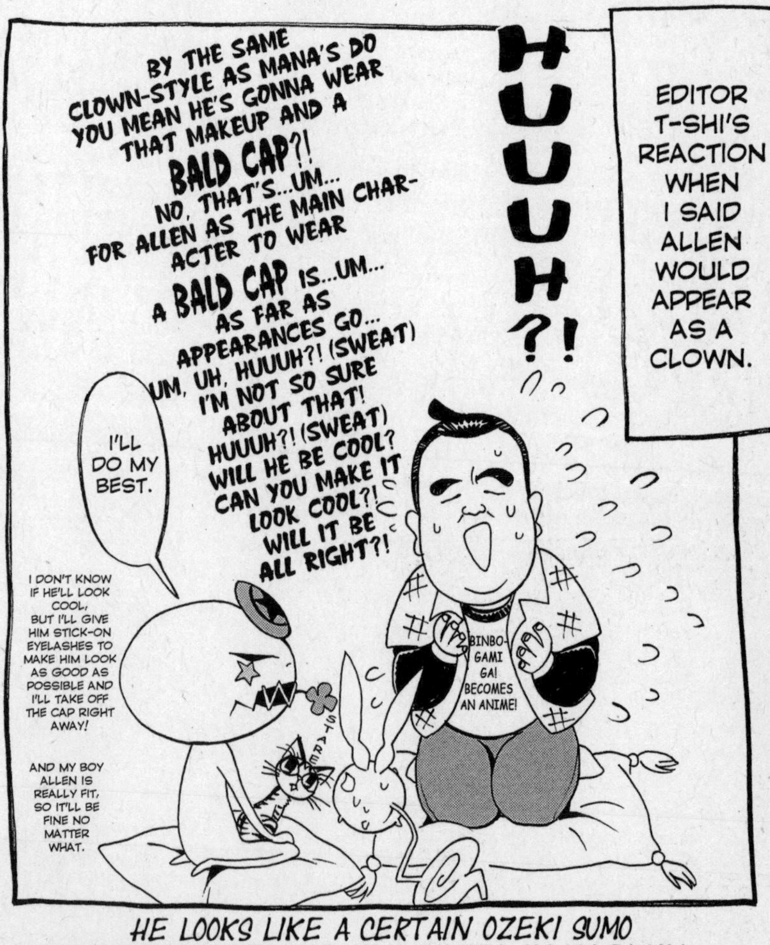
EDITOR T-SHI'S REACTION WHEN I SAID ALLEN WOULD APPEAR AS A CLOWN.
HUUUUH?!
BY THE SAME CLOWN-STYLE AS MANA'S DO YOU MEAN HE'S GONNA WEAR THAT MAKEUP AND A BALD CAP?! NO, THAT'S...UM... FOR ALLEN AS THE MAIN CHARACTER TO WEAR A BALD CAP IS...UM... AS FAR AS APPEARANCES GO... UM, UH, HUUUH?! (SWEAT) I'M NOT SO SURE ABOUT THAT! HUUUH?! (SWEAT) WILL HE BE COOL? CAN YOU MAKE IT LOOK COOL?! WILL IT BE ALL RIGHT?!
BINBO-GAMI GA! BECOMES AN ANIME!
I'LL DO MY BEST.
I DON'T KNOW IF HE'LL LOOK COOL, BUT I'LL GIVE HIM STICK-ON EYELASHES TO MAKE HIM LOOK AS GOOD AS POSSIBLE AND I'LL TAKE OFF THE CAP RIGHT AWAY!
AND MY BOY ALLEN IS REALLY FIT, SO IT'LL BE FINE NO MATTER WHAT.
STARE

HE LOOKS LIKE A CERTAIN OZEKI SUMO WRESTLER BECAUSE OF A FILTER IN MY BRAIN.

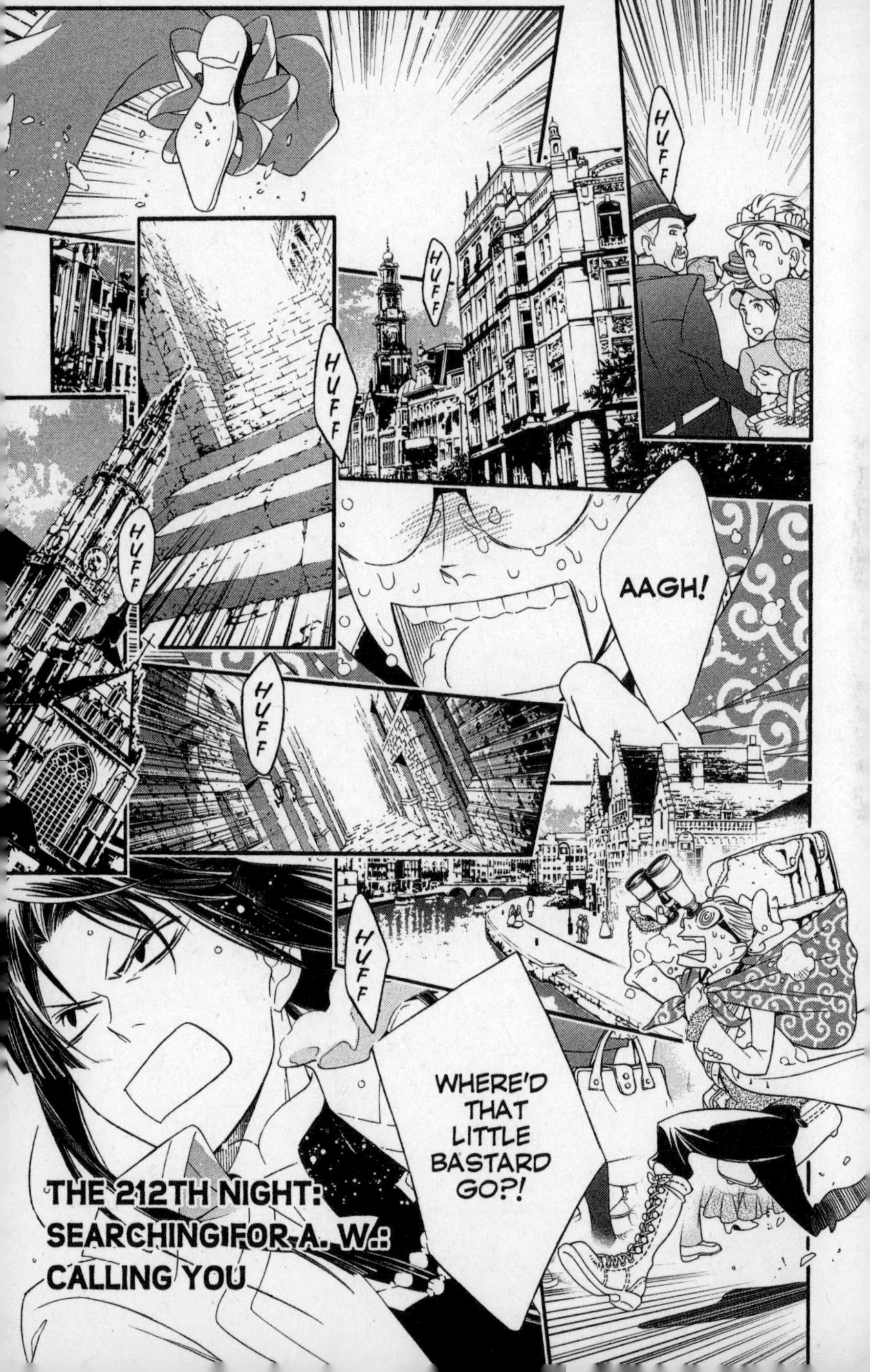
HUFF HUFF
HUFF HUFF
HUFF HUFF
AAGH!
HUFF HUFF
HUFF HUFF
WHERE'D THAT LITTLE BASTARD GO?!
HUFF HUFF
THE 212TH NIGHT: SEARCHING FOR A. W.: CALLING YOU

THE 212TH NIGHT:
SEARCHING FOR A.W.: CALLING YOU

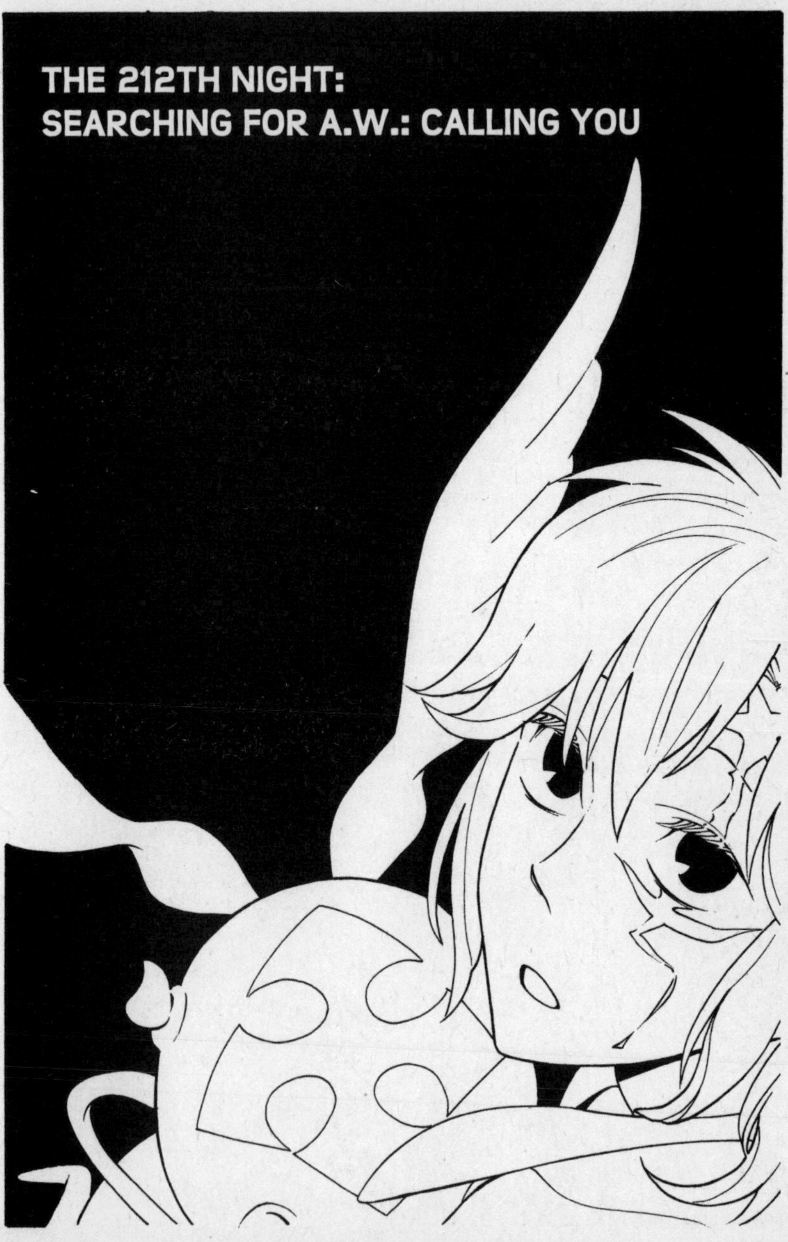

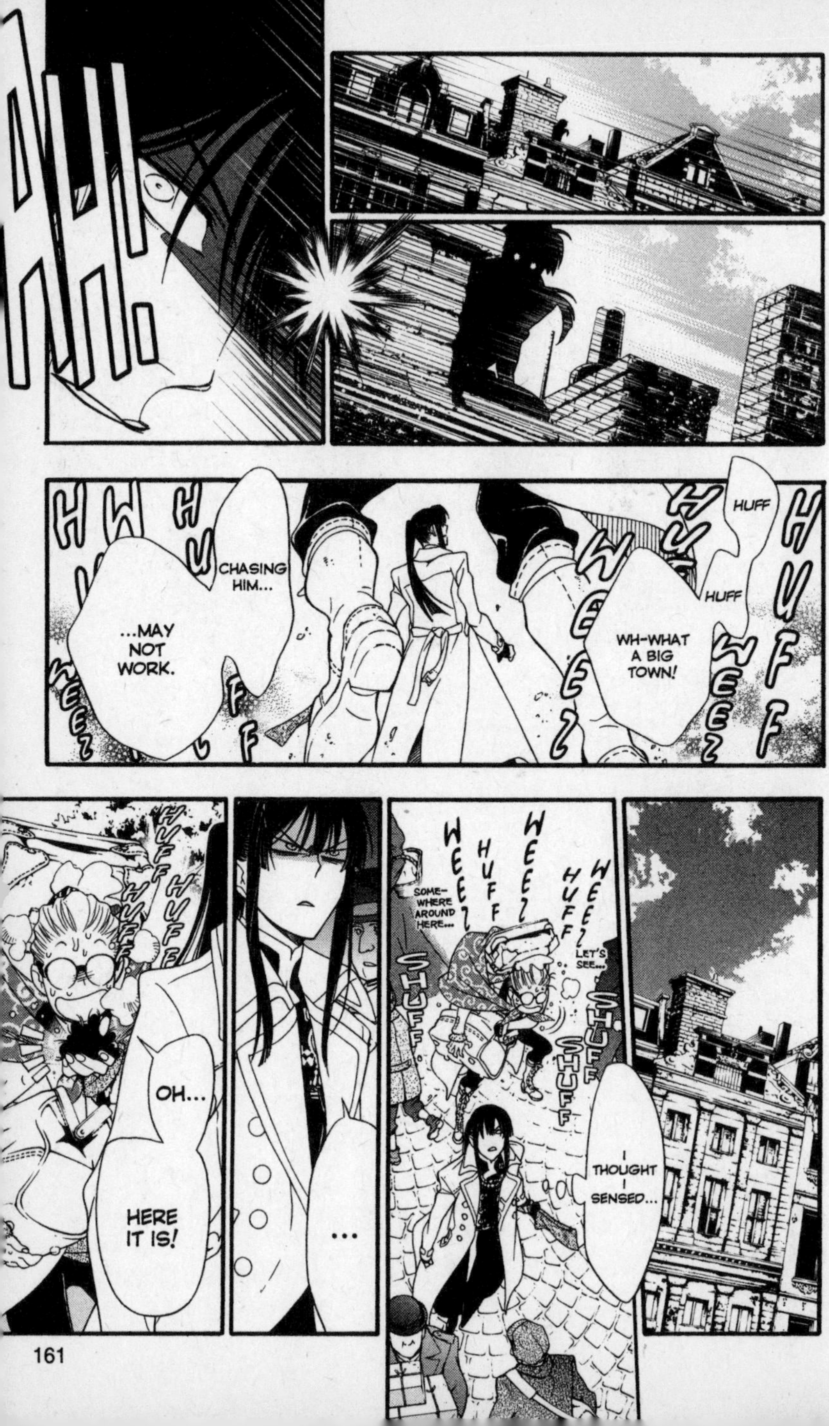
HUFF
HUFF
WH-WHAT A BIG TOWN!
CHASING HIM...
...MAY NOT WORK.
SOME-WHERE AROUND HERE...
LET'S SEE...
I THOUGHT I SENSED...
...
OH...
HERE IT IS!

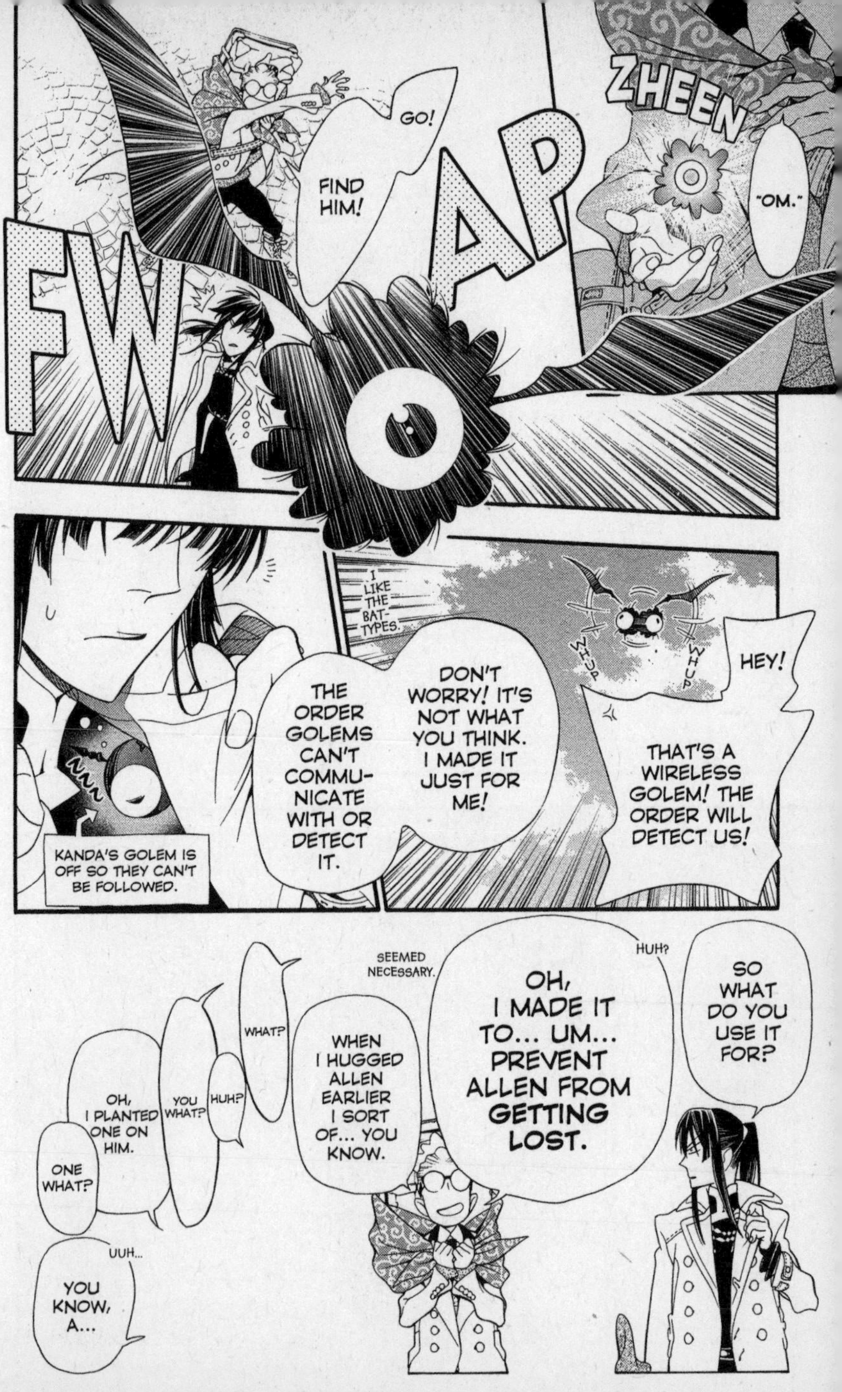

ZHEEN
"OM."
GO!
FIND HIM!
FWAP
HEY!
THAT'S A WIRELESS GOLEM! THE ORDER WILL DETECT US!
WHUP
WHUP
I LIKE THE BAT-TYPES.
DON'T WORRY! IT'S NOT WHAT YOU THINK. I MADE IT JUST FOR ME!
THE ORDER GOLEMS CAN'T COMMUNICATE WITH OR DETECT IT.
KANDA'S GOLEM IS OFF SO THEY CAN'T BE FOLLOWED.
SO WHAT DO YOU USE IT FOR?
HUH?
OH, I MADE IT TO... UM... PREVENT ALLEN FROM GETTING LOST.
SEEMED NECESSARY.
WHEN I HUGGED ALLEN EARLIER I SORT OF... YOU KNOW.
WHAT?
HUH?
YOU WHAT?
OH, I PLANTED ONE ON HIM.
ONE WHAT?
UUH...
YOU KNOW, A...

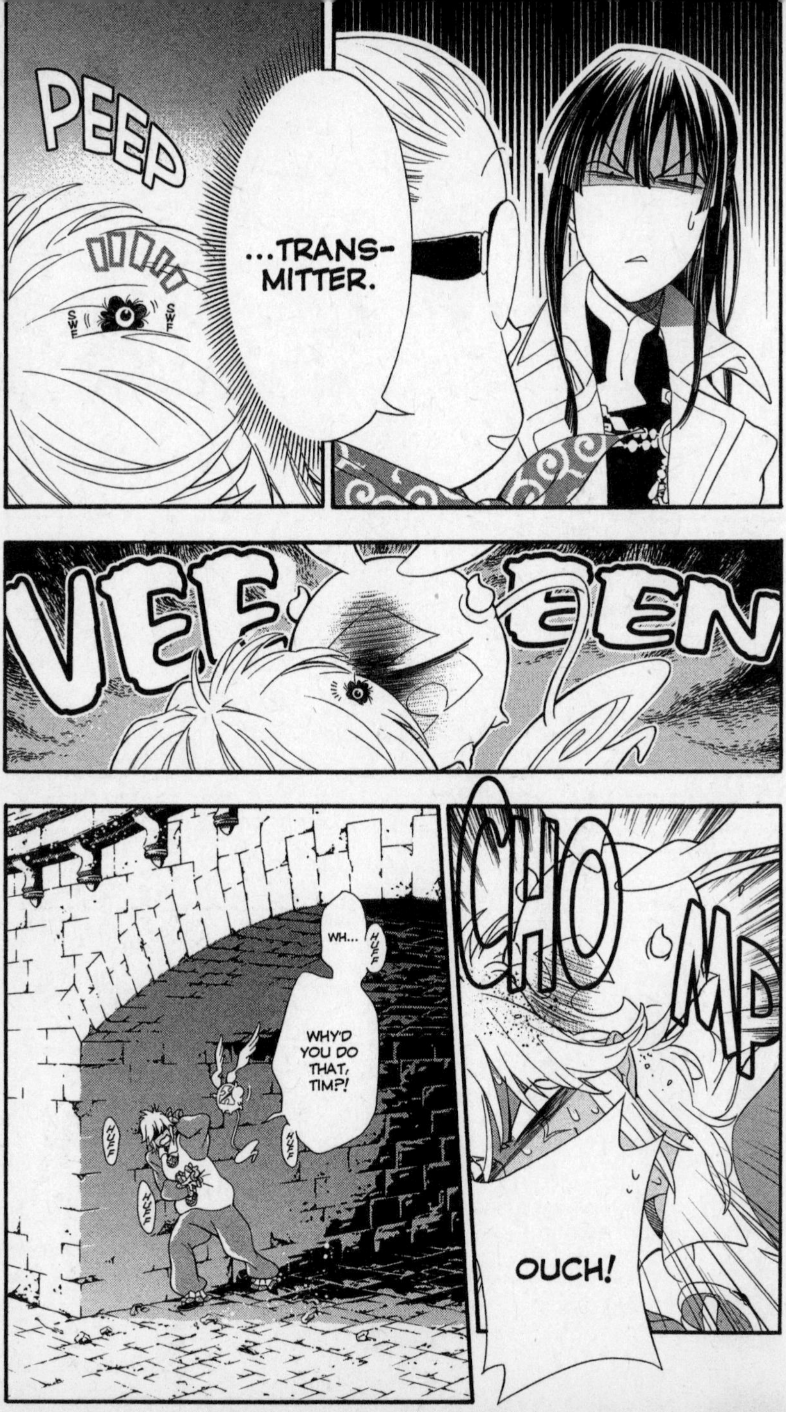
...TRANSMITTER.
PEEP
SWF
SWF
VEEEEN
CHOMP
OUCH!
WH...
HUFF
WHY'D YOU DO THAT, TIM?!
HUFF
HUFF
HUFF

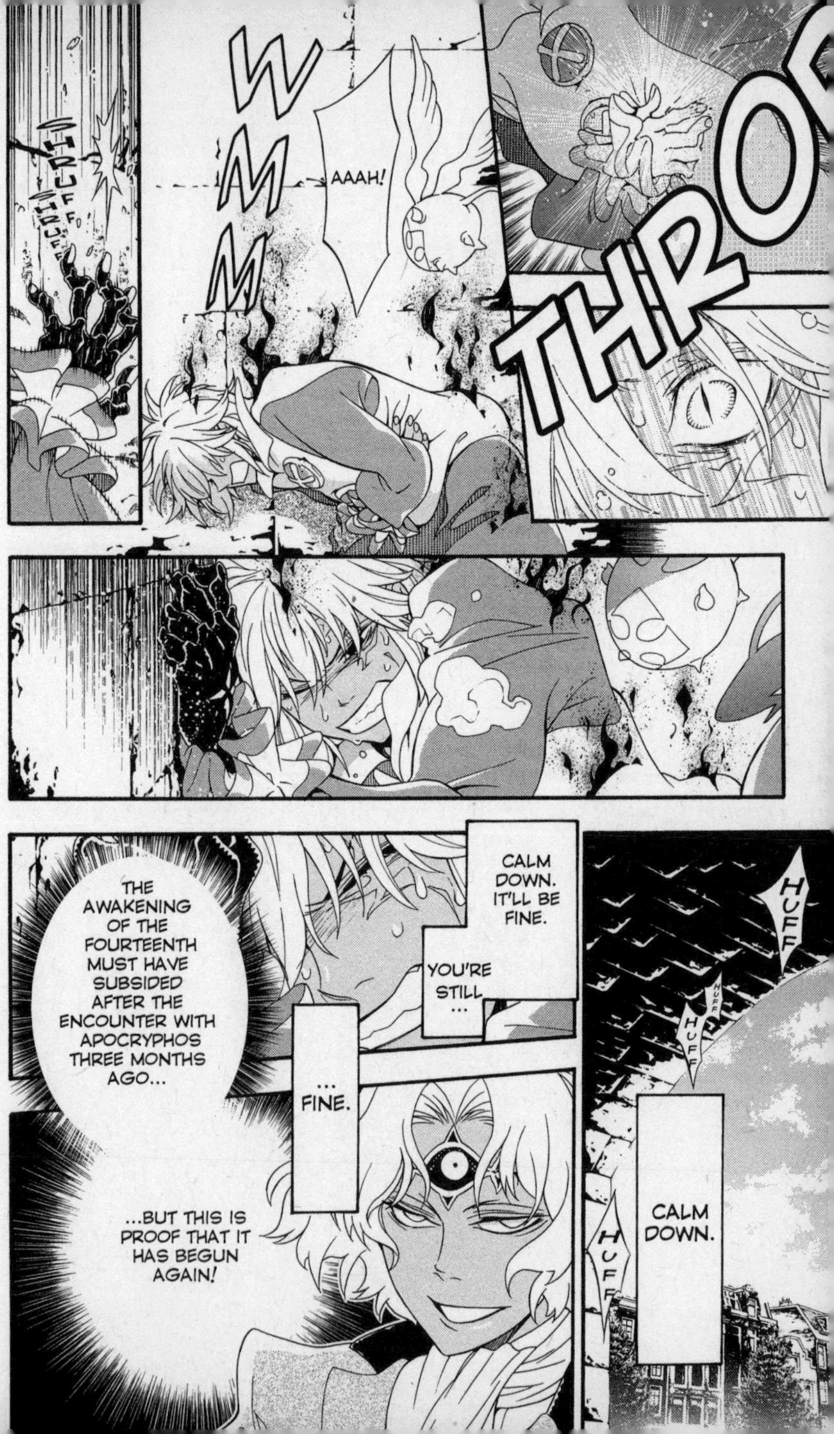
THRO
AAAH!
WMM
SHRUFF
SHRUFF
HUFF
HUFF
HUFF
CALM DOWN.
HUFF
CALM DOWN. IT'LL BE FINE.
YOU'RE STILL ...
... FINE.
THE AWAKENING OF THE FOURTEENTH MUST HAVE SUBSIDED AFTER THE ENCOUNTER WITH APOCRYPHOS THREE MONTHS AGO...
...BUT THIS IS PROOF THAT IT HAS BEGUN AGAIN!

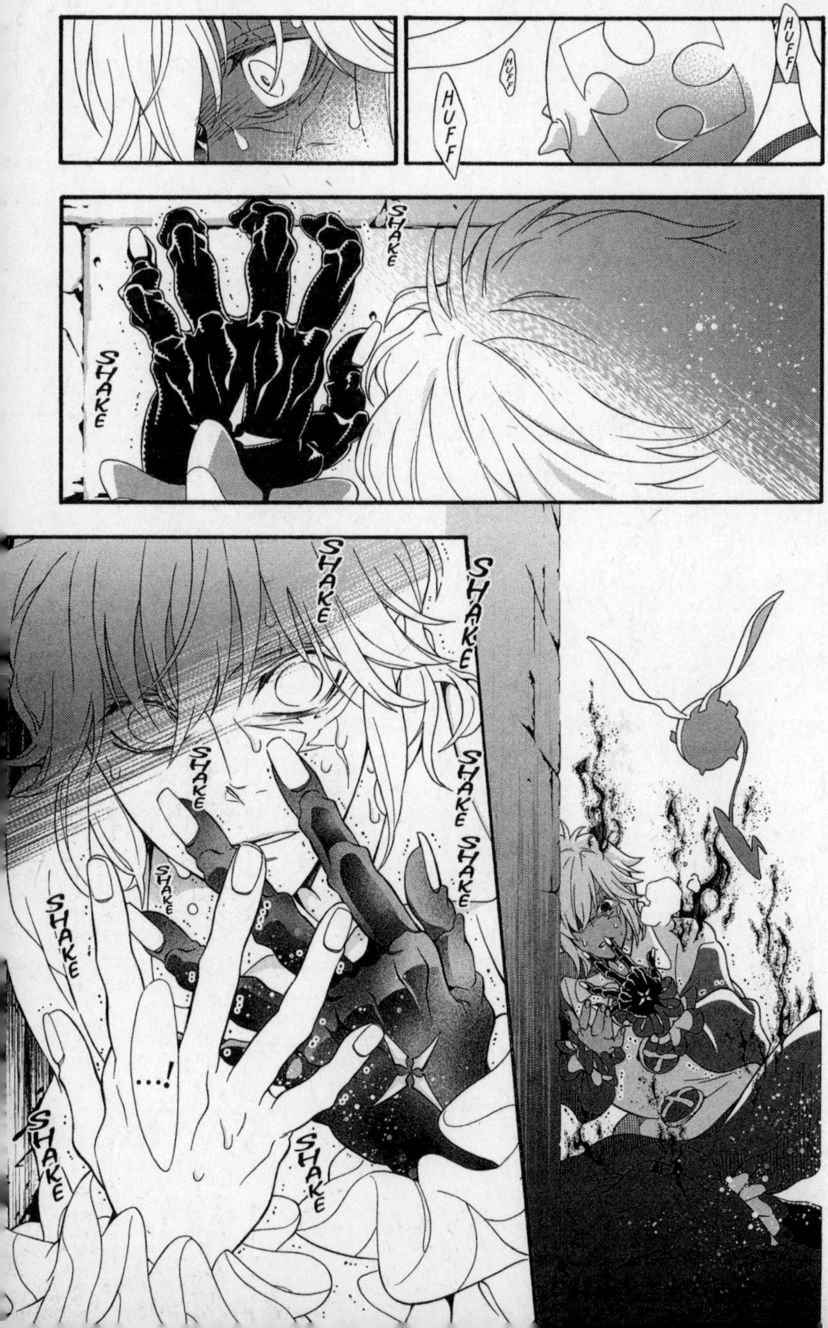
HUFF
HUFF
HUFF HUFF
SHAKE
SHAKE
SHAKE
SHAKE
SHAKE
SHAKE
SHAKE
SHAKE
SHAKE
...!
SHAKE
SHAKE

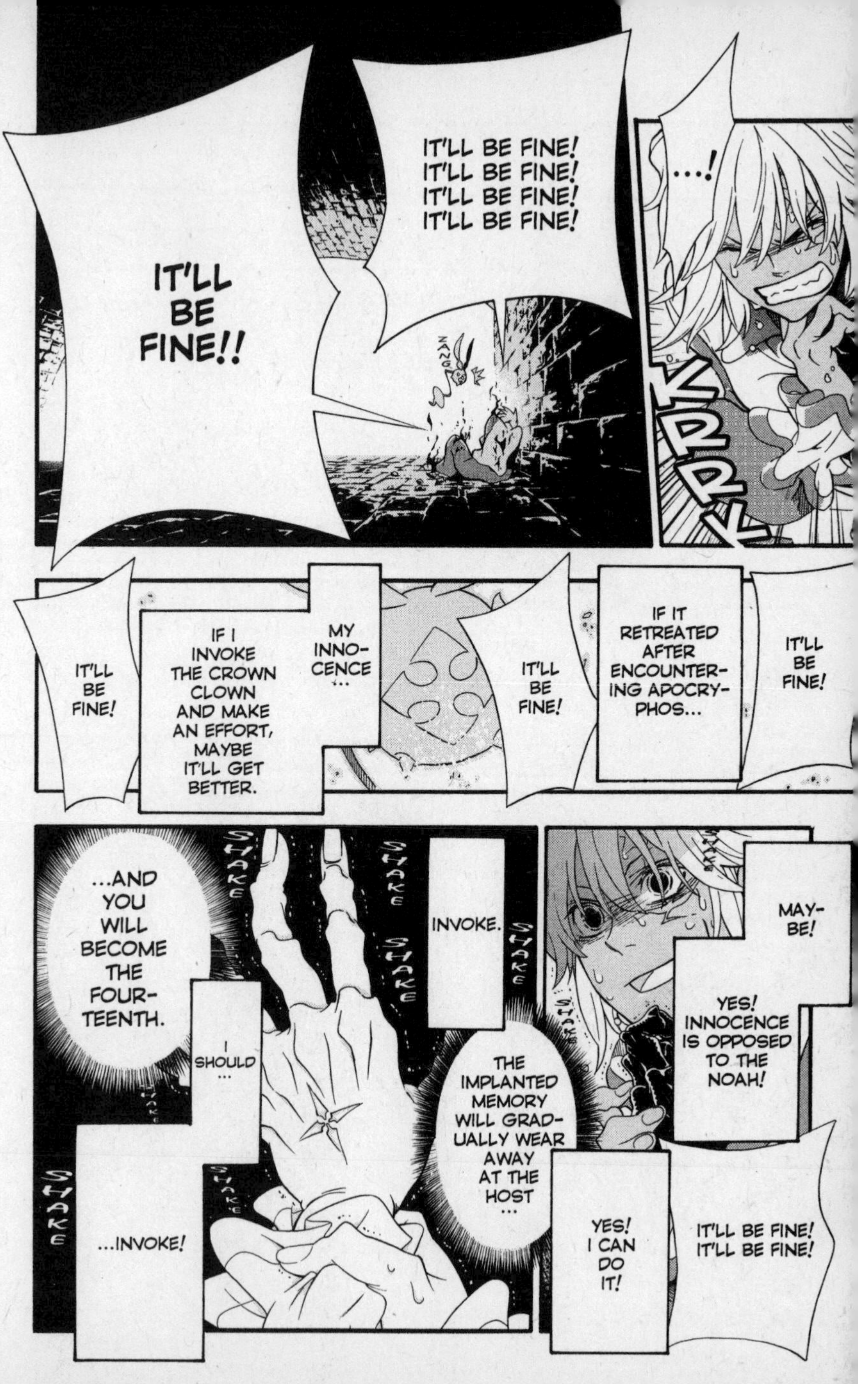
...!
KRRK
IT'LL BE FINE! IT'LL BE FINE! IT'LL BE FINE! IT'LL BE FINE!
IT'LL BE FINE!!
ZANG
IT'LL BE FINE!
IF IT RETREATED AFTER ENCOUNTERING APOCRYPHOS...
IT'LL BE FINE!
MY INNOCENCE...
IF I INVOKE THE CROWN CLOWN AND MAKE AN EFFORT, MAYBE IT'LL GET BETTER.
IT'LL BE FINE!
SHAKE
MAYBE!
YES! INNOCENCE IS OPPOSED TO THE NOAH!
IT'LL BE FINE! IT'LL BE FINE!
YES! I CAN DO IT!
THE IMPLANTED MEMORY WILL GRADUALLY WEAR AWAY AT THE HOST...
SHAKE
INVOKE.
SHAKE SHAKE SHAKE
...AND YOU WILL BECOME THE FOURTEENTH.
I SHOULD...
SHAKE
...INVOKE!
SHAKE

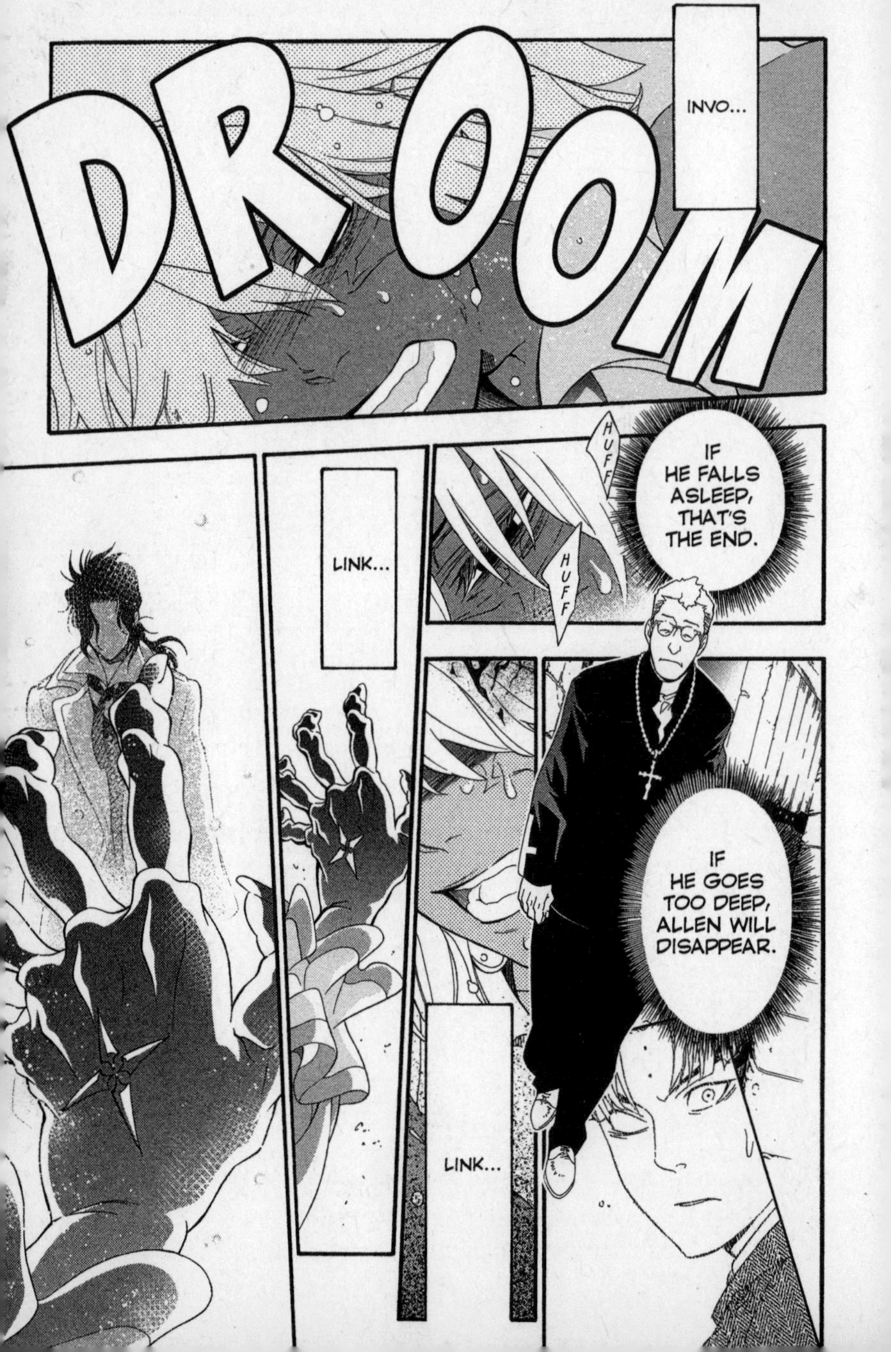
INVO...
DROOM
IF HE FALLS ASLEEP, THAT'S THE END.
HUFF
HUFF
LINK...
IF HE GOES TOO DEEP, ALLEN WILL DISAPPEAR.
LINK...

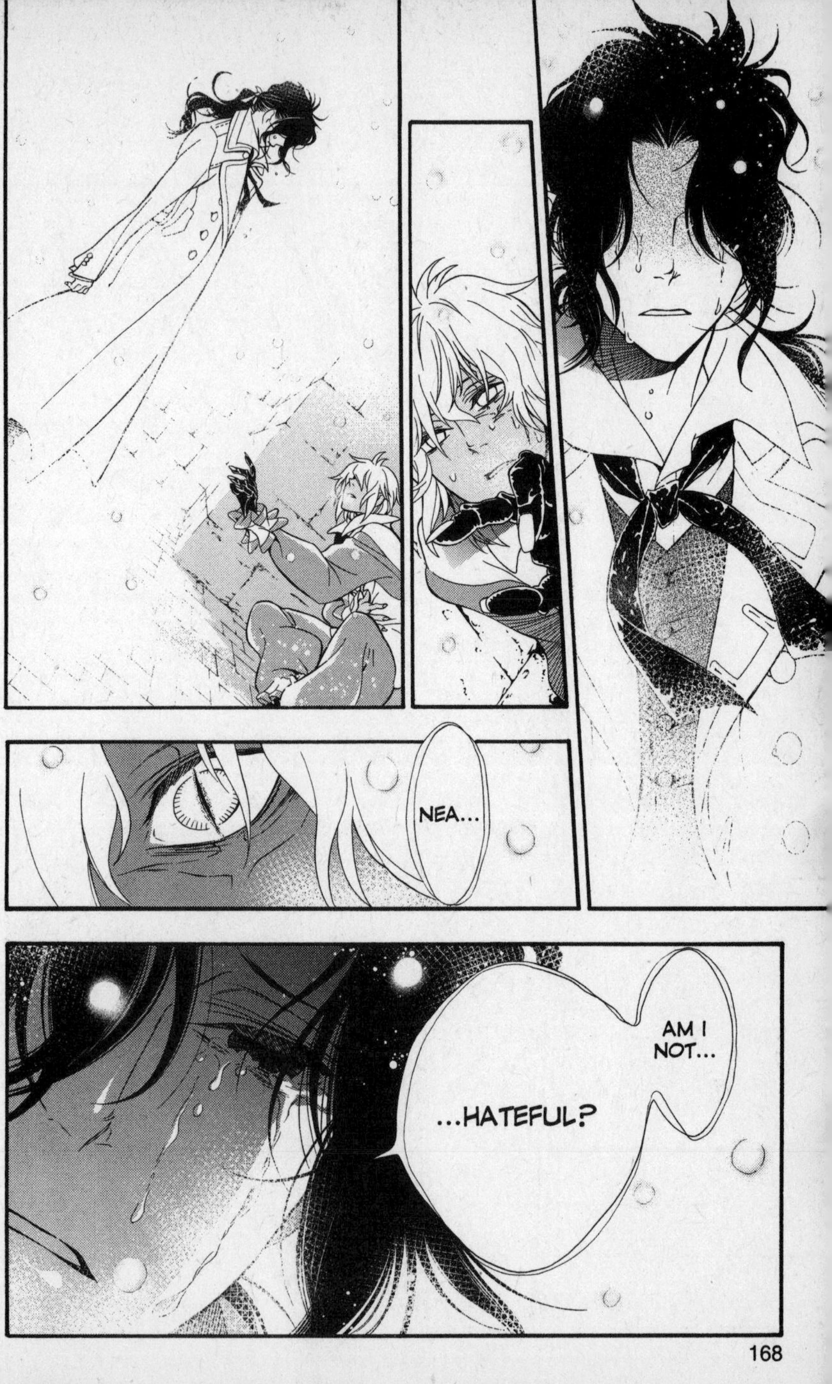
NEA...
AM I NOT...
...HATEFUL?

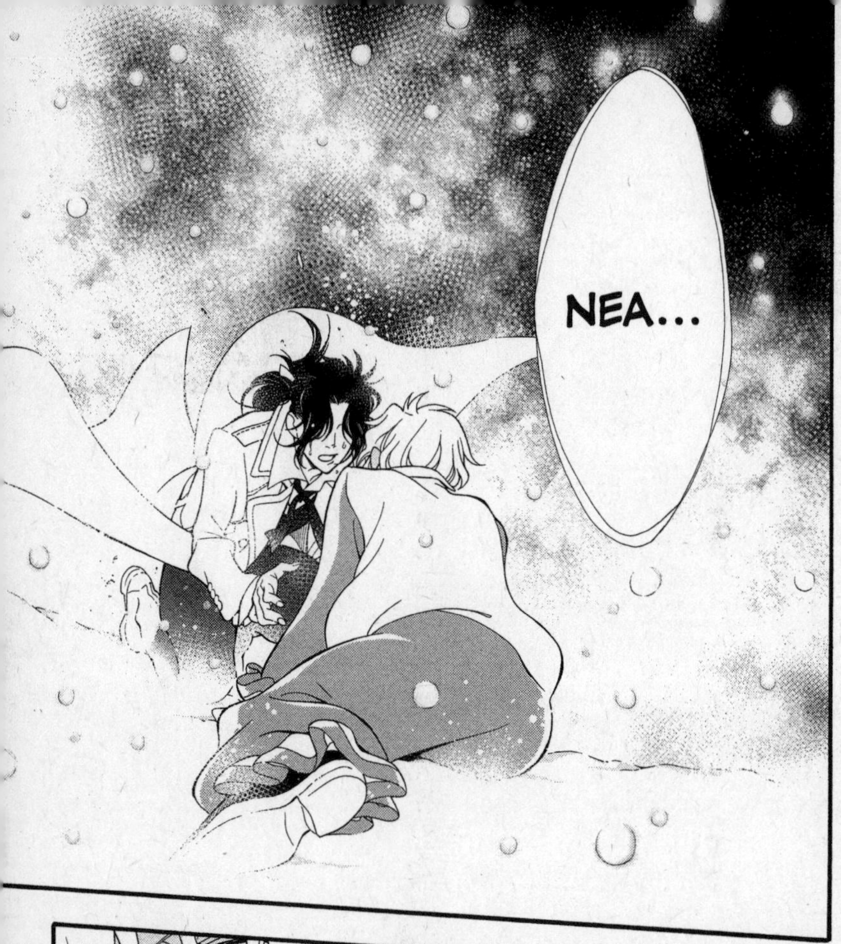
NEA...
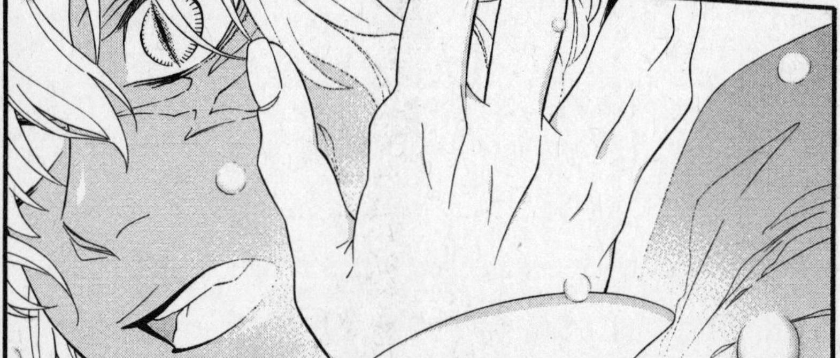

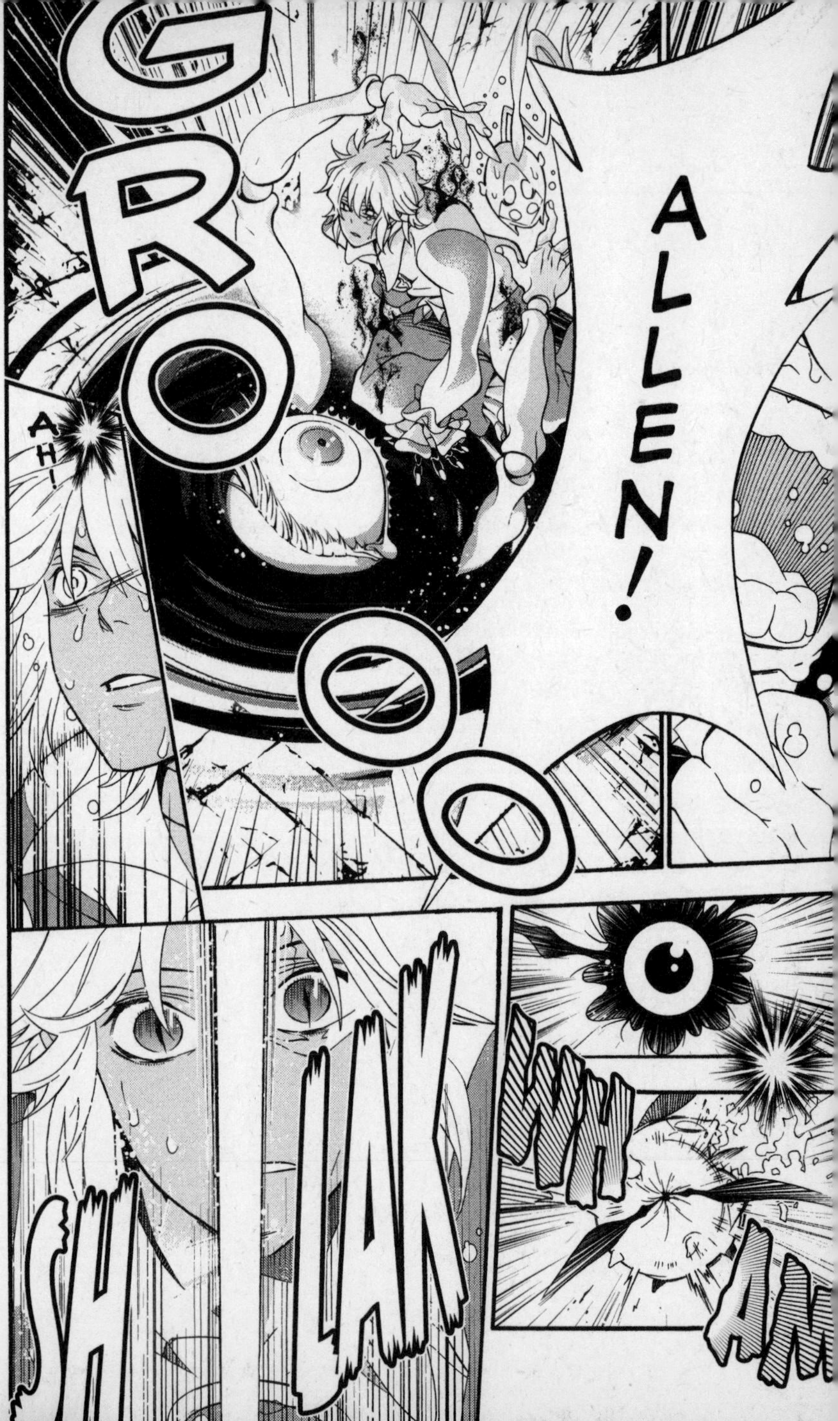
ALLEN!
GROOO
AH!
WH
AM
SHLAK

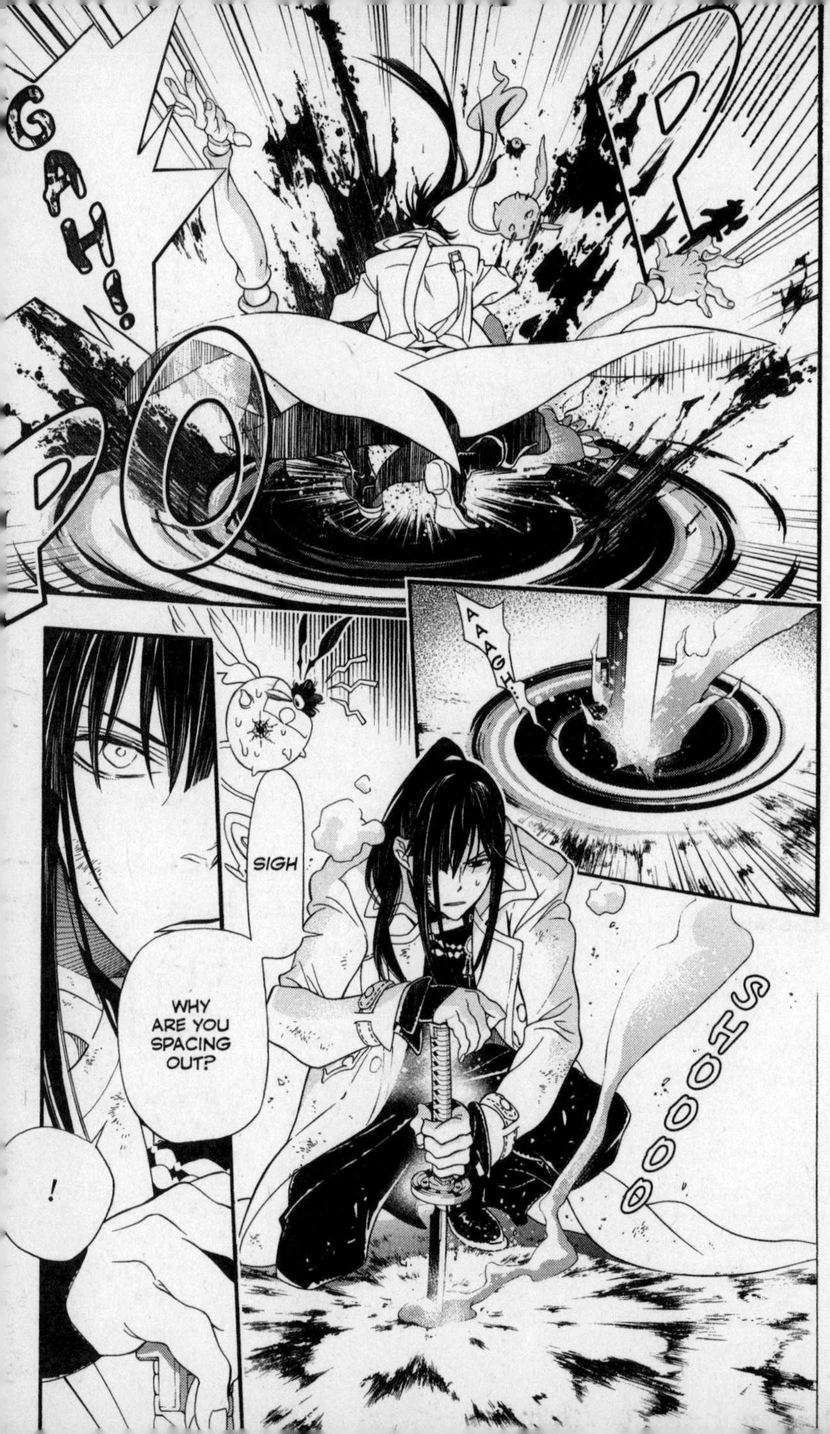
GAH!!
AAAGH...
SHOOOOO
SIGH
WHY ARE YOU SPACING OUT?
!

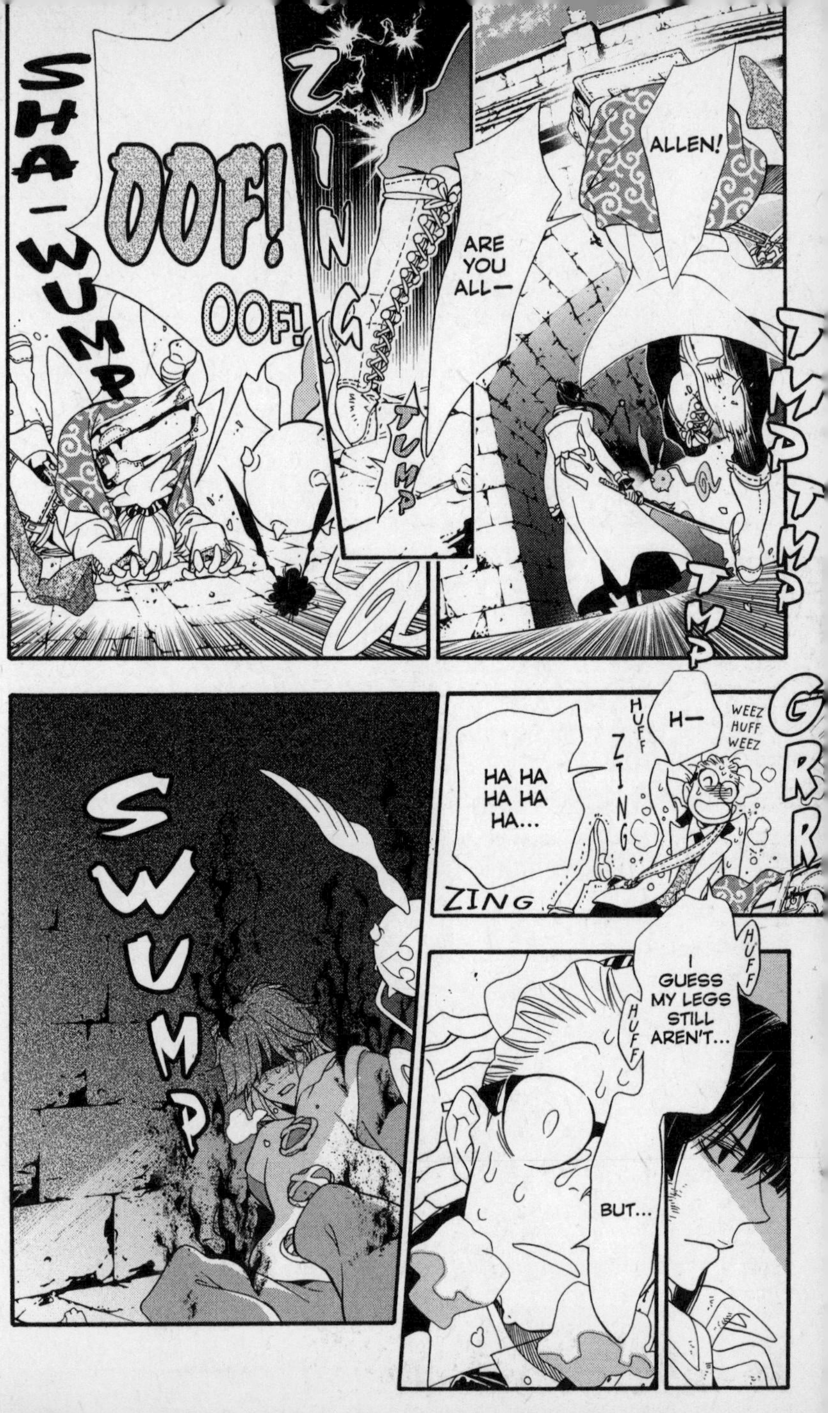
ALLEN!
ARE YOU ALL—
TMP TMP TMP TMP
ZING
TUMP
OOF!
OOF!
SHA-WUMP
GRRR
WEEZ HUFF WEEZ
H—
HUFF
ZING
HA HA HA HA HA...
ZING
I GUESS MY LEGS STILL AREN'T...
HUFF
HUFF
BUT...
SWUMP

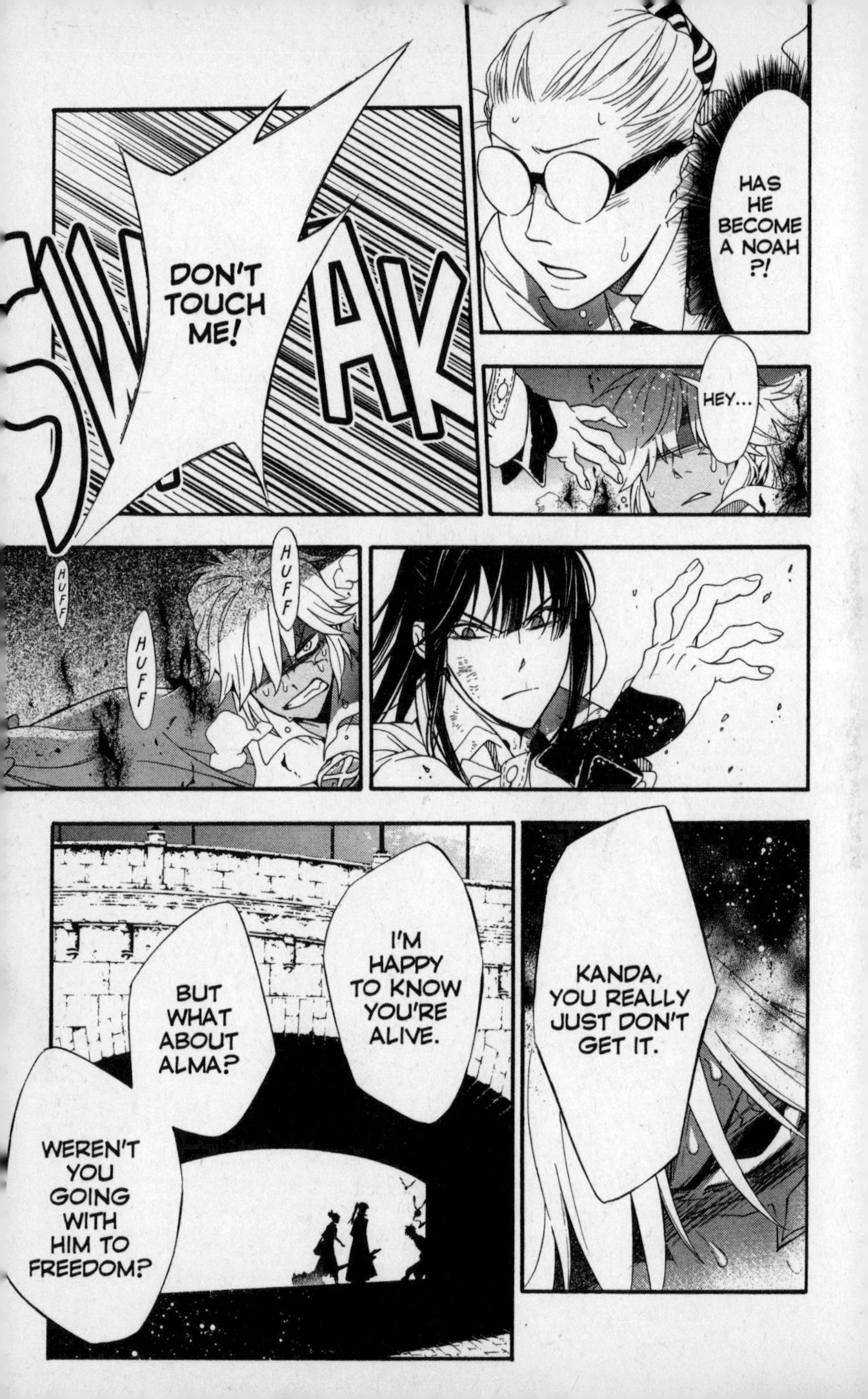
HAS HE BECOME A NOAH ?!
HEY...
DON'T TOUCH ME!
SWAK
HUFF
HUFF
HUFF
KANDA, YOU REALLY JUST DON'T GET IT.
I'M HAPPY TO KNOW YOU'RE ALIVE.
BUT WHAT ABOUT ALMA?
WEREN'T YOU GOING WITH HIM TO FREEDOM?

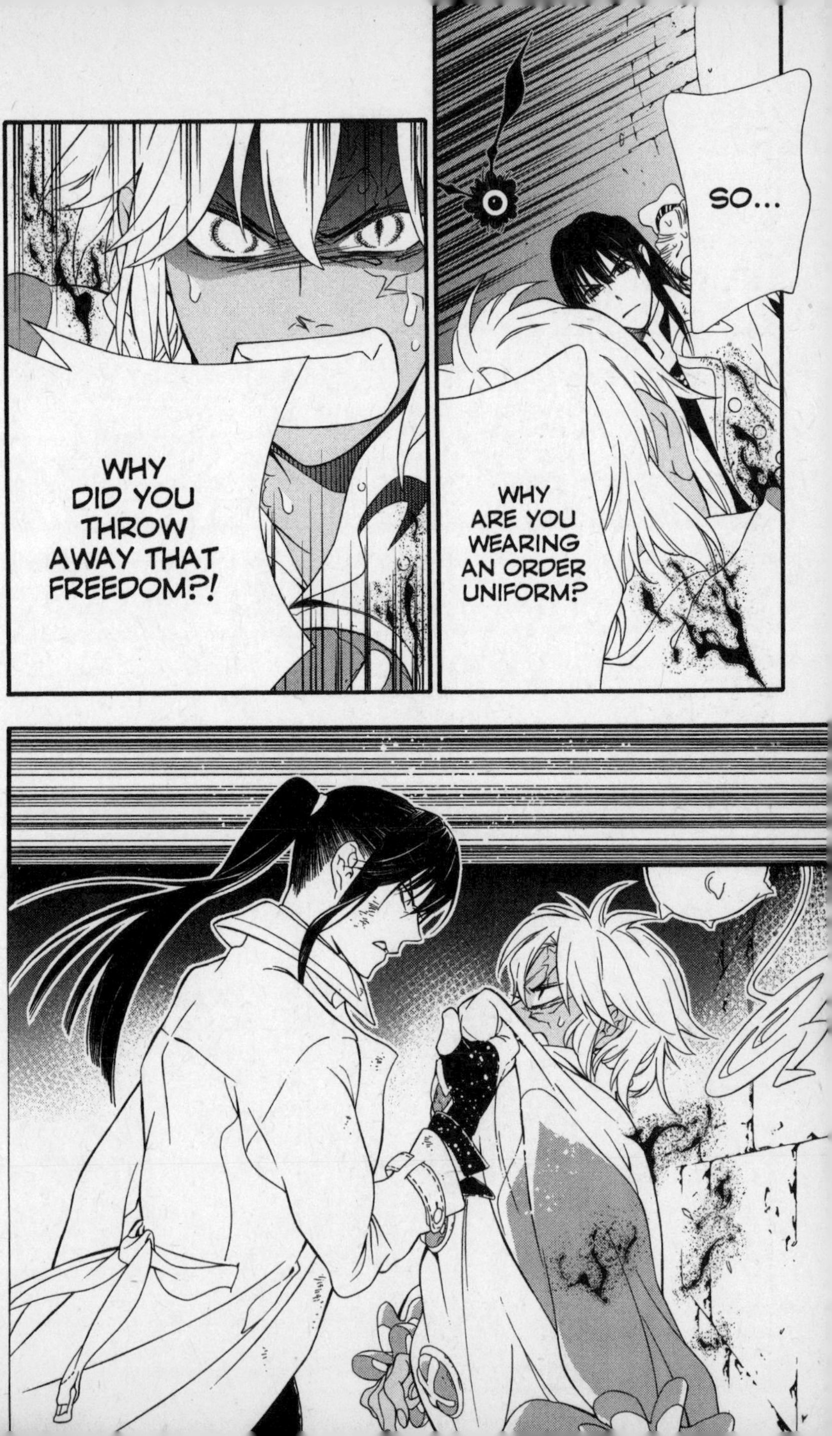
SO...
WHY ARE YOU WEARING AN ORDER UNIFORM?
WHY DID YOU THROW AWAY THAT FREEDOM?!

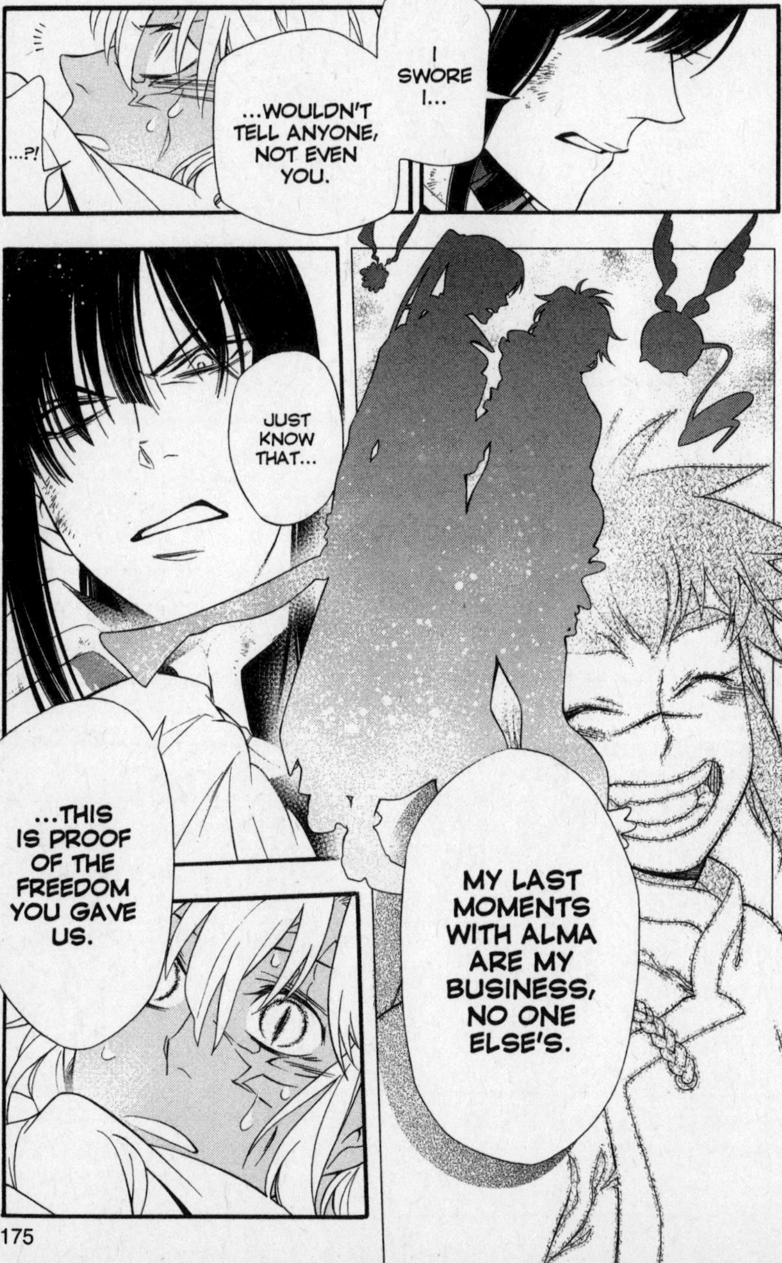
I SWORE I...
...WOULDN'T TELL ANYONE, NOT EVEN YOU.
...?!
MY LAST MOMENTS WITH ALMA ARE MY BUSINESS, NO ONE ELSE'S.
JUST KNOW THAT...
...THIS IS PROOF OF THE FREEDOM YOU GAVE US.

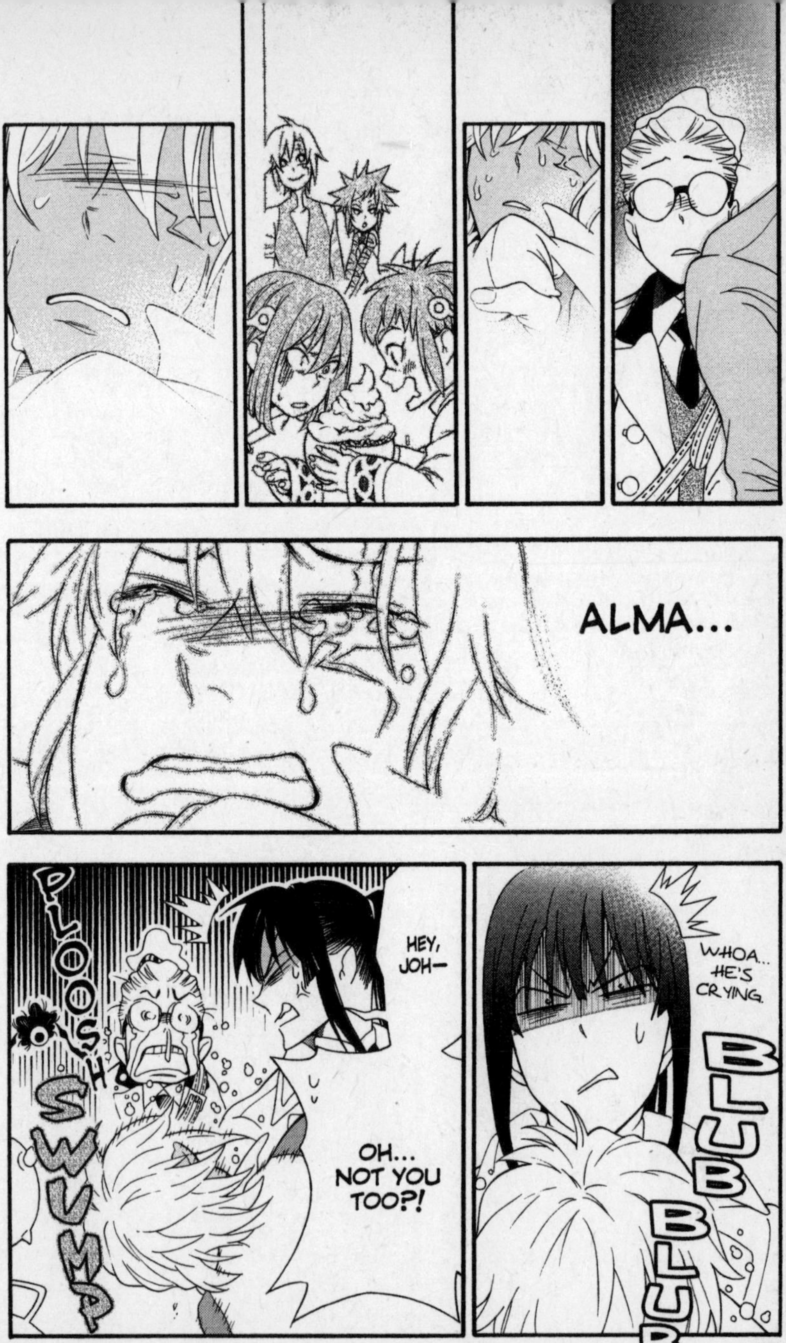
ALMA...
WHOA... HE'S CRYING.
BLUB BLUB BLUB
HEY, JOH—
PLOOSH
SWUMP
OH... NOT YOU TOO?!

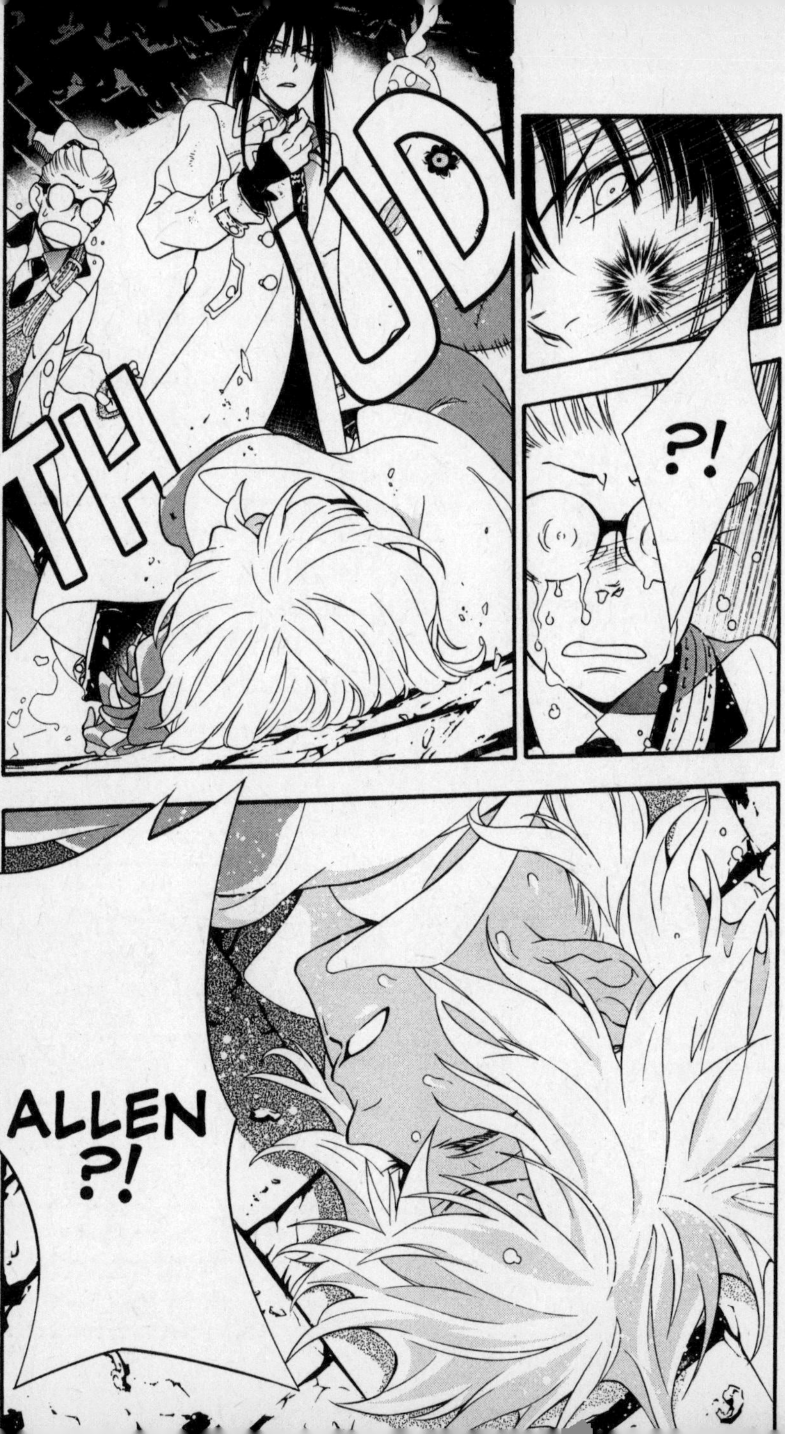
?!
THUD
ALLEN ?!

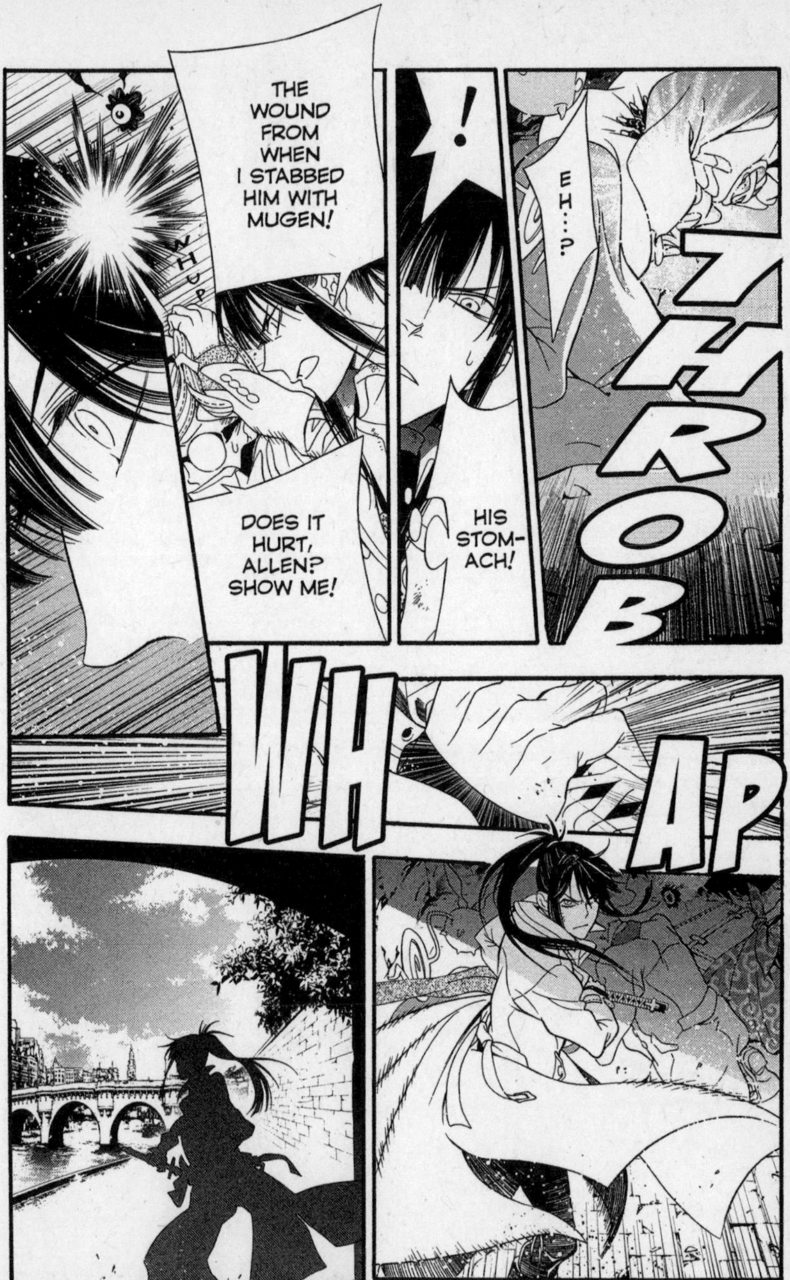
EH...?
THROB
!
HIS STOM-ACH!
THE WOUND FROM WHEN I STABBED HIM WITH MUGEN!
WHUP
DOES IT HURT, ALLEN? SHOW ME!
WHAP

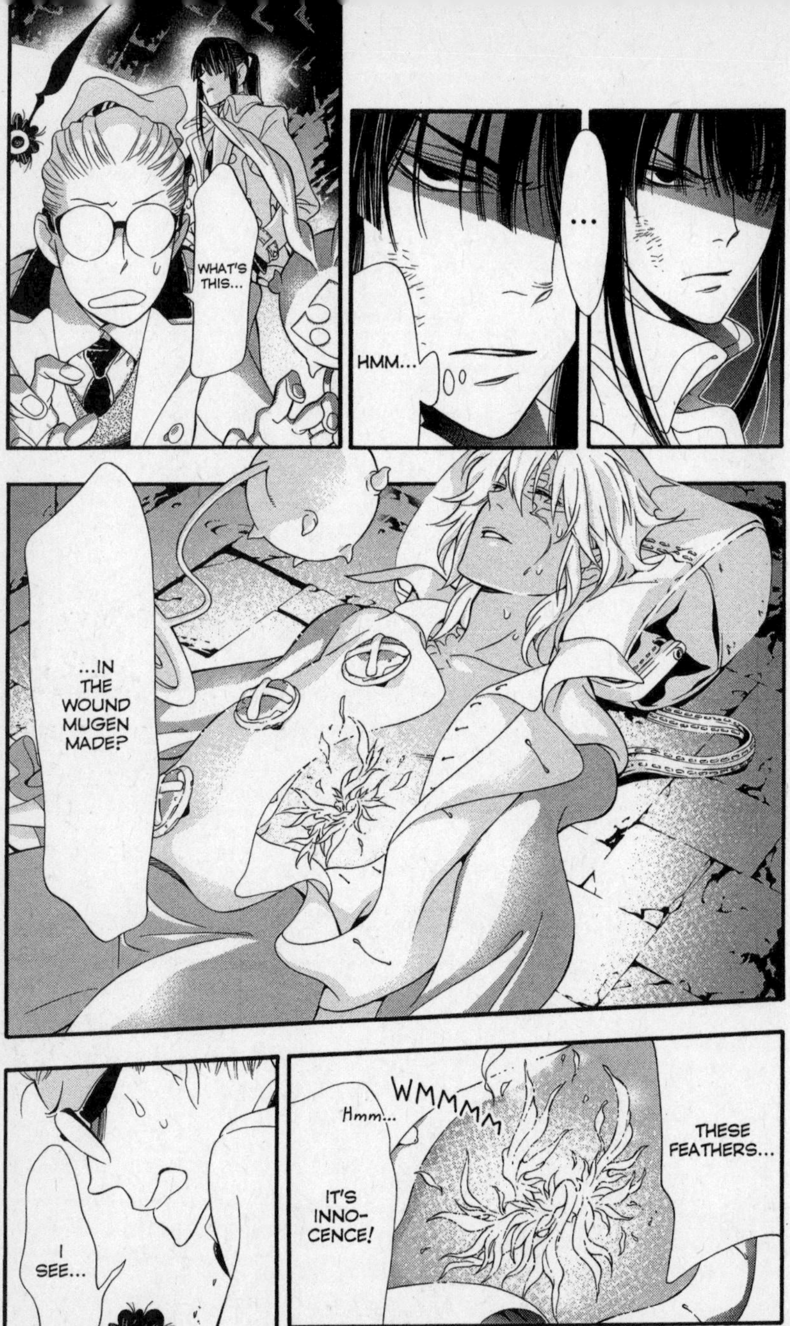
...
HMM...
WHAT'S THIS...
...IN THE WOUND MUGEN MADE?
THESE FEATHERS...
WMMMMM
Hmm...
IT'S INNO-CENCE!
I SEE...

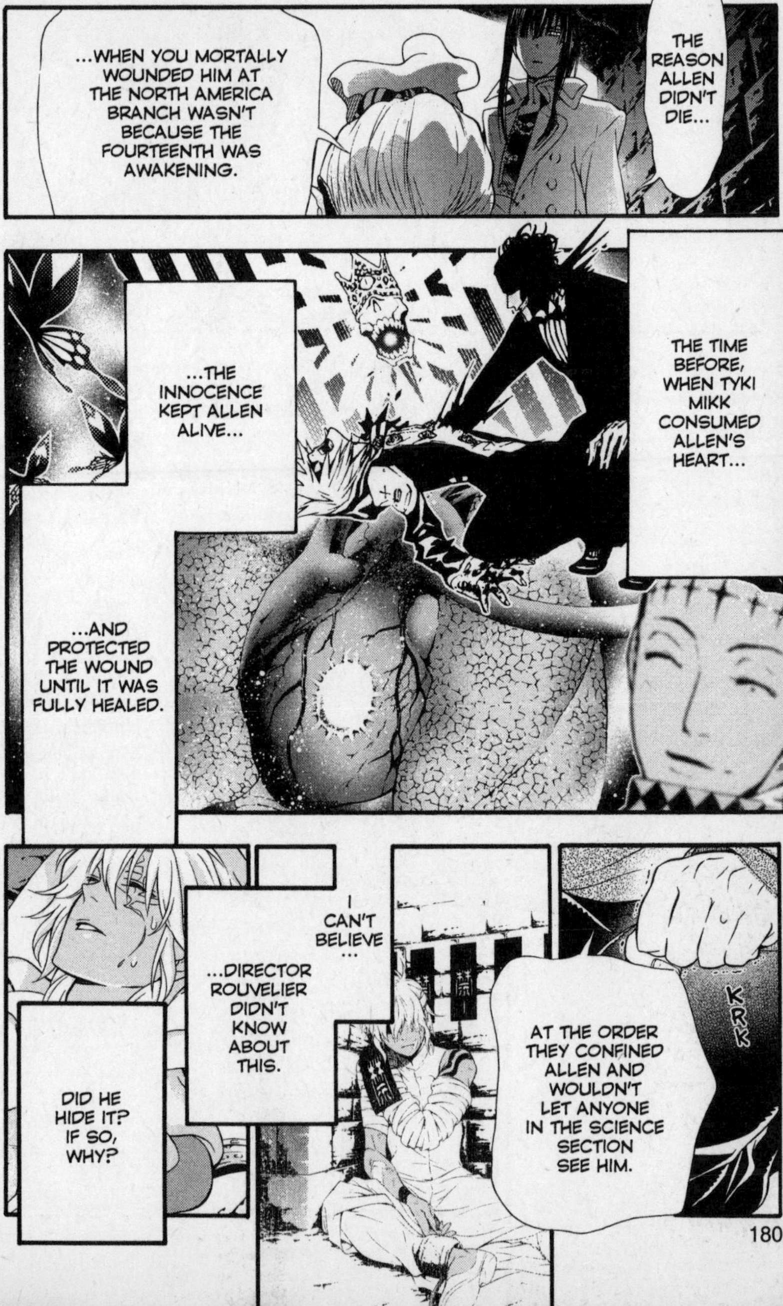
THE REASON ALLEN DIDN'T DIE...
...WHEN YOU MORTALLY WOUNDED HIM AT THE NORTH AMERICA BRANCH WASN'T BECAUSE THE FOURTEENTH WAS AWAKENING.
THE TIME BEFORE, WHEN TYKI MIKK CONSUMED ALLEN'S HEART...
...THE INNOCENCE KEPT ALLEN ALIVE...
...AND PROTECTED THE WOUND UNTIL IT WAS FULLY HEALED.
KRK
AT THE ORDER THEY CONFINED ALLEN AND WOULDN'T LET ANYONE IN THE SCIENCE SECTION SEE HIM.
I CAN'T BELIEVE ...
...DIRECTOR ROUVELIER DIDN'T KNOW ABOUT THIS.
DID HE HIDE IT? IF SO, WHY?

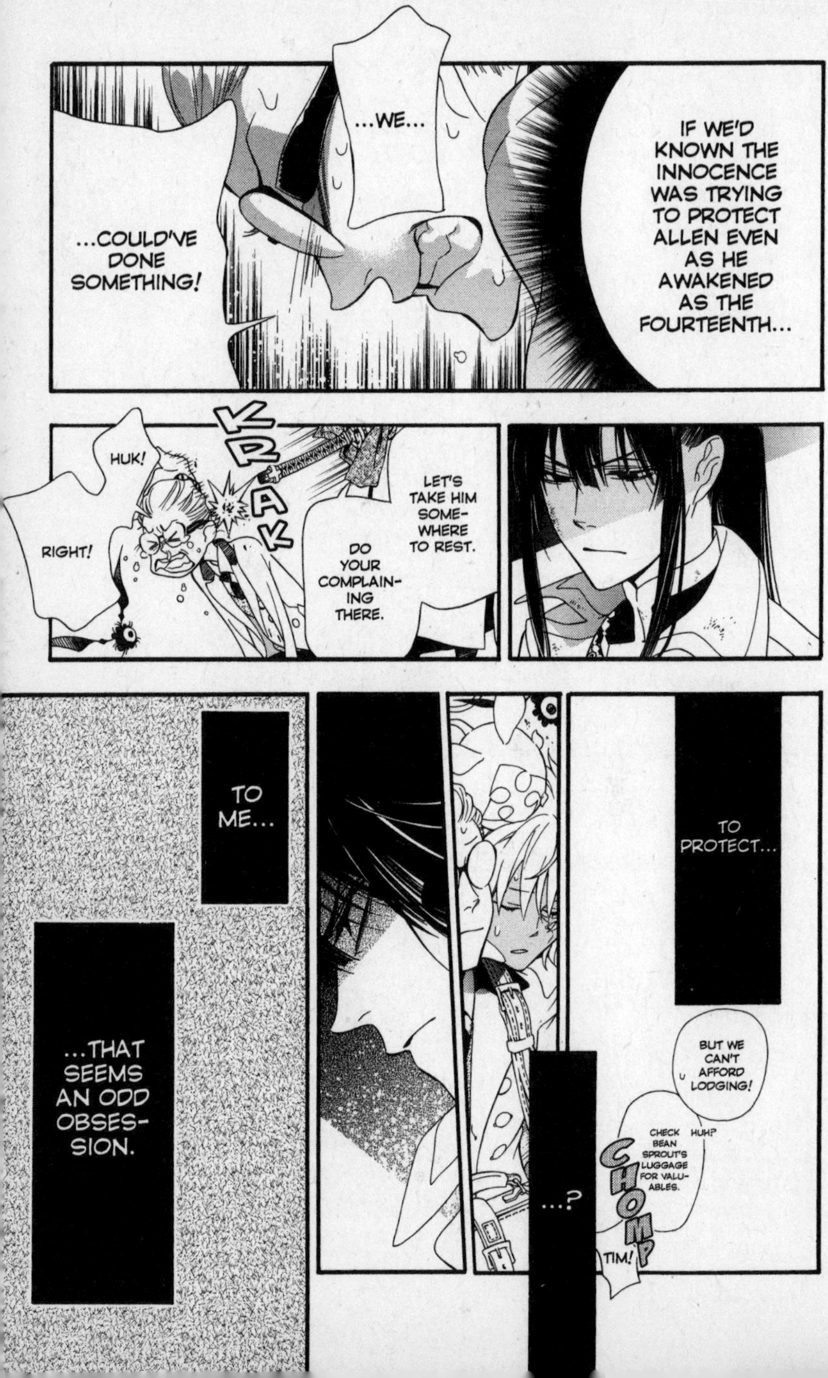
IF WE'D KNOWN THE INNOCENCE WAS TRYING TO PROTECT ALLEN EVEN AS HE AWAKENED AS THE FOURTEENTH...
...WE...
...COULD'VE DONE SOMETHING!
LET'S TAKE HIM SOMEWHERE TO REST.
DO YOUR COMPLAINING THERE.
KRAK
HUK!
RIGHT!
TO PROTECT...
BUT WE CAN'T AFFORD LODGING!
HUH?
CHECK BEAN SPROUT'S LUGGAGE FOR VALUABLES.
CHOMP
TIM!
...?
TO ME...
...THAT SEEMS AN ODD OBSESSION.

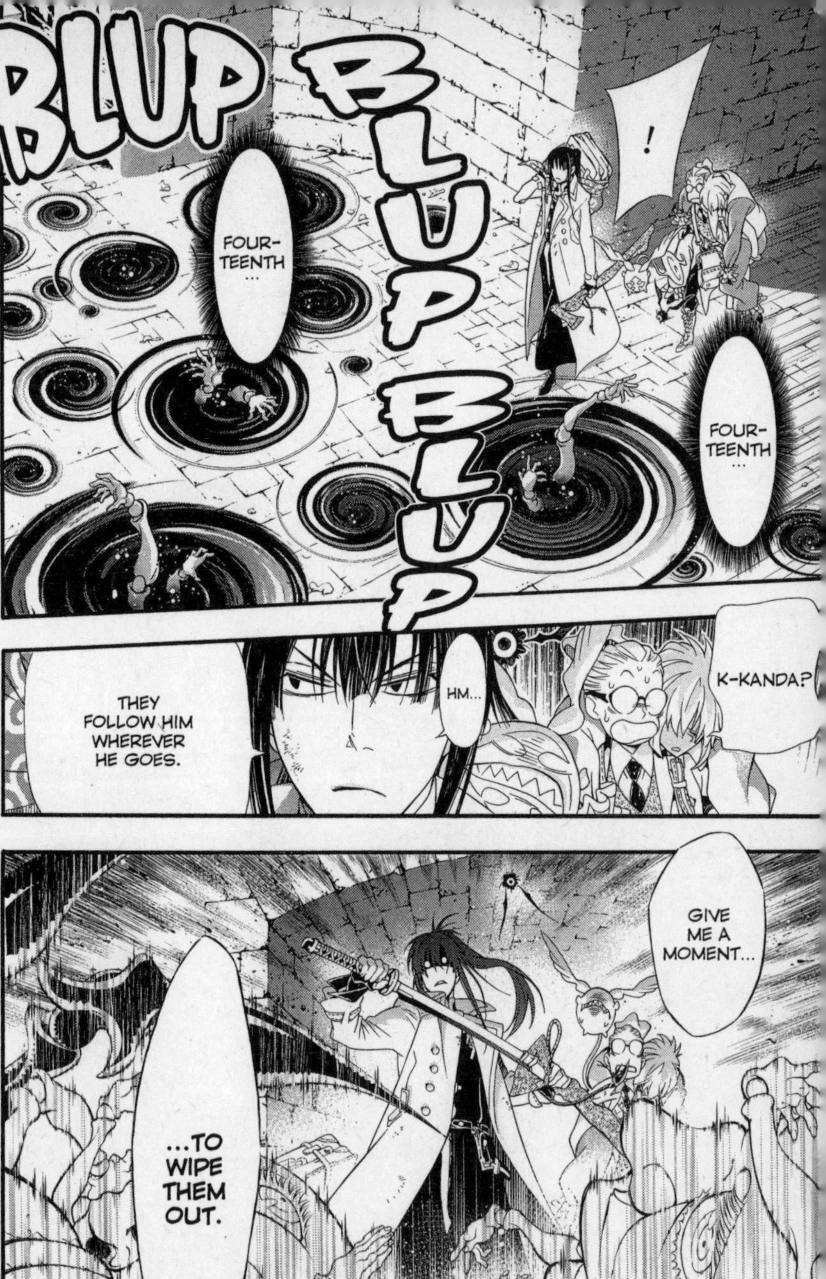
!
FOUR-TEENTH...
BLUP BLUP
FOUR-TEENTH...
BLUP
K-KANDA?
HM...
THEY FOLLOW HIM WHEREVER HE GOES.
GIVE ME A MOMENT...
...TO WIPE THEM OUT.

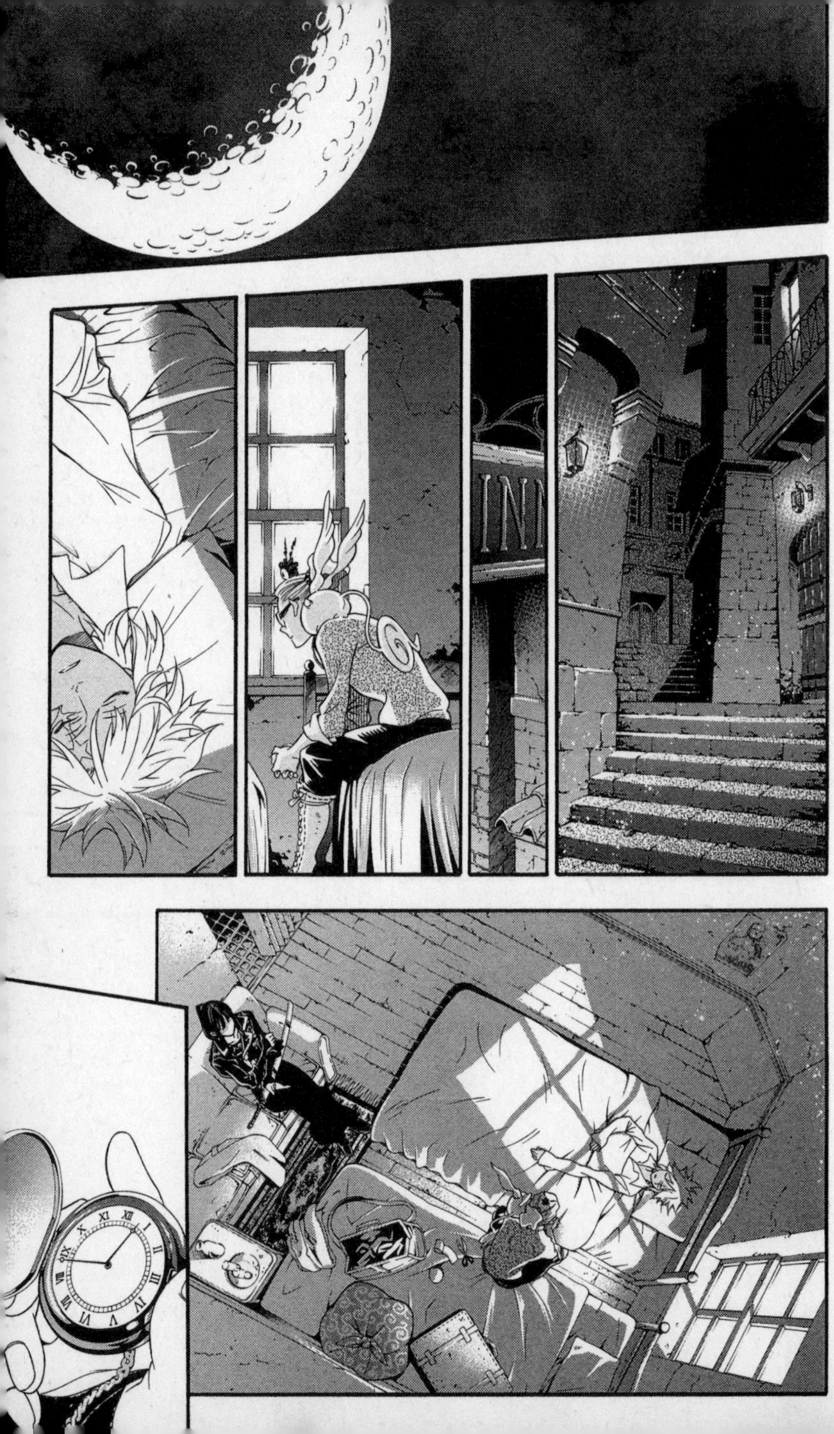
INN

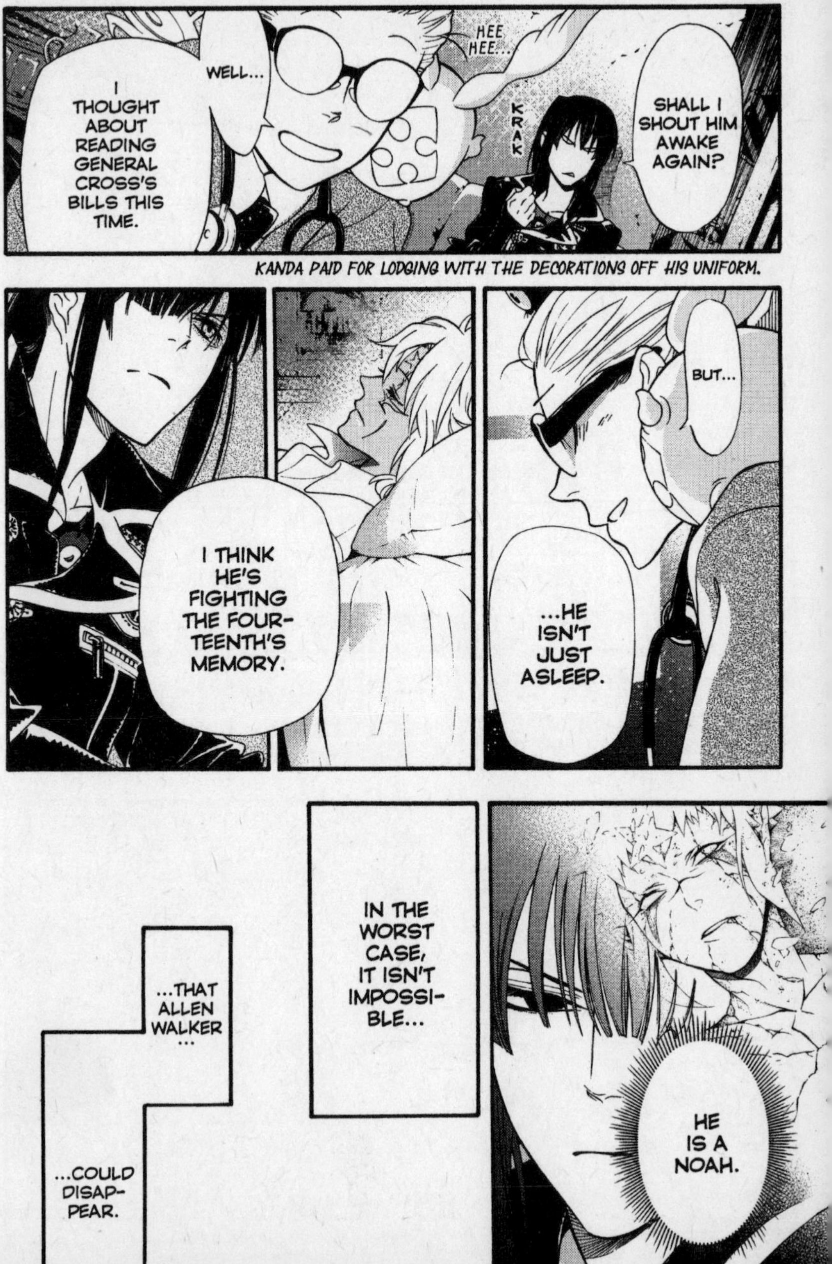
SHALL I SHOUT HIM AWAKE AGAIN?
KRAK
HEE HEE...
WELL...
I THOUGHT ABOUT READING GENERAL CROSS'S BILLS THIS TIME.
KANDA PAID FOR LODGING WITH THE DECORATIONS OFF HIS UNIFORM.
BUT...
...HE ISN'T JUST ASLEEP.
I THINK HE'S FIGHTING THE FOURTEENTH'S MEMORY.
HE IS A NOAH.
IN THE WORST CASE, IT ISN'T IMPOSSIBLE...
...THAT ALLEN WALKER...
...COULD DISAPPEAR.

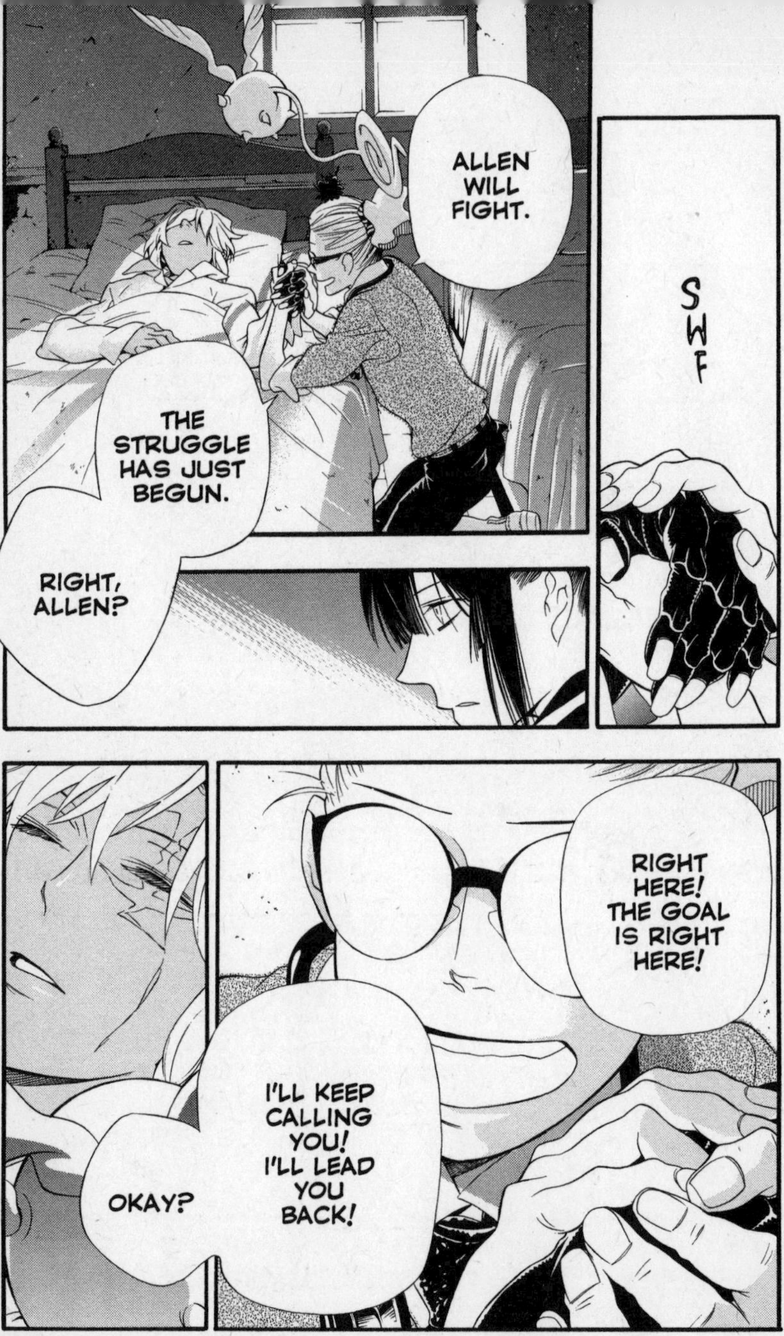
SWF
ALLEN WILL FIGHT.
THE STRUGGLE HAS JUST BEGUN.
RIGHT, ALLEN?
RIGHT HERE! THE GOAL IS RIGHT HERE!
I'LL KEEP CALLING YOU! I'LL LEAD YOU BACK!
OKAY?

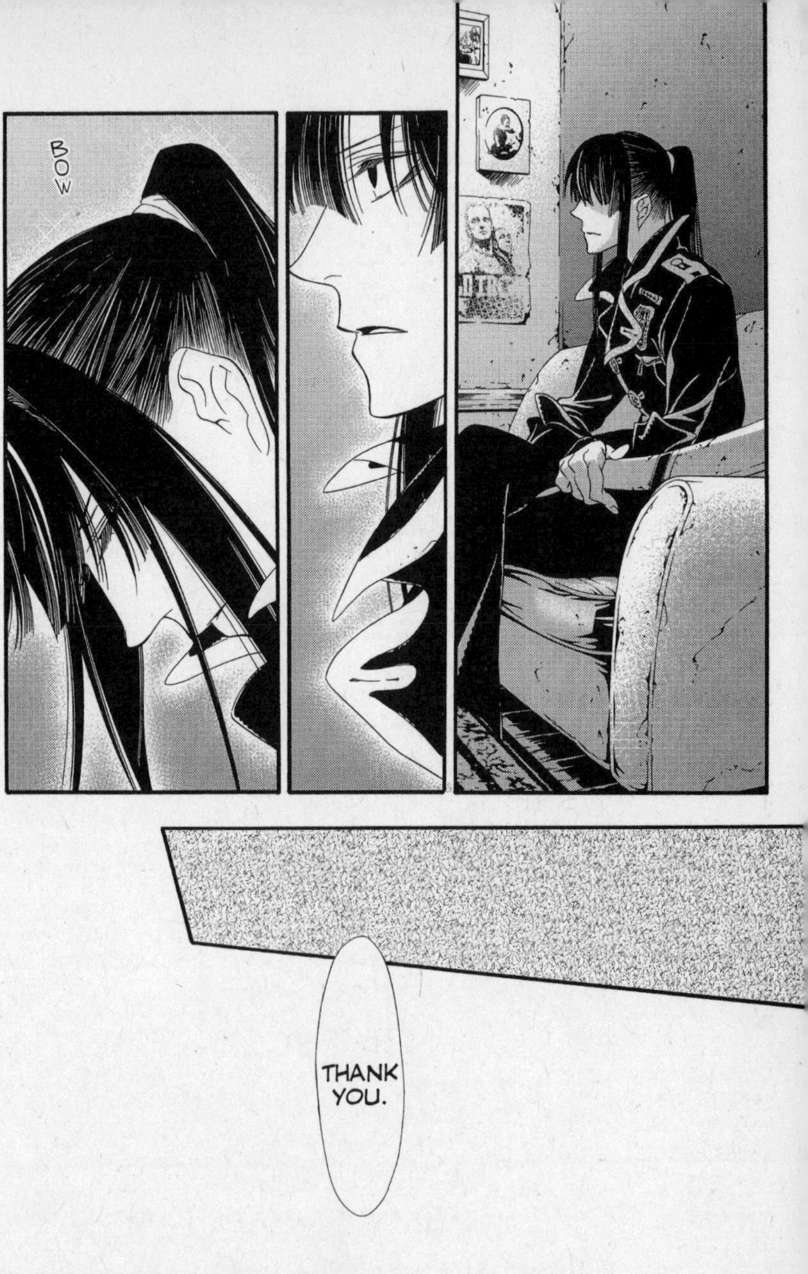
BOW
THANK YOU.

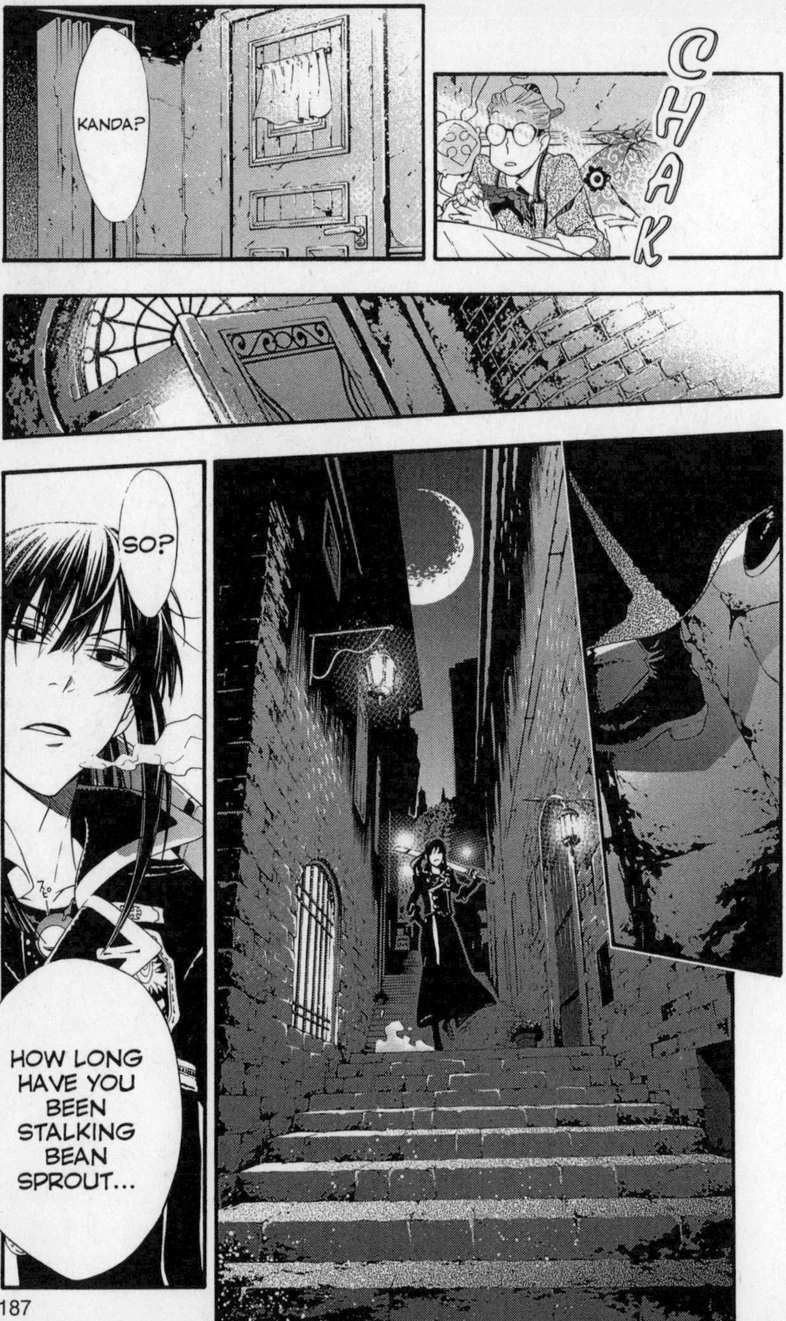
CHAK
KANDA?
SO?
HOW LONG HAVE YOU BEEN STALKING BEAN SPROUT...

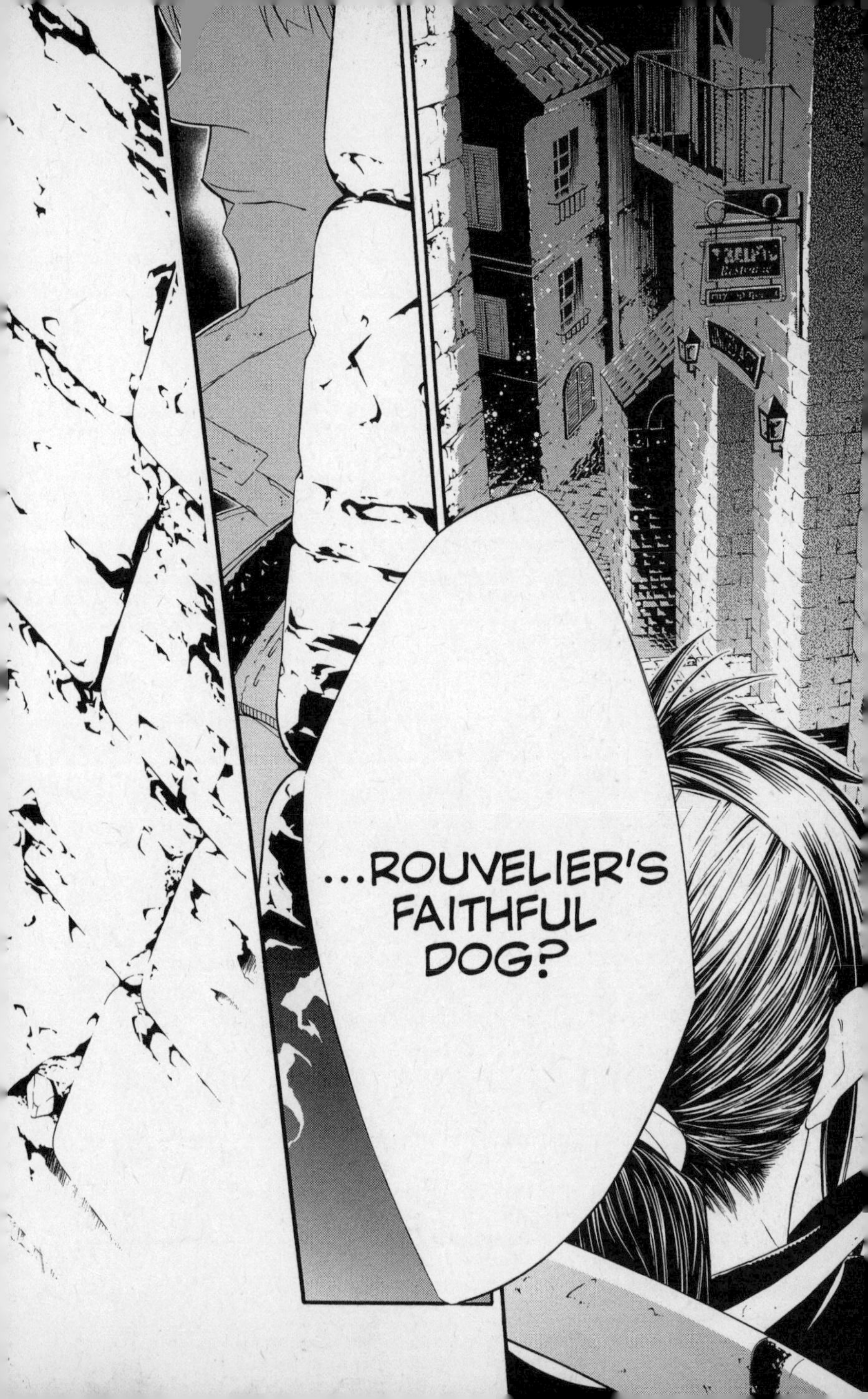
...ROUVELIER'S FAITHFUL DOG?

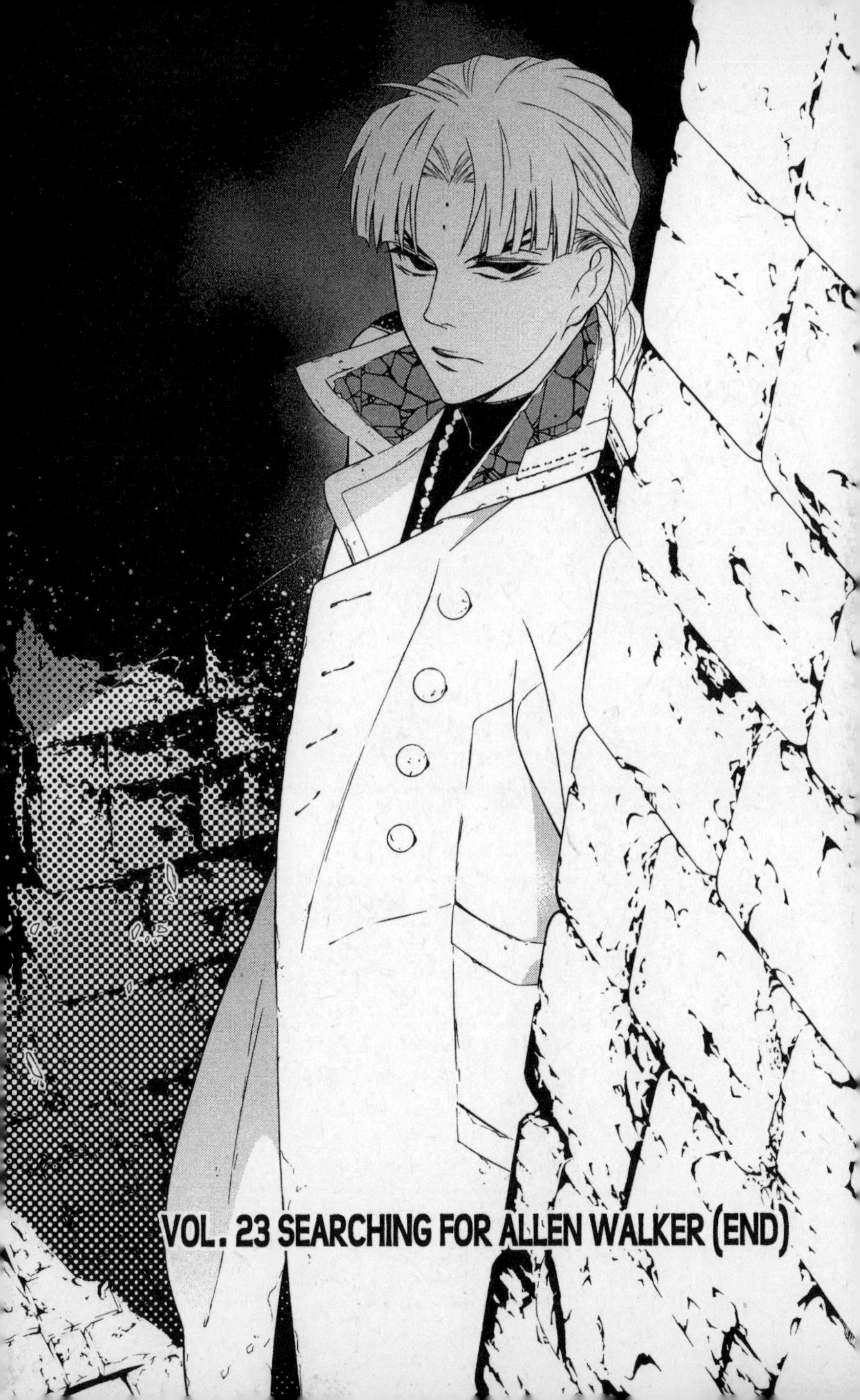
VOL. 23 SEARCHING FOR ALLEN WALKER (END)

SEARCHING FOR A.W. - BONUS MANGA

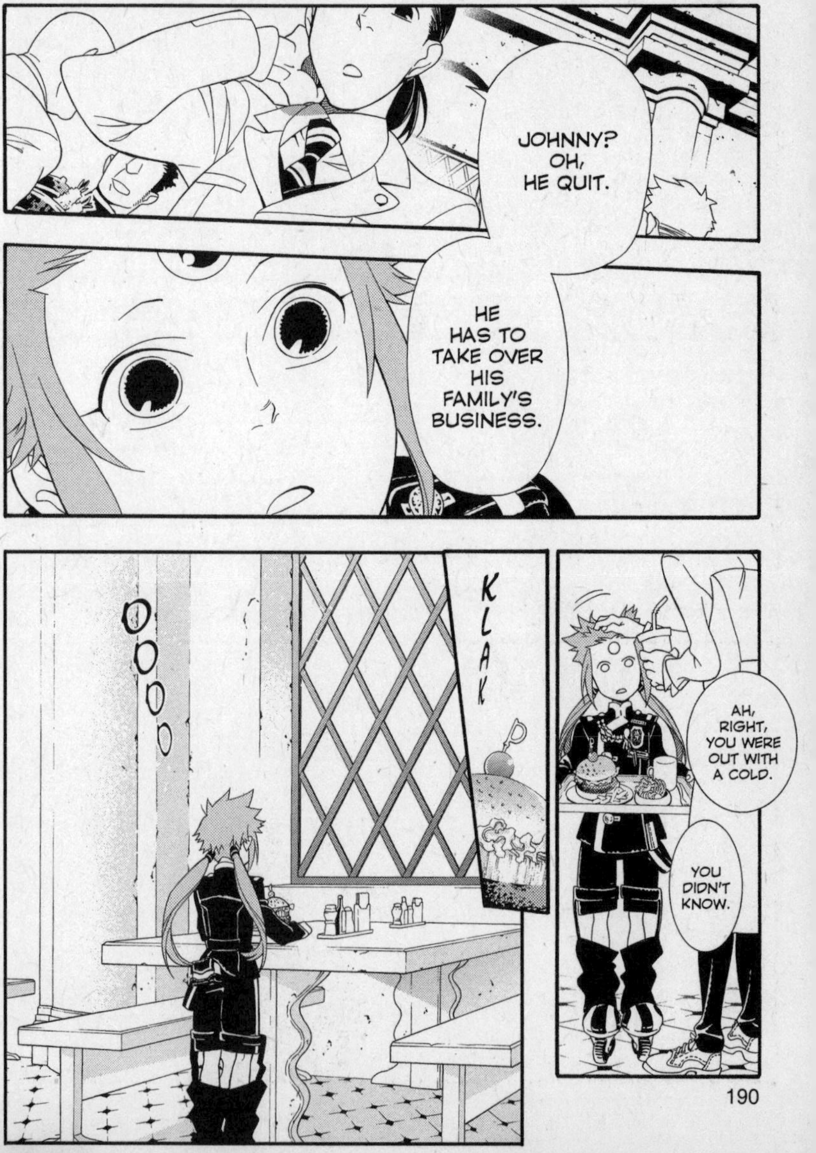
JOHNNY? OH, HE QUIT.
HE HAS TO TAKE OVER HIS FAMILY'S BUSINESS.
AH, RIGHT, YOU WERE OUT WITH A COLD.
YOU DIDN'T KNOW.
KLAK

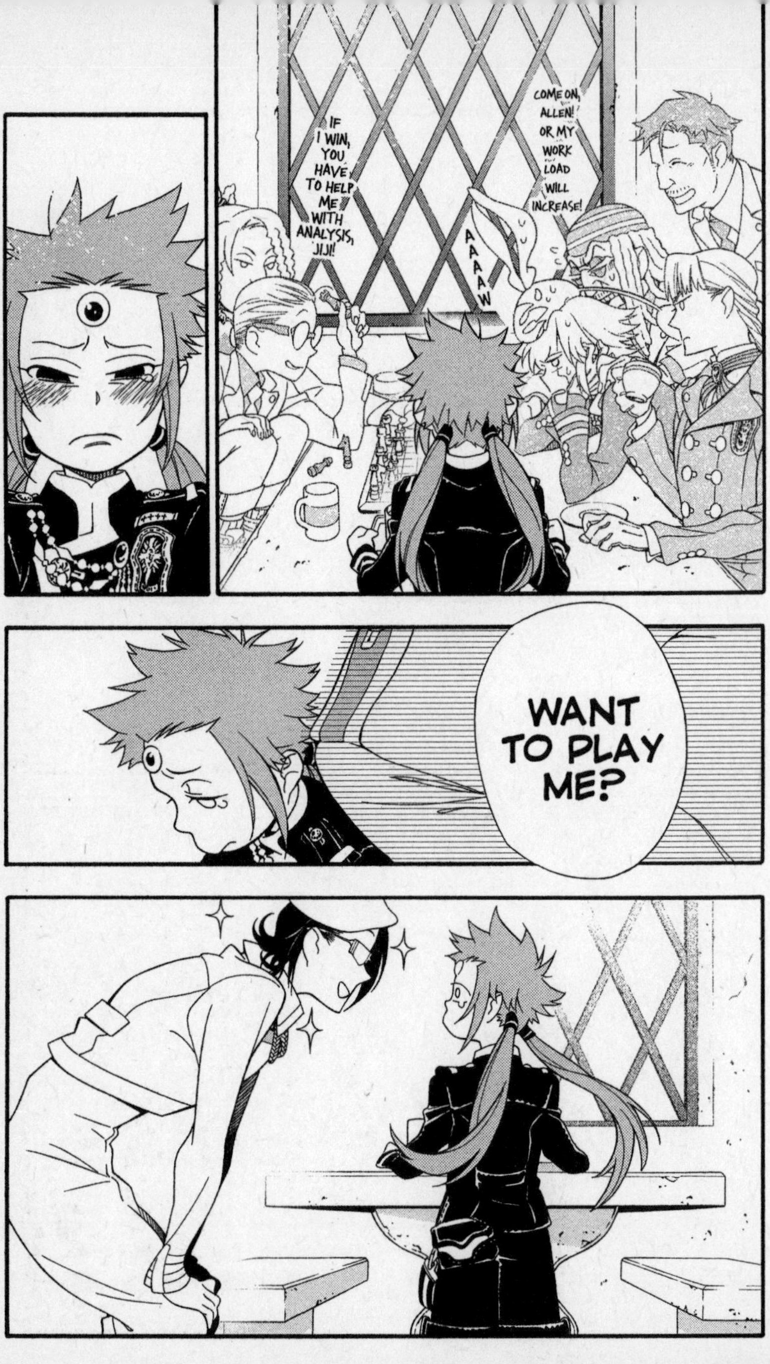
COME ON, ALLEN! OR MY WORK LOAD WILL INCREASE!
AAAAW
IF I WIN, YOU HAVE TO HELP ME WITH ANALYSIS, JIJI!
WANT TO PLAY ME?

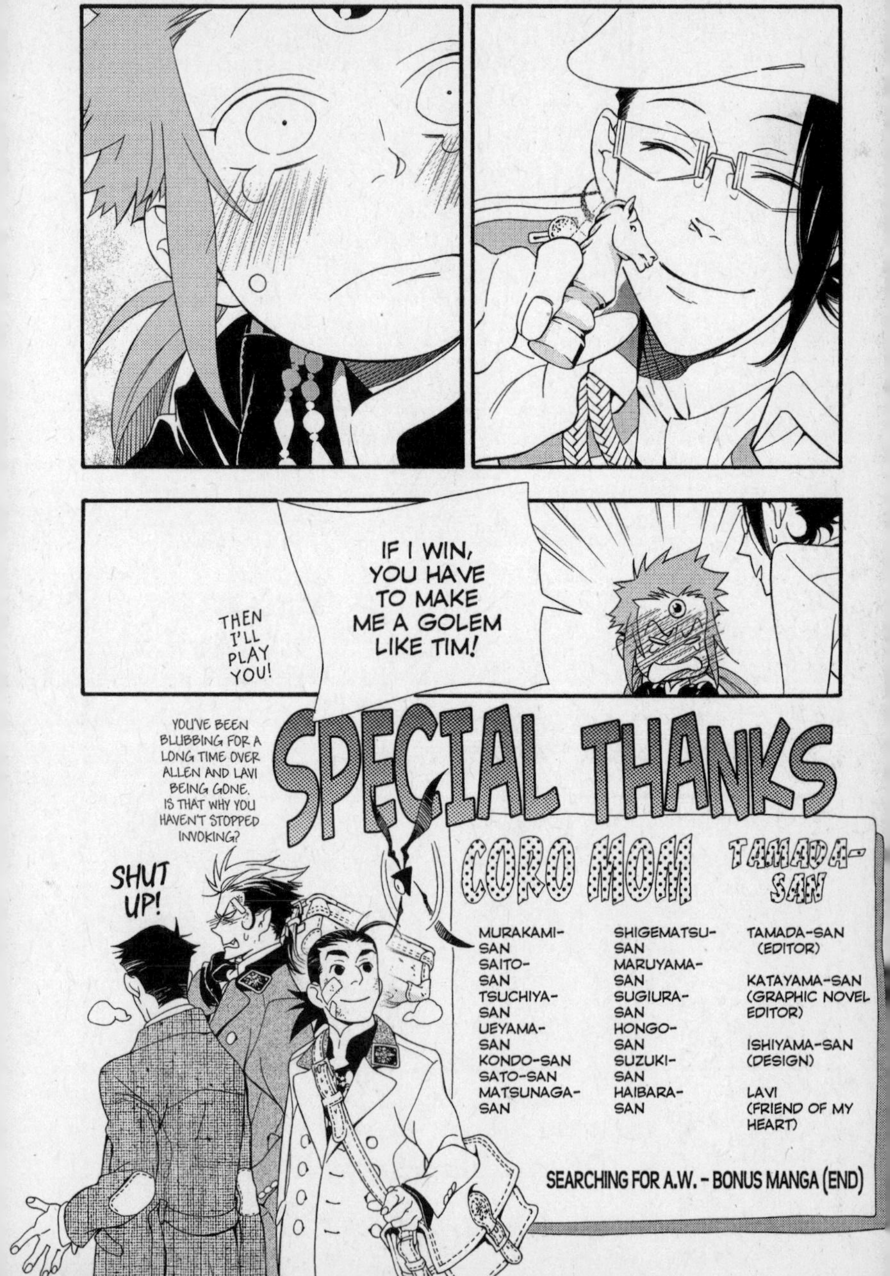
IF I WIN, YOU HAVE TO MAKE ME A GOLEM LIKE TIM!
THEN I'LL PLAY YOU!
SPECIAL THANKS
CORO MOM
TAMADA-SAN
MURAKAMI-SAN
SAITO-SAN
TSUCHIYA-SAN
UEYAMA-SAN
KONDO-SAN
SATO-SAN
MATSUNAGA-SAN
SHIGEMATSU-SAN
MARUYAMA-SAN
SUGIURA-SAN
HONGO-SAN
SUZUKI-SAN
HAIBARA-SAN
TAMADA-SAN (EDITOR)
KATAYAMA-SAN (GRAPHIC NOVEL EDITOR)
ISHIYAMA-SAN (DESIGN)
LAVI (FRIEND OF MY HEART)
YOU'VE BEEN BLUBBING FOR A LONG TIME OVER ALLEN AND LAVI BEING GONE. IS THAT WHY YOU HAVEN'T STOPPED INVOKING?
SHUT UP!
SEARCHING FOR A.W. - BONUS MANGA (END)

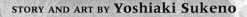

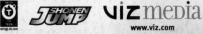